RePresenting Bisexuali

RePresenting Bisexualities
Subjects and Cultures
of Fluid Desire

Edited by
Donald E. Hall and
Maria Pramaggiore

NEW YORK UNIVERSITY PRESS
New York and London

NEW YORK UNIVERSITY PRESS
New York and London

Library of Congress Cataloging-in-Publication Data

RePresenting bisexualities : subjects and cultures of fluid desire /
edited by Donald E. Hall and Maria Pramaggiore.
     p. cm.
   Includes index.
   ISBN 0-8147-6633-1 (alk. paper). — ISBN 0-8147-6634-X (pbk. :
alk. paper)
   1. Bisexuality.   2. Bisexuality in literature.   3. Sexuality in
popular culture. I. Hall, Donald E. (Donald Eugene), 1960– .
II. Pramaggiore, Maria, 1960– .
   HQ74.R46   1996
306.76'4—dc20   96-8977
               CIP

Manufactured in the United States of America
10 9 8 7 6 5 4 3 2 1

Contents

Acknowledgments

This collection reflects the individual and collaborative work of twelve scholars, geographically and theoretically disparate individuals who have become colleagues and friends along the sometimes tortuous path from concept to reality. We thank our contributors for their creativity, perseverance, and good cheer: qualities which helped to make this process both intellectually provocative and enjoyable.

We thank Greta Gaard, who organized the ill-fated MLA panel which laid the groundwork for this anthology. Lila Hanft's input early on furthered the development of our ideas. We thank our colleagues at California State University at Northridge, Emory University, and North Carolina State University for supporting this project.

We thank Niko Pfund, Kathleen May, and Despina Papazoglou Gimbel at New York University Press, who were extremely knowledgeable and supportive at every point in the process.

"I felt a Cleaving in my Mind" by Emily Dickinson, reprinted by permission of the publishers and the Trustees of Amherst College from *The Poems of Emily Dickinson*, edited by Thomas H. Johnson. Cambridge, Mass.: The Belknap Press of Harvard University Press, copyright © 1951, 1955, 1979, 1983 by the President and Fellows of Harvard College.

Contributors

CHRIS CAGLE is a graduate student in English at Brown University working in film studies and queer theory. He has contributed to the forthcoming anthology *In the Streets, between the Sheets: Lesbian and Gay Documentary.*

ERIN G. CARLSTON received her Ph.D. in modern thought and literature from Stanford University, where she currently is an instructor. She lives in San Francisco and is now researching a project on race and American modernism.

TRACI CARROLL is an astrologer, bluegrass musician, and massage therapist in training. When she is not self-actualizing, she professes American literature at Rhodes College in Memphis, Tennessee. She is working on a book about food, aesthetics, and race in the nineteenth century.

MICHAEL DU PLESSIS is Assistant Professor of Comparative Literature and English at the University of Colorado at Boulder and is working on a book about lesbian, bisexual, and gay film, which is forthcoming from the University of Minnesota Press.

MARIAM FRASER is completing her doctoral thesis on bisexuality, which she employs as a key through which to explore a number of theories of the self. She also runs a course on representations of the body in popular culture at Lancaster University, U.K.

DONALD E. HALL is Associate Professor and Associate Chair of the English Department at California State University, Northridge. He is the editor of *Muscular Christianity: Embodying the Victorian Age* (Cambridge University Press, 1994) and the author of *Fixing Patriarchy: Feminism and Mid-Victorian Male Novelists* (New York University Press, 1996).

MARCY JANE KNOPF is a doctoral student in English at Miami University. In her spare time she moves between practicing bisexuality and working as a queer activist.

BRIAN LOFTUS is currently finishing his dissertation, "Suture, Sex, and the Subject of Modernism," at the University of California at Irvine, where he specializes in queer theory, Joyce, modernism, visual culture, and pornography.

FRANN MICHEL teaches English and women's studies at Willamette University in Salem, Oregon. She has published essays on Djuna Barnes, William Faulkner, Mary Shelley, contemporary cinema, and feminist and queer theory.

KI NAMASTE has a doctorate in semiotics from the University of Quebec in Montreal and has written a dissertation on the social semiotics of queer-punk culture.

MARIA PRAMAGGIORE adopts greyhounds and Manx cats and is a would-be massage therapist in training. She is Assistant Professor of Film Studies and Women's Studies at North Carolina State University in Raleigh and is working on a book about gender, sexuality, and ethnicity in postwar U.S. cinema.

LIDIA YUKMAN received her Ph.D. from the University of Oregon. She is the editor of *two girls review*. In addition to and in spite of her critical writing, she writes fiction; her work has appeared in the *Northwest Review, Puerto del Sol, Postmodern Culture, Left Bank*, the *Rain City Review, Quarry West, NWHQ*, and elsewhere. She is bi, loves glen livet, dogs, and devin.

BI-ntroduction I:
Epistemologies of the Fence

Maria Pramaggiore

Good fences make good neighbors.

—Robert Frost, "The Mending Wall"

When *Newsweek*'s July 17, 1995, cover story proclaimed "Bisexuality: Not Gay. Not Straight. A New Sexual Identity Emerges," many of us who have identified ourselves as bisexual for some time wondered what exactly could be considered "new" about bisexuality except the kind of public recognition enacted by the *Newsweek* cover, particularly since the article itself refers to a number of famous "historical" bisexuals (Cary Grant, Billie Holiday, and James Dean).[1] Does making the cover of *Newsweek* put bisexuality—the "wild card of our erotic life"—on a peak (or in a valley) of our sexual topography, and how does such a mapping affect politics and/or theory? Does Marjorie Garber's claim in that article that "[w]e are in a bisexual moment" (46), reinforced by her recently published book *Vice Versa: Bisexuality and the Eroticism of Everyday Life* (1995), authorize academics and activists to explore sexualities beyond the categories of straight, gay, and lesbian? Do appearances by "out" bisexuals on "The Maury Povich Show" (June 7, 1995)

1

and on "Leeza" ("Not Gay, Not Straight: Bisexual and Proud," September 7, 1995) embody and lend credibility to a set of sexualities that has been called bisexual, often for lack of a better word? And from what location did this "new" sexual identity "emerge" anyway?

The issue of mass culture's production and circulation of sexualities—from suitably citational scholarly inquiry to blatant mass-market titillation—is anything but secondary to the questions this collection of essays on bisexualities raises. If we heed the lessons contained in one of the founding documents of gay and lesbian studies, Eve Kosofsky Sedgwick's *Epistemology of the Closet* (1990), then this recent flurry of interest in bisexuality, and the generalized mainstreaming of previously closeted deviant sexualities, should remind us that ascribing newness to any sexuality (or any cultural phenomenon) is a peculiarly flexible trope of U.S. consumer culture. The practices that comprise bisexualities are hardly new; furthermore, they may not precisely be called the basis for sexual identities in many cases, which in itself is one of the paradoxes of bisexualities.

The *Newsweek* article on bisexuality, predictably, focuses on an individual's personal choice of sexual partner(s). "In the end, it is really about the simple, mysterious pull between [but not among?] warm human bodies when the lights go out," the writers conclude (50), but they neglect to examine why bisexuality might appear to be "new" at this moment in time. Is bisexuality merely the most recently acknowledged taboo-breaking sexual fashion trend under the sun? Or, as the authors of the essays in this volume suggest, do bisexual epistemologies go further than trendiness, charting the politics of sexualities in Western culture, redistricting and redistributing desire, and creating new cartographies for our cultural erotics?

It is our contention that the fence, a position attributed to bisexuals, and, in this collection, claimed by those of us who theorize from it, is more than merely the latest sexual position. In fact, fence-sitting is not a new position at all, as a number of essays in this volume demonstrate. Articles by Erin Carlston on Mary Renault's *Friendly Young Ladies*, by Chris Cagle on Alfred Hitchcock's *Strangers on a Train* and Kenneth Anger's *Fireworks*, and by Lidia Yukman on H. D.'s *Hermione* historicize bisexual representation, examining the political and aesthetic concerns of these early and mid–twentieth-century texts. Although they may not appear on any map, fences dot the cultural landscape in this century and others: well-worn, splintered, and split, sometimes uncomfortable and, until very recently, untheorized.

In *Epistemology of the Closet*, Sedgwick maintains that the relations of the closet, dependent as they are on distinctions between knowing and not knowing, seeing and not seeing, reveal both the power-laden nature of speech acts and the dynamics of what counts as a speech act.[2] She writes that "[t]he special centrality of homophobic oppression in the twentieth century ... has resulted from its inextricability from the question of knowledge and the processes of knowing in modern Western culture at large" (33–34). Sedgwick's recognition that the closet helps to define our ways of knowing the world informs but does not circumscribe the work in this volume, writing which directs our attention to a related location—the fence—and its attendant epistemologies. "Something there is that doesn't love a wall ... and makes gaps two can pass abreast," writes Robert Frost.[3] Those gaps rewrite the wall as fence, opening up spaces through which to view, through which to pass, and through which to encounter and enact fluid desires.

Sedgwick's closet is a rich visual and spatial metaphor—a location and a way of viewing and dividing the world. But closets are not definitive: they continuously dissolve and reproduce themselves. Nor are they comprehensive: the logic of the closet does not define all sexualities, despite that metaphor's resonance across modern and postmodern Western cultures. Cognizant of the connections between theorizing bisexualities and intervening in "the question of knowledge and processes of knowing" in Western culture, this collection reflects on and fences with the processes of knowing and enacting gender, sex, and sexuality—dynamics which are themselves implicated in cultural speech acts of writing, reading, filmmaking, spectatorship, and political activism. Michael Du Plessis's "Blatantly Bisexual," for example, speaks to the conflicted relations surrounding the politics of naming bisexuality from within queer theory and seeks to radicalize the "middle ground" bisexuality often stakes out. Ki Namaste's "From Performance to Interpretation" is concerned with postmodern, performative queer theory's reproduction of monosexual assumptions through its invocation of binary conceptions of the sign and its neglect of the potential for a historically grounded, social semiotics of sexuality.

The fence, in its nominal form, identifies a place of in-betweenness and indecision. Often precariously perched atop a structure that divides and demarcates, bisexual epistemologies have the capacity to reframe regimes and regions of desire by deframing and/or reframing in porous, nonexclusive ways. Fence-sitting—an epithet predicated on the presumption of the superiority of a temporally based single sexual partnership—is a practice that refuses the restrictive formulas that define gender according to binary categories, that associate one gender or one sexuality with a singularly gendered object choice, and that equate sexual practices with sexual identity. Bisexual epistemologies—ways of apprehending, organizing, and intervening in the world that refuse one-to-one correspondences between sex acts and identity, between erotic objects and sexualities, between identification and desire—acknowledge fluid desires and their continual construction and deconstruction of the desiring subject.

Marjorie Garber writes that "eroticism and desire are always to some degree transgressive, politically *in*correct" (31), yet it is also the case that eroticisms and desires are structured and policed at individual and cultural levels. Cultures, conceived of both as Foucault's disciplinary apparatuses and as constructive mechanisms, continually hem in and border our desires; enacting those desires produces institutional and psychological structures which are necessarily punctured by gaps through which "other" modalities of sexuality can be apprehended and performed. Thus the fence, a permeable and permeating structure, is most akin to the mutually inclusive "both/and" rather than the exclusive "either/or," just as Frost's mending wall is reconstructed and reinforced by persons on both sides: "And on a day we meet to walk the line/And set the wall between us once again./We keep the wall between us as we go" (23). The attention required to maintain this exclusionary wall forces those on either side to recognize not only both sides of the wall but also the wall's position as a third term in between them which continually deconstructs itself.

Sedgwick points toward the complexity of examining the "both/andness" of our sexual choices and behavior, not only in terms of gendered object choice, but also in relation to race, class, age, and species: "Without a concept of gender there could be, quite simply, no concept of homo- or heterosexuality. But many other dimensions of sexual choice (auto- or alloerotic, within or between generations, species, etc.) have no such distinctive, explicit definitional connection with gender; indeed, some dimensions of sexuality might be tied, not to gender, but instead to difference or similarities of race or class" (31).

One of the challenges of this volume is to create a space for fencing with oppositions that, Möbius-strip–like, sometimes become identities. This space overlaps and is adjacent to queer and feminist theories and also absorbs and infuses theories of race and class. Yet we are often fenced in by existing practices and discourses even as we theorize sexualities around, through, and beyond gender and object choice to address distinctions and identities of race and class.

The fence, in its verb form, implies sparring, dodging, and parrying with a single opponent. In the context of this anthology, our "opponents" assume the varied forms of literary theories, gay and lesbian theories, and theories of visual culture. But fencing, like many martial arts, is also a kind of dance: opponents are also partners. If monosexual models of hetero- and homosexuality can be conceived of as our sparring partners, then bisexualities are also unreliable third parties, refusing the agreed-upon rules of engagement and questioning the dualistic sport itself. Our theoretical points of contact and conflict, though often set up as oppositional terms, often shift to become points of mutuality. Good fences make good friends, indeed.

We recognize that bisexual theorizing and activism are implicated in the fencing match already under way: bisexual theories have come of age in an environment of newly prominent queer movements of the 1980s and 1990s and might be unthinkable outside that context.

One area in which theories of bisexuality have developed through a productive and sometimes painful interaction is within lesbian feminist discourse and politics, partly in response to the lingering postulate, prominent in Freudian psychoanalysis, of women's unique relation to bisexual desire and partly because of the significant body of lesbian and feminist politics and theory which addresses the pleasures and dangers of sexuality. A number of the papers on bisexuality presented at the "In Queery/Theory/Deed" Conference in November of 1994, for example, focused on the experiences of lesbians who come out as bisexuals, on differences in the construction of bisexual/lesbian identities, and on the fraught political alliances among bisexual women and lesbians.[4]

Anthologies of bisexual coming out stories published in the early 1990s point to the important role constructs of gender play in theorizing and enacting bisexualities for those who define their gender identities and sexualities according to heterosexual difference and for those who do not. The cluster of recent books, including *Bi Any Other Name: Bisexual People Speak Out* (1991), *Closer to Home: Bisexuality and Feminism* (1992), *Women and Bisexuality* (1993), and *Dual Attraction: Understanding Bisexuality* (1994),[5] raises the question of how gender differences are or should be important to bisexual theories and practices. In "Locating Bisexual Identities," Clare Hemmings speaks to the relationship between contemporary feminist theory and bisexuality, claiming that theorizing bisexuality offers a means of "making sense of the impasse that seems to have occurred between theories (and theorists) of identity and those of difference(s)" within feminism since the 1970s.[6] In this collection, Frann Michel's "Do Cats Eat Bats?" brings together feminist theory and postmodern performativity to ask what bisexuality "does" in the context of feminist, lesbian, and queer politics and theory, rather than to define what "it" "is."

Perspectives on bisexualities do seem to me to have a gender inflection: men's work on bisexuality, including the essays in this collection, more often deals with transgender issues, androgyny, and polymorphous perversity, whereas women's and feminist-inflected work often looks at the ways in which bisexuality, despite its binary implications, is a useful term precisely because it acknowledges that the world is divided by and governed according to gendered power relations. The papers written by the coeditors of this volume, as well as many others contained within it, look at bisexuality in strikingly different ways: Donald E. Hall works with concepts of polymorphous perversity in Victorian pornography, while I examine the problematic opposition between identification and desire posited by theories of film spectatorship that are based in heterosexual difference and Freud's constitutional model of bisexuality. The differences between these two essays are tempered, but not erased, by a shared concern with conceptualizing fluidities of sexual desire in and around the gendered political and aesthetic terminology currently available.

Because the fence stakes out a position between visibility and invisibility, a location "between two worlds," models of racial identity and passing often are adopted and elaborated upon in order to examine bisexualities, as Marcy Jane Knopf does in her essay on Jane Bowles's *Two Serious Ladies* and Traci Carroll does in her essay on E. Lynn Harris's *Invisible Life* and *Just as I Am*. Both authors revision the concept of passing as a racial *and* sexual activity, a movement between identities rather than a masquerade concealing an essential identity. Poet, essayist, and activist June Jordan has drawn an analogy between bisexuality and interracial or multiracial identities. In "A New Politics of Sexuality," she writes of her hope that a bisexual politics, an "emerging movement [that] politicizes the middle ground ... [and] invalidates either/or formulation, either/or analysis" will help to make possible a freedom in which a person is neither predictable nor controllable and need not choose between or among identities.[7] Jordan addresses the fact that making connections between and among racial and sexual identities is often controversial: "I do not believe it is blasphemous to compare oppressions of sexuality to oppressions of race and ethnicity" she states. "Freedom is indivisible or it is nothing at all besides sloganeering and temporary, short-sighted advancement for a few" (190). When E. Lynn Harris's Raymond refers to himself as "a bisexual: a sexual mulatto," he raises the prospect of the productive interplay between theories of sexuality and race and directs our attention toward those figures of powerful and too often tragic ambiguity: the bisexual and/or the mulatto.[8]

Echoing the various visual and spatial metaphors of the fence, passing, and visibility, several essays in the collection explore certain visual aspects of bisexual ambiguity—particularly in terms of the impossibility of codifying a bisexual body for private or mass consumption. Brian Loftus coins the term "biopia" to describe the simultaneous production and suppression of bisexualities through oppositions that construct and delimit sexuality according to the visibly signed body: male/female, masculine/feminine, and heterosexual/homosexual. Mariam Fraser discusses popular press representations of Simone de Beauvoir as a case study in "framing," a practice that defines its object only in relation to stable preexisting categories of identity. She argues that de Beauvoir is framed in terms of existentialism, as a "bohemian" and in relation to Jean-Paul Sartre, but cannot be framed bisexually.

We emphasize fluidity and mutual inclusion, yet bisexual epistemologies are not without particular conventions and concerns. Theoretical issues that appear throughout this volume in our readings of literary, film, and other texts include, but are not limited to: (1) the manner in which bisexualities disrupt and displace mono-sexual models of identity, most notably the Freudian model; (2) the relationship between temporality and sexuality; (3) triangulated structures of desire within and across genders (tellingly echoed in both the cover photograph for the *Newsweek* article, which depicts two men and a woman, and the cover of *Vice Versa*, which depicts three "pears/pairs"); (4) notions of invisibility and passing that differ from those posited by gay and lesbian models of the closet and models of essentialized racial difference; (5) the difficulty of distinguishing between/among identifications and desires; (6) the resonances between and among notions of sexual, gender, and racial ambiguity; (7) the search for ways of thinking about identity which do not rigidly codify sexuality in terms of gender; and (8) the tensions between and among gay, lesbian, queer, transgendered, transsexual, and bisexual studies and politics.

These concepts and reconceptualizations by no means encompass all of the concerns represented in this collection. Nor do the perspectives we present foreclose the possibilities for further theorizing, politicizing, and radicalizing the various "in-betweens" of gender, race, or sexuality. We hope that this volume contributes to a process of exploring the many epistemologies of many fences and provides a way of conceiving the fluidity of the various locations from which we examine and enact sexualities and desires.

BI-ntroduction II: Epistemologies of the Fence

Donald E. Hall

Don't/Stop

I felt a Cleaving in my Mind—
As if my Brain had split—
I tried to match it—Seam by Seam—
But could not make them fit.

The thought behind I strove to join
Unto the thought before—
But Sequence ravelled out of Sound
Like Balls—upon a Floor.[1]

* * *

porno-nation, evaluation
what's this, "time for segregation" . . .
bible-belt 'round anglo-waste, putting sinners in their place
yeah, right, great if you're so good explain the shit stains on
your face
white trash get down on your knees, time for cake and sodomy
time for cake and sodomy[2]

Multiplicities confuse, sometimes terrify, yet almost invariably intrigue us. Collapsed binaries, whether imploded or exploded, mystify *and* mesmerize us. Something there is that loves/doesn't love a wall. In *Powers of Horror*, Kristeva lingers over the apocalyptic, the wall-breaching, that which inhabits "the fragile border (borderline cases) where identities (subject/object, etc.) do not exist or only barely so—double, fuzzy, heterogeneous, animal, metamorphosed, altered, abject." Kristeva's is, and exalts, a literature of indeterminacy, of "murky waters," disappointing, frustrating, and hollowing the "demarcating imperative," "disturb[ing] identity, system, order," produced by "the artist who, even if he does not know it, is an undoer of narcissism and of all imaginary identity as well, sexual included."[3] Such is the case in the passages above, where Emily Dickinson's scattered balls and Marilyn Manson's desegregated, dis-placed, and politicized oral/anal gratifications simultaneously in(e)voke and transgress comforting categories, knowable orientations. Even so, they are clearly not the same. While Marilyn Manson links behind and before in strategic, seamless, yet finally reductive ways, Dickinson remains scattered and cleaved. Oddly, perhaps, Dickinson is the most noticeably "postmodern" of the two, even as she still seems rather regrettably reticent to find/allow pleasure in pluralities, in scattered balls.

They could learn a lot from each other (and from Kristeva). They *could* serve as key figures in the great, woefully neglected "bisexual" tradition in western culture.

If one wanted to construct and defend such a thing. To demarcate yet again. Sappho, Shakespeare, Byron, Marge Piercy . . . Where does that take us? Toward a tentative table of contents for a new, Nortonesque anthology of bisexual literature? [Yet imagine—if everyone who has ever had sexual contact, fantasies, sensual pleasures, across orientational lines were to buy a copy . . . oh, *please/support* your people] NO, the guest list for the first telethon [performances by David Bowie, Joan Baez, Michael Stipe, and Sophie B. Hawkins] UNITY

makes me nervous, at the same time that it *is* politically, critically, inter-personally (inter-communicatively) efficacious [though, frankly, I have always thought that Deleuze and Guattari make schizophrenia seem *ever* so much more attractive than paranoia].

I will [try to] put a belt around it.

A proposition: BISEXUALITY = POSTMODERNISM EMBODIED

This collection takes as one of its foundational premises that BISEXUALITY cannot be definitively REPRESENTED. There are oh so many sexualities that do not fit into the reductive, though eminently useful, binary of hetero- and homosexuality. Clearly "bisexuality" is a highly problematic term as it attempts to (or has been deployed to) embrace the dauntingly wide variety of these. [serial monogamists who have loved men and women who usually masturbate thinking about women who fuck men who play with men and women together whose sexualities have changed dramatically since adolescence(ts) who hate being categorized for sleeping with other young women or men who enjoy being anally penetrated and it doesn't matter if it is a man or a woman who finds role-playing more exciting than the biological sex of the role-player who watches heterosexual pornography and sometimes identifies with the woman and sometimes with the man who finally just likes a warm, moist embrace] Thus this collection does not work uniformly, seamlessly, to naturalize *a* bisexual state. Indeed, I am uncomfortable with all of the last four words in the previous sentence, especially when they are linked; even John Stuart Mill (no postmodern, certainly) would agree that "nature" and "fixity" are wholly irreconcilable terms. Exploring such problematic language, celebrating pluralities, reading multiplicities, engaging sexual diversities that queer the binary (the bina-*ries*)—yes, these are the pleasures and practices that you will [well, uh, may] encounter in the coming pages.

Like Balls—upon a Floor.

A question: WHY HAS THERE NEVER BEEN A BISEXUAL STONEWALL?

A quick, partial answer: as I explore in my essay included in this collection, what we might loosely term "bisexuality" (as a healthy sexual manifestation, anyway) has been substantially erased from (indeed, seems *almost* unknown to) twentieth-century cultural representations, ordered by, validated by, binary-based discourse. Resistance is one polyvalent possibility when one/something is discursively scripted; resistance is difficult when one/something does not exist, or exists only in a state of murky fluidity rather than discursive fixity.

Yet not impossible, certainly. I remember as a child being drawn to those horror films that had in their title role not clawed, toothy, upright monsters but those, like *The Green Slime*, *The Blob*, and any number of undersea thrillers, with viscous antagonists, ones who slide along, slug about amoebically, ooze menacingly, and barely manage to retain their bodily intactness as they surround and incorporate their confused victims.

Stone/wall? no. I want something moist, preferably gelatinous.

Mashed-up cake and gooey sodomy. What is inside/What is outside?
Like Balls—into the Batter.

REALITY CHECK: BISEXUALITY ≠ POSTMODERNISM EMBODIED + OK
AUTHORIZE YOUR SELF

One rather annoying (though admittedly successful) editor to whom we tried to market this collection asked us to "spice" things up a bit—"What do bisexuals do in bed?" was his barely veiled question.

OK—I usually grade papers and sleep in mine.
"Oh . . . yes . . . hmmm . . . BUT, what do you *dream* about"

"Emily/Dick/in/*what*?"

Well, if you *must* know, I do not often self-identify as "bisexual." I am "queer" mostly, "gay" when I am forced to be strategically political, "polymorphously perverse" when I can be loquacious. I have had and will have sex with both women and men, can be aroused by assorted tactile, visual, and mechanical "things," and am wholly dissatisfied with identity politics as currently configured. [unless . . . MECHANO-SEXUAL RIGHTS!] Indeed, I (speaking *only* for myself) especially dislike the term "bisexual," for it inescapably encodes binarism. I am not sure that there are only two sexes in an age when body parts are easily acquired and altered, am certainly not "split" in two as the term signals (am split, in fact, into parts/aspects too numerous and changing to count), and have had some of my most intense orgasms by myself anyway [uh, with the help of friendly, consenting machines, of course].
Is that spicy enough? Do I . . . *pass*?

BISOCIALITY/BISEXUALITY: An Epistemology of the Fence

Yes, something there is that loves/doesn't love a wall. Kristeva/we return time and again to that which demarcates, the walls that keep *us* in and *them* out, for an always potentially breaching sensuality pervades [practically?] all of our lives, is inescapable. Desiring beings, we touch one another, establish emotional ties, view/admire/envy each other's bodies, comfort and cajole—bisocially. Indeed, funny, sometimes scary, slippages between the social and the sexual are mainstays of films such as *When Harry Met Sally* and episodes of *The Simpsons*, *Seinfeld*, and *Roseanne*.

Categories constantly crumble and then are energetically reinstated as our culture toys with and hastily retreats from acknowledging the circuit-exploding, channel-overflowing nature of superabundant human desire, the ridiculous reductiveness of binarized notions of sexual identity. [A lesbian friend, who has had admittedly joyous, orgasmic sex with both male and female partners, confronted me recently with, "Sure, I understand bisexuality as a *concept*, but how would it work on a day to day basis?" I had no answer, but thought, "Buy a good daily planner!"] What becomes clear is that we still do not even know how to talk about (much less, pass credible judgment upon) the wide range of bodily pleasures that most of us experience every day, as we look at, smell, hear, and tactilely encounter one another. I do not know if we are all potentially, ideally "bisexual." I do know that we *are* pan-sensual and that the murky line between the sensual and the sexual has led to a general suspicion and derision of those who self-identify as "bisexual," who are scapegoated for the thorough erotic confusion that hides just under the surface of most of our lives.

Even so, such confusion has always been both threatening and useful to those forces structuring culture and society. Most immediately, the in-between, the unidentifiable, the viscously confounding work against the conveniences that allow easy social interaction. But they are also base matter(s):

Granted that disorder spoils pattern; it also provides the materials of pattern. Order implies restriction; from all possible materials, a limited selection has been made and from all possible relations a limited set has been used. So disorder by implication is unlimited, no pattern has been realised in it, but its potential patterning is indefinite. This is why, though we seek to create order, we do not simply condemn disorder. We recognize that it is destructive to existing patterns; also that it has potentiality. It symbolizes both danger and power.[4]

Such reactions to, usages of, disorder have been particularly pronounced since the paradigm shifts that led to the overwhelming reliance upon binary definitions characterizing Euro-American culture since the eighteenth century. A categorizing imperative, making specifically zero-sum sense of perceived disorder, has propelled the sciences and the numerous pseudosciences of cultural studies. Desire is [sooo] inherently disorderly. Is it at all surprising that for Freudians, childhood bisexuality is the base matter of properly channeled adult sexuality? After all, social/cultural/personal "PROGRESS" builds upon such broad bases, moving upward pyramidically in regular rows of seamlessly linked, solid little blocks, ones with reliable, regular boundaries and hard constitutions. Surely *no one* wants to go back and do foundational work when finally, almost, finishing the roof.

Oh yes, we do and must:

We live today in the age of partial objects, bricks that have been shattered to bits, and left-overs. We no longer believe in the myth of the existence of fragments that, like pieces of an antique statue, are merely waiting for the last one to be turned up, so that they may all be glued back together to create a unity that is precisely the same as the original unity. We no longer believe in a primordial totality that once existed, or in a final totality that awaits us at some future date. We no longer believe in the dull gray outlines of a dreary, colorless dialectic of evolution, aimed at forming a harmonious whole out of heterogeneous bits by rounding off their rough edges.[5]

Well, we don't, but *they* do.

Metaphors hold awful sway over many of our lives, over aspects of all of our lives. Confront them we must; live within and among them we always will. Sexuality is not a hard little brick. A binary-based notion of "progress" is hardly the deity that it once seemed. But are there replacement paradigms? Scattering balls, coagulate frosting, slip/hard sodomy—certainly these are more to my taste. And (finally/obviously) I am not alone. The essays that follow (ones that coagulate into three groupings) seek to disrupt traditional epistemologies, challenge the ways we continue to define literary/representational/theoretical "progress." Is "queer" the/a telos? Can we scrap narrow notions of identity politics? Should we? And what else is scrappable—monogamy? Narrative form? Can we read "bisexually" when we do not even agree on what "bisexuality" means? Is the latter even a useful term given its history and overloaded deno/connotations?

The contributors to this collection do not provide uniform answers.

There are many seams that simply do not fit.

SO WHY THIS BOOK?

It is clear that the binarily, often reactively, defined field of lesbian and gay studies has not done justice to the diverse "nonstraight" expressions of desire that have been represented literarily and visually, and that are theorizable. And as several of the essays that follow argue at length, "queer theory" has not performed much better. "Bisexuality" has barely begun to "trickle up" from "popular" to "high" culture. The forces of gravity are mighty.

Yet . . . we *are* making progress, aren't we? So now (join hands, please), what we *ALL* need to visualize is a big BISEXUAL CONTINUUM, one that this collection (why, *thank you!*) discovers . . . explores . . . *maps*—a useful paradigm and one that has a certain ring (*of marketability!*) to it.

STOP! Such a "progressive" notion is wholly antithetical to what I see as the more pressing need to disrupt such facile model-building, especially as it concerns the many fluid forms, vectors, and possible manifestations of desire. *RePresenting Bisexualities* engages pluralities and partitions throughout, lingering over problems and potentials, but not working to *fix* them conclusively. "Bisexuality" is a practical, even inevitable, rubric under which to place the diverse essays that make up this collection:

it is a Library of Congress subject heading

even though it does not adequately re/present the sexualities and sensualities that are explored in the coming pages. Something there is that *needs* a wall, at least for marketing and cataloging purposes.

Juxtapositions ≠ Walls

you give me the anger. you give me the nerve. carry out the sentence.
i get what i deserve. i'm just an effigy to be defaced. to be disgraced.
your need for me has been replaced. and if i can't have everything
well then just give me a taste.
it comes down to this. your kiss. your fist. and your strain.
it gets under my skin. within. take in the extent of my sin.[6]

* * *

Then they started from their places,
moved with violence, changed in hue,
Caught each other with wild grimaces,
Half-invisible to the view,
Wheeling with precipitate paces
To the melody, till they flew
Hair and eyes and limbs and faces,
Twisted hard in fierce embraces,
Like to Furies, like to Graces,
Dash'd together in blinding dew;
Till, kill'd with some luxurious agony,
The nerve-desolving melody
Flutter'd headlong from the sky.[7]

Sin across the centuries. Sexually obscure and undifferentiated erotics. Boundary-breaching pain/pleasures. SYNCOPE: that rapturous dissolution of SELF.[8] Destruction (even) of the i. Yet ... oh ... the stories/states we have to create simply to do what we want to do (or, more often, *not* do what we want to do). Fiercely embraced, twisted, defaced, nerve-dissolved. *Please.* please ...

Their sex still frightens them. Their bodies, which they haven't dared enjoy, have been colonized.[9]

Cixous on the (queered?) sex/es (FORMERLY KNOWN AS . . .): "let us imagine a real liberation of sexuality, that is to say, a transformation of each one's relation to his or her body (and to the other body), an approximation to the vast, material, organic, sensuous universe that we are."[10] Yet, where do we start and where do we stop?

with ravelled cake? with cleaved frosting flows?

with seams and balls out of sound . . .

Notes to BI-notroduction I

1. "Bisexuality. Not Gay. Not Straight. A New Sexual Identity Emerges," *Newsweek* (July 17, 1995), 44–50.

2. Eve Kosofsky Sedgwick, *Epistemology of the Closet* (Berkeley: University of California Press, 1990), 3.

3. *Selected Poems of Robert Frost*, introduced by Robert Graves (New York: Holt, Rinehart and Winston, 1963), 23. The definitive edition of Frost's works is *The Poetry of Robert Frost*, ed. Edward Connery Lathem (New York: Henry Holt, 1969).

4. The panel "Bisexual Positions," moderated by Robyn Ochs, is a good example. That panel included Amanda Udis-Kessler, "Identity/Politics: A History of the Bisexual Movement"; Amber Ault, "Bifurcated Consciousness: Lesbian Feminists and the Erasure of Bisexuality"; Jill Nagle, "Bisexuality in a Gender Container: The Tupperware Theory"; and Beth Firestein, "How Biphobia Hurts the Struggle for Queer Liberation." The "Identities" panel, moderated by Mickey Eliason included Julia Wallace, "Biphobia: Gay and Lesbian Dismissals of Bisexuality"; Arlene Stein, "Leaving the Fold: Ex-Lesbians and the Maintenance of Sexual Binarism"; and Paula Rust, "To Identify or Not Identify: The Process of Becoming or Not Becoming Bisexual Identified."

5. Sue George, *Women and Bisexuality* (London: Scarlet Press, 1993); *Bi Any Other Name: Bisexual People Speak Out,* ed. Loraine Hutchins and Lani Ka'ahumanu (Boston: Alyson Publications, 1991); Martin S. Weinberg, Colin J. Williams, and Douglas Pryor, *Dual Attraction: Understanding Bisexuality* (New York: Oxford University Press, 1994); and *Closer to Home: Bisexuality and Feminism*, ed. Elizabeth Reba Weise (Seattle: Seal Press, 1992).

6. Clare Hemmings, "Locating Bisexual Identities: Discourses of Bisexuality and Contemporary Feminist Theory," in *Mapping Desire*, ed. David Bell and Gill Valentine (London: Routledge, 1995), 45.

7. June Jordan, "A New Politics of Sexuality," in *Technical Difficulties* (New York: Vintage Books, 1992), 193.

8. E. Lynn Harris, *Just As I Am* (New York: Doubleday, 1994), 4.

Notes to BI-ntroduction II

1. Emily Dickinson, "937," in *The Complete Poems of Emily Dickinson*, ed. Thomas H. Johnson (Boston: Little, Brown and Company, 1960), 439–40.

2. Marilyn Manson, "Cake and Sodomy," on *Portrait of an American Family*, Interscope Records, 1994.

3. Julia Kristeva, *Powers of Horror*, trans. Leon S. Roudiez (New York: Columbia University Press, 1982), 207, 4, 210, 68, 208.

4. Mary Douglas, *Purity and Danger: An Analysis of the Concepts of Pollution and Taboo* (New York: Ark, 1984), 94.

5. Gilles Deleuze and Felix Guattari, *Anti-Oedipus: Capitalism and Schizophrenia*, trans. Robert Hurley et al. (Minneapolis: University of Minnesota Press, 1983), 42.

6. Nine Inch Nails, "Sin," on *Pretty Hate Machine*, TVT Records, 1989.

7. Alfred Lord Tennyson, "The Vision of Sin," *Victorian Poetry and Poetics*, 2d ed., ed. Walter E. Houghton and G. Robert Stange (Boston: Houghton Mifflin, 1968), 39–40.

8. See Catherine Clément, *SYNCOPE: The Philosophy of Rapture*, trans. Sally O'Driscoll and Deirdre M. Mahony (Minneapolis: University of Minnesota Press, 1994).

9. Hélène Cixous and Catherine Clément, *The Newly Born Woman*, trans. Betsy Wing (Minneapolis: University of Minnesota Press, 1986), 68.

10. Cixous and Clément, *The Newly Born Woman*, 83.

Part One

Unthinking Queer/
Theorizing Bisexually

Chapter 1

Blatantly Bisexual;
or, Unthinking Queer Theory

Michael du Plessis

Not Half Gay, Not Half Straight, But Totally Bisexual!
—Sticker, Queer Terrorist Network, c.1993

Unthinking Bisexuality

Given the highly contradictory accounts to which it has been subject, bisexuality may well seem fated to confusion. We have been told that bisexuality veers between homosexuality and heterosexuality as two distinct sexual orientations, without ever becoming an orientation in its own right; we have also been informed that it oscillates between two genders because it already androgynously contains masculine and feminine within itself. Experts and laypersons alike have wondered in a variety of ways whether it might be some rare fusion of sexuality, gender, and object choice. But we have also heard, over and over again, that bisexuality is merely a behavior which is fairly common but does not have an identity to back it up. To make matters worse, bisexuality seems to lend itself to exaggeration—all or nothing; everyone is bisexual or no one is. Bisexuality carries extreme values, so that it can be extolled as progressive, "chic," as a panacea, a fantasy, a promised land, mythologized as origin of all desires, or vituperated as reactionary, infantile, regressive, a red herring, a cop-out, a lie, a dead-end street. "Bisexuality" can even be many or all of these things at once: there has never been, it seems, one single bisexuality, but only more or less incoherent *versions* of bisexuality.

Given this state of affairs, what is the critical task for people who identify, against all odds, as bisexual? (And what, one may also ask, does it mean, socially and critically, to identify as "bisexual"?) We could adjudicate among the various fantasies of bisexuality, such as those sketched above, as we try to spell out what real bisexuality, devoid of myth and stereotype, would be. And, in time perhaps, we could even soberly come out with the plain truth about bisexuality. But these options always run the risk of making bisexuality be only a single thing and therefore simply promoting one of the many well-worn versions of bisexuality as the only one that all bisexuals should embrace. Whatever we do, we should, I think, avoid the temptation to have the last word on bisexuality, but without throwing caution to the wind and uncritically embracing every stereotype of bisexuality that has ever existed. We can, instead, painstakingly identify and elaborate the models of bisexuality that have had currency at particular places and times, all the while understanding that those "bisexualities" necessarily have some strategic import. Why *this* bisexuality, and not that? What does a particular model of bisexuality *do* in a given place and time?

In coming up with a theory of what all "bisexuality" *is*, without regard to the bisexualities available in precise situations, we risk generalization, no matter how generous or accommodating our conceptual model might be, or how persuasive its effects. For example, overgeneralization seems an inherent danger of Marjorie Garber's *Vice Versa*, an exhaustive account of bisexuality that is part tabloid and part encyclopedia.[1] She shows again and again (and very convincingly) that there are links between bisexuality, the stories people make of their sexual lives, and what the subtitle of *Vice Versa* calls "the eroticism of everyday life." But Garber does not clarify or even consider why, more than any other sexuality, bisexuality should have such an affinity for both "narrative" and a fluid and almost indefinable "eroticism" (as Garber appears to see the latter). Indeed, "sexuality," "narrative," and "eroticism" are terms that Garber simply takes for granted. *Vice Versa* undoubtedly opens many conceptual possibilities for reading bisexuality (sometimes for reading bisexuality in, as well), but it does so only by promoting one, highly tendentious, version of bisexuality which makes the latter the equivalent of "eroticism" and "narrative" (all eroticism, all narrative).[2] Because *Vice Versa* turns on sweeping statements, it tends to disregard history, which, after all, concerns specific meanings in specific situations.

While her book is amply filled with detail, the detail always amounts to the same thing: a link between narrative, the everyday, and bisexuality, all of which are then understood as entities characterized by their fluid natures. Garber's neglect of historical precision and specificity leads her to dismiss "politics" in contemptuous, quite ahistorical terms. Thus, she uses the loaded term "politically correct," which is particular to a very well-defined right-wing political agenda in the North America of the late 1980s, to celebrate bohemian bisexuality in Bloomsbury and Harlem during the 1920s. "And lives, it turns out, are no more politically correct than art," she claims, setting "life" and "art" against "politics" and "political correctness."[3] The epigrams which show up in *Vice Versa* generalize beyond any usefulness. For example, Garber can confidently assure the reader: "Politics is always belated."[4]

The shortcomings of *Vice Versa* can be traced to a desire to have that last word, or, in the colloquial expression, to write the book on bisexuality, and to state, once and for all, what bisexuality *is*. (To say, repeatedly, that the essence of bisexuality is fluid, as Garber does, by no means makes this attempt to fix essences less sure of itself or less essentialist.) Perhaps analyzing what bisexuality is *not*, rather than insisting on what it is, could help in understanding bisexuality historically. We need to look at the ways in which various bisexualities have been constructed, interpreted, or excluded. And we would need to do so, again, in specific situations. We may well insist on our visibility by working through the conditions of our invisibility. To insist on the social viability of our present bisexual identities, as "blatant" rather than shady or latent, we may need to turn the tables on high- or low-brow, recondite or popular, models of sexuality that appear unthinking when it comes to bisexuality. Such models have omitted, denied, disavowed, and even appropriated bisexuality. Now is the time, actively and critically, to unthink them.[5]

In this essay, I examine the ways in which something called "bisexuality" has been made to play in a specific set of writings, namely, those texts that academics recognize under the label of "theory." Such an examination may be one way of beginning the task that is crucial to bisexual politics: understanding how we have come to be unthought, made invisible, trivial, insubstantial, irrelevant. While this theory may seem far from the urgencies of bisexual politics, theory itself is a practice, and a practice which reaches far beyond its own confines. For example, the ways in which the self-declared theory of psychoanalysis has spelled out definitions of "bisexuality" continues to inform just how we are understood; much more recent forms of theory, such as "queer theory," have repercussions far beyond the simply academic in their treatment of bisexuality. The greater part of my paper is devoted to outlining what theory has said about us and how we might speak back to its pronouncements on our own terms.

We can begin naming ourselves and our various bisexual identities by, paradoxically, negation: we can scrutinize the pronouncements of which we have been either the objects or the missing others in order to spell out the process of erasure that has taken place. In my readings of various forms of "theory," I do not mean to suggest ill intentions and individual malice; on the contrary, I wish to highlight an ideologically bound inability to imagine bisexuality concretely which is common to various "theories," from the apparently radical to the politically reticent, from Freudian to "French feminist" to Anglophone film theory, from popular sexology to queer theory. In order to name ourselves not once-and-for-all but tactically, through the very utterances that would un-name us, bisexuals have drawn on what I call and analyze as a politics of *para*-naming, or a naming which is in, through, and alongside the misnaming to which we are subject. (According to *Webster's*, *para*, as a prefix, means "beside, alongside of, beyond, aside from, or closely related to.") Such para-naming provides one way in which we can assert ourselves as "totally bisexual." A brief example: the sticker that I quote as a motto comes up with the slogan, "Not half gay, not half straight, but totally bisexual," in which "bisexual" achieves its meaning through its refusal of both adjacent terms, "straight" and "gay." However, the politics of naming or para-naming *alone* is not enough, as our ongoing battles over health care, citizenship and immigration, family structures, multiple or single partnerships, housing, employment, social services, and survival all testify.

Through para-naming "bisexuality" can work in ways not unlike the "oppositional consciousness" of which Chela Sandoval writes in relation to the contradictions of "U.S. third world feminism." Sandoval describes how "differential consciousness represents the variant, emerging out of correlations, intensities, junctures, crises. What is differential functions through hierarchy, location, and value— enacting the recovery, revenge, or reparation."[6] For Sandoval, location, place, and hierarchy produce differences, out of which resistance can come, precisely as the effect of those differences.

As bisexuals we can enact a "recovery, revenge, or reparation" across a number of terrains, which would be similar to that envisaged by Sandoval for all forms of oppositional consciousness, once we come out of the interstices of theories and speak back to, and through, the systems and groups that have tried to think us away. An entry in an entire series of "ultimate bisexual comebacks" offered by the bisexual fanzine *Anything That Moves* puts it best: "Well, I don't think you exist either."[7] This is un-thinking with a vengeance.

Place is crucial to both oppositional consciousness and to the tactical recovery of bisexuality as something adjacent or alongside, a *para*-identity. Accordingly, this essay ends by reimagining the place of bisexuality. The commonplace of bisexuality as some "middle ground" between other entities, whether sexualities, genders, or social groups, has often been the only place to which bisexuality gets relegated.

Perhaps that middle ground can lose some of its commonplaceness and be made radical as the site for a new bisexual activism. Yet I do not want to impose anew the cliché of bisexuality as a borderline or borderland that affirms two, and only two, other identities that are understood to be securely in place. Instead, I wish to suggest that, ideally, bisexuality would make for an identity politics that involves, unavoidably, an identity-in-coalition politics. The *topos* of "middle ground" occurs frequently in discussions that link bisexuality to what has come to be called "multi-culturalism" in the United States, and this frequency seems to be more than coincidental and bears investigation. While the model of multiculturalism is itself highly time- and place-bound, I want to suggest that such a situation of bisexuality in and through the issues of multiculturalism can offer the hope of identity politics beyond identity politics, a site on which bisexuals can stand, firmly, in coalition and solidarity with many other groups and identities.[8]

Why Bi Theory?

It's 1991, and two other queer graduate students and I are talking about the upcoming Rutgers Lesbian and Gay Conference. To reiterate: *Lesbian and Gay,* for it soon turns out that I'm the only bisexual in our group, and that I'm also (not surprisingly) the only one who knows about the conference organizers' decision to drop "Bisexual" from the official title. I've heard a great deal of gossip about this decision, including one rumor that intrigues and infuriates me: supposedly, a reason given for the noninclusion of bisexuals is that *bisexuals have not produced good theory.* (Like all veritable rumors, this one has remained unverified.)[9] "The organizers certainly aren't giving bisexuals a chance to produce theory," muses the more sympathetic of my two interlocutors, before adding, "What *would* a bisexual theory look like?" Suddenly angry, I respond, "We don't need a bisexual theory. We need bisexual *bodies.*" The conversation, then, turns to other things.

Robyn Ochs and Pam Ellis tell the story of the conference in more detail in a short article, "Conference Organizers 'Confused'" from *Anything That Moves.* They note that when the conference was held at Harvard the previous year, "bisexual" did feature in the conference title, which was "The Fourth National Lesbian, Bisexual, and Gay Studies Conference: 'Pleasure and Politics'" (Harvard, 26–28 October 1990).[10] Conference organizers at Rutgers, however, told Ochs and Ellis that their decision to drop the word—*that* word—from the conference title was "unanimous": the organizers felt justified that, by leaving "bisexual" out, they were being "more inclusive." Confused conference organizers indeed! Ochs and Ellis comment, "Categorizing all sexual behavior which cannot be categorized as heterosexual as 'lesbian and gay' is an oppressive act in language"[11]—oppressive in more than just language, just as language is always more than "just" language.[12] Ochs and Ellis called for a letter-writing zap, but the situation seems to have been "resolved," not entirely satisfactorily, by giving a few panels to bisexuals without "bisexual" as such making its way back into the conference title.[13] The ad hoc "Stick It Back In" committee also busied itself with protests against the Rutgers committee's paternalistic assumption that we would feel happy to be reclassified as "lesbian and gay" without our consent and to be included, according to the committee's double-talk, by being left out.[14]

A simple appeal to bisexual bodies (like my call for bodies as opposed to theories) risks the presumption that bodies can somehow be enough, that is, self-evident, or outside a world of already existing meanings.[15] The relations between bisexual bodies and theories of bisexuality become even more vexed when we realize that bisexuality is very often only apprehended as something "in theory," that is, as a speculation or hypothesis which does not, in fact, exist "in reality" (wherever *that* may be). In the instance of the Rutgers conference, we were expelled because, supposedly, we had not done enough good theory, but bisexuals may very well be only good *in theory*—hence, perhaps, the reluctance even to name us as such. Also, a simple "commonsense" appeal to the body can serve the ends of heterosexism, for which anatomy, relentlessly, is destiny. Yet the bland belief that "theory" itself does not *do* a politics and does not produce an immediate practice can have very particular—if implicit—political goals, as the rumor about bisexuals not making good enough "theory" evidences.[16] Whatever the reasons for the disappearance of "bisexual" from the title of the 1991 Rutgers conference, "theory" can be read as a pretext for biphobia and may operate in many situations as a straightforward act of elitism and exclusion.[17]

Since we have already been faulted for our theoretical failures, bisexuals may gain something by keeping our distance from the thriving scene of queer theory. From our critical distance—perhaps from our very position on the fence on which we are so often accused of sitting—we can raise a different set of issues. For example, we might ask why and how "theory" rather than "queerness" has become the credit card—indeed, the credibility card—of "cultural capital" inside the Anglo-American academy?[18] In ways that a nascent bisexual criticism can find useful, one critic, Donald Morton, has begun to question the spectacular success of "queer theory" and its self-sustaining "narrative of break and break-through . . . as if from within [the academy itself]."[19] Morton astutely reveals the commodification process by which the same old theory can be given a make-over, and he claims that what is really going on in "queer theory" amounts to an uncritical and ubiquitous reassertion of a liberal-humanist appeal to "experience."[20] In the end, it is less "theory" *queered* (or even defamiliarized) than the usual business of theorizing "queerness."[21]

Persuasive as Morton is, he does not tell the full story. The rise of queer theory in the United States may be linked to an increased loss of political force and direction inside the United States academy. The past decade and a half have witnessed Republican dominance; neglect and cruelty in the AIDS crisis; assaults on immigrants, welfare, and affirmative action; and, in the academy, cuts in educational budgets, an ever-weakening liberal understanding of the role of the university (that understanding limited from the start); the debacles of deconstruction; the attacks on what came to be denounced as "political correctness"; and all of this along with the still tentative institutionalization of women's studies. In such a context, joining "theory" to some almost all-purpose "queerness" seems to promise a kind of magical resolution to conflicts over the social role of the university by granting whoever purveys "queer theory" the illusion of direct action *via* theory. Academic decorum and protocols tend to work as class-based constraints and to minister to class interests.

Given all these considerations, the question becomes not so much why bi theory as why buy theory (or who buys which theory), but that question has to be taken up elsewhere. I can only suggest that as bisexuals, our interests might be served better if we begin with historical and social analyses. At issue is not whether we can find our place in queer theory but the way in which our asserted presence can transform the problematic of sexuality and gender as it has been posed in the academy. Take the ubiquity of the concept "homophobia" in the work of queer theory. We may well ask if "homophobia" *alone* can explain the complicated oppressions to which everyone living outside a normative sex-gender system is subject. As a critical concept "homophobia" tends to suggest psychological, hence individualized, explanations for social oppression, regardless of whether that psychology is personal or collective. Despite the formation of the term "biphobia" by analogy with "homophobia," it is useful to insist that "biphobia" is a specific term which has a political, if not linguistic, closeness to "heterosexism." Indeed, "heterosexism" may name our oppression far more effectively than "homophobia" does, and using "heterosexism" to name a structure of oppression can lead to considerably more powerful ways of thinking against it.[22]

Heterosexism may have much to do with many bisexuals: take, for example, the couple culture that makes itself an institution everywhere, even in the ostensibly liberal movement by which partnership benefits are extended from one set of couples ("opposite-sex") to another ("same-sex"). Such heterosexism understands the two-partner model of heterosexuality as the only acceptable basis for relationships, and denies the full and urgent complexities of lived social networks of support, affection, and lust. On the issue of multiple partners, the AIDS crisis might be understood very differently by insisting on the validity, rather than the guilt, of bisexuality.

In terms of gay culture, as bisexuals we have many reasons to be skeptical of the way in which the story of the Stonewall riots is now told. "Stonewall" has come to be canonized (and amply commercialized) as the point of origin of contemporary queer culture in a master narrative which relies on the even grander master narrative of "American" nationalism and the onward and upward progress of "American democracy." Given that bisexuals have always been in lesbian and gay communities, whether acknowledged or not, perhaps we can help lesbians and gay men tell history in less rigid and damagingly nationalistic ways. What about the models of "polymorphous perversity" that were available at the time of Stonewall? What about the initial transnational, coalitionist, and anti-imperialist politics of the various groups identified with Gay Lib?[23] What about earlier moments, such as Magnus Hirschfeld's Institute for Sexual Research in Berlin prior to World War II? To assume bisexuality as a point of departure rather than as an afterthought can prevent some of the mistaken presumptions of lesbian and gay history/theory, which has tended to understand all same-sex and cross-sex behaviors according to a contemporary lesbian and gay norm.[24]

Unthinking Theory (Freud, French Feminist, Film, Queer . . .)

Freud's "Innate Disposition"

The relation of "bisexuality" to "theory" has the air of a dangerous liaison. "Theory" seems always to be attempting to make "bisexuality" *merely* "theoretical," that is, masterable and knowable, an object for which it can finally account and which it can ultimately explain away. In its turn, "bisexuality" threatens to undo, if not throw into crisis, some of the certainties of theory. Their dangerous liaison, moreover, appears to consist of a series of missed encounters and broken dates, in which "theory" continues to postpone its engagement with the "bisexuality" that "theory" either relegates to some distant anterior time or anticipates in an unspecified future. The end result is that bisexuality can always be held off, never to interrupt the present moment.[25]

The empiricism of the early sexologists found evidence of bisexual behavior everywhere, a ubiquity which led them to invent all kinds of names for the sexuality they believed they were discovering.[26] But the links, missing and otherwise, between "theory" and "bisexuality" can be traced back to Sigmund Freud's *Three Essays on the Theory of Sexuality* (*Drei Abhandlungen zur Sexualtheorie* [1905]). As Freud's title makes clear, "sexuality" and "theory" are henceforth to run in tandem. (And this pairing takes place before queer theory, although queer theory continues to give priority to psychoanalysis, often over other more obviously socially based theories.) In *Three Essays*, Freud carefully distinguishes his own "science"[27] from "the theory of bisexuality [which] has been expressed in its crudest form by a spokesman of the male inverts."[28] He further warns against the untheoretical understandings of "the lay circles" in which Otto Weininger is credited with "the hypothesis of human bisexuality," a hypothesis which, according to Freud, Weininger made "the basis of a somewhat unbalanced book."[29] Freud thus salvages his version of bisexuality for science and theory, precisely *against* lay circles, crude forms, unbalanced books, and popular misconceptions. Moreover, he guarantees a proprietorship over a bisexuality which almost becomes his patent, and it is this (his) bisexuality which his theory will call up only to expel time and time again.

Freud has indeed made a *theory* of bisexuality completely his own: in his famous never-delivered lecture of 1933 on "Femininity," he declares roundly that his science and he "are standing on the *ground* of bisexuality" when making their irrefutable claims about the "riddle of femininity."[30] Simply put, bisexuality is entirely Freud's turf by the early 1930s.[31] In a slightly earlier (1931) piece on "Female Sexuality," bisexuality again guarantees Freud's knowledge: "First of all, there can be no doubt that the bisexuality, which is present, as we believe, in the innate disposition of human beings, comes to the fore much more clearly in women than in men."[32]

His gendering of bisexuality as an attribute of "women" resolves an ongoing confusion in Freud's theory over whether bisexuality is to be comprehended as a form of hermaphroditism, "psychic" or otherwise, or as a primary sexual matrix for later homosexual or heterosexual object choice and sexual orientation. Freud had taken the word "bisexuality" from Wilhelm Fliess, for whom bisexuality was a physical rather than a psychic fact, and Freud never could decide once and for all if bisexuality designated the coincidence of two anatomical sexes in the same body or the conjunction of two—or more—kinds of desire in the same subject. The *Three Essays* begins with an allusion to Plato's myth of the division of an original hermaphrodite into two sexes, and both "anatomical" and "psychical hermaphroditism" stand as signs for such an originary bisexuality in Freud's work.[33]

His widely quoted remarks about the bisexual disposition of everyone, whether "homosexual" or "heterosexual," are made even earlier, in 1920, in "The

Psychogenesis of a Case of Homosexuality in a Woman," which, as the title alone shows, concentrates on the gendering of sexualities other than heterosexual as *female*:

Such an achievement—the removal of genital inversion or homosexuality—is in my experience never an easy matter. On the contrary, I have found success possible only in specially favorable circumstances, and even then the success essentially consisted in making access to the opposite sex (which had hitherto been barred) possible to a person restricted to homosexuality, thus restoring his full bisexual functions. After that it lay with him to choose whether he wished to abandon the path that is banned by society, and in some cases he has done so.[34]

Freud goes on to warn his presumed-to-be-straight-and-male readers of the obvious, that, since bisexuality must ostensibly go both ways, heterosexuality, like homosexuality, can seem like a truncated or arrested bisexuality. "One must remember that normal sexuality too depends upon a restriction in the choice of object. In general, to undertake to convert a fully developed homosexual into a heterosexual does not offer much more prospect of success than the reverse, except that for good practical reasons the latter is never attempted."[35] With the rather jovial phrase "good practical reasons," Freud alludes to the entire institution of hetero-sexism, which his postulate of universal bisexuality does not shake. The theorization of a bisexuality, even a universal one, seems less than earth-shattering.[36]

Juliet Mitchell, a later feminist commentator on Freud, describes the vagaries of bisexuality in Freudian theory: he reaches bisexuality via his belief in the "polymor-phous" character of the sexual drive.[37] The latter *has* to be polymorphous and thus potentially bisexual to save the Oedipus complex from simple gender determinism. Commenting on Freud, Mitchell notes that in this process of making meaning, bisexuality "[shifts] its meaning and [comes] to stand for the very uncertainty of sexual division itself."[38] Far from being shifty, bisexuality can be put to work as an all-purpose theoretical stopgap: it now signifies, in Freud's writings, the "very uncer-tainty" of sexual division and sexuality, so that "bisexuality" itself signifies "uncer-tainty." This maneuver ensures that everyone has *some* of that original bisexual disposition left over in them, but the assertion of an actual "full bisexual disposition" in the present becomes impossible. Any bisexuality becomes a dangerous reversion to the "polymorphousness" of a sexuality *before* male/female and hetero/homo divi-sions. In the quotation from "The Psychogenesis of a Case of Homosexuality in a Woman," given earlier, Freud makes it clear that a "[restoration of] . . . full bisexual functions" necessitates a choice between "homosexuality" ("the path that is banned by society") and "heterosexuality." Once more, he does not envisage "bisexuality" as a choice so much as a return. He gives pride of place to a "bisexuality" that he puts outside the culturally possible, always *before, after,* or *outside* (rather than alongside) the imposition of cultural order.[39]

Bisexuality is always out of time in a Freudian scenario. Even in a very recent retelling of Freud's story of bisexuality, critic Jonathan Dollimore, not unlike Freud, places bisexuality in any time except the present:

> In the attempt to remold deviant desire Freud discovers its obstinacy, even or especially in that incompleteness which it shares with normal desire; an incompleteness which, again in the case of both the deviant and the normal, bears their histories.... But it is also an incompleteness which in raising the possibility of a "full bisexuality," affirms a future potential beyond the normal, incorporating the latter in the act of displacing it. It is in such ways that the narrative of the polymorphous perverse may, as I say, be at once nostalgic and utopian, as in the remark of Freud, picked up by Marcuse: "the subsequent fulfillment of a prehistoric wish."[40]

I have quoted Dollimore at some length because he reiterates in such a clear way what temporal shifts occur in this particular version of "bisexuality." However "utopian" (forward-looking) or "nostalgic" (regressive) the account may be, it banishes the plenitude of "full bisexuality" to some (any) other time. Dollimore's own backward glance at the "sexual politics" associated with the 1960s (via Marcuse) leaves bisexuality at two removes: it appears to have existed solely in the past, but even then it was either too late or too early, as the "subsequent" realization of a "prehistoric" desire. As such, bisexuality must remain ever and only a theoretical wish.

French Feminism and the "Two-In-One"

Freud's version of bisexuality has continued to provoke theoretical responses. His gendered linkage of bisexuality to *women*, in particular, amply evident from the citations above, has engaged a number of feminist critics.[41] Two different accounts and critiques of Freudian bisexuality emerge from the work of "French feminist" critics, Hélène Cixous and Sarah Kofman, but, while they are overtly critical in their appropriations of Freud, in ways opposed but complementary, both Cixous and Kofman perpetuate problems for a political and social understanding of bisexuality.[42]

Cixous takes up bisexuality when she rewrites Freud's account of how the little "bisexual" human being (understood as polymorphous or androgynous) acquires its gender to become a girl and then grows up to be a woman. Like Marcuse, and perhaps also Dollimore, Cixous makes "bisexuality" an origin and a utopian promised land.[43] She holds out for what she calls "the *other bisexuality*," both like and unlike Freud's, which would be in close proximity to woman's body and, hence, derived from what Cixous considers to be a specifically feminine economy of two-in-one.[44] She thus maintains Freud's gender scheme for bisexuality as that "innate disposition of human beings, [which] comes to the fore *much more clearly in women than in men*."[45] Even while Cixous sets out to controvert Freud's models of gender, she keeps bisexuality the province of women, and thus gendered (as female) in some way *before* gender.

Kofman, too, rewrites Freud, but in a manner quite the opposite of Cixous. Unlike Cixous, Kofman does not envisage a future paradise of bisexuality as the realization of a "prehistoric wish" for women. In *The Enigma of Woman: Woman in the Writings of Freud*, Kofman's wily tactic is to make Freud the analysand: she subjects him to his own analysis and tests exactly how shaky the "ground" of "bisexuality" can be for the (straight) male analyst. She argues that by shutting bisexuality up inside the figure of "woman," Freud manages to ward off bisexuality in men, and in himself in particular.[46] Kofman's rereading of Freud is richly ironic, as the tables are turned and the knife of "bisexuality" cuts the other way—cuts, to mix a metaphor, the very "ground" of bisexuality out from under Freud's feet.

In the mid-1990s neither Cixous nor Kofman receives much consideration in queer theory, even though Freud, Lacan, and Luce Irigaray are still widely discussed.[47] One reason for this may be that Cixous and Kofman deal with bisexuality, homosexuality, and heterosexuality *only* insofar as those relate to gender. What is difficult about both their versions of Freud—what is difficult, indeed, about the very Freud they revise and rewrite—is this *gendered* understanding of "bisexuality" as part and parcel of a generalized "femininity." Bisexuality becomes something like a metaphor or a synecdoche for an idealized "woman," which begs all manner of questions concerning sexuality and gender. Cixous, for example, may link bisexuality to homosexuality from time to time,[48] but the connection lacks social weight, since it is so obviously metaphorical and de-essentialized.[49]

Bisexual critics can still benefit from a consideration of Cixous and Kofman's critiques of Freud's phallocentric assumptions, but what both theorists offer in the last analysis is another version of the fantasy that everyone is bisexual (*all* women are bisexual, Cixous reiterates). This is not an especially helpful fantasy in formulating a bisexual politics. If *everyone* is bisexual, "bisexuality" can no longer be a specific or a pertinent feature. At this point a deeply biphobic logic, which may appear as utopianism or nostalgia, emerges, according to which no one would *really* be bisexual. Or everyone was *once* bisexual, or will be bisexual *in the future*, yet no one is bisexual *here and now*. Thus, no one has to take responsibility for bisexual identities, issues, or politics. Such theories work almost like the popular counselors who reassure nervous heterosexual correspondents to advice columns that bisexual fantasies are OK as long as they stay fantasies (*"Everyone* has them, but hardly anyone *acts* on them"). When all is said and done, these theories of "bisexuality" are themselves finally only fantasies, incapable of sustained social change and unable to confront heterosexism, genderphobia, or couple culture.

Bisexuality was also understood as a midpoint between genders in feminist film theory of the 1970s and 1980s, when it enjoyed a vogue as the way out of an apparent theoretical impasse that set male gaze against female spectacle.[50] This led to a flirtation with the notion of a bisexual spectator, which was a peculiar, but unfortunately not *queer*, fantasy of getting "that way" at the movies, as if the cinematic apparatus somehow really could turn out bispectators. Again, such theories have fallen out of favor, because their "bisexuality" was *always* only potential, on screen, or somewhere between film and spectator, but never outside the theater. Academic writings can subject a term to a kind of conceptual exhaustion which then makes it hard to reopen a serious discussion of that term. This was the fate of "bisexuality" in film theory by the mid-1980s: hence the summary dismissal of "bisexuality" as nothing but a theoretical *and* social fantasy in Teresa de Lauretis's essay "Film and the Visible," when she writes, "For it seems to me that this notion of female bisexuality, with its emphasis on androgyny . . . is itself a fantasy. And a not very engaging fantasy for lesbians."[51] So off we go, airily banished from the "visible." In the same collection, Judith Mayne makes the point that "either you [as a film theoretician] end up affirming some notion of a wishy-washy bisexual human subject—'wishy-washy' in the sense that such a subject-position carries very little political impact in our society—or you are accused of essentialism."[52] Trends, academic or otherwise, bring the danger of turning issues into commodities to be discarded once a particular trend is over. Bisexuality is especially vulnerable to such trendiness, given the widespread fantasies about bisexuality as either a thing of the past or sign of the times. Perhaps the only response to the many appropriations and dismissals of bisexuality is to say, along with Lily Braindrop, former editor of the queer fanzine *A Taste of Latex* and avowed "bisexualtress," "I'm a pervert, not a trend."[53]

Queer Theory inside, outside, and around 1991 (A Story of Parentheses, and All Kinds of Ellipses)

While the title of this section alludes to Jane Gallop's *Around 1981: Academic Feminist Literary Theory,*[54] the allusion is less than serious. Although I will be offering a very brief consideration of some texts, particularly anthologies, that appeared around 1991, my goal is not to do for "queer theory" what Gallop does for the strangely depoliticized hybrid "academic feminist literary theory," namely, to defend an academic practice through an endlessly recursive rereading. Instead, I wish to examine the ways in which particular texts either crystallized or contained some of the symbolic force of a politics that had begun, around 1991, to call itself "queer."

What was this politics? Gayatri Spivak argues that moments of social change are best considered in their historical context when they are "pluralized and plotted as confrontation"; such moments are "signaled or marked by a functional change in sign-systems," she adds.[55] Thus, in 1991, the signifier "queer" marked such change and confrontation as it was mobilized across a range of social fields, from queer fanzines to club scenes, from Queer Nation to the officially delimited "gay" against which "queer" strove to define itself. This mobilization both registered and resulted in a switch in the public sign systems which had regulated sexed/sexualized/gendered identities in the United States in the 1980s. Unfortunately, the change that took place is now very often represented, after the fact, as some leap into a barely articulable new zone of sexuality and gender, where "queer" simultaneously means everything and nothing. Here Sedgwick's "T Times" (*sic*) and "Queer and Now" and Butler's "Critically Queer" come to mind.[56]

The "antiassimilationist" drive of Queer Nation and of "queer" in general has received much attention,[57] but the impetus of "queer" to name under one rubric "lesbian" and "gay" *and* "bisexual" and "transgender" has not. When, in Los Angeles in the spring of 1991, I saw a Queer Nation sticker that said "BI POWER/TRANS POWER/QUEER NATION" and another that announced tersely ". . . AND BISEXUAL/GET USED TO IT," I knew I could be, or was already, a Queer National. "Queer" named or misnamed a politics of coalition among bisexuals, transgenderists, lesbians and gay men, and any other person who refuses the dominant system of sex, gender, and sexuality. The work of the word "queer" was contextual and strategic, not permanent, and the coalition it established could also break down, as indeed it did some two years later.

Queer theory, unlike Queer Nation, has been far from the troubled world of actual coalition-building, and has, more often than not, treated bisexuality and transsexuality quite shabbily. Part of the difficulty that queer theory has with bisexuality (and indeed with any form of sexual or gender identity that does not, in the last analysis, translate into "lesbian" or "gay") comes from the way it conceives of the categories of "sexuality" and "gender" as wholly separate.[58] Instead of exploring the radical connections of gender and sexuality, queer theory commonly makes "sexuality" by extension stand for "homosexuality" or "heterosexuality," while "gender" comes to designate "women" or "men." Although queer theory often sets up cross-dressing or drag as practices that ostensibly undo the categories of "sex," "sexuality," and "gender," cross-dressing is almost always treated from the outside, with vested indifference, to misquote the title of Garber's widely read book.[59] The fixation queer theory has on drag ends up seeming shallow, like the diversion of a tourist who can go home to the security of those very categories.[60]

Eve Sedgwick's early and influential piece, "Across Gender, across Sexuality: Willa Cather and Others," already makes the split between gender and sexuality clear.[61] Sedgwick provides much of the conceptual machinery of what has become queer theory by mapping what she calls "our culture's crystallization of *gay identities* over the past hundred years" (my emphasis) onto a chart of two separate columns, "gender" and "sexuality."[62] While her model has its uses, it keeps "gender" distinct from "sexuality" as one column from another and cannot accommodate people for whom sexuality and gender may match up differently. Quite revealingly, bisexuals only feature on Sedgwick's chart under the cliché of "bisexual potential" as a form of "sexuality" that makes universalizing claims. (This is hardly the only current image of bisexuality.) Transgender people do not show up at all, unless implicitly under the rubric of "gender" in its minoritizing forms.[63] (Sedgwick does not seem to be ready to imagine a "transsexual potential" here.)

The limits of Sedgwick's project reveal themselves immediately in her failure to put bisexuals and transgender people on the map. Her theory of gender and sexuality does damage to the realities of transgender sexualities and bisexual genders. Imagine for a moment if Sedgwick's piece had not been called "*Across* Gender, *across* Sexuality," where "across" presupposes a distance to be forged and traversed, but "*Trans* Gender, *Trans* Sexuality," or "*Bi* Gender, *Bi* Sexuality," or any and every mixture of the two.[64] To imagine that would be to think of the power of a renaming that would change Sedgwick's project.

Bisexual people often make productively contradictory assertions about our relation to genders in sexualities. Kathleen Bennett summarizes some of these statements in the bisexual feminist anthology *Closer to Home*, when she observes that both heterosexism and monosexism "are upheld by a sexist myth that the genders are mutually exclusive—thus, anything other than a clear preference for one or the other must be a phase or a pathology of identity confusion."[65] Bennett suggests that bisexuals resist the binarism of gender in ways that are different from either lesbians and gay men or heterosexuals: "[S]ome bisexuals say they are blind to the gender of their potential lovers and that they love people as people; others are aware of differences between their male and female partners but are able to be attracted to each in different (but overlapping) ways. For the first group, a dichotomy of genders between which to choose doesn't seem to exist; the second group simply disregards the social obligation to choose."[66] This provides a useful point from which to begin a reconsideration of gender and sexuality together.

In her more recent work, Sedgwick continues to uphold the distinctions which bisexuals controvert, and bisexuals are thus given short shrift in *Tendencies*. Bisexuals appear in the introduction to *Tendencies* in a particularly tortuous sentence which juxtaposes and contrasts "the moment of Queer (*sic*)" with "*other moments*" (Sedgwick's emphasis).[67] "[P]eople [who organize] around claiming the label bisexual, the steady increase in AIDS-related deaths, Clinton's impending presidency, and the 'massive participation by African Americans and Latinos' in the New York Gay Pride Parade" are all part of the "other moments" which are set off from the "Queer" moment by Sedgwick's use of parentheses and italics, almost as if the text needed to differentiate typographically between what is "Queer" and what is not.[68] Why are African Americans, Latinos, and bisexuals all shuffled off from the center of queerness here? Are there no people of color who are queers or bisexuals or even bisexual queers? This kind of putting-in-parenthesis has come to exemplify how queer theory deals with issues such as bisexuality and race.

While the year 1991 may have been crucial for Queer Nation and for the forging of links between bisexuals, transgenders, and lesbians and gay men, a very different understanding of the term "queer" operated in both academic circles and in some of the venues for "lesbian-and-gay" journalism. There the term "queer" functioned, as in *Tendencies*, to shut bisexuals either out or up. This is how an article in the *Village Voice* chose to represent the Rutgers conference:

[W]hen representatives of the bisexual caucus piped up, demanding to be named, they were often shrugged off—not for the old hardcore political reasons ("you're with us or against us, make up your mind"), but because they represented a theoretical throwback. Just when the field starts calling itself *queer* theory, as a means of avoiding strict, oppositional boundaries, the insistence on bisexuality—suggesting that people are inhabited by two sexual orientations—reinscribes the very categories that bisexual identity claims to blur.[69]

Alisa Solomon's comments here may seem at first to be nothing more than *Village Voice* bi-bashing.[70] Unfortunately, Solomon's biases anticipate clearly what would happen to bisexuality under the regime of "the field [that started] calling itself *queer theory*" around 1991. Solomon omits any mention of the organizers' decision to drop "bisexual" from the title, which allows her, in some ways like Sedgwick in the passage from *Tendencies*, to reduce any bisexual politics or theorization to a squeaky (or shrill?) "pip[ing] up, demanding to be named." The implication is clear: even in a situation where we have been violently un-named, our demand for naming has no political dimensions.

Once bisexuality has been stripped of politics, Solomon can dismiss bisexuals, without bothering to spell out any explicitly "political" (or "hardcore," as she puts it) pretexts. Because we are out of fashion, *passé*, a phase either passing or past, we are neither "theoretical" nor "queer" enough to be part of "queer theory." We may look deconstructive, but we "[reinscribe] the very categories that bisexual identity claims to blur." Our deconstruction, then, is a fake, an illusion, a lie, presumably like our sexualities and our identities, which are, in Solomon's view, a "throwback." Bisexuals must be discounted politically *and* theoretically: Solomon imagines politics and theory in separate realms at the very instant when "theory" is put to the political end of erasing bisexuality. Even stranger is Solomon's agentless, objectless appositional phrase, "suggesting [by whom? to whom?] that people are inhabited by two sexual orientations." For want of a better subject, does the word "*bi*sexuality" itself insinuate this? While "bisexuality" as a word-concept may perform a certain deconstructive labor on "homosexuality" and "heterosexuality" alike, to understand "bisexuality" simply as a term that veers dialectically between undoing and affirming the "homo/hetero" opposition seems to be a sure way of assigning blame to bisexuals when all is said and done.

For another example of how bisexuals can be vilified for being simultaneously "homosexual" and "heterosexual," we need only move to another institution, one which may seem far away from the *Village Voice*'s cozy "gay-affirmative" liberalism but which operates according to Solomon's logic. The United States military has a definition of bisexuals which sounds disturbingly like Solomon's description of bisexuals as people illegitimately "inhabited by two sexual orientations": "Bisexual means a person who engages in, desires to engage in, or intends to engage in homosexual and heterosexual acts."[71] There are thus only homosexual and heterosexual *acts*; the person who enacts them (whether in desire or fact or fantasy) would be a "bisexual," one who has no identity except insofar as she or he behaves as a "homosexual" or a "heterosexual." Even a bisexual *act* as such does not exist within this biphobic schema. United States military policy specifically legislates bisexual identity out of existence, while nevertheless policing that same nonidentity with some ferocity.[72] In an extreme version of the two-in-one scenario on which Cixous draws, bisexuality becomes not an interzone but a nowhere.

Such enforced binarism turns the bisexual into a kind of vanishing point where the apparently parallel lines of homosexuality and heterosexuality converge. Conceptually, the bisexual can then only be an antisubject. As bisexuals, for instance, we are denied specific safer-sex information, even though we continue to be reviled in the AIDS crisis. In this matter Jan Zita Grover has reflected helpfully on how bisexuality appears in policies and representations concerning AIDS. She cites popular medical texts which claim that "*because of their double lives,* [bisexuals] may be the most difficult group to reach and counsel" (my emphasis).[73] Here we come across either another version of Solomon's two orientations that don't add up to another, separate one, or the frequent trope of double lives, or even the "dual attraction" of a recent text.[74] The medical authorities Grover cites also opine that "it takes only one bisexual to introduce the AIDS virus [*sic*] into the heterosexual community. . . . The risk is easily hidden when they are having sex with women."[75] (In the last quotation, note the [hetero]sexist presumptions that "they," the bisexuals having sex with women, are men, or that bisexuals can only have homosexuals or heterosexuals as our partners.) For Grover, bisexuals, who are placed outside of earshot and reason in these discourses, bear the burden of symbolically maintaining the boundaries between "homosexuals" and "heterosexuals": "sexual desire is parceled into two realms, the heterosexual and homosexual 'communities,' with the bisexual—understood as a homosexual *posing* as a heterosexual—acting as the secret conveyor of the diseases of the former to the healthy bodies of the latter."[76] Another presupposition is that bisexuals cannot have sexual relations between and among ourselves, for we can only prey on unsuspecting heterosexuals or homosexuals as their partners, while presumably concealing our own lack of identity under the cloak of either homosexuality or heterosexuality.[77]

Discussions of bisexuals and bisexuality are now inevitably framed, implicitly or explicitly, by the AIDS crisis, even though, as Alexis Danzig points out, "Safer-sex and drug use education rarely addresses those of us who are bisexually active."[78] Instead we are insistently blamed. Danzig amends Grover to note that public discussions of AIDS have made bisexual women as well as men visible in extremely threatening ways. She refers to the biphobic assumption that "bisexual women spread HIV to lesbians."[79] Bisexuals of all genders have been framed within the AIDS crisis time and time again.[80] But in response to the immense media energy devoted to vilifying bisexuality, bisexuals have found a reverse discourse to speak back, an oppositional consciousness with which to begin forming our own politics, coalitions, and agendas.[81]

The association of bisexuality with a deconstruction of sorts, which is explicitly forged in middlebrow journalism like Solomon's and tacitly at work in the military's definition of "bisexual" and public discourses on AIDS, leaves bisexuals at a disadvantage. It is ironic that the only reference, and a glancing one at that, to "bisexuals" in Cindy Patton's otherwise admirable *Inventing AIDS* should occur within the context of "the linguistic turn in current critical practice," or deconstruction:[82]

Race and sexuality function in structurally similar ways—both are cultural continua pressed into a socially constructed pair of opposites. In this context, the idea of passing (acquiring the signifiers of the normative category) of claiming "Black is beautiful" or "gay is good," and the increasing visibility of "racially mixed" persons and "bisexuals" constantly function to call into question the lines of demarcation between socially constructed opposites.[83]

As we will see, in passages from *Bi Any Other Name*, there are considerable links between cross-cultural and biracial identities and bisexuality or transsexuality, but Patton's summary view of some vague homology between "racially mixed" people and "bisexuals" (which Patton keeps, for whatever reason, in quotation) evens out common causes instead of analyzing them. This is all done in the service of calling "into question . . . socially constructed opposites," but again, for whom? Such glib commenting, not for but *about* bisexuals and/or people of mixed race descent and biracial heritage, reinforces the lines that divide inside from outside and leaves the very social subjects which the commentary calls upon to do its work stranded beyond both "inside" and "outside."

On that subject, the figure of the "inside/out" has achieved considerable currency in "queer theory," largely through its use in a much-cited anthology from 1991, *Inside/Out: Lesbian Theories, Gay Theories*, edited by Diana Fuss.[84] Pondering the intricacies of the inside and the out, Fuss asks: "And what gets left out of the inside/outside, heterosexual/homosexual opposition, an opposition which could at least plausibly be said to secure its seemingly inviolable dialectical structure only by assimilating and internalizing other sexualities (bisexuality, transvestism, transsexualism . . .) to its own rigid polar logic?"[85]

What might escape the "seemingly inviolable dialectical structure" is called upon, in passing and in parentheses, only to be given no more than a glancing reference which trails off in an ellipsis. We are not very far from Solomon's view of bisexuality as a deconstruction that falls short. Given this introduction, as an anthology *Inside/Out* continues the process of making "bisexuality, transvestism, transsexualism . . ." marginal and parenthetical. In effect, Fuss does not so much describe as reinforce that process. The identities she lists as somehow in excess of "homosexuality" and "heterosexuality" are cordoned off by those parentheses from the body of her own text, taken into consideration only in order to be more insidiously expelled.[86]

Fuss's maneuver, which can be summarized as inside/out/outside, takes place again in Teresa de Lauretis's introduction to the self-styled "Queer Theory" issue of the journal *differences*, also from 1991.[87] This issue is subtitled "Lesbian and Gay Sexualities." "Theory" is qualified here as "queer" with "sexuality" in second billing, its plural neatly lining up with gender as "Lesbian and Gay." In a kind of diminishing return, in the special "Essays in Lesbian and Gay Studies" issue of *Discourse* a year later, bisexuals and transgenders have been entirely written out of Cheryl Kader and Thomas Piontek's introduction, which takes de Lauretis to task for being too eager to embrace "queerness."[88] Kader and Piontek caution ominously, "Lesbians and gay men have every reason to be suspicious of 'queerness' and its promise of an instant identity."[89] An instant identity *other* than "lesbian" and "gay male"? Or *between* lesbian and gay man? Might "bisexuality" and "transsexuality" be here in their absence, as rhetorical ellipsis? Kader and Piontek call on (a sadly reduced) "feminism" as a (monocular) "gender-based perspective,"[90] presumably to help them reinstate those gender boundaries that the "instant identity" of "queerness" was about to snatch away. Once more, bisexuals and transgenders must remain nameless, lest the mere uttering of our identities jeopardize those ensconced monosexual non-transgenders that pontificate so comfortably about themselves as the sole arbiters of "queerness."

Blatantly Bisexual: The Politics of Para-Naming

An overt and necessary politics of naming and renaming emerges from the anthology of testimony edited by Loraine Hutchins and Lani Ka'ahumanu, *Bi Any Other Name Bisexual People Speak Out*, which appeared in 1991 as well. In the epigraph to their text, Hutchins and Ka'ahumanu quote the "rose by any other name" passage from *Romeo and Juliet* and then gloss it as follows: "Shakespeare's tragedy, *Romeo and Juliet*, is about lovers whose warring families prevent their love. We bisexuals are also caught between our homosexual and heterosexual families. We're called by *every* other name but bi, and still we dare attempt our love. Thus, the title for our book."[91]

Hutchins and Ka'ahumanu name bisexuality and a bisexual collectivity through a set of commonplaces of doomed heterosexual love (*Romeo and Juliet*, Romeo and Juliet, roses), but they do it in such a way that a new entity, a "differential consciousness," as Sandoval might say, emerges between, in relation to, and in contrast to the terms "heterosexual" and "homosexual."[92]

The rhetorical figure which Juliet invokes here is *prosonomasia*, or "calling by a name or nickname," so that the generic name of the rose can become the place of "any other name."[93] In his text on rhetorical terms, the critic Richard Lanham notes that prosonomasia (renaming) is often confused with another figure, paronomasia,[94] which involves "punning; playing on the sounds and meanings of words . . . [where] the words punned on are similar but not identical in sound."[95] The confusion of prosonomasia with paronomasia would itself be an instance of paronomasia. (Another rhetorical critic, Keir Elam, defines paronomasia literally as "change of name.")[96] When Hutchins and Ka'ahumanu substitute "bi" for the preposition "by," they, perhaps unwittingly, use paronomasia. Both linguistically and socially, the title of their book and the space they open for bisexuals can be figured as a kind of paronomasia, or a naming by/bi any other name through which we can insist on our own names, identities, and loves. The *Oxford English Dictionary* (2d ed.) gives "paronomasia" as a variant for "paronomasia," and the sense of name which is alongside or adjacent to (*para*) another name which it renames conveys some of the transformative force of bisexuality. The Queer Nation sticker which reads, ". . . AND BISEXUAL/GET USED TO IT," uses the ellipses which precede "AND BISEXUAL" to stand for all the contexts to which our name can be added. This is a politics of paranaming, of naming alongside, through, and by means of all kinds of other names to make our multiple proper identities stick.[97]

In *Bi Any Other Name*, among many other demonstrations of how such a politics might work, there is Obie Leyva's piece, "¿Que es un *bisexual*?";[98] Kei Uwano's "Bi-Lovable Japanese Feminist";[99] and Shu Wei Chen-Andy's "A Man, a Woman, Attention"[100]—all of which place bisexuality in cross-cultural contexts. In Leyva's account, in Chicano and Latino communities there is a "polarized view of male sexuality with the belief that a man is either macho or *joto*, leaving no room for bisexuality (sound familiar?)."[101] His answer to the question, "¿*Que es un* bisexual?" then works paronomasically, substituting himself, his own name, or the pronoun or shifter of *yo* for that untranslatable other word "bisexual": "Now when people ask, '¿*Que es un* bisexual?' I smile and proudly answer, '¡*Yo soy!*'"[102] Leyva shifts interrogatives as well, replacing the "what" of *que* with his own "who."

Somewhat differently, by naming herself "bi-lovable," Uwano has already substituted an adjacent term, "lovable," for the available one, "sexual." She writes, "When I was growing up in Japan there was no concept, no word for sexuality. When we say heterosexual, it translates to heterosex-love. The word for gay or lesbian is homosex-love. Bisexual is only referred to in slang and translates as 'one who uses both souls.'"[103] Uwano next goes on to ask what name to give herself in a series of semantic paronomasias, based on the simultaneous imperative and impossibility of translating a name, "bisexual," as any other name. "I identify myself based on the structure of love. Technically, I am bi-lovable and monogamous. My soul is androgynous, which means I am fully human. Should I call myself a human lovable? A whole sexual?"[104]

Shu Wei Chen-Andy situates bisexuality within a relationship between a Filipina transsexual and an Asian bisexual-transgender: "I began telling her [Christina, the

Filipina transsexual] how difficult it was to be an Asian bisexual, and how disappointed I was by not being accepted by gays and straights when I crossed from male to female."[105] Together, Andy and Christina then "[understand their] double minority status and how [their] cross-gender lifestyle [is] not taken seriously."[106] The title of this piece, "A Man, a Woman, Attention," which appears to name the elements of heterosexual/heterosexist romance, instead turns out to name, once more—paronomasically—a double or multiple gender-cross. The ostensibly dualistic formula, "a man, a woman," now designates both bisexuality and transsexuality at one and the same time, as an identity of "a man, a woman," and as a simultaneous desire for "a man, a woman," and for the transgenders who are "men, women."[107] Another paranomasia is at play here too, namely, "attention," which can also be read or heard as "a tension," thus naming the attractions between, among, and across the categories "man" and "woman."

Another adjacent term by which bisexuality renames itself in *Bi Any Name* is "queer." Carol A. Queen (whose own name speaks volumes) writes, "I use my bisexual wits to cross boundaries, crack codes, and bring back a store of information that society would like to use to keep us *all* in thrall. . . . It is the queer in me that empowers—that lets me see those lines and burn to cross them."[108] In her description, "bisexual wits" and "the queer in me" name one and the same entity, but without simply silently subsuming "bisexual" to "queer." The kind of double naming that runs throughout *Bi Any Other Name* is crucial, I would suggest, to marking a politically effective symbolic space for bisexuals. Unfortunately, various "theories" of bisexuality achieve the opposite and reach, consciously or inadvertently, the same end: they make that space impossible to occupy.

Of Cunts, Cocks, Cloven Hooves, and Communities: Toward New Horizons and Middle Grounds Made Radical

> Bisexuality: Our Basic Instinct
>
> —BIONIC (Bisexuals Organizing with Noise,
> Insurrection, and Confrontation), pamphlet

> We want it ALL!!!
>
> —Letter in response to "What Do Bisexuals Want?"
> *OutLook* 15 (Summer 1992): 9

So what *do* bisexuals want?[109] In a text that does not necessarily identify itself as "bi," Myrna Elana nevertheless seems to speak to my (however idiosyncratic) bisexual desire and identity. The text is called, self-reflexively, one might say, "Define 'Community': This Is a Test":

> If my lover had a cunt
>   yet passed as a man
>   and I had to explain
>
> If my lover wore a dress
>   but shaved and pissed standing up
>   and I had
>   to explain that
>   to everyone
>
> If my lover
>   had a cloven hoof
>   and a cunt and a penis
>   and we went along
>   the horizon line
>   shouting about it
>
> only the people who mattered
>   would be left
>   anywhere near us[110]

Speaker and lover disappear along the horizon line in an ever-proliferating series of sexual and gender possibilities, with only "the people who [matter]" as part of their community. How large or how small would such a "community" be? Would it be a sexual/gender minority or an as yet unimaginable majority? We cannot know in advance who the "people who [matter]" and who are "near" (again, para) us would be.

The endlessly retreating horizon line which marks a different kind of community formation would also be something of a middle ground. Elana's poem dares us to twist the commonplace of a middle ground so that it can be everywhere, somewhere altogether new, and perhaps, "on the fence" (as bisexuality is always supposed to be) all at once. Picture a middle ground that is not static but on the move, as we go shouting toward a horizon, like the lovers of Elana's poem. That is the space for new bisexualities that can be exorbitant, eccentric, ecstatic, beside themselves.

Bisexuality challenges given notions of how sexual communities or so-called sexual "minorities" are formed. This challenge is especially important in the United States, since bisexuality runs counter to received notions about sexual identity as something in which the subject has no choice. Lesbian and gay communities in the

United States have sometimes tended to define their community with reference to a model of ethnicity, in order to claim civil rights. This model implies that sexual identity is an immutable feature, just as race or ethnicity is, supposedly, fixed.[111] Clearly, the model is deeply flawed: it essentializes both race and sexual identity as somehow prepolitical "givens," and it draws its analogy between race and sexual identity only by separating the two, so that sexual identity appears somehow to be a *white* ethnicity. Lesbians, gay men, bisexuals, and transgender people *of color* are not considered in this model except as additions to an already established white "gay community," which maintains the covert racism of that "community." By claiming civil rights on the basis of a kind of ethnicity, white lesbian and gay groups end up exacerbating a situation in the United States where ethnic and racial groups are constructed so as to be pitted against one another for a share of the rights and resources which the dominant white, middle-class order withholds or grants arbitrarily.[112] Bisexuality exposes the failures of such an ethnic identity model.

Bisexuality has been associated with race, however, in ways that depart from an ethnicity model in recent statements about the politics of multiculturalism as an anti-racist, anti-imperialist struggle within the United States. Even *Newsweek* has noticed that "multiculturalism has begun to embrace multisexualism."[113] Far more eloquently, activists June Jordan and Lani Ka'ahumanu have both redefined the notion of "middle ground" in a radical relation to bisexuals and our common cause with many other struggles.

Speaking at the 1993 March on Washington for Lesbian, Gay and Bi Equal Rights and Liberation, Lani Ka'ahumanu spoke of her identity as a "mixed race bisexual woman of color" and the relation between that identity and social transformation: "Like multiculturalism, mixed race heritage and bi-racial relationships, both the bisexual and transgender movements *expose and politicize* the middle ground. Each shows there is no separation: that each and everyone of us is part of a fluid social, sexual, and gender dynamic. Each signals a change, a fundamental change in the way our society is organized."[114] The middle ground of which Ka'ahumanu speaks so eloquently is the place for which as bisexual-transgender people we are fighting, most certainly not a neutral zone in between, but a highly politicized terrain, in which identities can nevertheless come together. Like Ka'ahumanu, Jordan evokes the middle ground to place bisexuality within urgent conflicts over race:

I need to speak on bisexuality. I do believe that the analogy is interracial or multiracial identity. I do believe that the analogy for bisexuality is a multicultural, multiethnic, multiracial world view. Bisexuality follows from such a perspective and leads to it as well. . . . *This emerging movement politicizes the so-called middle ground:* Bisexuality invalidates either/or formulation, either/or analysis. Bisexuality means I am free and I am as likely to want and to love a woman as I am likely to want and to love a man, and what about that? . . . If you are free you are not predictable, and you are not controllable. To my mind, that is the keenly positive, politicizing significance of bisexuality.[115]

What do we want? We are not predictable; we are not uniform. We are women, transgenders, men. We run off to the horizon and leave behind the borders on which monosexual, non-transgender theories, edifices, and institutions have been built. We are of necessity an *identity-in-coalition*. Our middle ground may yet move the world.

There is, obviously, no last word in bisexual politics. We are often accused of being too fluid to form or to ground a material politics, an accusation to which Garber gives credence when she suggests that bisexual politics would be simply about a watery "eroticism."[116] Through our identity politics in coalition, we can begin to live out an ethics and a politics of connectedness in which our identities are not defined by fluidity, but by the quality of our closeness and the strength of our alliances.

Notes

1. Marjorie Garber, *Vice Versa: Bisexuality and the Eroticism of Everyday Life* (New York: Simon and Schuster, 1995).
2. Garber's thesis, namely, that "bisexuality [has] something fundamental to teach us about the nature of human experience" (Garber, *Vice Versa,* 15), is repeated, with variation, a number of times in the course of her book. One example: "[T]he question of whether someone was 'really' straight or 'really' gay misrecognizes the nature of sexuality, which is fluid, not fixed, a narrative that changes over time, rather than a fixed identity, however complex. The erotic discovery of bisexuality is the fact that reveals sexuality to be a process of growth, transformation, and surprise, not a stable and knowable state of being" (66). According to Garber, we are dealing with the very "nature of sexuality" and the "fact" of sexuality as a "process of growth." The assumption that sexuality *has* a nature, albeit a fluid one, seems tendentious, just as the belief that sexuality somehow involves "growth" seems open to question.
3. Garber, *Vice Versa,* 134.
4. Garber, *Vice Versa,* 87.
5. I am alluding, of course, to Gayle Rubin, "Thinking Sex: Notes for a Radical Theory of the Politics of Sexuality," in *Pleasure and Danger: Exploring Female Sexuality*, ed. Carole S. Vance (London: Routledge, 1984), 267–319.
6. See Chela Sandoval, "U.S. Third World Feminism: The Theory and Method of Oppositional Consciousness in the Postmodern World," *Genders* 10 (Spring 1991): 14.
7. *Anything That Moves* 5 (1993): n. p.

8. For a carefully considered critique of multiculturalism, see Gayatri Spivak, "Extreme Eurocentrism," interview with Edward Bell, in *The Abject America*, ed. Catherine Liu (New York: Lusitania, n. d.), 55–60.

9. Rumors abounded during this time among bisexuals in and out of the academy; for a while, discussions of the erasure of "bisexual" functioned as a way of identifying other bisexuals (and biphobes). This seems a perfect example of Patricia Meyer Spacks's contention that gossip as a shared activity "demands a process of relatedness among its participants; its *I*'s inevitably turn into *we*." Spacks, *Gossip* (New York: Alfred A. Knopf, 1985), 261.

10. Robyn Ochs and Pam Ellis, "Conference Organizers 'Confused,'" *Anything That Moves* 3 (1991): 15.

11. Ochs and Ellis, "Conference Organizers 'Confused,'" 15.

12. Pierre Bourdieu discusses "symbolic power" and "symbolic violence" in language as acts that are both determined by and determining of a host of material conditions: "*linguistic relations are always relations of symbolic power* through which relations of force between the speakers and their respective groups are actualized in transfigured form." Pierre Bourdieu and Loïc J. D. Wacquant, *Invitation to Reflexive Sociology* (Chicago: University of Chicago Press, 1992), 142. It is through acts of symbolic power such as the refusal to name bisexuals and transgender people that lesbians and gay men can exercise social control without necessarily enjoying the same symbolic/material privileges as straight-identified white middle-class men, for example.

13. Thus, the Fifth Annual Lesbian and Gay Studies Conference took place at Rutgers University, 1–3 November 1991. A symposium was held with Pierre Saint-Armand, Pam Ellis, Elias Farajaje-Jones, Cora Kaplan, Robyn Ochs, and Warren Blumenfeld, with the worrying title, "Lesbian, Gay . . . and Bisexual?" on 2 November 1991. Two other panels were held, both of which seemed to address, while in effect affirming, the marginalized status of "bisexuality": "Boundary Politics: Bisexuals in Lesbian and Gay Communities" and "(Re)Contextualizing Bisexuality," 2 November 1991 and 3 November 1991, respectively. I thank Nan Alamilla Boyd for this information.

14. I thank Ki Namaste for bringing the "Stick It Back In" campaign to my attention.

15. Judith Butler strikes a cautionary note about simple appeals to the matter of the body. "What about the materiality of the body?" she asks at the start of *Bodies That Matter: On the Discursive Limits of "Sex"* (Routledge: New York, 1993), ix. She explains that recourse to the body might be nothing more than a rhetorical move to reassert a bedrock of common sense, in the form of "a bodily life that [can] not be theorized away" (ix).

16. Consider Bourdieu's criticism of the "typically scholastic opposition" which contrasts an all-knowing "theory" with a practice somehow at a loss: "Those who treat [language] as an *object* of analysis rather than use it to think and speak with are led to constitute language as a *logos*, in opposition to a *praxis*, as a 'dead letter,' without practical purpose or no purpose other than that of being interpreted, in the manner of a work of art. . . . The illusion of autonomy of the 'purely' linguistic order which is asserted by the privilege granted to the internal logic of language, at the expense of the social conditions and the correlates of its usage, opens the way

to all subsequent theories which proceed as if the theoretical mastery of the code sufficed to confer practical mastery of socially appropriate uses." Bourdieu and Wacquant, *Invitation to Reflexive Sociology*, 141–42.

17. Sandoval has shown in a different context that the opposition between what comes to count as "theory" proper and what is devalued as "description" can lead to the dismissal of work by feminists of color. Sandoval, "U.S. Third World Feminism," 9.

18. Bourdieu explains that "cultural capital" is a form of "dissimulation, or more precisely, *euphemization*" of objectively economic practices in such a way that those practices cannot directly be recognized within the social field *as* economic. Cultural capital is thus "institutionalized in the form of academic qualifications," and is "convertible, on certain conditions, into economic capital." Pierre Bourdieu, "The Forms of Capital," in *Handbook of Theory and Research for the Sociology of Education*, trans. Richard Nice, ed. John G. Richardson (New York: Greenwood, 1986), 243. The opacity of "theory" itself to analysis or theorization—how did "theory" come to be this way?—signals a kind of accretion of specialized academic credentials, a stockpiling of cultural value, around the practice of theory.

19. Donald Morton, "The Politics of Queer Theory in the (Post)Modern Moment," *Genders* 17 (Fall 1993): 122.

20. Morton, "The Politics of Queer Theory in the (Post)Modern Moment," 128, 133–39. I am not at all sure, however, that Morton's own brand of "critique-al [*sic*] practice" (123) is the radical break which he seems to think it is and not just another brand name competing in the academic marketplace. Thus, Morton can claim that "critical cultural studies sees theory not as something to be resisted in general but as itself ... a form of resistance" (126), a rather easy defense of Morton's own investment in a particular version of "theory." Moreover, Morton's genealogy of "liberal humanism" (his personal bogey) is so sweeping that it can encompass not only Eve Sedgwick, Judith Butler, and Teresa de Lauretis, but also Jacques Derrida, all of phenomenology, and Georges Bataille (139–41)! At this point, an historically specific ideology like Anglo-American liberal humanism loses whatever specificity it once might have had simply to include whatever Morton happens to dislike.

21. Thus, Sedgwick notes that 1992 may be "the queer moment" in what she designates rather un-self-consciously or -critically as "the American marketplace of images." Eve Sedgwick, *Tendencies* (Durham: Duke University Press, 1993), xii. Sedgwick then goes on to provide "queer" with a pedigree that does not draw on the histori-cally specific contexts of its use (semiologically, a pragmatics), so that she disre-gards, for example, Joan Nestle's important critical use of the term as far back as 1987, a use which in itself was a recollection of a previous particular context: Nestle describes "the first layer of my history: the memory of being a queer, my inheritance from the fifties." Joan Nestle, *A Restricted Country* (Ithaca: Firebrand, 1987), 111. Sedgwick gives "queer" a lineage by attempting to uncover the word's "Indo-European root" (xii): such a use of etymology to legitimate is, of course, a highly culture-bound maneuver.

22. See Ronald R. Butters, John M. Clum, and Michael Moon, eds. *Displacing Homo-phobia: Gay Male Perspectives in Literature and Culture*, (Durham: Duke University Press, 1989), for an example of how central the concept of "homophobia" has

become. For brief, yet helpful, discussions of the terms "homophobia" and "hetero-sexism," see the glossary in Loraine Hutchins and Lani Ka'ahumanu, eds., *Bi Any Other Name: Bisexual People Speak Out* (Boston: Alyson, 1991), 369.

23.   For a reasonable account of the multitude of political groups associated with Gay Lib, see Donn Teal, *The Gay Militants* (New York: Stein and Teal, 1971).

24.   Thus, Terry Castle: "In my opening paragraph I refer to Greta Garbo as a lesbian, despite the fact, *as some readers will know*, she occasionally had affairs with men as well as women. Why not refer to her, more properly, as a bisexual? Because I think it more *meaningful* to refer to her as a lesbian." Terry Castle, *The Apparitional Lesbian: Female Homosexuality and Modern Culture* (New York: Columbia University Press, 1993), 15, first emphasis mine. "*Meaningful*" for whom, one might wonder, since Castle's decision is arbitrary and all too clearly based on the exclusion of the nameless few readers who might know that Garbo was bisexual. Castle also supposes—incorrectly—that there was no context for bisexual self-understanding or subculture formation in Garbo's day.

25.   Amanda Udis-Kessler, "Present Tense: Biphobia As a Crisis of Meaning," in *Bi Any Other Name*, ed. Hutchins and Ka'ahumanu, 350–58, has been very important in shaping my thoughts on this issue.

26.   Jeffrey Weeks gives a very useful overview of sexology in his *Sexuality and Its Discontents: Meanings, Myths, and Modern Sexualities* (London: Routledge and Kegan Paul, 1985), 61–95. Garber discusses Havelock Ellis, Freud and Wilhelm Fliess in *Vice Versa*, 237–48 and 169–206.

27.   Sigmund Freud, *Three Essays*, trans. James Strachey (New York: Basic Books, 1962), 7.

28.   Freud, *Three Essays*, 8. Freud is referring to Karl Heinrich Ulrichs.

29.   Freud, *Three Essays*, 9.

30.   Sigmund Freud, *Standard Edition of the Complete Psychological Works*, vol. 22, trans. James Strachey (London: Hogarth Press, 1964), 117.

31.   David T. Evans gives a good, if short, account of other sexologists, either predecessors or contemporaries of Freud, who mobilized notions of bisexuality: Ulrichs, Moll, Krafft-Ebing, Arduin, Havelock Ellis, Hirschfeld, Herman, Fliess, Moebius, and Bloch. David T. Evans, *Sexual Citizenship: The Material Construction of Sexualities* (London: Routledge, 1994), 149.

32.   Sigmund Freud, *The Standard Edition*, vol. 21, trans. James Strachey (London: The Hogarth Press, 1964), 227–28.

33.   See the entry "Bisexualité" in Jean Laplanche and J.-B. Pontalis, *Vocabulaire de la psychanalyse* (Paris: Presses Universitaires de France, 1967), 49–51. See also Freud, *Three Essays*, 2 and 7–10. The phrases "psychic hermaphroditism" and "anatomical [hermaphroditism]" to designate bisexuality come from the latter.

34.   Sigmund Freud, *Standard Edition*, vol. 18, trans. James Strachey (London: Hogarth, 1955), 151. Also of note is Teresa de Lauretis, *The Practice of Love: Lesbian Sexuality and Perverse Desire* (Bloomington: Indiana University Press, 1994), 38–57, in which de Lauretis asks about Freud's persistent identification of "bisexuality" with women.

35.   Freud, *Standard Edition*, vol. 18, 151.

36.   Interestingly, Weeks finds the postulate of universal bisexuality helpful in combatting homophobia. Weeks, *Sexuality and Its Discontents*, 150.

37. Juliet Mitchell, "Introduction-I," in Jacques Lacan, *Feminine Sexuality: Jacques Lacan and the École Freudienne*, trans. Jacqueline Rose (New York: Norton, 1982), 12.

38. Mitchell, "Introduction-I," 12.

39. Judith Butler accurately and bi-affirmatively describes what Freud is up to as "the construction of an 'outside' that is nevertheless fully 'inside,' not a possibility beyond culture, but a concrete cultural possibility that is refused and redescribed as impossible." Judith Butler, *Gender Trouble: Feminism and the Subversion of Identity* (New York: Routledge, 1990), 77.

40. Jonathan Dollimore, *Sexual Dissidence: Augustine to Wilde, Freud to Foucault* (Oxford: Clarendon, 1991), 217.

41. Freud's essays "Female Sexuality" and "Femininity" have gathered a considerable number of feminist responses, including, but not limited to, Luce Irigaray, *Speculum de l'autre femme* (Paris: Editions de Minuit, 1974); Hélène Cixous, "Sorties: Out and Out: Attacks/Ways Out/Forays," in Hélène Cixous and Catherine Clément, *The Newly Born Woman*, trans. Betsy Wing (Manchester: Manchester University Press, 1986), 61–132; Sarah Kofman, *The Enigma of Woman: Woman in Freud's Writings*, trans. Catherine Porter (Ithaca: Cornell University Press, 1985 [1980]); Shoshana Felman, "Rereading Femininity," *Yale French Studies* 62 (1981): 19–44; and Teresa de Lauretis, "Desire in Narrative," in *Alice Doesn't: Feminism, Semiotics, Cinema* (Bloomington: Indiana University Press, 1984), 103–57.

42. Spivak provides an excellently skeptical account of "French feminism" in "French Feminism in an International Frame," in *In Other Worlds: Essays in Cultural Politics* (New York: Routledge, 1988), 134–53, although she falls into the trap of describing Hélène Cixous's version of "bisexuality" as a denial of sexual difference (here understood narrowly as the difference between "real"—genetic—women and "real"—genetic—men) (146–47). Spivak also goes on to link her discussion of "bisexuality" in Cixous to statements about "the impossibility of remaining in the in-between" (147), statements which cannot but have a biphobic ring.

43. One might remember here that the etymology of "utopia" is from the Greek *ou*, not, and *topos*, place: utopia is no-place.

44. See Cixous, "Sorties," 84, 85–86. Cixous reiterates this appeal to a bisexuality, "the one with which every subject, who is not shut up inside the spurious Phallocentric Performing Theatre, sets up his or her erotic universe" (85), in a number of other texts. Many of these were translated and distributed in the United States and England at more or less the same time and became highly influential in "feminist literary theory," to the extent that the passages on this "other bisexuality" were cited with great theoretical, if somewhat uncritical, zeal.

Cixous, "The Laugh of the Medusa," trans. Keith Cohen and Paula Cohen, *Signs* 1.4 (1976): 875–99, includes a very similar passage on "bisexuality" (883–84). In Cixous, "Castration or Decapitation?" trans. Annette Kuhn, *Signs* 7.1 (1981): 41–55, there is a footnote in which Cixous includes a passage apparently excised from the body of the text: "Female sexuality is always at some point bisexual. *Bisexual doesn't mean, as many people think, that she can make love with a man and a woman, it doesn't mean she has two partners, even if it can at times mean this.* Bisexuality on an unconscious level is the possibility of extending into the other, of being in such a relation with the other that *I* move into the other without destroying the other" (55, first emphasis mine). So Cixous moves from one sort of "bisexuality"—its common sense—to a version of latency that figures an ethical relation to the Other. The inclusion of Cixous's "Laugh of the Medusa" in the widely heralded anthology *New French Feminisms*, ed. Elaine Marks and Isabelle de Courtivron (Amherst: University of Massachusetts Press, 1980), explicitly in the section "Utopias" and as the last entry in the anthology (245–64), also did much to disseminate the notion of "an other bisexuality" as the last word of the "new" French feminism.

45.   Freud, *Standard Edition*, vol. 21, 227–28, my emphasis.

46.   Kofman, *The Enigma of Woman*, 134–35.

47.   Garber mentions Cixous a few times in passing in *Vice Versa*, without engaging with any of Cixous's points. See *Vice Versa*, 169, 174, 183, and 515. Garber neglects to mention Kofman.

48.   See, for example, Cixous, "Sorties," 85.

49.   Here one might observe that while appeals to "maternity" in Cixous have drawn a great deal of critical debate about whether they are "essentialist" or not, "bisexuality" has remained oddly underexamined, as though, unlike "maternity," everyone knows what *that* means. For an overview of debates on essentialism in Cixous (that once again tends to talk about "maternity"), see Katherine Binhammer, "Metaphor or Metonymy? The Question of Essentialism in Cixous," *Tessera* 10 (1991): 65–79.

50.   See, for example, Michelle Citron, Julia Lesage, Judith Mayne, B. Ruby Rich, and Anna Maria Taylor, "Women and Film: A Discussion of Feminist Aesthetics," *New German Critique* 13 (1978): 83–107; Janet Bergstrom, "Sexuality at a Loss: The Films of F. W. Murnau," *Poetics Today* 6.1–2 (1985): 185–203, especially 200–2, in which Freud's *Three Essays on the Theory of Sexuality* is explicitly evoked as a way out of the rigid gender theorization of film, to "help us see new possibilities for the cinematic representation of sexual identities" (202).

51.   Teresa de Lauretis, "Film and the Visible," in *How Do I Look? Queer Film and Video*, ed. Bad Object Choices (Seattle: Bay, 1991), 237–38.

52.   Judith Mayne, "Lesbian Looks: Dorothy Arzner and Female Authorship," in *How Do I Look?* 136–37.

53.   Lily Braindrop, *A Taste of Latex* 9 (1993): 9.

54.   See Jane Gallop, *Around 1981: Academic Feminist Literary Theory* (New York: Routledge, 1992). Gallop writes, "If feminist criticism is not just 'academic,' meaning 'of no practical or useful significance,' then its greatest resources are its 'points of connection,' points where the research, teaching, and writing are attached to actual material life" (10). Of course, such a set of binaries sustains the simple 'academic'/'material' opposition that Gallop seems to want to undo here. She notes that around 1981, "American feminist literary criticism entered the heart of a contradiction. It became secure and prospered in the academy while feminism as a social movement was encountering major setbacks in a climate of new conservatism.... [I]n the American academy feminism gets more and more respect while in the larger society women cannot call themselves feminist" (10). I am profoundly worried that "queer theory" will end up with the same relation to an "actual material life" which it will necessarily imagine as its opposite, while its chroniclers will be able to note, but not explain, what institutional forces brought about these divisions.

55. Spivak, "Subaltern Studies: Deconstructing Historiography," *In Other Worlds: Essays in Cultural Politics* (Routledge: New York and London), 197.

56. See Sedgwick, *Tendencies*, xi–xvi, 1–20, and Butler's "Critically Queer," in *Bodies That Matter*, 223–42. Michael Warner, for example, writes: "I've heard people worry that the political experience of lesbians and gays is being trivialized [through the use of the word 'queer']. Through the rhetoric of queer, they say, straight people score coolness points without suffering. *It may very well be impossible for the sentence 'I am queer' to be false. I can't say this bothers me.*" Michael Warner, "Something Queer about the Nation-State," *Alphabet City* 3 (1993): 14, my emphasis. "Queer" is here understood as an umbrella term for lesbians, gay men, and cool straights. Missing are "bisexuals" and "transgenders": this does worry me, unlike Warner. Like Freud's unconscious, "queer," in this version, knows no "no."

57. See Allan Bérubé and Jeffrey Escoffier, "Queer/Nation," *OutLook: National Lesbian and Gay Quarterly* 11 (Winter 1991): 13–14, for an account of Queer Nation as "confrontational" and against "assimilation" to the point of supposedly practicing an incoherent politics which preaches total inclusivity and pure marginality at one and the same time. I disagree very strongly with this analysis, which has seriously distorted subsequent academic accounts of Queer Nation in particular and "queerness" in general: see Lauren Berlant and Elizabeth Freeman, "Queer Nationality," in *Fear of a Queer Planet: Queer Politics and Social Theory* (Minneapolis: University of Minnesota Press, 1993), 193–229, in which Berlant and Freeman make the queer fanzines seem like the Frankfurt School's negative dialectics for a Xerox generation.

In the *OutLook* article, Escoffier and Bérubé write of how "the new generation [*sic*] calls itself *queer*, not *lesbian, gay and bisexual*," which they go on to suggest are "awkward, narrow, and perhaps compromised words" (13). Since the masthead of *OutLook* named its readership as exclusively "Lesbian and Gay," one has to wonder how "and bisexual" so conveniently slips out of the discussion: not right for *OutLook*, passé for "queer." It is significant that Bérubé and Escoffier disregard how particular Queer Nationals articulate "queer" with transgender and bisexual politics—these comments are printed in the sidebars of the article but do not feature in its body. In the sidebar quotations both Jason Bishop and Rebecca Hensler's testimonies to why they are Queer Nationals involve much more than a simple *preference* of one term over another: Bishop talks about transgender people, as well as about AIDS and HIV, and Hensler mentions bisexual women specifically and nonconformist women in general (16–17). Through this tactical overlooking of "bisexual," along with "transgender," Escoffier and Bérubé arrive at their picture of a politics void of everything except the glamor of the fringe. This account has, in a variety of ways, whether critical or celebratory, become the dominant version of Queer Nation.

58. The conceptual divorce of "sexuality" from "gender" goes all the way back to Gayle Rubin's important essay "Thinking Sex," in which she tried to theorize a domain of experience and practice, that is, "sexuality," distinct from the regulation of "masculine" and "feminine" roles in a patriarchal culture, that is, "gender." See Rubin, "Thinking Sex" (267–319) and especially her comment, "Feminism is the theory of gender oppression. To automatically assume that this makes it the theory of sexual oppression is to fail to distinguish between gender, on the one hand, and erotic desire, on the other" (307). Rubin here suggested a strategic separation that

responded to particular politics in the early 1980s and clearly never intended to separate sexuality from gender for all time, as if the two could be thought apart. Her most recent work has called for a renewed understanding of the category "gender" within theories and politics of "sexuality": "I have wanted to diversify conceptions of butchness, to promote a more nuanced conceptualization of gender variation among lesbians and bisexual women, and to forestall prejudice against individuals who use other modes of managing gender." See Rubin, "Of Catamites and Kings: Reflections on Butch, Gender, and Boundaries," in *The Persistent Desire: A Femme-Butch Reader*, ed. Joan Nestle (Boston: Alyson, 1992), 476.

59. See Marjorie Garber, *Vested Interests: Cross-Dressing and Cultural Anxiety* (New York: Routledge, 1991).

60. For example, when Butler reiterates a variant of her much-criticized dictum that the theatrical is the political at the end of *Bodies That Matter*, it is telling that after a pious invocation of ACT UP and Queer Nation, she should refer to Lypsinka, a drag queen whose repertoire consists of overtly lipsynching the usual pantheon of divas (Judy Garland et al.) (233). It is clear that Butler prefers drag performance over transgender substance. Leslie Feinberg provides a strong and angry critique of the absence of both the word "transgender" and self-identified transgender criticism from recent academic work on "cross-dressing." Leslie Feinberg, "The Power of the Performance," *Lambda Book Report* 4.4 (May/June 1994): 23–24.

61. Eve Sedgwick, "Across Gender," in *Displacing Homophobia*, ed. Butters, Clum, and Moon, 53–72.

62. Sedgwick, "Across Gender," 57.

63. Sedgwick, "Across Gender," 58. The chart is repeated in Eve Sedgwick, *Epistemology of the Closet* (Berkeley: University of California Press, 1990), 13.

64. Sedgwick is still stuck with "across" in *Tendencies*: "Titles and subtitles that at various times I've attached to the essays in *Tendencies* tend toward 'across' formulations: *across genders, across sexualities, across genres, across 'perversions'*" (xii). While she maintains that "the *queer* of these essays is transitive—multiply transitive" (i), the *across* substitutes or stands in for *trans/bi* in a way that negates the latter two.

65. Kathleen Bennett, "Feminist Bisexuality: A Both/And Option for an Either/Or World," in *Closer to Home: Bisexuality and Feminism*, ed. Elizabeth Reba Weise (Seattle: Seal Press, 1992), 207.

66. Bennett, "Feminist Bisexuality," 207.

67. Sedgwick, *Tendencies*, xii.

68. Sedgwick, *Tendencies* , xii.

69. Alisa Solomon, "Strike A Pose," *Village Voice* (November 1991): 13–19.

70. After all, only a few weeks earlier in the *Village Voice* lesbian critic B. Ruby Rich wrote the following absurd generalization about bisexuals in an interview with Camille Paglia, whom Rich identified as "this alleged ex-lesbian, self-professed fag hag, proud bisexual, and resentfully *de facto* celibate." See B. Ruby Rich, "Like A Virgin," *Village Voice* (8 October 1991): 29. Rich mused about bisexuals: "Bisexuals, in my experience, are frequently the product of only-child families, caught in a double bind: included too completely in the mommy-daddy unit, they end up paralyzed, unable to fix an object choice of either male or female, alternating between the two in a replay of the childhood tangle. Paglia was an only child until she was

14" (29). Instead of any criticism of Paglia's work, her identification as "bisexual" is used to discredit and infantilize her. Note the recurrence of the commonplace of "bisexuality" as a temporality that does not occur in the present but is forever seeking in the future what it was in the past. Note also that Rich believes in "object choice" in its Freudian form (rather than as a matter of sex toy selection) and that such object choice is rigidly determined as "either male or female," and then overdetermined by the derivation of these gender positions from the "mommy-daddy unit." What about bisexuals who make transgender "object choices"?

71. The regulation is 32 C.F.R. pt. 41, app. A (1992) and is reprinted in William Rubenstein, ed., *Lesbians, Gay Men, and the Law* (New York: New, 1993), 335. I have not been able to ascertain whether the wording which defines "bisexual" has been substantially changed under the "new" policy of Clinton.

72. The United States school system, as another institution, has also dismissed bisexual teachers, while turning such bisexuality into a variant of "homosexuality." See the case of *Rowland v. Mad River School District,* discussed, without perhaps an adequate consideration of bisexuality, in Janet E. Halley, "Misreading Sodomy: A Critique of the Classification of 'Homosexuals' in Federal Equal Protection Law," in *Body Guards: The Cultural Politics of Gender Ambiguity,* ed. Julia Epstein and Kristina Straub (New York: Routledge, 1991), 371–72.

73. Jan Zita Grover, "AIDS Keywords," in *AIDS: Cultural Analysis, Cultural Activism,* ed. Douglas Crimp (Cambridge: MIT Press, 1988), 21.

74. See Martin S. Weinberg, Colin J. Williams, and Douglas W. Pryor, *Dual Attraction: Understanding Bisexuality* (Oxford: Oxford University Press, 1994). See also Marcy Sheiner's perceptive criticism of the book in her review, "Either/Or Both," *San Francisco Bay Guardian Literary Supplement* 2.30 (27 April 1994): 1, 3, 4. Sheiner notes that the book postulates as theory that in bisexuality, "homosexuality is often an 'add-on' to heterosexuality" (3) and that bisexual and transsexual activists alike have attacked the work: "*Dual Attraction* has drawn comments from activists such as 'So are we "add-ons" or what?' Transsexuals have joined the fray, condemning the study for drawing conclusions about them based on 11—yes, 11—transsexual bisexuals, of whom only one was a female-to-male"(3). At least Weinberg, Williams, and Pryor recognize the existence of transsexual bisexuals.

75. Quoted in Grover, "AIDS Keywords," 21.

76. Grover, "AIDS Keywords," 21.

77. Garber also discusses Grover's analysis and the effects of the AIDS crisis and the scapegoating of bisexuals, although she turns toward proto-bisexual images of vampires and bodily fluids, at which point the political edge of her argument gets blunted. Garber, *Vice Versa,* 91–104.

78. Danzig, "Bisexual Women and AIDS," in *Women, AIDS, and Activism,* by ACT UP/NY/Women and AIDS Book Group (Boston: South End, 1990), 197.

79. Danzig, "Bisexual Women and AIDS," 197.

80. See Ki Namaste, "Le déplacement et la crise du réel: La socio-sémiotique et la biphobie de *Basic Instinct,*" *Cinémas* (Spring 1993): 223–38.

81. "'Reverse' discourse" from Foucault, *The History of Sexuality: Volume One,* 101. I would wager the hypothesis that the current rise of bisexual activism has happened in part in relation to the AIDS crisis and the double scapegoating of bisexuals as

outsiders shadily inside "homosexual" and "heterosexual" communities alike. BiTen, the bi affinity group of Queer Nation/Los Angeles, for example, was founded out of a common need among bisexual Queer Nationals to educate other Queer Nationals about the specific needs of bisexuals in the AIDS crisis. There is a worried silence in works by self-identified lesbians and gay men about bisexuals and AIDS, as in Douglas Crimp and Adam Rolston, *AIDS Demo/Graphics* (Seattle: Bay Press, 1990). Oblique but forceful links between bisexuals and AIDS can be established, as in Sarah Schulman's novel *People in Trouble.* It seems hardly incidental that Schulman should filter her novel about AIDS activism through the lens of a lesbian's relationship to a bisexual woman, in which the latter is presented as irresponsible, manipulative, unable to commit, deeply immersed in heterosexual privilege, and on and on. See Sarah Schulman, *People in Trouble* (New York: Penguin, 1991). Evans writes, on the issue of the AIDS crisis for bisexuals, "negative stereotypy [*sic*] of sexual deviations [*sic*] has always been formally discouraging whilst at the same time informally raising the profile and presence of the forbidden phenomena" Evans, *Sexual Citizenship*, 161.

82. Cindy Patton, *Inventing AIDS* (New York: Routledge, 1990), 121.
83. Cindy Patton, *Inventing AIDS*, 122.
84. Diana Fuss, *Inside/Out* (New York: Routledge, 1991).
85. Fuss, *Inside/Out*, 2.
86. "Bisexuality" is brought up only one more time in D. A. Miller's reading of Hitchcock's *Rope*, and it shows up in the margins of the text, in a footnote with the very word enclosed in supercilious scare quotes (*Inside/Out*, 140).
87. *differences* 3.2 (1991): iii–xviii.
88. Kader and Piontek, Introduction to *Discourse* 15.1 (1992): 7–9.
89. Kader and Piontek, Introduction, 9.
90. Kader and Piontek, Introduction, 9.
91. Hutchins and Ka'ahumanu, *Bi Any Other Name*, vi.
92. By a curious coincidence, Julia Kristeva invokes Romeo and Juliet precisely as emblems for "transgression love, outlaw love" (209) in a chapter of her *Tales of Love* entitled "Romeo and Juliet: Love-Hatred in the Couple." *Tales of Love*, trans. Leon Roudiez (New York: Columbia Univ. Press, 1987), 209–33. As in each of the other sections of *Tales of Love*, one of Kristeva's case histories from her practice as a psychiatrist is written up at the end. This particular one involves a woman who is involved with both a heterosexual and a homosexual man (228–33). Kristeva predictably fails to consider what dynamic bisexuality might have for any of the participants in the threesome and does not seem even to consider how the "homosexual" man must be bisexual. Bi any other name . . . Kristeva's psychoanalytic project is hardly antiheterosexist.
93. The definition of "prosonomasia" I have used here is from Richard A. Lanham, *A Handlist of Rhetorical Terms*, 2d ed. (Berkeley: University of California Press, 1991), 123.
94. Lanham, *A Handlist of Rhetorical Terms*, 121 and 123.
95. Lanham, *A Handlist of Rhetorical Terms*, 121.
96. See Elam, *Shakespeare's Universe of Discourse: Language-Games in the Comedies* (Cambridge: Cambridge University Press, 1984), 314.

97. To be sure, this is not, in any way, to suggest that one single linguistic figure can answer all questions and resolve all conflicts. Instead, my reading of prosonomasia/paronomasia works somewhat like a figure itself, prosonomasically/paronomasically renaming a politics of bisexualities. Given the powerful quality of *Bi Any Other Name*, I am drawing out the theoretical/political force of what might be regarded only as "testimony." I am suggesting, in effect, that "theory" is where you find it, and that "theory" is what works.

98. Obie Leyva, "¿Que es un *bisexual?*" in *Bi Any Other Name*, ed. Hutchins and Ka'ahumanu, 201–2.

99. Kei Uwano, "Bi-Lovable Japanese Feminist," in *Bi Any Other Name*, ed. Hutchins and Ka'ahumanu, 185–87.

100. Shu Wei Chen-Andy, "A Man, a Woman, Attention," in *Bi Any Other Name*, ed. Hutchins and Ka'ahumanu, 179–80.

101. Leyva, "¿Que es un *bisexual?*" 202.

102. Leyva, "¿Que es un *bisexual?*" 202

103. Uwano, "Bi-Lovable Japanese Feminist," 185.

104. Uwano, "Bi-Lovable Japanese Feminist," 185.

105. Chen-Andy, "A Man, a Woman, Attention," 179.

106. Chen-Andy, "A Man, a Woman, Attention," 179.

107. I have devoted attention primarily to *Bi Any Other Name* instead of the anthology *Closer to Home* because *Bi Any Other Name* seems to move beyond the set of binaries that effectively holds *Closer to Home* in a particularly defensive position, namely, women = lesbianism = feminism and men = heterosexuality = patriarchy. I am not especially invested in salvaging the category of "men," but an ongoing assumption in *Closer to Home* seems to be that there are two genders, female and male, which translate into two sexes, women and men, and then into two sorts of sexualities, lesbianism and heterosexuality. (This is despite Kathleen Bennett's comments about genders, which I cited earlier.) Beyond a passing reference, *Closer to Home* does not place bisexuality as consistently in a transgender context as *Bi Any Other Name* does.

108. Carol A. Queen, "The Queer in Me," in *Bi Any Other Name*, ed. Hutchins and Ka'ahumanu, 20.

109. Here I echo Freud's notorious question—"What does woman want?"—and the apparently unironic repetition of that question with regard to bisexuals in "What Do Bisexuals Want?" *OutLook* 4, no. 4 (Spring 1992).

110. Myrna Elana, "Define 'Community': This Is a Test," in *The Persistent Desire*, ed. Nestle, 440–41.

111. One of the first writers actively to advance this claim is Steven Epstein, who writes that, "Just as blacks cannot fight the arbitrariness of racial classifications without organizing *as blacks*, so gays could not advocate the overthrow of the sexual order without making their gayness the very basis of their claims." "Gay Politics, Ethnic Identity: The Limits of Social Constructionism," *Socialist Review* 17. 3/4 (May/August 1987): 19.

112. For a useful criticism of the "ethnic identity model" in gay politics, see Steven Seidman, "Identity and Politics in a 'Postmodern' Gay Culture: Some Historical and Conceptual Notes," in *Fear of a Queer Planet: Queer Politics and Social Theory*, ed. Michael Warner (Minneapolis: University of Minnesota Press, 1993), 116–17.

113. David Gelman with Debra Rosenberg, "Tune in, Come Out," *Newsweek* (15 November 1993): 44.

114. Lani Ka'ahumanu, "A 1993 March on Washington for Lesbian, Gay, and Bisexual Rights and Liberation Speech," *Anything That Moves* 5 (1993): 16.

115. June Jordan, "A New Politics of Sexuality," *Technical Difficulties* (New York: Vintage, 1994), 192–93, my emphasis.

116. Garber, *Vice Versa*, 90.

Chapter 2

Do Bats Eat Cats?
Reading What Bisexuality Does

Frann Michel

In Aesop's fable of "The Bat, the Birds, and the Beasts," the Bat is the creature who refuses to take sides in the war between the birds and the beasts, and ends up exiled from both groups.[1] Why does this sound so familiar, this tale of someone who might belong to either group, or neither—the unreliable figure who abandons potential allies? And why is there only one Bat? Why not a slightly more naturalistic setting, with a community of bats, who might agitate for bat visibility? To be sure, the birds and the beasts make peace at the last moment, and no battle takes place; the indecisive Bat may be "poised ... between ... two mutually exclusive ... cultures," but we never learn which of the two might have "the power to exercise violent repression against the other."[2]

Not so in our unfabulous world. The recent spate of anti-queer-rights measures proposed (and sometimes approved) across the United States makes abundantly clear that the birds and the beasts are at war, and the place of the bats has been subject to debate.

As an intervention in that debate, this essay argues that studying bisexuality is important because of the ways it has helped shape extant discourses of sexuality and the ways it reveals the limitations of our customary readings of sexuality. We can locate constructions of bisexuality in both static image and diachronic narrative.[3] But the image of the bisexual woman typically aligns her with the femme lesbian, while narrative constructions may separate these two figures by emphasizing a monosexual ending. I trace the play between image and narrative of this figure of the bi/fem from inversion theories of homosexuality presented by nineteenth-century sexologists and by psychoanalysis and lesbian representations, through 1950s lesbian communities and fictions, to 1970s lesbian-feminist condemnations of butch-femme as an imitation of heterosexual roles, and finally to more recent queer feminist reclamations of butch-femme. Throughout, I suggest that bisexuality has been constructed in conjunction with other sexualities, and that neglect of this construction has been an artifact of conventional habits of reading. Thus bisexuality is neither immanent in static images nor determined by narrative closure. Rather, reading bisexuality involves reading the process of narrative, the tensions between end and image, between the pull toward closure and the dilation of spectacle.

What, then, is the political place of theorizing about bisexuality? As Loraine Hutchins and Lani Ka'ahumanu have noted, "The main focus of the bisexual movement has been and continues to be the visibility and liberation of all bisexual people."[4] And an earlier incarnation of this paper evoked from a lesbian-identified listener the concern that attending to bisexuality constitutes a distraction from pressing political attacks against lesbians and gay men.

Such concerns affect even those who are otherwise committed to exploring bisexuality. In an essay arguing for the importance of bisexuality to queer ethics, for instance, Elisabeth Däumer states that "it remains to be seen . . . if and how . . . increased [bisexual] visibility would contribute to our struggle against homophobia, sexism, and heterosexism."[5] Däumer acknowledges that visibility might "boost the psychological well-being of many bisexual people," but she neglects to note that that psychological well-being, in turn, can affect our ability to engage in political action.[6]

The question here, then, is not "What is bisexuality?" but "What does bisexuality do?" Eve Kosofsky Sedgwick has recently advocated this approach to the issue of bisexuality and the politics of bisexual identification. She notes that what "bisexuality" does well, within the context of discourses that organize sexuality according to gender of object choice, is to make a space for people for whom that is not exclusive; in other words, it disrupts the notion that hetero/homo or straight/gay is an exhaustive dichotomy. But, Sedgwick notes, the tripartite structure of hetero/homo/bi, or gay, straight, and in between, risks seeming to make gender of object choice a matter that can really exhaustively describe sexuality, and it leaves out all the other axes along which people describe and experience and organize their sexuality.[7]

Many bisexual activists, too, have expressed dissatisfaction with the term. For instance, Paula Rust suggests that since "we do not choose our partners based upon" their gender, it is "self-defeating" to define ourselves with a word that emphasizes the gender of our partners.[8] According to Sedgwick, the rubric under which the centrality of the axis of gender of object choice is being challenged is not "bisexual" but "queer." So within the context of straight/gay, Sedgwick argues, "bisexual" makes space; within the context of "queer," it reduces the possibilities.[9]

Why then use the term "bisexual" rather than "queer" to signal such space-making subversions? Clearly, we do not need to choose always to use one and never to use the other, but can preserve both "bisexual" and "queer" as two available possible terms among many. Moreover, what some others see as a limitation, I see as offering an advantage. As long as gender retains its salience as a structuring of power, there is a use for terms that recognize the extant binary constructions of gender. Where the term "queer" displaces the centrality of gender as an axis of sexual object choice, "bisexual" calls attention to both sexuality and gender. Commenting on the movie *Batman Returns*, Judith Halberstam writes:

When Batman and Catwoman try to get it on sexually, it only works when they are both in their caped crusader outfits.... [T]heir flirtation in capes looked queer precisely because it was not heterosexual, they were not man and woman, they were bat and cat, or latex and rubber, or feminist and vigilante: gender became irrelevant and sexuality was dependent on many other factors.... [I]n other words, the sexual encounter is queer because the genders of the partners are less relevant. Just because Batman is male and Catwoman is female does not make their interactions heterosexual—think about it, there is nothing straight about two people getting it on in rubber and latex costumes, wearing eyemasks and carrying whips and other accoutrements.[10]

"Queer" focuses, then, on sexuality rather than gender. But despite Halberstam's gesture toward a queer utopia where gender is "irrelevant," the practical existence of a dichotomous gender system reemerges in the comment that gender is "less rele-vant." It emerges, too, in the acknowledgment that Batman is male and Catwoman is female, however "many other factors" sexuality depends on.

There are, to be sure, queer representations less anchored in gender than is possible in a mainstream feature film. In "The Femme Tapes," Madeline Davis notes that "Some of my partners were very feminine men. They were Sal Mineo when he was a pretty, big-eyed, soft-looking baby-butch type.... I went with a couple of guys who were faggots and were quite effeminate."[11] Although Davis's narrative suggests the independence of "butch" from gender, she locates these relationships as part of her process of coming out as lesbian. Conversely, the protagonist of Leslie Feinberg's

Stone Butch Blues refrains from making love with her drag queen friend and neighbor only out of fear of emotional vulnerability, but she later acknowledges "it doesn't matter whether it's women or men—it's always high femme that pulls me by the waist and makes me sweat."[12] Kate Bornstein argues that "[t]here are plenty of instances in which sexual attraction can have absolutely nothing to do with the gender of one's partner."[13]

For others, by contrast, the gender play itself is the crux of desire. Bornstein, for instance, notes that there's a "whole group of people who really *like* gender ambiguity, it turns them on."[14] But of course reading ambiguity involves reading the genders that are made ambiguous. Thus, though she wants to go beyond the binary structuring of gender, Bornstein also recognizes the importance of one's gendered history in, for instance, the lingering effects of male privilege.[15] Bornstein points out that some transsexual women display a sense of entitlement they have actually gained from their experiences as men, and she affirms the importance of transsexual women recognizing the difference between their positioning and that of born women. That is, although the binary hierarchy of gender is constructed, it certainly has significant effects. Thus I would agree with Karin Baker that it is worth asking what it means "for bisexual women to remain open to relationships with women and men, the latter being members of a group that oppresses us as women?"[16] "A bisexual politics that does not acknowledge the inevitable differences between the social and personal consequences of relationships with women and relationships with men, that is, one that pretends it is presently possible to 'go beyond gender,' is misguided."[17]

Just as the constructions of gender persist, so too do previous constructions of bisexuality. In asking what "bisexuality" does, we might also ask what it has done, the ways it "already has been, and is, shaping the discourse of sexual politics and theory," as Clare Hemmings puts it.[18] Moreover, we might ask what has been done to it, since even in discourses that explicitly address bisexuality, readings have constructed stories that reabsorb women's bisexuality in lesbian or heterosexual identity. Paula Rust suggests that "bisexuality is only invisible because it is not seen. . . . The failure to see bisexuality lies in the observer, not the observed."[19] The question of bisexual visibility thus becomes a question of a kind of reader response.

Bisexuality has been constructed through both image and narrative. As image, as static spectacle, it has a notable affinity with fem-butch imagery, aligning the bisexual woman and the femme. The cover illustration for the Spring 1992 *Out/Look* issue on bisexuality is an image from Jaime Hernandez's *Love & Rockets* comics. Titled "What Do Bisexuals Want?" it shows a woman with long hair, in a short, tight dress and high heels; her arm is linked with a man's, and she looks questioningly toward another woman with short hair, wearing short heels and a tux.[20] Freud wondered about femininity; *Out/Look* seemed to wonder about femmes.

In contrast, the overlapping of these images—of the figures of the bisexual and the femme—can be disrupted or disentangled by a monosexual narrative telos. As Lisa Walker has noted, femme and butch styles have been understood primarily in terms of their visibility, and the "point often made about femmes . . . is that they, unlike butches, are indistinguishable from straight women in their sexual style."[21] Consequently, as Pat Califia puts it, "butches think of femmes as straight girls taking a sapphic vacation from serving the patriarchy."[22] Thus the visual indistinguishability of the femme from the straight or bisexual woman is frequently resolved through narrative, one version of which collapses bisexuality into a wayward heterosexuality. In a discussion of femme identity, for instance, Joan Nestle comments on the way that 1950s psychologists represented the femme as childish and narcissistic, and then quotes what she calls "the final blow: 'She is more apt to be bisexual and also apt to respond favorably to treatment.'"[23] Nestle's reading of this sexological portrait asserts that "the femme lesbian is stripped of all power, made into a foolish woman who can easily be beckoned over into the right camp."[24] Assuming that the bi/fem is "'apt to respond favorably to treatment'" or that she "can easily be beckoned over into the right camp," as Nestle puts it, locates the bi/fem as potentially and ultimately heterosexual.[25]

As these comments suggest, the 1990s reclamation of butch-femme emerges from and against a long history that locates the femme as bisexual. The genealogy of this figure of the bi/fem can be traced to inversion theories of homosexuality presented by nineteenth-century sexologists and by psychoanalysis and lesbian representations, through 1950s lesbian communities and fictions, to 1970s lesbian-feminist condemnations of butch-femme as an imitation of heterosexual roles. Both sexological reclamation of the femme and lesbian-feminist condemnation of her tend to resolve her potential bisexuality through a narrative that recasts her as finally heterosexual. More recent queer feminist revalorizations of butch-femme have had a dual imperative. On one side, they are part of a queer movement interested in disrupting and denaturalizing the socially normative links among sex, gender, sexual desire, and sexual object choice through gender play; on the other, they continue to mobilize a feminist investment in the woman-identification of the lesbian couple.

Inversion theory accounts for homosexual relationships in terms of heterosexual desire. The woman who desires another woman is an "invert," a man trapped in a woman's body, a masculine woman. Thus she desires a feminine woman. But the feminine woman is by definition not an invert, and thus her desire for another woman is not so easily accounted for. The most famous femme in Anglophone lesbian literature is probably Mary Llewellyn, Stephen Gordon's lover in *The Well of Loneliness*. Radclyffe Hall's novel explains and defends female homosexuality by dramatizing the model of gender inversion supplied by Havelock Ellis, Krafft-Ebing, and other early sexologists, for whom the lesbian was gender-inverted, a masculine woman. This theory is embodied in the heroine Stephen, but cannot account for her feminine lover Mary, to whose consciousness the reader has virtually no access. Teresa de Lauretis comments, "Even today, in most representational contexts, Mary would be either passing lesbian or passing straight"; but, de Lauretis suggests, neither of these readily available designations would really be adequate.[26] At the novel's end, Stephen gives Mary up to a male lover so she will have a chance at a "normal" life. Mary is thus represented as essentially passive and becomes the precursor to the negative image of the bisexual woman who leaves her woman lover for a man.

Sexologists and psychologists of the 1940s and 50s drew on earlier inversion theory to explain butch-femme relationships, and these accounts appear to have had an impact on popular lesbian representations. One narrator in the Buffalo Women's Oral History Project notes that in the forties, "There was a great difference in looks between a lesbian and her girl."[27] The lesbian's girl, the femme, was evidently not herself a lesbian. As Joan Nestle has observed, twentieth-century sexologists' characterizations of the femme pictured her as an "imperfect deviant."[28]

Lesbian literature of the 1950s in some ways suggests an understanding of butch-femme less based on dichotomized heterosexual models. Unlike Hall's Mary, whose desire is indirectly expressed in a novel focalized through the invert Stephen, Ann Bannon's Laura in *Women in the Shadows* feels active desire for butch women: "the big ones, the butches . . . were the ones who excited Laura the most."[29] Yet the butches Laura desires "acted like men and expected to be treated as such."[30] Although 1950s lesbian popular fiction represented a more positive and fully developed lesbian subculture than earlier works like *The Well of Loneliness*, it remained influenced by inversion theory.

This problematic representation of the bisexual woman appears in other works of lesbian fiction of the era as well. In Ann Bannon's *Beebo Brinker*, for instance, butch Beebo first falls for Mona, who is described as "both" "gay" and "straight."[31] The naive Beebo at first finds it difficult to believe the apparently femme Mona is gay, because she has long hair and "doesn't look like a buck private."[32] But Beebo's date with Mona is interrupted when they find a man waiting in Mona's apartment, and Mona lies to Beebo about who's inside. Mona turns out to be the villain of the novel, as much of a bitch as Beebo's friend Jack says she is. Promiscuous with men as well as women because, according to Jack, men are good ego-boosters, Mona is involved, too, with Beebo's next love, the decidedly femme Paula.[33] Finally, Mona disrupts Beebo's affair with the famous Venus Bogardus. Venus, too, has been sexually involved with both women and men, but though she insists that she's gay, at the end of the novel she's too attached to her child, marriage, and acting career to give up her family and position for Beebo. While Venus is a sympathetic figure, then— not the malicious bitch Mona is—she is also fundamentally a coward.

The choice between the conformity of heterosexual marriage and the independence of lesbian subculture is a recurring theme in lesbian pulp novels of the 1950s. In those texts, as Angela Weir and Elizabeth Wilson have argued, "[l]esbianism stands as a metaphor for personal autonomy and, openly or implicitly, heterosexuality is posed as inauthentic for women, precisely because it involves financial dependence."[34] That is, in engaging with a more general concern of U.S. culture during that period—conventionality as opposed to bohemianism—lesbian pulp novels correlate lesbian subculture and relationships with personal freedom and with intellectual, artistic, financial, and spiritual self-fulfillment.

The alignment of femme identity with bisexuality and of both with politically conservative heterosexuality becomes even more emphatic in post-Stonewall lesbian-feminist articulations, although with the formulation and promulgation of the idea of "The Woman-Identified Woman," understandings of sexual identity dominant among queer women broke away from inversion models of lesbian identity, and from sexology in general.[35] For instance, Sue-Ellen Case critiques Del Martin and Phyllis Lyon's *Lesbian/Woman* (1972), arguing that Martin and Lyon present femmes as "lost heterosexuals who damage birthright lesbians by forcing them to play the butch roles. The authors assert that most femmes are divorced heterosexual women who know how to relate only to men and thus force their butches to play the man's role, which is conflated with that of a butch."[36] Thus a butch is butch only because she is responding to the desire of a woman who is really straight. The 1970s rejection of butch-femme roles and emphasis on woman-identification found its culmination in Adrienne Rich's 1980 essay "Compulsory Heterosexuality and Lesbian Existence," in which femme-butch roles no longer merit a mention, and bisexuality is mentioned only as a utopian humanist ideal that could be used to blunt the political critique achieved by focusing on heterosexuality as a political institution.[37] As Lyndall MacCowan points out, "By the 1980s, femmes were named 'sellouts' who reclaimed heterosexual privilege and used it to oppress butch lesbians."[38]

The 1970s and 80s lesbian-feminist condemnation of butch-femme relationships hinged on their supposed replication of heterosexual roles: the model inherited and adapted from inversion theory came to be seen as inauthentic. Consequently, the 1990s reclamation of butch-femme has entailed demonstrating its difference from heterosexuality, generally by emphasizing its parody of heterosexual roles, celebrating its inauthenticity. Moreover, since the figure of the femme has been historically problematic for lesbians because of her ostensible heterosexuality, promiscuity, confusion, and cowardice (i.e., her stereotypical bisexuality), feminist queer theorists interested in revalorizing butch-femme have been at particular pains to assert the purity of the femme's lesbianism, as well as the impurity or inessentiality of her gender.

For instance, in Sue-Ellen Case's analysis of the Split Britches productions of Peggy Shaw and Lois Weaver, "Toward a Butch-Femme Aesthetic," Case locates "the feminist subject, endowed with the agency for political change" in the butch-femme couple.[39] But for Case, as for other theorists of butch-femme, decoding the lesbianism of the femme proves difficult: how to assure the femme is not hetero or bi? Case argues that butch-femme roles "qua roles lend agency and self-determination to the historically passive subject" and, "with the aid of camp," also offer "an irony that allows [the feminist subject's] perception to be constructed from outside ideology."[40] Her argument draws on Joan Riviere's theory of womanliness as masquerade. For Riviere, all women wear the mask of womanliness "to disguise," as Case puts it, "the fact that they have taken their father's penis in their stride, so to speak," though "the heterosexual women don't claim possession openly, but through reaction-formations; whereas the homosexual women openly display their possession of the penis."[41] According to Case, "the butch is the lesbian woman who proudly displays the possession of the penis, while the femme takes on the compensatory masquerade of womanliness."[42] But since this would seem to indicate the femme is heterosexual, Case hastens to add that the "femme, however, foregrounds her masquerade by playing to a butch, another woman in a role."[43] Emphasizing visual display while repudiating the narratives that have recuperated the femme for heterosexuality, Case argues of Weaver and Shaw's work that "no narrative net can catch them or hold them, as they wriggle into a variety of characters and plots," and that "[t]his exciting multiplicity of roles and narratives signals the potency of their agency."[44] Counterposing narrative realism to the agency of seduction, Case suggests that "[t]he closure of . . . realistic narratives chokes . . . women to death and strangles the play of symbols, or the possibility of seduction."[45]

Similarly to Case, Judith Butler argues that the butch is not an "invert," but that she parodies rather than replicates heterosexuality, and that it is the recontextualizing and parody of masculinity that the femme finds desirable.[46] As Carole-Anne Tyler notes, "Butler discusses the butch as the subject of gender play but the object of desire, which enables the lesbian to be consistently associated with transvestic subversion. The discussion would not work as well in reverse."[47] Indeed, Tyler argues, the idea that the femme "recontextualizes" her role by playing it to another woman relies on "an essentialist tautology":

[B]utch-fem or drag is gender play because it is gay; it is gay and drag because it is gender play. In short, a "gay sensibility" is implicitly invoked to determine in advance what counts as gender play, keeping straight the difference between enlightened drag and unenlightened masquerade or parade. . . . But perhaps the most troubling consequence of this homosexual essentialism is its paradoxical reinforcement of the idea that the "authentic" or "natural" self is heterosexual, even as it inverts the hierarchy by proclaiming the "fake" or artificial gay self to be the "better," smarter—more smartly dressed—self, which deconstructs itself by knowing its difference from itself and the gender role it only assumes like a costume.[48]

That is, Tyler suggests, the emphasis on demonstrating that the femme is lesbian and that femininity is a masquerade paradoxically leads to a reinforcement of straight femininity as the ground on which the ensuing queer gender play is staged. Thus the femme is both the point at which the heterosexist model of lesbian sexuality as inversion breaks down and the most problematic point for feminist queer theory which seeks to argue for lesbian sexuality as parodic revelation of the inessentiality of gender. Like the bisexual, the femme constitutes a point of crisis in representation, resolved by attempting to freeze a monosexual image or to move toward a monosexual narrative telos.

The telos of stories about bisexuality has also frequently meant the subordination of bisexuality to a lesbian narrative. The constitution of bisexuality as narrative is evident, for instance, in the Gay Revolution Party Women's Caucus's 1971 essay, "Realesbians and Politicalesbians":

The claim to bisexuality is commonly heard within the movement, and while bisexuality is not physiologically impossible, the term cannot be used to characterize a stable socio-sexual orientation. Because no heterosexual relationship is free of power politics and other masculine mystifications, women who assert that they are bisexual retain their definition by men and the social advantages accruing from this. Bisexuality is a transitional stage, a middle ground, through which women pass from oppressive relationships to those of equality and mutuality. It is a struggle with privilege and fear, and not all women come through it to their sisters on the other side.[49]

In the intervening years lesbian relationships have been somewhat demystified, and can no longer be so easily romanticized. Relationships between women can no longer be assumed to be free of power politics and necessarily characterized by equality and mutuality, for instance. Yet the presentation of bisexuality formulated here still has a good deal of currency. Many lesbian feminists still read bisexuality as complicity with the institution of heterosexuality and a rejection or denial of the critique of that institution. In this account, bisexuality is necessarily part of a larger narrative, and indeed it manifests the disequilibrium that D. A. Miller has argued is characteristic of narrative.[50] Construing bisexuality as an unstable transitional stage on the way to the telos of lesbian identification frames it as part of a conventionalized, linear, lesbian coming-out narrative.

As Biddy Martin has noted, the contributions to collections like *The Coming Out Stories*, *The New Lesbians*, and *The Lesbian Path* offer narratives constructed through cultural feminist analyses that locate "the key to opposing male supremacy" in "withdrawal from men, now named lesbianism."[51] Emphasizing woman-identification as the authenticating unity of sexuality, subjectivity, and political stance, these narratives offer a linear progression from confusion or lies to a return to an essential, true self and desire, "grounding identity and political unity in moral right and truth."[52] Thus the ending of the story—the arrival at lesbian identity—shapes the meaning of what has come before. Such essentializing narratives postulate a purely constative mode, one that obscures the extent to which discourse constructs rather than merely reflects the truth of experience and identity. Thus in both the hetero and lesbian versions of such narratives, whom one ends up with indicates what one's sexuality really is.[53]

In contrast, the more recently developed genre of the bisexual feminist coming-out narrative problematizes its conventional precursor. Amending the lesbian coming-out narrative by adding another chapter, the bisexual story destabilizes the teleological closure of linear narrative. For instance, Ruth Gibian implicitly acknowledges and repeats the gesture of the lesbian coming-out story when she writes, "When I came out as a lesbian, I, like many other women, felt I was giving voice and life to my true self, releasing what had remained stifled and denied for too long."[54] Yet this retrospective account follows its repetition: the essay opens with an account of dawning attraction, which turns out to be for a man, and then turns out to echo a prior experience of awakening love for a woman, which, in turn, it thus decenters. Gibian goes on to ask, "And what if we do change? What if our feelings vary? Does that negate our previous experience, make it any less important?"[55] The title of Gibian's essay is "Refusing Certainty: Toward a Bisexuality of Wholeness." While the reference to "wholeness" indicates the utopian impulse that would deny the necessary exclusions of signification, the emphasis on process rather than closure indicated by "toward" confirms the refusal of certainty.[56]

Reading bisexuality thus involves neither, on the one hand, just a reading of a static moment outside its history, a specular performance, nor, on the other hand, simply a teleological reading of narrative, in which the ending determines the significance of particular moments that have come before. It involves, instead, reading the tensions of an ongoing construction.

As I have suggested, images of the bisexual woman overlap with images of the femme. Theorizations of butch-femme relations tend to focus on spectacle: static images, acts, moments that emphasize the visual impact of the pair. But these images risk destabilization by the narratives in which they are often embedded: the femme might turn out not to be a lesbian after all; the queerness of her sexuality is not visually marked and threatens to be disconfirmed by what happens next, by her potential bisexuality. Bisexuality, in turn, may be undermined by being embedded in a narrative with a monosexual telos, rather than being read as itself a narrative process. Bisexuality is thus neither immanent in the specular nor determined by an imminent end.

The specular and teleological modes of interpretation have been discussed by Judith Mayne with respect to lesbian readings of classical films such as *Morocco* and *Queen Christina*. Reading specific cinematic moments as lesbian requires

a convenient forgetfulness or bracketing of what happens to these images, plot and narrative-wise, in the films in which they appear, where heterosexual symmetry is usually restored with a vengeance. Depending on your point of view, lesbian readings of isolated scenes are successful appropriations and subversions of Hollywood plots, or naive fetishizations of the image. Put another way, there is a striking division between the spectacular lesbian uses to which single, isolated images may be applied and the narratives of classical Hollywood films, which seem to deaden any such possibilities.[57]

Mayne argues for a "'both/and'" reading of the conflict between narrative and spectacle as fundamentally ironic and herself connects this reading process with a bisexuality that provokes a "crisis in representation."[58] But Mayne emphasizes the importance of keeping "these two dynamics of sameness and difference in some kind of tension" so as not to "end up affirming some notion of a wishy-washy bisexual human subject—'wishy-washy' in the sense that such a subject-position carries very little political impact in our present society."[59] It has little political impact, as I take it, because of its "human," that is to say, ungendered and presumably otherwise unspecified, status, its apparently undiluted universalizing absorption of other sexualities, its posture as "everysubject."

But the development of a bisexual movement dedicated to visibility and liberation, to ending heterosexist and sexist oppressions, is giving bisexual subject positions increasing political impact. We have the tools to begin reading bisexuality as an ongoing construction, the provocation of a crisis in representation. "Bisexual" can retain an awareness of the constraints of gendering, even while, like "queer," it gestures toward a utopian wonderland beyond gender, where it really would not matter whether one ended up with a partner who was a boy or a girl or neither. In *Alice's Adventures in Wonderland*, as she falls down the rabbit-hole, Alice thinks of her cat, Dinah, and the absence of available rats for Dinah to catch. "'Do cats eat bats?' Alice wonders, and sometimes, 'Do bats eat cats?' for, you see, as she couldn't answer either question, it didn't much matter which way she put it."[60]

Notes

1. *Folklore and Fable: Aesop, Grimm, Andersen* (New York: Collier, 1937), 21.
2. Lisa Orlando, "Loving Whom We Choose," in *Bi Any Other Name: Bisexual People Speak Out*, ed. Loraine Hutchins and Lani Ka'ahumanu (Boston: Alyson Publications, 1991), 224–25.
3. Marjorie Garber similarly suggests that bisexuality "is . . . a narrative" (87), but she also suggests that all sexuality is narrative (86). Despite the apparent essentialism of her language here, she also argues that sexuality is constructed (e.g., 184), though she locates a number of textual instances other then those I trace here. See *Vice Versa: Bisexuality and the Eroticism of Everyday Life* (New York: Simon and Schuster, 1995).
4. Loraine Hutchins and Lani Ka'ahumanu, "Overview; Politics: A Queer among Queers," in *Bi Any Other Name*, 222.
5. Elisabeth D. Däumer, "Queer Ethics; or, The Challenge of Bisexuality to Lesbian Ethics," *Hypatia* 7.4 (Fall 1992): 97.
6. Däumer, "Queer Ethics," 97.
7. Eve Kosofsky Sedgwick. (August 17, 1994). "Bi," QSTUDY-L@UBVM.CC.BUFFALO.EDU.
8. Paula C. Rust, "Who Are We and Where Do We Go From Here? Conceptualizing Bisexuality," in *Closer to Home: Bisexuality and Feminism*, ed. Elizabeth Reba Weise (Seattle: Seal Press, 1992), 299.
9. Sedgwick, "Bi."
10. Cited in Kate Bornstein, *Gender Outlaw: On Men, Women, and the Rest of Us* (New York and London: Routledge, 1994), 35–36.
11. Madeline Davis, Amber Hollibaugh, and Joan Nestle, "The Femme Tapes," in *The Persistent Desire: A Femme-Butch Reader*, ed. Joan Nestle (Boston: Alyson Publications, 1992), 254–67, esp. 256.
12. Leslie Feinberg, *Stone Butch Blues: A Novel* (Ithaca, N.Y.: Firebrand Books, 1993), 274.
13. Bornstein, *Gender Outlaw*, 35.
14. Bornstein, *Gender Outlaw*, 10.
15. Bornstein, *Gender Outlaw*, 101, 110.
16. Karin Baker, "Bisexual Feminist Politics: Because Bisexuality Is Not Enough," in *Closer to Home*, 260.

17. Baker, "Bisexual Feminist Politics," 260.

18. Clare Hemmings, "Resituating the Bisexual Body: From Identity to Difference," in *Activating Theory: Lesbian, Gay, Bisexual Politics,* ed. Joseph Bristow and Angelia R. Wilson (London: Lawrence and Wishart, 1993), 118.

19. Rust, "Who Are We and Where Do We Go from Here?" 305.

20. *Out/Look* 4.4 (Spring 1992): 1.

21. Lisa Walker, "How to Recognize a Lesbian: The Cultural Politics of Looking Like What You Are," *Signs: Journal of Women in Culture and Society* 18.4 (Summer 1993): 867.

22. Cited in Walker, "How to Recognize a Lesbian," 868.

23. Joan Nestle, "The Femme Question," in *The Persistent Desire*, 143.

24. Nestle, "The Femme Question," 143–44.

25. The continuing salience of this connection can also be seen in *The Femme Mystique*, ed. Leslea Newman (Boston: Alyson Publications, 1995). The first selection in that anthology, Amy Warner Candela's "Not What You Might Think," begins "I am not heterosexual. I am not bisexual" (17). That a number of writers in the collection do identify themselves as bisexual in the contributors' notes, however, indicates that with the increase of bipride, there is less need among queer women to distinguish firmly between bisexual and femme identities.

26. Teresa de Lauretis, "Sexual Indifference and Lesbian Representation," in *The Lesbian and Gay Studies Reader,* ed. Henry Abelove, Michèle Aina Barale, and David Halperin (New York and London: Routledge, 1993), 155.

27. Madeline D. Davis and Elizabeth Lapovsky Kennedy, "Oral History and the Study of Sexuality in the Lesbian Community: Buffalo, New York, 1940–1960," in *Unequal Sisters: A Multicultural Reader in U.S. Women's History,* ed. Ellen Carol DuBois and Vicki L. Ruiz (New York and London: Routledge, 1990), 387–99, esp. 388.

28. Nestle, "The Femme Question," 143.

29. Cited in Angela Weir and Elizabeth Wilson, "The Greyhound Bus Station in the Evolution of Lesbian Popular Culture," in *New Lesbian Criticism: Literary and Cultural Readings,* ed. Sally Munt (New York: Columbia University Press, 1992), 107.

30. Cited in Weir and Wilson, "The Greyhound Bus Station," 107.

31. Ann Bannon, *Beebo Brinker* (Tallahassee, Fla.: Naiad Press, 1986 [1962]), 193.

32. Bannon, *Beebo Brinker,* 38.

33. Bannon, *Beebo Brinker,* 37.

34. Weir and Wilson, "The Greyhound Bus Station," 101.

35. See Radicalesbians, "The Woman Identified Woman," reprinted in *Radical Feminism,* ed. Anne Koedt, Ellen Levine, and Anita Rapone (New York: Quadrangle, 1973), 240–45. Like lesbian political discourse and fiction, sexology no longer relies exclusively on the inversion model to explain same-sex sexuality. Indeed, George Chauncey has argued that "medical opinion began to shift from an exclusive focus on 'inversion' as gender reversal to 'homosexuality' as deviant sexual orientation" as early as the 1930s." Cited in Esther Newton, "The Mythic Mannish Lesbian: Radclyffe Hall and the New Woman," in *The Lesbian Issue: Essays from Signs,* ed. Estelle B. Freedman, Barbara C. Gelpi, Susan L. Johnson, and Kathleen M. Weston (Chicago: University of Chicago Press, 1985), 16 n.19. But, as Newton observes, "The change has had only limited effect on popular ideology" (16 n.19). Moreover,

the model of inversion (though not the term) persists in some medical studies, including the widely cited work of Simon LeVay. He argues that the third interstitial nucleus of the anterior hypothalamus is smaller in women and in men he presumed to have been homosexual, larger in men he presumed to have been heterosexual. In other words, gay men resemble women.

36.   Sue-Ellen Case, "Toward a Butch-Femme Aesthetic," in *Making a Spectacle: Feminist Essays on Contemporary Women's Theatre*, ed. Lynda Hart (Ann Arbor: University of Michigan, 1989), 283. See also Del Martin and Phyllis Lyon, *Lesbian/Woman* (New York: Bantam, 1972), 79.

37.   See Adrienne Rich, "Compulsory Heterosexuality and Lesbian Existence," in *Powers of Desire: The Politics of Sexuality*, ed. Ann Snitow, Christine Stansell, and Sharon Thompson (New York: Monthly Review Press, 1983), 177–205, esp. 182. For a useful rereading of this essay, see Rebecca Kaplan, "Compulsory Heterosexuality and Bisexual Existence: Toward a Bisexual Feminist Understanding of Heterosexism," in *Closer to Home*.

38.   Lyndall MacCowan, "Re-Collecting History, Renaming Lives: Femme Stigma and the Feminist Seventies and Eighties," in *The Persistent Desire*, 299–328, esp. 315.

39.   Case, "Toward a Butch-Femme Aesthetic," esp. 283.

40.   Case, "Toward a Butch-Femme Aesthetic," 292.

41.   Case, "Toward a Butch-Femme Aesthetic," 291.

42.   Case, "Toward a Butch-Femme Aesthetic," 291.

43.   Case, "Toward a Butch-Femme Aesthetic," 291.

44.   Case, "Toward a Butch-Femme Aesthetic," 295.

45.   Case, "Toward a Butch-Femme Aesthetic," 297.

46.   See Judith Butler, *Gender Trouble: Feminism and the Subversion of Identity* (New York and London: Routledge, 1990), 123.

47.   Carole-Anne Tyler, "Boys Will Be Girls: The Politics of Gay Drag," in *Inside/Out: Lesbian Theories, Gay Theories*, ed. Diana Fuss (New York and London: Routledge, 1991), 32–70, esp. 55.

48.   Tyler, "Boys Will Be Girls," 56.

49.   Gay Revolution Party Women's Caucus, "Realesbians and Politicalesbians," in *Out of the Closets: Voices of Gay Liberation*, ed. Karla Jay and Allen Young (New York: Douglas Book Corp., 1972), 179–80.

50.   D. A. Miller, *Narrative and Its Discontents: Problems of Closure in the Traditional Novel* (Princeton: Princeton University Press, 1981), ix.

51.   Biddy Martin, "Lesbian Identity and Autobiographical Difference[s]," in *Life/Lines: Theorizing Women's Autobiography*, ed. Bella Brodzki and Celeste Schenck (Ithaca and London: Cornell University Press, 1988), 86.

52.   Martin, "Lesbian Identity and Autobiographical Difference[s]," 89.

53.   Marjorie Garber discusses such stories as "conversion narratives" (347) and notes, "We begin with the 'end' of the story, and retell it so that it 'comes out right,' producing, as if inevitably from the materials of a life, the person we (think we) are now" (324).

54.   Ruth Gibian, "Refusing Certainty: Toward a Bisexuality of Wholeness," in *Closer to Home*, 3–16, esp. 3.

55.   Gibian, "Refusing Certainty," 4.

56. Similar narratives appear in many of the essays in *Closer to Home* (see those by Dvora Zipkin, Stacey Young, Sharon Gonsalves, Kathleen Bennet, and Beth Elliott) and *Bi Any Other Name* (see those by Elizabeth Reba Weise, Lisa Orlando, Lani Ka'ahumanu, and Karen Klassen). Paula Rust has noted in her study "'Coming Out in the Age of Social Constructionism: Sexual Identity Formation among Lesbian and Bisexual Women," that "coming out is not a linear, goal-oriented, developmental process," and that its description as such is a function of the limits of most available models. *Gender & Society* 7.1, (March 1993): 50–77, 50.

57. Judith Mayne, "Lesbian Looks: Dorothy Arzner and Female Authorship," in *How Do I Look? Queer Film and Video*, ed. Bad Object Choices (Seattle: Bay Press, 1991), 103–35, esp. 103.

58. Mayne, "Lesbian Looks," 117, 131.

59. Mayne, "Lesbian Looks," 136–37.

60. Lewis Carroll, *The Annotated Alice: Alice's Adventures in Wonderland and Through the Looking Glass*, intro. and notes by Martin Gardner (New York: New American Library, 1960), 28.

Chapter 3

From Performativity to Interpretation: Toward a Social Semiotic Account of Bisexuality

Ki Namaste

It seems to be one of those things where we have a word for it [bisexual], but the word, you can never really use it, you know? It's like, you can never really use it [the word "bisexual"] because you're going to be classified in one way or the other [as heterosexual or homosexual].

—Lucy, CKUT-FM, Montreal, July 29, 1994

Lucy's comment on language and sexual identity illustrates the theoretical and political problems which accompany the articulation of bisexuality. That the term "bisexual" can be uttered without specifying a particular referent indicates a theoretical problem of meaningless words and barren semantic fields. At the same time, this theoretical issue is bound within obstacles of a more political nature— i.e., the impossibility of enunciating a critical bisexual identity and politics (or any bisexual identity and politics, for that matter).

This paper is concerned with the relations between language and identity, with an emphasis on how to conceptualize bisexual subject-positions and, equally important, how to make sense of their erasure. Recent criticism in the field known as "queer theory" turns its attention to these kinds of questions.[1] This area of inquiry is heavily influenced by both semiotics and deconstruction. Broadly speaking, semiotics refers to the ways in which meaning is generated and interpreted, while deconstruction examines the production of binary oppositions, such as that between "men" and "women."[2] Queer theory combines these perspectives in order to account for the generation and effacement of hetero- and homosexualities. It invokes the trope of "inside/out" to explain how heterosexuality requires homosexuality for its internal coherence.

As numerous scholars have shown, however, critics in queer theory neglect sociological approaches to sexuality, privileging textual meanings over social context.[3] While many social scientists would argue that we need to abandon interpretive methodologies such as semiotics and deconstruction, and while these debates are especially heated in the context of poststructuralist theory,[4] I want to suggest that we continue our examination of discourse but develop a methodology which is capable of theorizing how social relations are expressed in language.

An absence of social scientists in queer theory is, as Steven Seidman puts it, "somewhat ironic in light of the gesturing of queer theory towards a general social analysis."[5] In this paper, I examine the kinds of semiotic theories critics in queer theory employ, as well as how these methodological choices prevent an adequate conceptualization of the connections between language and society. Social semiotics, I propose, offers a perspective which accounts for the realization of ideology in discourse. This approach is especially useful for thinking about bisexuality, since bisexual identity is undermined in the very instance it is uttered. By forging a social semiotic methodology, we can examine the connections between representation, discourse, and society. Such a transdisciplinary endeavor allows us to be both semioticians and sociologists. Laboring on the borders of traditional academic disciplines, this kind of fence-sitting also responds to both the theoretical and political problems involved in the articulation of bisexual identities, communities, and activism.

A warning should be issued at this point: since I am concerned with investigating the epistemological underpinnings of queer theory,[6] this paper will necessarily suffer from an excess of vocabulary, terminology, and theory. It goes without saying that the remainder of this exposé will be quite dry (*sec*).

"Performativity": A Brief Archaeology

The notion of "performativity" has been influential in the development of queer theory.[7] Specific invocations of the concept, however, are marked by ambiguous and contradictory understandings of what constitutes "performativity," as well as its linguistic, discursive, and/or political effects. A brief survey of the idea as it is used in speech act theory, deconstruction, linguistics, and queer theory is in order. A historical overview of "performativity" will illuminate the ways in which the idea is used differently by scholars in these fields. An analysis of these differences can in turn inform a theory which accounts for the effacement and/or inscription of bisexual subject-positions.

"Performativity" is first associated with the speech act theorist J. L. Austin, whose work is a central reference point for critics in queer theory.[8] Austin proposes a new way for philosophers and grammarians to think about a particular statement. He introduces a distinction between performative and constative utterances. In the case of performative speech acts, a specific act is achieved in the very process of its utterance. In the phrase "I promise," for example, the promise is carried out when it is said. A constative speech act, in contrast, describes an external reality, as in the sentence, "He promised to come out as bisexual." In this instance, the statement describes a commitment on the part of an individual to come out as bisexual, but it does not realize the process of coming out. While Austin begins his lectures by differentiating between performative and constative speech acts (Lecture I), he subsequently demonstrates the difficulty of maintaining any neat separation between these categories (Lectures II–XII). Austin offers several examples to make his point. When the captain of a ship performs a marriage ceremony and says the phrase, "I now pronounce you husband and wife," he consolidates the bond of marriage in his words. Saying is doing. Yet this can only be valid in a context where the captain is authorized to conduct marriage ceremonies—i.e., on sea, not on land. Austin reflects on this context and realizes that this performative utterance in turn depends on conventional circumstances (being on a ship), procedures (the ritual of a marriage ceremony), words ("I now pronounce you husband and wife," not "I now pronounce you mutual sex slaves"), and participants (one male and one female, not three male-to-female transsexuals). If one of these conditions is not met, then the phrase "I now pronounce you husband and wife" can still be uttered, but it will not have validity. Austin states that an utterance is "infelicitous" or "unhappy" when the conventions of speech are not respected (Lecture III).

The provisional definition of a performative speech act requires that an utterance be conjugated in the first-person, present tense, indicative mood, active voice. Thus, phrases such as "I promise," "I declare," "I wish," and "I bet" are all performative speech acts. Since Austin demonstrates the ways in which these phrases already require an extraverbal situation in which to secure their validity, he reveals the limitations of a theory of speech acts which isolates an individual's discourse.

In an attempt to elucidate the notion of performativity, Austin distinguishes different types of performative verbs (Lecture VII). In the case of an explicit performative, such as the expression "I apologize," the act of apologizing is carried out in the utterance of the words. Austin differentiates this kind of performative verb from one which is "not pure," or "half descriptive," such as the statement "I am sorry."[9] In this example, the phrase both achieves and describes a certain effect in its utterance; to say "I am sorry" is to apologize and to relate that one already feels remorse. The locution is simultaneously performative and constative.

Austin then abandons his original distinction between performatives and constatives and instead turns his attention to the particular effect an utterance achieves (Lecture VIII). In his framework, a statement may have locutionary, illocutionary, or perlocutionary force—which is to say that it may designate a certain sense and reference (locutionary), it may achieve its effects in its utterance (illocutionary), or it may bring about an effect (perlocutionary). The move away from the concept of "performativity" is important, since it allows Austin to focus on the particular force of a statement; not merely its meaning, but how it is used and what it accomplishes. Austin contends that if we examine "what one is doing in saying something," we will necessarily theorize the speech situation in its totality.[10]

Jacques Derrida extends Austin's ideas considerably.[11] He invokes the example of launching a ship and claims that the performative utterance associated with naming a vessel (e.g., "I name this ship *Betsy*") can only succeed if it follows an identifiable formula. Although the ship is named in the act of utterance, this is only possible given an implicit understanding of what these words mean in a particular context. Derrida introduces the notion of citationality to advance his position. It is only in citing the context of utterance that the naming of a ship makes sense. If I say "I name this ship *Betsy*" while standing at the front of a classroom delivering a lecture, the statement can not be classified as a performative, since it does not achieve what it says. Derrida asks a rhetorical question: "Could a performative statement succeed if its formulation did not repeat a 'coded' or iterable statement, in other words, if the expressions I use to open a meeting, launch a ship or a marriage were not identifiable as conforming to an iterable model, and therefore if they were not identifiable in a way as 'citation'?"[12] Derrida's concept of citationality repeats Austin's work on infelicities and demonstrates the ways in which an utterance is part of a complex speech situation. Discourse cannot be isolated from its context and must be theorized in relation to the norms and codes within which it appears and to which it belongs.

While Austin admits that performative speech acts must follow established conventions, he paradoxically ignores most instances of "unhappy" and/or "non-serious" discourse. At the same time, he returns throughout his work to statements produced in the first-person present indicative active (e.g., "I promise"). By ignoring infelicitous statements, and by focusing much of his analysis on the intention of a speaker, Austin offers a theory of speech acts which privileges an individual's ostensibly unconstrained choice in the organization of grammar, syntax, and semantics. Derrida disputes these two aspects of Austin's theory, and it is in this challenge that he makes a valuable contribution.

Since a performative can only be successful when it is already located within an identifiable context, Derrida echos Austin to argue that a "pure" performative does not exist. The contextual coding of specific acts of discourse defines what constitutes a performative utterance. In this light, Derrida suggests, it would be useful to think about locutions which are not considered performatives. They would illustrate some of the ways in which social discourse is already coded. A reflection on nonserious and "parasitic" statements[13] forces us to relinquish a theory which locates a self-present speaking subject as the source of all utterance. This regard for identifiable norms of speech, citationality, means that an individual speaker's intention will not be the central focus of study. Derrida does not go so far as to say that intentionality will vanish entirely; he simply raises an important question about its origin. If the utterance can only be understood in terms of its social context, then a theory which attempts to account for the "totality" of a speech situation should not place the speaking subject at its core.[14] Since Austin constantly reverts back to the first-person present indicative active ("I" statements), and since he consistently ignores instances of "non-serious" discourse, his project cannot account for a total speech situation. Derrida's concept of citationality thus proposes an alternative conception of speech acts.[15] At the same time, it illustrates the ways in which Austin's theory belongs to a broader Western epistemological tradition which posits an all-knowing, self-present subject—man—at its very core.

While Derrida addresses Austin's notion of performativity only to elaborate the theory of citationality, Paul de Man (who is also associated with the strand of literary criticism known as deconstruction) approaches the issue from a different perspective.[16] De Man draws on the theory of rhetoric espoused by Nietzsche. Nietzsche proposes that we focus on the use of figures and tropes in language rather than on linguistic and argumentative methods of persuasion, as theorized in classical rhetoric. This achieves an important shift in focus: tropes, defined as figures of extended meaning, mediate intricate relations between thought, meaning, and expression.[17] To suggest that rhetoric turn its attention to these operations, as Nietzsche does, is to privilege figural rather than literal meaning. Language does not exist to express some concrete object and/or thought; its function is more complex than a referential or representational framework can allow. An emphasis on the figural and rhetorical aspects of language allows Nietzsche to demonstrate that, since the delineation of simple referents is always more complicated than this process first appears, the entire notion of objective "truth" is undermined.

De Man continues this project. In the introduction to his book *Allegories of Reading*, de Man proposes that the linguistic sign mediates both referential and figural meanings.[18] He then incorporates elements of speech act theory into his project, taking up the distinction between constative and performative language.[19] Constative language is associated with rhetorical persuasion and some extralinguistic referent, while performative language involves rhetorical figures and strategies.

Yet if one is to privilege questions of rhetoric in language, one necessarily admits the impossibility of producing a definitive statement in the act of interpretation, because tropes and figures involve extended meanings. De Man refers to this predicament under the title "misreading." Given the rhetorical nature of language, all interpretations are misreadings of an "original" text, and these commentaries serve to establish other (mis)readings of the same text. Even de Man's own enterprise is not immune to this condition. He points out that while his theory of (mis)reading demonstrates the rhetorical operations which motivate a text, this is only possible when the interpretation of the text acts as its own referent. Here is the essential paradox: deconstruction can illuminate the workings among grammar, reference, and rhetoric and, in that very process, can undermine a referential conception of language. Nevertheless, this in turn depends on the ability of this (mis)reading to know itself as an object of study, a referent. For these reasons, de Man admits that a return to the referent is inevitable, that interpretation demands "a relapse from a language of figuration into a rhetoric of signification."[20] De Man uses this insight to critique speech act theory. He maintains that since one cannot distinguish between the self-reflexive and referential functions of language, the division between performative and constative statements is equally suspect. This predicament means that we can only ever offer readings which are, in de Man's words, "aberrant."

Like Derrida, De Man addresses one of the central tenets of speech act theory—the distinction between performative and constative utterances. Both Derrida and de Man explain how this distinction does not hold and consequently extend the project initiated by Austin. Derrida and de Man also share similar critiques of the theoretical presuppositions which inform speech act theory. Derrida's work on citationality undermines the intentions of a speaking subject, while de Man's emphasis on misreading privileges the rhetorical devices and structures of language, rather than the professed desires of individual authors and critics.

Deconstruction thus rejects the performative-constative opposition. The distinction is preserved, however, within the field of semio-linguistics, most especially in the work of Émile Benveniste.[21] In his article "La philosophie analytique et le langage," Benveniste summarizes Austin's arguments.[22] For Benveniste, we can continue to define performative statements, although we must apply strict criteria in so doing.

Foremost among these conditions is that a performative statement is an act in itself; it achieves its validity in its utterance. Since performatives can only accomplish an act, having no descriptive or prescriptive power, they remain singular and unique: "Étant acte individuel et historique, un énoncé performatif ne peut être répété. Toute reproduction est un nouvel acte qu'accomplit celui qui a qualité. Autrement, la reproduction de l'énoncé performatif par un autre le transforme nécessairement en énoncé constatif."[23] This condition means that a performative statement constitutes itself; it is "sui-référentiel."[24] The statement (*l'énoncé*) produced identifies itself with its utterance (*l'énonciation*), so that the object to which a statement refers is the same as what is signified linguistically. "Le signifié est identique au référent."[25]

Scholars who espouse deconstruction and those trained in linguistics approach the performative-constative distinction in radically different ways. For practitioners of deconstruction, the task is to expose the bankruptcy of the opposition. Linguists, on the other hand, refine their diagnostic criteria of what constitutes performativity and turn their attention to the specific pronominal, verbal, and temporal markings of the category.

We can now ask how critics in the field of "queer theory" understand performative statements, as well as how they designate a specifically "queer performativity."[26] Queer theory seeks to offer a model which can account for the social inscription of sexual and gender identities. It does this through an invocation of "performativity"—a notion which, following Benveniste, refers to individual acts of discourse which cannot be repeated. The contradiction is flagrant: on the one hand, queer theory is interested in the social, historical, and cultural locations of sexual and gender identities. On the other, it uses a theoretical model which forecloses consideration of these historical, social, and cultural factors. Reflection on this paradox will suggest crucial methodological starting points for a social semiotic account of (bi)sexuality. Due to limitations of space, I shall confine my comments to the writings of Eve Sedgwick and Judith Butler.

Sedgwick provides a reading of the phrase "Shame on you" in terms of performativity. She begins with this construction in part because it questions the conditions which define Austin's performative utterance (first-person present indicative active). For Sedgwick, this is a performative statement, because the conferral of shame is achieved in the act of utterance. Moreover, this is an interesting example because the first-person pronoun "I" effaces itself through an invocation of the pronoun "you." Finally, the phrase does not have an explicit verb, in contrast with the examples of performative locutions which Austin offers (e.g., "I do"). Sedgwick contends that the expression "Shame on you" challenges Austin's definition of performativity and that it achieves this at the level of grammar.[27]

Sedgwick goes on to claim the political relevance of working with the notion of shame. She does not want to advocate "a queerness drained of specificity or political reference" and therefore locates "queer performativity" as "the name of a strategy for the production of meaning and being, in relation to the affect shame and later to the related fact of stigma."[28] In this framework, "shame-consciousness and shame-creativity do intimately cluster around lesbian and gay worldly spaces," many of which are subsequently listed in Sedgwick's article.[29]

If we read speech act theory alongside Sedgwick, we are confronted with a number of pressing theoretical questions. Although Sedgwick maintains that the phrase "Shame on you" is performative, a careful reading of Austin's theory would recognize that this expression is not an explicit performative but is rather "not pure" or "half descriptive."[30] To say the words "Shame on you" is not the same as saying "I confer shame on you." In the latter case, the conferral of shame is achieved in the act of utterance; it is an explicit performative. The locution "Shame on you," in contrast, is fundamentally concerned with invoking an addressee (what Sedgwick rightly labels "the interpellation of witness")[31] and creating a sense of shame in and for that individual.[32] The remainder of Sedgwick's essay is devoted to considering the ways in which shame and stigma are created and resisted in relation to lesbian and gay spaces. Her own use of the utterance "Shame on you" extends beyond its unique linguistic production. To that end, she offers a reading of this expression which is concerned with the effects it creates rather than those it achieves. In the language of speech theory, this is the realm of *perlocutionary* (not illocutionary) force.

Judith Butler's writings on the performativity of gender are marked by similar terminological difficulties.[33] Butler uses the term "performativity" to express the implicit norms and social relations in which gender is located. Once it is viewed this way, gender is not a fixed entity, but rather something which must be continually repeated in order to secure its legitimacy. Gender is not something which a volitional subject elects to perform but is precisely those social relations which would establish the subject prior to performance. The critical task at hand, for Butler, is the invention of innovative strategies of repetition which demonstrate the fabricated nature of gender relations.

Since the notion of repetition is central to her argument, it is curious that Butler chooses to discuss the disruption of sexual and gender norms under the rubric of "performativity." As we have already observed, the concept of performativity can only be used if, following Benveniste, we do not discuss the repetition or reproduction of a particular utterance. Given that gender is something which is constantly maintained and reproduced in the social world (a position which Butler would not dispute), a theoretical model which does not account for this reproduction is insufficient.

Terminological contradictions are also evident when Butler designates gender as performative, stipulating that "'performative' itself carries the double meaning of 'dramatic' and 'non-referential.'"[34] Butler seems to be drawing on de Man here, and it is noteworthy that he is referenced in one of her later essays on this question.[35] But while de Man problematizes a simplistic, referential concept of language, he at no point endorses a "non-referential" theory. Rather, he is interested in the rhetorical operations which produce and require incessant play between literal and figural readings.

Consider, as well, Butler's discussion of the role that signs play in social life: "Political signifiers, especially those that designate subject positions, are not descriptive; that is, they do not represent pregiven constituencies, but are empty signs which come to bear phantasmatic investments of various kinds. No signifier can be radically representative, for every signifier is a site of a perpetual *méconnaisance* [*sic*]; it produces the expectation of a unity, a full and final recognition that can never be achieved."[36] In the field of semiotics, the phrase "empty signs" is associated with the linguist Benveniste. Benveniste discusses pronouns such as "I" and "you" in terms of their linguistic conditions of utterance (*l'énonciation*).[37] He argues that these pronouns have no reference to an external reality but only make sense when they are uttered: "Dépourvus de référence matérielle, ils [*je* and *tu*] ne peuvent pas être mal employés. . . . C'est en s'identifiant comme personne unique prononçant *je* que chacun des locuteurs se pose à tour comme 'sujet.' L'emploi a donc pour condition la situation de discours et nulle autre."[38]

In many respects, Butler's use of the phrase "empty signs" is the antithesis of Benveniste's model. While Benveniste limits himself to a very precise linguistic site ("la situation de discours et nulle autre"), Butler insists that "political signifiers" such as "women" cannot be exhaustive, thus refusing to confine her analysis to one particular site. Indeed, were Butler to follow Benveniste's program, she would not be able to speak about the implicit rules and conventions of gender, since this would shift the discussion from a linguistic instance of utterance to a social context. For these reasons, Butler's decision to use a collocation associated with Benveniste—"empty signs"—is regrettable.

Despite an invocation of the vocabulary developed within speech act and semio-linguistic theories, Butler is not concerned with "performativity," "non-referentiality," or "empty signs." She is, however, interested in thinking about the ways in which gender norms must be cited: "[p]erformativity is a matter of reiterating or repeating the norms by which one is constituted."[39] In this context, Butler follows Derrida's work on *citationality* and demonstrates the ways in which compulsory sex/gender relations require subjects to repeat or "cite" socially sanctioned practices.[40]

Theoretical reflection on Austin's theory of performative statements is characterized by two mutually exclusive positions. Critics such as Derrida and de Man continue Austin's project by demonstrating the impossibility of distinguishing between performative and constative utterances. Linguists like Benveniste, in contrast, continue to speak of performative verbs, although they maintain strict definitional criteria for these cases. Paradoxically, queer theory confuses these approaches by using the language of speech act theory and linguistics ("performativity") in a theory of citationality.[41] This choice of vocabulary is unfortunate, because the rich and complex history associated with performative statements is forgotten. At every twist and turn, Sedgwick and Butler move from a linguistic instance of utterance to an extratextual reality. Which is to say that queer theory exhibits a decidedly *aberrant* relation to the very concept of performativity.

These remarks on the historical and contemporary uses of performative utterances provide an important point of departure for a social semiotic account of sexual and gender identities. As we have observed, critics in queer theory are fundamentally concerned with the conditions which govern sexual and gender positions—the effects of shame, and/or the unwritten rules which regulate sex/gender relations. For two reasons a theory of "performativity" is not the best place from which to begin such an analysis: first, the idea of "performativity" refers to unique instances of discourse which cannot be repeated; and second, the framework presupposes the existence of lesbian, gay, and/or "queer" subjects. Such a perspective does not explain how these subjectivities emerge or disappear. A social semiotic theory of sexuality and gender is faced with the challenge of accounting for these workings of ideology in discourse.

Queer Theory's Saussurian Legacy

Sedgwick and Butler are both interested in the social conditions in which identities such as "queer" are located. Unfortunately, they draw on theoretical models which are often ill-equipped to theorize how social relations are realized in discourse. This is evident in a contradictory use of the vocabulary associated with semio-linguistic and speech act theories. It can also be observed in the manner in which critics in queer theory espouse a Saussurian conception of the sign.[42]

Ferdinand de Saussure suggests that we consider language both as a structure of rules (*langue*) and individual acts of utterance (*parole*). In his course on general linguistics, he proposes a well-known definition of the sign, as that entity which is composed of a signifier (an abstract concept) and its signified (the concept which is designated). For instance, the word "tree" is a sign, composed of tree (signifier) and the implicit image it evokes (a large plant with sap and leaves, the signified).

Returning to Butler's work on political signifiers, we see that she uses a Saussurian concept of the sign in her discussion of terms like "women" or "queer."[43] Although Butler contends that these signifiers do not designate predetermined subject-positions, her choice of vocabulary contradicts this argument. *Signifiers* function to denote a concept. While a particular term may only be loosely defined (e.g., "queer"), it nonetheless carries with it implicit mental and conceptual images. To speak of a "performative function of the signifier"[44] is to negate its denotative role. Butler's attempt to leave terms like "women" or "queer" open is admirable and may indeed help to forge a unique form of political community. Nevertheless, one must acknowledge that any invocation of a "signifier" necessarily brings with it a corresponding concept. Therefore, one cannot properly classify signifiers under the rubric of performative statements. Performatives are verbs; their appearance is much more limited than the constative features of language present in the use of names such as "women."

A consideration of other thinkers in queer theory will clarify these methodological issues. D. A. Miller also relies on a Saussurian concept of the sign in his reading of Alfred Hitchcock's film *Rope*.[45] To be more precise, Miller works with the theory of connotation proposed by Roland Barthes,[46] who himself accepts a signifier/signified split. Following the work of Danish linguist Louis Hjelmslev,[47] Barthes maintains that a particular signifier can denote some concept or other. But this same signifier can also indicate a second order of meaning, what Barthes refers to as connotation. Whereas the signifier's primary signified is denoted, the realm of connotation is only implied. Miller uses this framework to claim that within *Rope*, homosexuality can never be stated explicitly. It is always relegated to a parenthetical status—the realm of connotation, not denotation.[48]

The argument is seductive and certainly helps explain the lack of representation of sexual and gender minorities within mass culture. Yet it is marred by significant methodological difficulties. As numerous scholars have shown,[49] a neat separation between the realm of denotation and connotation assumes that language only designates things and thus obscures the ways in which meaning, interpretation, and context intersect. The words of Terry Threadgold, "[I]deological struggle in discourse is realised at the lowest (the denotative) lexico-grammatical level and cannot be treated only as a connotative semiotic.... [T]his problematises the whole question of the adequacy of the necessity of a connotative semiotic level to handle ideology in discourse."[50]

A reflection on some of the common insults directed against bisexuals demonstrates the weakness of a theory of connotation. Words like "fence-sitter," "closet case," "swinger," and "confused" all imply that bisexuals are both sexually and politically uncommitted. Biphobia thus instantiates itself at the denotative, semantic level. Similarly, when Alexander Doty provides readings of queerness in mass culture, he can only refer to bisexuality in the conditional tense, as when he cites a number of films "that could be discussed as bisexual texts."[51] The inscription of bisexuality as a mere possibility—never a reality—is achieved through the use of the conditional verb tense.[52] Biphobia is also realized in grammar.

A final comment on Miller's use of Barthesian semiotics is needed, in order to show how Miller elides the workings of ideology in discourse. If homosexuality is relegated to connotation, then heterosexuality is, by implication, that which one can denote. Yet Barthes maintains that ideology is located on a connotative level. Because Miller aligns homosexuality with connotation, he presupposes that hetero- sexuality exists outside its ideological construction.[53] Consequently, Miller enacts conservative assumptions about the nature of sexuality.

An application of Barthesian semiotics to mass culture brings with it insur- mountable obstacles when it comes to theorizing the constitution and elision of sexual identities. Since biphobia manifests itself at the lexico-grammatical level (semantics, verb tense), we need a theory which can account for the micrological, linguistic operations which support a more macrological denial of bisexual identity.[54]

Thus far, we have remarked on some of the methodological presuppositions which inform the project of queer theory. Despite an invocation of the notion of "performativity," critics in queer theory are invested in a referential project—one in which hegemonic norms of gender and sexuality figure centrally and which can be witnessed through an appeal to a Saussurian conception of the sign. It would be difficult to imagine developing a critical sexual politics without some reference to the social context in which sexual practices, identities, and communities are located. The theoretical issue here is not that queer theory appeals to lesbian and gay identi- ties but that it does not offer an adequate framework for theorizing the sociopolit- ical circumstances which govern the inscription of sexualities and genders. While critics in the field of queer theory do not wish to delineate the borders of categories such as "queer," they nonetheless rely on a theoretical model which compels the denotation of identity. Since this area of study is fundamentally concerned with a referential politics, an investigation of the notion of reference is in order.

Reference, Use, and Mention

The field known as the philosophy of language has devoted a considerable amount of attention to the idea of reference.[55] One of the most important contributions is that of G. Frege, who asks how proper names and definite descriptions refer to things.[56] Frege answers this question by distinguishing between sense, the descriptive content of a name, and reference, the object referred to by that name. Reference is always achieved by way of sense. This proposition has been rejected by Bertrand Russell, who believes that descriptive expressions do not "refer" at all and can consequently only be analyzed in terms of their predicates and logical constraints.[57]

Ogden and Richards develop these insights and claim that we need to examine "the relations of words to ideas and of ideas to things."[58] In their perspective, symbol, thought, and referent are related in a triangular fashion. A symbol symbolizes a particular thought or reference, while this thought in turn refers to a specific referent. At the same time, the symbol stands for the referent.[59] The distinction between thought (or reference) and the object to which it refers (referent) is crucial, because the relation between a symbol and its referent is an imputed one. In contrast, thought is causally related to a referent, just as a symbol is causally related to thought. In their definition of the sign, we have (1) a sign which (2) refers to something and (3) is interpreted by a person.[60] Ogden and Richards emphasize that when we speak of the meaning of a sign, we should not confuse that with either the imputed relation between a sign and that to which it refers, or the referent (what is designated).

Ogden and Richards achieve an important shift from a Saussurian conception of the sign by focusing on the triadic process of interpretation in which signs are embedded (symbol, thought, referent). P. Strawson approaches this issue from a related perspective.[61] Strawson takes issue with Russell's theory of reference, reiterating his example of the phrase "The King of France is wise." Russell has a problem with this sentence: how can it be significant when there is no King of France? Strawson explains that Russell's question presupposes that the meaning of a sentence which requires an objective referent (the King of France) determines its significance. Strawson then suggests that we think not about what the sentence means but about how it is used. The differences between the use and mention of a sentence are most clear when we situate the expression within a specific context. Someone can utter the phrase "The King of France is wise" in the eighteenth century, as can someone in the nineteenth century. These two utterances reflect different occasions of use.

Strawson suggests that instead of talking about the truth or falsity of the sentence, we think about the ways in which it is used "to express a true or false proposition."[62] He criticizes Russell for confusing the use of an expression in a particular context with referring (mention). Like Ogden and Richards, Strawson points out the displacements enacted when meaning and use are collapsed. Thus, the "meaning of an expression cannot be identified with the object it is used, on a particular occasion, to refer to."[63]

These reflections on reference can help elucidate the ways in which practitioners of queer theory implicitly undermine bisexual identity. Reading the phrase "Shame on you," Sedgwick declares that shame "is an affect that delineates identity—but delineates it without defining it or giving it content. Shame, as opposed to guilt, is a bad feeling that does not attach to what one does, but to what one is."[64] Since she does not define the content of identity and shame (meaning), Sedgwick appears to theorize the *use* of the utterance "Shame on you." When she relates "shame-consciousness and shame-creativity" to "lesbian and gay worldly spaces," however, she assimilates the meaning of the expression "Shame on you" to the object it designates (lesbians and gay men). It is in a confusion of meaning and use that Sedgwick moves from performativity ("the conferral of shame")[65] to ontology ("what one is").[66]

Once again, we observe that queer theory elaborates a referential politics. As previously stated, the fact that there are lesbians and gay men to which the terms "lesbian," "gay," and/or "queer" refer is not in question. What is at issue are the terminological and theoretical slippages required in order to make this "queer" theory work. At this point, we can summarize three pressing methodological difficulties within this field: an inconsistent use of terminology, especially regarding the notion of performative statements; a Saussurian conception of the sign, which privileges denotation at the expense of social context; and a confusion of the meaning and use of an utterance. The appropriate response to these problems, I suggest, lies in a radically different conception of the generation and interpretation of meaning.

Beyond Saussurian Binaries: Peirce's Theory of the Sign

The theory of the sign elaborated by Charles Saunders Peirce avoids the methodological problems which plague queer theory, while still attending to the social production of meaning.[67] Peirce believes that binary definitions of the sign reduce it to a stagnant entity. He investigates the dynamic processes within which the sign is located, rather than offering a simple decodification of what a particular signifier denotes. To that end, Peirce proposes a triadic definition of the sign, composed of a representamen, an object, and an interpretant. Let us return to the sign "queer" in an effort to demonstrate the political potential of this model. The phonic utterance "queer" is the representamen, while the object is a mental image evoked through an utterance of the term—say, for instance, a leather dyke. This definition seems to parallel Saussure's signifier/signified split, in which "queer" designates a particular aesthetic, politics, and/or group of individuals. To move beyond such a static conception of the sign, Peirce introduces his notion of interpretant: the entire network of relations associated with the lexeme /queer/ in the English language (since the term was uttered in English).[68]

For Peirce, an interpretant is not a thing, much less a person, but is rather a function. The interpretant of the sign "queer" in turn generates other signs. Once the mental image of a leather dyke has been evoked, we enter into the sign system of leather, as well as a conjunctural relation between leather and women. In Peirce's terminology, the interpretant becomes the ground of a new sign, composed of a representamen, an object, and another interpretant. Peirce argues that this generation of meaning is a defining condition of the sign, such that we are presented with a situation of semiosis ad infinitum. There are numerous categories of the sign in Peirce's framework (ten classes, organized into levels of firstness, secondness, and thirdness) and a variety of ways in which the interpretant's function can be carried out (immediate, dynamic, and final interpretants). The specifics of these categories can be left to Peircian scholars, at least for the purposes of this paper. What is important to underline is the shift from a theory of denoting a particular signified to a framework which accounts for the intertextual relations in which semiosis is located.[69]

We have already observed some of the ways in which queer theory's reliance on a signifier/signified split enacts conservative assumptions about sexuality, as well as how its use of reference (a collapse of meaning and use) situates its project within a gendered, monosexual discourse. Furthermore, we have examined some of the syntactic and lexico-grammatical devices employed to undermine bisexual identity, such as the use of the conditional tense. All of these examples investigate how monosexuals designate bisexuality. An analysis of how bisexuals articulate our own identities is useful at this point, since activists engage strategies of reference markedly different from those employed by critics in queer theory.

A pamphlet produced by the group BIONIC (Bisexuals Organizing with Noise, Insurrection, and Confrontation) speaks directly to members of the lesbian and gay communities who believe the myth that bisexuals are politically uncommitted.[70] The pamphlet lists common myths that monosexuals utter about bisexuality, including the following example:

YOU SAY: Bisexuals are confused about their sexuality.
WE SAY: It is you who are confused about our sexuality.[71]

The issue raised here is one of reference. When biphobic lesbians and gay men invoke the sign "bisexual," the tract suggests, they do so with a particular image of bisexuality in mind—one in which bisexuals are sexually confused. Bisexuals respond by challenging the implicit referent evoked in the "you say" statement. Rather than a delineation of who is bisexual, however, the pamphlet simply declares that the "you say" statement lacks an understanding of bisexual specificity. In this manner, the reader's attention is drawn to the ways in which statements about bisexuality are used rather than what the signifier "bisexual" designates. This strategy recognizes the difference between the assertion of a proposition and the act of referring.

Having distinguished between use and mention, BIONIC goes on to problematize any simple denotation of bisexual identity. A list of definitional criteria is presented, with the term "bisexual" at the top of the page followed by two columns under the headings "Are . . ." and "Aren't. . . ." The list of what "bisexuals are . . ." includes adjectives such as "queer," "single," "non-monogamous," "lesbian-identified," "black," "transsexual," "bi-identified," and "here." The list of what "bisexuals aren't . . ." contains phrases such as "an AIDS risk," "ashamed," "straight," "invisible," "a cop out," and "going away." A warning is issued at the bottom of the page: "This list is not conclusive, to be continued. . . ." BIONIC undermines a definitive statement on bisexuality and demonstrates the ways in which signs are embedded in complex intertextual relations. The sign "bisexuals" can refer to the objects, people, and/or concepts specified under the words "bisexuals are . . ." and "bisexuals aren't. . . ." Yet these people, identities, and/or concepts are not absolute; bisexuality can mean many other things as well. In this light, BIONIC recognizes that the function of the interpretant is a crucial element of the sign: the act of referring to bisexuality is situated within a network of relations which is already both overdetermined (through biphobia) and infinite (through activism). Since the "list is not conclusive," BIONIC appreciates that the interpretant of one sign in turn becomes the ground of a new sign, and so on ad infinitum.

Like BIONIC, the editors of the magazine *Anything That Moves* suggest that we cannot simply assimilate the meaning of the utterance "Bisexuals are confused" with the particular object to which this expression refers (bisexuals). The introduction to the magazine subverts some of the most common ways in which biphobic assertions manifest themselves in discourse: "Do not assume that bisexuality is binary or duogamous in nature . . . or that we MUST be involved simultaneously with both genders to be fulfilled human beings."[72] In a strategy which parallels that of BIONIC, this discourse locates sexual identities within their rhetorical propositions (monosexuality), rather than merely denoting bisexual referents. Through an emphasis on the reflexive, open-ended nature of bisexuality, *Anything That Moves* focuses its attention on the interpretant's function in processes of semiosis. The sign of bisexuality goes on to generate new signs, which in turn become the ground for other signs.

This strategy is important, because it is by refusing referents that demarcate bisexuality that a broad-based movement can be established. The introduction to the magazine, for instance, highlights that monosexuality not only denies bisexuality but also requires a rigid, binary gender system. With the warning "don't assume there are only two genders," these bisexual activists create a coalition among transgenders and bisexuals—a coalition which is fostered and encouraged in the concrete, organizing efforts of bisexual communities.[73] In the introduction to their book *Bi Any Other Name: Bisexual People Speak Out,* Loraine Hutchins and Lani Ka'ahumanu emphasize that they will not provide an easy definition of what bisexuality is. They view this in a positive light, however, and contend that this refusal of closure is crucial for the development of a "multicultural feminist bisexuality."[74] A stress on the dynamic process of meaning enables a bisexual politics which is actively feminist, antiracist, and transgender-positive.

Theorizing Bisexuality: From Denotation to Interpretation

As we have observed, biphobia is realized at the lexico-grammatical level. This presents a formidable challenge to activists, because the utterance of the category "bisexual" does not guarantee the realization of a bisexual identity and/or community. Here, then, is the ultimate problem: the discourses of monosexuality evacuate any and all referential meanings for the term "bisexual," beyond states of confusion and a severe lack of political commitment. Biphobia is the persistent attempt to undermine the very possibility of bisexual identity.

The examples of bisexual activism discussed in this paper recognize how biphobia instantiates itself in social discourse. To that end, they do not simply repeat "We're bisexual!" over and over again. Rather, they ask us to think about how bisexuality is conceptualized and used in specific occasions and stagings of the social text. The issue is not one of what bisexuality is, or whom it includes, but of how the category is used. Since such a strategy locates sexual and gender identities within their social contexts, it responds to Marxist and social scientific concerns about the solipsistic nature of queer theory in America.[75]

The differences between the semiotic strategies of critics in queer theory and bisexual activists can be explained in terms of Saussure and Peirce. Whereas Saussure proposes a binary conception of the sign, in which signifiers denote some concept, Peirce offers a triadic definition, where a sign is composed of its representamen, object, and interpretant. In this approach, the sign "bisexual" can refer to a particular object (individual bisexuals), but it is also oriented to an entire network of social relations (monosexuality). By focusing on the function of the interpretant, activists struggle against heterosexism and monosexuality, without foreclosing a diversity of bisexualities. Theoretically, this effects a shift from a semiotics of decodification to one of interpretation.

There are some strong arguments to be made for investigating sexuality (and culture more generally) from a Peircian framework. Firstly, much of Peirce's writings complement the antifoundationalist sentiment which critics in queer theory espouse. With the concept of an interpretant, Peirce demonstrates the intertextual relations in which all utterances are located. His idea of the "ground" goes somewhat further than this, to illustrate how one particular sign becomes the defining condition of other signs, in a process without end. This emphasis on the generation of meaning, I submit, parallels Derrida's work on citationality, where communication is only possible given a prior code, and de Man's writings on aberration, in which referentiality is at once impossible and inevitable.

The theoretical issues explored by Peirce are often made explicit within deconstruction. De Man refers to Peirce's theory of the sign[76] and endorses the stress on a continuous process of interpretation, although de Man designates this with the term "misreading." The invocation of Peirce is entirely appropriate for an anti-Cartesian program, since Peirce suggests that subjects do not master thought; they are constituted in it.[77] If we return to Derrida's article "Signature Event Context," we find he advances a theory of the sign not unlike Peirce's, although Derrida examines the concept of the sign advanced by Condillac.[78] Condillac's ideas are too detailed to present here, but let us recall his argument that a passage from sensation to reflection occurs through fundamental faculties of understanding, including perception, consciousness, attention, reminiscence, memory, and imagination. In this framework, signs are themselves produced by these faculties of understanding, enabling various modes of thought and logic (discrimination, abstraction, judgment, reason). Condillac's interest in classifying spheres of interpretation is not merely pedantic: he wrote against the grammarians of Port-Royal, who, heavily influenced by Descartes, offered a binary conception of the sign.[79] Despite their different historical and national locations, one can see a great deal of continuity between Condillac and Peirce; they both contend that communication is a complex process and that the sign achieves much more than the mere designation of a concept.

Insofar as Peirce forces an acknowledgment of the intertextual relations in which a sign is embedded, he reorients the field of semiotics.[80] Despite this considerable achievement, Peirce does not fully succeed in developing a social semiotic analysis. There are a variety of sites one could explore for such an approach: one thinks of Valentin Voloshinov, whose work on reported speech and syntax demonstrates the ways in which a dialogic utterance is inscribed into a monologic context;[81] systemic functional linguistics developed in Australia, which emphasizes the functional components of language—not just what words mean but the effects they achieve;[82] Italian social semiotics, which theorizes the sign in terms of macrological communication process;[83] and québècois social discourse analysis, which combines semiotic, rhetorical, and argumentative theories to explain the workings of ideology in discourse.[84] While all of these perspectives offer more technical, linguistic analyses than Peirce, they nonetheless share his conception of semiosis.[85]

The focus in this paper on the role and function of a sign's interpretant should thus be read as a crucial step in the development of a social semiotic analysis.

The shift from a semiotics of decodification to one of interpretation is of concern not only to scholars interested in bisexuality but to activists as well. The examples presented clearly demonstrate that the greatest challenge facing bisexual activism is an exposition of the rhetorical propositions which govern utterances on sexual and gender identities. Social semiotics offers an important contribution in this regard, because it elucidates the propositions which underlie sexual and gender identities. This perspective is most relevant to activism, since it forces us to think about the ways in which categories of sexuality and gender are used, deployed, and coded.

Critics in queer theory merely presuppose the existence of lesbians, gay men, and/or "queers" as possible referents of the sign "queer." Furthermore, they collapse the meaning and use of utterances on sexuality and gender and rely on a Saussurian conception of signification, which compels the static denotation of a signified. A social semiotic examination of sexuality and gender, in contrast, accounts for the dynamic process of meaning embodied in signs like "bisexual" or "queer." Instead of focusing on the referent of the term "bisexual" (whether implicitly or explicitly), social semiotics investigates how the category "bisexual" is coded, as well as the propositions it is used to support. This involves a theory of meaning concerned with the circulation of signs, rather than with what particularly signifiers denote.

Like critics in queer theory, social semiotics takes up the challenge of semiotics and deconstruction. At the same time, such a perspective remains faithful to socio-logical inquiry, because it explains the instantiation of social relations in discourse. Social semiotics thus involves the development of a truly transdisciplinary, praxis-oriented methodology. It is, of course, no accident that a "theory" best suited to accounting for bisexuality refuses disciplinary divisions of labor as vigorously as it refuses sexual and gender binaries.

Notes

Many of the ideas presented in this paper were developed in conversation with Michael du Plessis, particularly the ways in which critics in queer theory use speech act theory. I am also grateful to Maria Pramaggiore for her editorial comments, and to Lorna Weir for numerous conversations on the importance of a social semiotic analysis. Finally, I thank Judith Marshall for her activist work, as well as her humorous reflection on the rather serious problems involved in articulating bisexual identity.

1.   See, among others, Diana Fuss, *Inside/Out: Lesbian Theories, Gay Theories* (New York: Routledge, 1991); Eve Sedgwick, *Epistemology of the Closet* (Berkeley and Los Angeles: University of California Press, 1990); Sedgwick, "Queer Performativity: Henry James's 'The Art of the Novel,'" *GLQ* 1.1 (1993): 1–16; Judith Butler,

"Critically Queer," *GLQ* 1.1 (1993): 17–32; Butler, *Bodies That Matter: On the Discursive Limits of "Sex"* (New York: Routledge, 1993); Butler, "Performative Acts and Gender Constitution: An Essay in Phenomenology and Feminist Theory," in *Performing Feminisms: Feminist Critical Theory and Theatre*, ed. Sue-Ellen Case (Baltimore: John Hopkins University Press, 1991), 270–82.

2. For an introduction to semiotics, see Terence Hawkes, *Structuralism and Semiotics* (Berkeley and Los Angeles: University of California Press, 1977). For an overview of deconstruction, see Vincent Leitch, *Deconstructive Criticism: An Advanced Introduction* (New York: Columbia University Press, 1983).

3. Steven Seidman, "Symposium: Queer Theory/Sociology: A Dialogue," *Sociological Theory* 12.2 (July 1994): 166–77; Donald Morton, "The Politics of Queer Theory in the (Post)Modern Moment," *Genders* 17 (Fall 1993): 121–50.

4. See, for instance, Bryan Palmer, *Descent into Discourse: The Reification of Language and the Writing of Social History* (Philadelphia: Temple University Press, 1990). For an overview of poststructuralism and postmodernism in the Anglo-American social sciences, see Pauline Rosenau, *Insights, Inroads, Intrusions: Postmodernism and the Social Sciences* (Princeton: Princeton University Press, 1992).

5. Seidman, "Symposium," 174.

6. One should point out that queer theory has developed within departments of film, literature, and cultural studies in America; its project is thus overdetermined by these disciplinary and national locations. Attention to different national and disciplinary sites would offer alternative models for theorizing sexuality. For an overview of English Canadian research—which is primarily situated in the social sciences and which remains bi-positive—see Barry Adam, *The Making of a Gay and Lesbian Movement* (Boston: Twayne, 1987); Gary Kinsman, *The Regulation of Desire: Sexuality in Canada* (Montreal: Black Rose Books, 1987); and Mariana Valverde, *Sex, Power, Pleasure* (Toronto: Women's Press, 1985).

7. Butler, "Critically Queer," "Performative Acts," and *Bodies That Matter*; Sedgwick, "Queer Performativity."

8. J. L. Austin, *How to Do Things with Words* (New York: Oxford University Press, 1973 [1962]). Austin's ideas were first delivered in a series of lectures at Harvard University in 1955. Readers may wish to consult his article "Performatif-Constatif," in *Cahiers de Royaumont, Philosophie no. IV, La philosophie analytique* (Paris: Editions de Minuit, 1962), 271–304, which was originally presented in French in 1958. The published French version offers a transcription of the discussion following his presentation. An English translation of this article is available: Austin, "Performative-Constative," in *The Philosophy of Language*, ed. John Searle (New York: Oxford University Press, 1971 [1963]), 13–22. This article does not include the subsequent discussion with conference participants.

9. Austin, *How to Do Things with Words*, 83.

10. Austin, "Performative-Constative," 22.

11. Jacques Derrida, "Signature Event Context," in *Margins of Philosophy*, trans. Alan Bass (Chicago: University of Chicago, 1982 [1972]), 307–30.

12. Derrida, "Signature Event Context," 326; emphasis in original.

13. Austin, *How to Do Things with Words*, 22; Derrida, "Signature Event Context," 325.

14. Austin, "Performative-Constative," 22.

15.   For another opportunity to understand the concept of citationality, see the debate between speech act theorist John Searle, "Reiterating the Differences: A Reply to Derrida," *Glyph* 1 (1977): 198–208 and Derrida, "Limited Inc. abc," *Glyph* 2 (1977): 162–254. When Searle accuses Derrida of misreading Austin, Derrida responds with the charge that Searle has not grasped the notion of citationality. In his reply, Derrida cites the original article to which Searle objects (Derrida, "Signature Event Context")—thereby demonstrating the concept of citationality on the level of semantics (the content of words) and syntax (how they are arranged and presented). For an excellent overview of this debate, see Gayatri Spivak, "Revolutions That As Yet Have No Model: Derrida's Limited Inc," *Diacritics* 10 (December 1980): 29–49.

16.   Paul de Man, *Allegories of Reading: Figural Language in Rousseau, Nietzsche, Rilke, and Proust* (New Haven: Yale University Press, 1979); de Man, "Semiology and Rhetoric," in *Textual Strategies: Perspectives in Post-Structuralist Criticism*, ed. Josué Harari (Ithaca: Cornell University Press, 1979), 121–40.

17.   For useful working definitions of tropes, see R. M. Dumarsais, *Des tropes ou des différents sens* (Paris: Flammarion, 1988 [1730]) and Pierre Fontanier, *Les figures du discours* (Paris: Flammarion, 1968 [1821]).

18.   de Man, *Allegories of Reading*, 10.

19.   An excellent discussion of the ways in which de Man uses (and rejects) speech act theory is provided by Randolphe Gasché, "Setzung and Übersetzung: Notes on Paul de Man," *Diacritics* 11 (1981): 36–57. Also see Geoffrey Bennington, "Aberrations: de Man (and) the Machine," in *Reading de Man Reading*, ed. Lindsay Waters and Wlad Godzich (Minneapolis: University of Minnesota Press, 1989), 209–22.

20.   de Man, *Allegories of Reading*, 49.

21.   Émile Benveniste, *Problèmes de linguistique générale*, vol. 1 (Paris: Gallimard, 1966).

22.   Benveniste, *Problèmes*, 267–76.

23.   Benveniste, *Problèmes*, 273.

24.   Benveniste, *Problèmes*, 274.

25.   Benveniste, *Problèmes*, 274.

26.   Sedgwick, "Queer Performativity," 1; Butler, "Critically Queer," 17.

27.   Sedgwick, "Queer Performativity," 12.

28.   Sedgwick, "Queer Performativity," 11.

29.   Sedgwick, "Queer Performativity," 13.

30.   Austin, *How to Do Things with Words*, 83.

31.   Sedgwick, "Queer Performativity," 4.

32.   Although Sedgwick remarks that "Shame on you" has no explicit speaking subject ("I"), she does not provide an analysis of the ways in which "I" and "you" are mutually bound. For an elaboration of these ideas, see Benveniste's essay "La nature des pronoms," in *Problèmes*, 251–57.

33.   Butler, "Critically Queer," *Bodies That Matter*, "Performative Acts."

34.   Butler, "Performative Acts," 273.

35.   See Butler, "Critically Queer," 29 n.2.

36.   Butler, *Bodies That Matter*, 191, emphasis in original.

37.   "La nature des pronoms," in Benveniste, *Problèmes*, 251–57.

38.   Benveniste, *Problèmes*, 254.

39.   Butler, "Critically Queer," 22.

40.   Given her commitment to a Derridean project, it is somewhat ironic that Butler pays little attention to the effects compulsory sex/gender relations have on subjects who live on the *margins* of sex/gender boundaries. Although Butler discusses gender outlaws, she does not do so with a consideration of our subjectivities, as for instance when she refers to the transsexual women in the film *Paris Is Burning* as "men" (*Bodies That Matter*, 128, 137). This erasure of transgender subjectivity continues the work Marjorie Garber began in *Vested Interests: Cross-Dressing and Cultural Anxiety* (New York: Routledge, 1992). Garber is an American humanities-based intellectual interested in "looking at"—but not speaking with—transvestites. She begins her work with the reduction of contemporary transgender politics to "the right to shop" (4).

        For a brilliant investigation of (post)transsexual subjectivity, see Sandy Stone, "*The Empire Strikes Back*: A Posttranssexual Manifesto," in *Body Guards: The Cultural Politics of Gender Ambiguity*, ed. Julia Epstein and Kristina Straub (New York: Routledge, 1991), 280–304. For a semiotic analysis of the ways in which transgender identity is undermined and reclaimed, see Ki Namaste, "L'idéologème de genre et l'énonciation transsexuelle," *Protée* 22.1 (Winter 1994): 81–88.

41.   It is noteworthy that while Sedgwick ("Queer Performativity," 1) and Butler ("Critically Queer," 17) speak of "performativity," Austin, de Man, Derrida, and Benveniste consistently speak of "performative statements" and "performative verbs." An analysis of the grammatical transformations enacted by Butler and Sedgwick ("performative," "performativity," "perform," "performance") would illustrate the modifications of both Austin's theory and deconstruction's response.

        Moreover, although Butler insists that gender is a performative and not a performance which an individual chooses to effect, her argument contradicts itself in the sense that, following linguistics and speech act theory, performatives are verbs. While Butler does not fully acknowledge the verbal component of performative utterances, she does end up changing the noun (and/or adjective) "queer" into a verb, as when she writes of "how it is that 'queering' persists as a defining moment of performativity" ("Critically Queer," 1). Once again, grammatical transformations underlie the ways in which Butler's use of the notion "performativity" follows neither speech act theory nor deconstruction.

42.   Ferdinand de Saussure, *Cours de linguistique générale* (Paris: Payot, 1972 [1913]).

43.   Butler, *Bodies That Matter,* 191.

44.   Butler, *Bodies That Matter,* 191.

45.   D. A. Miller, "Anal *Rope*," in *Inside/Out: Lesbian Theories, Gay Theories*, ed. Diana Fuss (New York: Routledge, 1991), 119–41.

46.   Roland Barthes, *S/Z* (Paris: Seuil, 1970). Also see Barthes, *Le degré zéro de l'écriture, suivi de éléments de sémiologie* (Paris: Seuil, 1964).

47.   Louis Hjelmslev, *Prolegomena to a Theory of Language*, trans. Francis Whitfield, rev. English ed. (Madison: University of Wisconsin Press, 1961 [1943]).

48.   Alexander Doty, *Making Things Perfectly Queer: Interpreting Mass Culture* (Minneapolis: University of Minnesota Press, 1993), follows Miller's work on the connotative inscription of homosexuality in mass culture. For a similar argument

in terms of lesbian identity, see Patricia White, "Female Spectator, Lesbian Specter: *The Haunting*," in *Inside/Out: Lesbian Theories, Gay Theories*, ed. Diana Fuss (New York: Routledge, 1991), 142–72.

49. Terry Threadgold, "Semiotics—Ideology—Language," in *Semiotics—Ideology—Language* (Sydney: Sydney Association for Studies in Society and Culture, 1986), 15–60; Robert Tremblay, "L'idéologie: Défense et illustration de la perspective socio-sémiotique," in *Cinq approches de symbolique*, Cahiers Recherches et Théories, Collection Symbolique et Idéologie, no. 59, ed. Josiane Boulad-Ayoub (Department of Philosophy, University of Quebec in Montreal, 1987), 69–97; Augusto Ponzio, *Signs, Dialogue, and Ideology*, ed. and trans. Susan Petrilli (Philadelphia and Amsterdam: John Benjamins, 1993).

50. Threadgold, "Semiotics—Ideology—Language," 31.

51. Doty, *Making Things Perfectly Queer*, 106 n.13, emphasis mine.

52. For a provocative analysis of the difficulties in living bisexuality in the present tense, see Amanda Udis-Kessler, "Present Tense: Biphobia as a Crisis of Meaning," in *Bi Any Other Name: Bisexual People Speak Out*, ed. Loraine Hutchins and Lani Ka'ahumanu (Boston: Alyson, 1991), 350–58.

53. An investigation of the social construction of heterosexuality can be found in Kinsman, *The Regulation of Desire* and Jonathon Ned Katz, "The Invention of Heterosexuality," *Socialist Review* 20.1 (January–March 1990): 7–34.

54. For an excellent analysis of semiotics in relation to the micro/macro juncture, see Paul Thibault, *Social Semiotics as Praxis: Text, Meaning-Making, and Nabokov's "Ada"* (Minneapolis: University of Minnesota Press, 1991).

55. See, among others, *Readings in the Philosophy of Language*, ed. Jay Rosenberg and Charles Travis (Englewood Cliffs, N.J.: Prentice-Hall, 1971 [1950]); John Searle, *Speech Acts: An Essay in the Philosophy of Language* (New York, London: Cambridge University Press, 1980 [1969]); C. Ogden and I. Richards, *The Meaning of Meaning* (London: Routledge and Kegan Paul, 1949).

56. G. Frege, *Philosophical Writings*, trans. P. T. Geach and M. Black (Oxford: Blackwell, 1952 [1884]).

57. Bertrand Russell, *Lectures on the Philosophy of Logical Atomism*, reprinted in Russell, *Logic and Knowledge*, ed. R. C. Marsh (London: Allen and Unwin, 1956 [1919]).

58. Ogden and Richards, *The Meaning of Meaning*, 7.

59. Ogden and Richards, *The Meaning of Meaning*, 11.

60. Ogden and Richards, *The Meaning of Meaning*, 21.

61. P. Strawson, "On Referring," in *Readings in the Philosophy of Language*, ed. Jay Rosenberg and Charles Travis (Englewood Cliffs, N.J.: Prentice-Hall, 1971 [1950]), 175–95.

62. Strawson, "On Referring," 180.

63. Strawson, "On Referring," 181.

64. Sedgwick, "Queer Performativity," 12.

65. Sedgwick, "Queer Performativity," 4.

66. Sedgwick, "Queer Performativity," 12.

67. Charles Saunders Peirce, *Collected Papers*. vols.1–6, ed. C. Hartshorne and P. Weiss; vols. 7–8, ed. W. Burks (Cambridge: Harvard University Press, 1931–58

[1867–1911]). For useful introductions to Peirce's work, see Jean Fisette, *Introduction à la sémiotique de C. S. Peirce*, (Montreal: XYZ, 1990); David Savan, *An Introduction to C. S. Peirce's Full System of Semiotic* (Toronto: Toronto Semiotics Circle, 1988); Gérard Deledalle, *Charles S. Peirce: Phénoménologue et sémioticien* (Amsterdam: John Benjamins, 1987); and Deledalle, *Théorie et pratique du signe: Introduction à la sémiotique de Charles S. Peirce* (Paris: Payot, 1979).

68. The network of relations of a particular term is often complicated in bilingual and polylingual contexts. For example, when walking through the halls of my francophone university, I overheard several of my colleagues reading the "BI-QUEER" sticker on my jacket. To an anglophone listener, their phonic utterance of the sticker sounded like "BE QUEER," thus forcing me to think about the ways in which an activist sticker produced in an Anglo-American setting (Queer Nation) could further and hinder the process of sexual liberation in a different cultural setting. In this case, the category "bi" was aligned with ontology ("be")—not an unhappy result, given the ways in which biphobia undermines the ontology of bisexuality. Moreover, the phonic utterance "queer" recalls the French word *cuir,* meaning leather, such that leather communities are included in a conception of "queer" politics—also a rather happy effect. The varied meanings of the phrase "bi-queer"—especially as evoked by its use in different cultural and linguistic settings—illustrates the ways in which a sign is a dynamic entity. (I discuss this idea below.) Having said this, one should also note that activists in Montreal have spent many an hour trying to find an adequate translation for the category "queer."

69. Peirce's emphasis on the ways in which a sign is oriented develops from his interest in phenomenology. An application of Peirce to questions of sexuality would prove fruitful, given queer theory's interest in phenomenology (Butler, "Performative Acts"). An acknowledgment of the ways in which signs of gender are already oriented, moreover, would allow one to appreciate the contributions made by ethnomethodology to gender studies. Although Butler references ethnomethodological research on gender ("Performative Acts," 279 n.12), she does not consider the specific ways in which this field theorizes a structure/agency dualism, in an explicit reformulation of phenomenology. For an introduction to the shift from phenomenology to ethnomethodology in social theory, see Ian Craib, *Modern Social Theory: From Parsons to Habermas* (New York: St. Martin's Press, 1984).

70. BIONIC, "For the urgent attention of all lesbians and gay men. The word from the bisexual movement is . . . ," educational pamphlet, n. p., 1992.

71. BIONIC, "For the urgent attention . . ." 1992.

72. *Anything That Moves* 4 (1992): 1.

73. See, for instance, Naomi Tucker, "The Natural Next Step: Including Transgender in Our Movement," *Anything That Moves* 4 (1992): 37. Consult, as well, the text of Lani Ka'ahumanu's speech at the march on Washington in 1993, reproduced in Ka'ahumanu, "A 1993 March on Washington for Lesbian, Gay, and Bisexual Rights and Liberation Speech," *Anything That Moves* 5 (1993): 16, 36. Ka'ahumanu's speech not only included transgenders within bisexual communities but went further, to point out how monosexuality denies both bisexual and transgender identities.

74. Loraine Hutchins and Lani Ka'ahumanu, eds. *Bi Any Other Name: Bisexual People Speak Out* (Boston: Alyson, 1991), xxii.

75.   Anglo-American social scientists may find it difficult to recognize their research programs in the theory of the sign espoused here, particularly given the rather quick dismissal of semiotics and deconstruction by social scientists in recent years (e.g., Palmer, *Descent into Discourse.*) Peirce's notion of an interpretant, I submit, complements the type of social theory which explores the relations between rhetoric and politics, as in the writings of Vico and Gramsci. See Giambattisa Vico, *Principles of the New Science of Giambattista Vico concerning the Common Nature of the Nations*, trans. and ed. T. Bergin and M. Fisch (Ithaca, N.Y.: Cornell University Press, 1968 [1725]); Antonio Gramsci, *Selections from the Prison Notebooks*, trans. and ed. Quentin Hoare and Geoffrey Nowell Smith (New York: International Publishers, 1971 [1947]); and Gramsci, *Letteratura e vita nazionale* (Torino: Einaudi, 1950).

76.   de Man, "Semiology and Rhetoric," 127–28.

77.   See Fisette, *Introduction*, 19. From an antifoundationalist perspective, Peirce's focus on the function of an interpretant is a significant advance over Ogden and Richards's theory of reference. Ogden and Richards privilege the interpretation of individual speakers and hearers and thus make recourse to the transcendental nature of "man." Note, however, their insistence that a "person actually interpreting a sign is not well placed for observing what is happening. We should develop our theory of signs from observations of other people." *The Meaning of Meaning*, 19.

78.   Derrida, "Signature Event Context," 311–14. Etienne Condillac, *Essai sur l'origine des connaissances humaines* (Paris: Galilée, 1947 [1746]). Readers interested in this question may wish to consult Derrida's other published work in this area, notably *L'archéologie du frivole: Lire Condillac.* (Paris: Gallimard, 1973).

79.   For more on the theory of grammar associated with the Port-Royal School—including its Cartesian roots—see François Récanati, *La transparence et l'énonciation: Pour introduire à la pragmatique* (Paris: Seuil, 1979); Jean-Claude Chevalier, *Histoire de la syntaxe: Naissance de la notion de complément dans la grammaire française* (1530–1750) (Geneva: Droz, 1968); L. Marin, *La critique du discours: Sur la "Logique du Port-Royal" et les "Pensées" de Pascal* (Paris: Editions de Minuit, 1975) and Michel Foucault, "La grammaire générale de Port-Royal," *Langages* 7 (1967): 7–15. This shift to a binary theory of the sign has been analyzed as part of a larger discursive formation, in which man placed himself at the center of inquiry. See Foucault, *Les mots et les choses: Une archéologie des sciences humaines* (Paris: Gallimard, 1966).

80.   Peirce was not, of course, the first to offer a nonbinary theory of the sign. The history of semiotics includes many such thinkers. Among others, see the Greek Stoic scholar Sextus Empiricus, *Opera*, ed. H. Mutschmann (Leipzig: Teubner, 1912–14 [ca. 150–225]); Petrus Hispanus, *Tractatus* (Assen: Van Gorcum, 1972 [ca. 1230]); and Condillac, *Essai.*

81.   Valentin Voloshinov, *Marxism and the Philosophy of Language*, trans. Ladislav Matejka and I. R. Titunik (Cambridge: Harvard University Press, 1986 [1929]). There is a significant dispute as to whether or not this work should be attributed to Voloshinov or the Marxist linguist Mikhail Bakhtin.

82.   Thibault, *Social Semiotics*; Threadgold, "Semiotics—Ideology—Language"; M. A. K. Halliday, *Language as Social Semiotic: The Social Interpretation of Language and*

Meaning (Oxford: Oxford University Press, 1978); Halliday and R. Hasan, *Language, Context, and Text: Language in a Social Semiotic Perspective* (Oxford: Oxford University Press, 1989). The journal *Social Semiotics* provides a useful overview of contemporary Australian research in this area.

83.   Ponzio, *Signs, Dialogue, and Ideology*; Ponzio, *Production linguistique et idéologie sociale* (Candiac, Quebec: Editions Balzac, 1992); Ferruccio Rossi-Landi, *Il linguaggio come lavoro e come mercato* (Milan: Bompiani, 1968).

84.   Marc Angenot, "Les idéologies ne sont pas des systémes," *Recherches sémiotiques/Semiotic Inquiry* 11.2–3 (1991): 181–202; Angenot, "Social Discourse Analysis: Outlines of a Research Project," *Social Discourse/Discours social* 1.1 (Winter 1988): 1–22; Michel van Schendel, "L'idéologème est un quasi-argument," *Texte* 5/6 (1987): 21–132. The Montreal journal *Social Discourse/Discours social* publishes scholarship in this field.

85.   Cf. van Schendel, "L'idéologème."

Part Two

ImPrinting Bisexualities:
Literary Readings

Chapter 4

Graphic Sexuality and the Erasure of a Polymorphous Perversity

Donald E. Hall

essay
by
bi
an essay *about*
bi-ology
bi(ø)sexuality
about bi(ø)graphy
porno-bi(ø)graphy
an essay about . . graphē
This is an *essay* about graphic sexuality
perversexuality
This is an essay about perversity
perver-city?
An essay about
an essay
about perver-site-y
essaying
about

ends

And about switching . . .

Westphal's famous article of 1870 . . . can stand as its date of birth. . . . The sodomite had been a temporary aberration; the homosexual was now a species.[1]

Foucault's often, perhaps over, quoted pronouncement does, of course, highlight the dramatic shift in the discourse on sexuality inscribed throughout texts of the late Victorian age. It is common now to recognize that with the proliferation of sexological materials during the last third of the nineteenth century, "homosexuality" became a site of both oppression *and* identification, potential confinement *and* liberation, insights that have helped propel lesbian/gay/queer studies. Yet these and other new theoretical potentials for gay-positive historiography and literary critique are not the only implications and consequences of Foucault's generally compelling work, for indeed he participates in many of the restrictive binaries that he usefully uncovers. I, among others, am left (figuratively) speechless, for Foucault points not only to a discursive birth in volume 1 of *The History of Sexuality* but also, and without remark, to a practical extinction. If the homosexual was now a "species," what then was the aberrational sodomite? If, as Alan Sinfield has recently pointed out, there arises out of the late nineteenth century a (more or less) recoverable "queer moment" in which the "libertine" identity underwent wholesale revision into an effeminate "homosexual" identity, such was clearly a moment of discursive loss as well as discursive gain.[2] Granted, "loss" is a problematic term here; Raymond Williams makes the cogent point that society "will always contain residual cultural elements" even as "new meanings and values, new practices, relationships and kinds of relationships are continually being created."[3] But can residua form a basis for identification? Certainly discourse can be quite differential in its processes of proscribing as well as prescribing, doing so imperfectly always, but with highly varying degrees of effectiveness in curtailing possibilities and proliferating polyvalent potentials. Sinfield's "queer moment" was not one that marked a bursting into discourse of a queerness that embraced bisexual potentials; rather, it was a discursive deflation of, at times taking the form of an energetic and effective repudiation of, a polymorphously perverse queerness, a paradigm shift that works to erase, or at best tokenize, bisexuals to this day. Even in the relatively fluid erotica of the nineteenth century, 1870 marks an era of death, as well as birth, for the polymorphous pervert: the aberrational, sodomitical male was now a (discursively) endangered species.

This is an essay *about* switches,
in language,
about men in (and out of) pornography,
about silences.

Essay discourse . . .

Silence itself—the things one declines to say, or is forbidden to name,
the discretion that is required between different speakers—is less the
absolute limit of discourse, the other side from which it is separated by a
strict boundary, than an element that functions alongside the things said,
with them and in relation to them within over-all strategies. There is no
binary division to be made between what one says and what one does not
say; we must try to determine the different ways of not saying such things.
. . . There is not one but many silences, and they are an integral part
of the strategies that underlie and permeate discourse.[4]

To be sure, the forces binarizing notions of hetero- and homosexuality did not
magically appear around 1870 with publications by continental sexologists such as
Westphal, Ulrichs, and Krafft-Ebing;[5] the regulatory processes erupting dramatically
into overt forms of discourse during the last third of the nineteenth century operated irregularly and built slowly through preceding decades. John D'Emilio has
argued that "new forms of gay identity and patterns of group life . . . reflected the
differentiation of people according to gender, race, and class that is so pervasive in
capitalist societies."[6] Indeed, capitalism demands specialization and categorization
for most efficient operation and is inextricably intertwined with patterns of social
organization beyond the realm of the strictly economic.[7] Through the eighteenth
century and with dramatically increasing valence during the nineteenth century, a
host of mutually reinforcing economic, social, scientific, and political principles
propelled a charting of human behaviors and functions that worked to fix individuals narrowly and delimit subjectivity binarily. Yes, there are "many silences," and
while some operate clearly within a broad model of Foucauldian polyvalence, where
discursive proscriptions allow points of identification and sites for resistance, there
are other silences for which that matrix-based model is far less appropriate. The rise
of a specifically, powerfully binary notion of heterosexual/homosexual identity,
energized by and parallel to the wide range of seductive, useful new binaries
ordering mid- to late Victorian life,[8] did not work to engender, so to speak, a
productively polyvalent bisexual identity; it worked instead to reorder the very

mechanisms by which subjectivity was constructed, and in such a way that the "either/or"ness of sexual "orientation" scripted new (per/de)formations of the desiring self, enforced a notion of only two possible (rigidly, mutually exclusive) sexual identities, and, to a remarkable degree, *un*polyvalently erased a bisexual fluidity from most discussions of enacted, and even fantasized, adult sexual desire. All of this imperfectly, of course, but with startling, enduring effectiveness.

Activities once encompassed within an overall notion of an ecstatic, perverse, libertine sexuality were dichotomized into notions of oppositional sexual*ities*, ones that determine, infect, render suspect the very language that I am using here. Bisexuality/libertinism/polymorphous perversity—particularly slippery signifiers when referring to previous eras, when drawing conclusions across centuries. As Foucault notes usefully in volume 2 of *The History of Sexuality*, our language is "plainly inadequate as a means of referring to an experience, forms of valuation, and a system of categorization so different from ours."[9] Yet language we must use, even when meanings are unstable, imprecise, productively *and* unproductively confounding, as Janet E. Halley confronts in her recent essay on the malleability of the term "sodomy," "that utterly confused category."[10] While none of the above terms is wholly adequate, and all carry heavy baggage, they are the only ones readily available, and all will be used here, for distinct purposes. "Polymorphous perversity," that Freudian infantile state, is a phrase that allows me to nod toward an ideal, impossibly extradiscursive erotic freedom; "*bi*sexuality" points toward desires and, perhaps (though not necessarily), bodily enactments that at times encompass, at times simply transgress, heterosexual and homosexual orientations in a binary-based world; "libertinism" is a lost, ideologically delimited role, one that in centuries past allowed considerable sexual play, though admittedly, only among the privileged.[11]

And while that factor of privilege cannot be ignored, it need not render a discussion hopelessly labyrinthian, for in examining most graphic sexual *writing*, literate-class male subjectivity is most immediately at issue—reflected in, revealed through, sometimes formed by, certainly imbricated within, the discourses directing the use of bodies, organs, and orifices that pornography foregrounds. Regulatory processes surrounding sexuality have operated variously among social groups, but while the centralization of certain forms of male desire provides an overall appearance of seamless male privilege, the simultaneous mandating, in very explicit fashion, of a rigid, "proper" masculine sexual role certainly renders any notion of unidirectional power suspect. It also engenders the following discussion, which examines processes of re-striction, of male re-deployment of male bodies, revealed in the pages of mid-to late Victorian pornography.

"Where" does desire originate? Frankly, I do not know, and rather than engage in a questionable search for origins, I follow Joan W. Scott, who exhorts us instead to break silence, to try "to understand the operations of the complex and changing discursive processes by which identities are ascribed, resisted, or embraced, and which processes themselves are unremarked and indeed achieve their effect because they are not noticed."[12]

Are we all theoretically, potentially bisexual? Perhaps.[13] Certainly discourse provides the base matter of perceptions of difference and sameness, the mechanism through which desire is articulated and deployed. In moving backward to a time "before" hetero- and homosexuality existed as explicit concepts, we *may* be exploring a "prelapsarian" era in which there were more people whom we today would call "bisexual," who engaged in erotic contact with members of both sexes; yet that is in no way provable and certainly fails to account for the greater personal valence of religious discourses that discouraged all forms of sexual contact outside of marriage. It is equally possible, I suppose, that there may have lived in the last and previous centuries roughly the same percentage of "bisexuals" as today, biologically determined through some mechanism that we still do not comprehend. But, at the very least, these were individuals whose words and activities were *present*, legible, in the underground world of erotic consumerism and whose relative free play seems to have been less threatening to male sexual transgressors of primarily same- or other-sex–desiring preferences. In pornography from the last half of the nineteenth century, one finds a continuing accommodation of polymorphous forms of desire, even as a gradual binarization emerges. "Bisexual"/polymorphous perverts, I have said, were an endangered species after 1870, for they were (and are), in fact, thoroughly *endangering*, undermining the binarisms through which life was (and is) rendered comprehensible and through which medical/political/sociological regimes were (and are) enforced and contested.[14]

Simply stated, bisexuals fucked, and continue to fuck, things up.

Essay this . . .

> I will fuck anything living . . . and some things dead.
> —Toilet graffiti, University of Illinois

> The Duc was having a marvelous time. Curval, recollecting what Martaine
> had offered the Bishop, stuffed her while he got his own ass stoppered.
> A thousand other horrors, a thousand other infamies accompanied and
> succeeded those.

> Curval had himself fucked, the Bishop and Durcet for their part did passing
> strange things with both sexes; then supper was served.

> [T]he Duc, half-drunk, abandoned himself in Zephyr's arms, and for thirty
> long minutes sucked that lovely child's mouth while Hercule, exploiting the
> situation, buried his enormous engine in the Duc's anus [who] was all
> complacency, and without stirring, without the flicker of an eyelash, went
> on with his kissing as, virtually without noticing it, he changed sex.
> —Sade, *The 120 Days of Sodom*[15]

Sadian libertinism has been amply and legitimately criticized for its violence and misogyny; it is wholly male-centered and revels in appalling acts of physical and psychological abuse. Yet even in its hyperbole, it does offer considerable insight into pre-Victorian discourses of sexual desire and identity. As Sinfield notes, "the dissolute aristocrat might indulge in any kind of debauchery."[16] Sade captures an era during which, as G. S. Rousseau has argued, "the old-style bisexual sodomite . . . held a male on one arm and female on the other while kissing both."[17] Randolf Trumbach, among others, has traced the polymorphousness of the libertine lifestyle during the seventeenth and eighteenth centuries, drawing on numerous case studies to conclude that "debauchery might be displayed indifferently towards male and females."[18] Such object-choice slipperiness is certainly apparent in John Cleland's *Fanny Hill* (1749), in which one debauched character concludes simply, "Pooh . . . my dear, any port in a storm," and another, who believes he has seduced a young man, seems quite flexible when he discovers that it is a young woman with whom he is dallying.[19] In Michel Delon's reading, Diderot's works also display such "polymorphousness," for "physical and affective life unceasingly overflow the small 'norm' of heterosexual monogamy."[20] That such freeplay is often recuperated as "heterosexual" or "homosexual" alone is addressed by Trumbach: "it is only the later theory of exclusive attachment to one gender that leads us to discount descriptions of European men as having male lovers and female mistresses simultaneously."[21]

Of course, sexual desire was discernibly ordered, clearly on the basis of class and sexual privilege, but also on the basis of preference. Sade, for example, is explicit in ascribing to his characters clear "tastes": in *The 120 Days of Sodom*, the Bishop is "a faithful sectary of sodomy, active and passive, he has an absolute contempt for all other kinds of pleasure" (255); Curval's "tastes induce him to prefer men; all the same he has no scorn for a maid" (256). Yet, as is clear here, such are preferences, not sexual identities of the twentieth-century variety; they are what Foucault would call "character trait[s]: men could be distinguished by the pleasure they were most fond of; a matter of taste ... not a matter of topology involving the individual's very nature,"[22] not a binarily fixed sexual orientation. These Sadian characters self-define as libertines: as the root suggests, men freed of moral restraints, devoted to self-indulgence. Chief among them is the Duc, who is "the depository of every vice" (255). His relatively polymorphous perversity and astounding fluidity in terms of sexual activity, as he moves in and among bodies and orifices, make him a useful starting point in charting a refiguration of desire, demarcation of new forms of identity, binarization of homo- and heterosexuality.

"What effortlessness, what ease, what detachment in libertinage!" (265) exclaims the narrator on the "first day" of *The 120 Days of Sodom*; this during a scene in which the Duc first "calmly down[s] three bottles of wine while lying embuggered upon" Invictus's "enormous prick" and afterward reels off to the "orgy salon," where women and young men lie about "promiscuously" and he and his friends fall "upon the flock like wolves assailing a sheepfold" (281). As Peter Cryle makes abundantly clear in *Geometry in the Boudoir: Configurations of French Erotic Narrative*, there is form here, not chaos, as the "infamies" and "excesses" increase geometrically.[23] Yet noteworthy is the fact that the narrative begins with and never loses an accommodation of male/male (and later female/female) erotic contact among many instances involving men and women; characters are defined primarily by an exuberant perversity, one that is explicitly naturalized:

The Duc undertook an encomium of libertinage, and proved that it was natural, and that the more numerous were its extravagances, the better they served the creator of us all. His opinion was generally acclaimed, enthusiastically applauded, and they rose to go and put into practice the doctrines which had just been established. (281)

His doctrines challenge directly the narrow configurations of a reproduction-centered society, but this admittedly inherently binary status in no way precludes activity that could lead to reproduction. Unlike Oscar Wilde during the next century, Sade here broadly accords the status of the "natural" to *ecstatic sexuality*, not just to a gendered object-choice-based sexuality that is parallel to, though wholly different from, an "other" sexuality, also defined by gendered object-choice.

porno-graphy

> [T]here was an attempt by some writers in the latter part of the Victorian period to publish pornography under the cover of anonymity. Some such works may be listed as erotic literature by the few, but, generally speaking, the crudity of their language, the sheer exploitation of pornography, frequently at far too great a length, make them anything but uplifting.[24]
>
> *uplifting?*

> Pornography is, after all, nothing more than a representation of the fantasies of infantile sexual life, as these fantasies are edited and reorganized in the masturbatory daydreams of adolescence. Every man who grows up must pass through such a phase in his existence, and I can see no reason for supposing that our society, in the history of its own life, should not have to pass through such a phase as well.[25]
>
> *just a phase!*

As is all communication, critical analysis is thoroughly riddled with problems. Our language is often baldly pompous, not to mention silly and self-subverting. As much as we might like to pretend, no critic is "outside" of ideological, personal, discursive contexts. I am clearly something of a sexual radical, eager to make people think about what they do with their bodies and why they do it. Other critiques of pornography are bound up with their own specific ideological agendas, differentiating "good" from "bad" pleasure, rendering judgments about what you (yes, you!) should or should not masturbate to: authoritatively, presumptuously, and usually without the body of the critic intruding. Yet bodies *do* intrude; desires are no less present for being simply unacknowledged or covered up. Critical distance is an odd concept when the critic is interacting with written works that have as their most obvious and immediate goal sexual arousal. As Stephen Marcus points out in his Freudophilic (not to be confused with my Fou-cault-philic) study of Victorian pornography, the cultural and social embeddedness of such works makes them highly compelling from a genealogical standpoint.[26] Yet what he does not discuss is the erotic interest that one can only suppose Victorian pornography holds for him. I was relieved, so to speak, to discover Victorian pornography a decade or so ago, given the orientational narrowness of almost all twentieth-century erotic works. For individuals whose sexuality cannot be contained within the heterosexual/homosexual binary, Victorian pornography has the potential for stimulating the body as well as the mind, providing fluid erotic images that one rarely finds today, as well as compelling artifactual material that allows some insight into a less rigidly binarized era.

Such is the case with *The New Epicurean* (1865),[27] a text which accommodates a relative freeplay of desire that marks it as preorientational, though not divorced from the paradigmatic changes that I mention above. Among the numerous erotic adventures of the male narrator, all involving young women, a telling passage appears, in which the narrator's wife, Lady Cecilia, seduces a teenage boy nicknamed "Daphnis." The narrator observes them as Cecilia has sex with Daphnis, while inserting "her delicate finger into his little rosy orifice behind":

> Now, whatever the ancients may have thought on the subject, I must confess I have never seen what the peculiar point of attraction could be in having beautiful boys, as they unquestionably did; yet when I saw [Daphnis's] lovely young bottom bounding up and down, and Cecilia's wanton finger frigging away, a strange dizziness seized me and I felt a lust, stronger than the lust for women, lay hold of me.

He ends by stating that "like a true Epicurean, I never let slip any pleasure within reach."[28] Seemingly, the "true Epicurean's" desire still encompasses a *potential* for something like "bisexual" fluidity; yet this scene and another voyeuristic one involving (in the words of the text) the "fucktious" Daphnis are all that remain of "true" libertinism, for the narrator does not slip his own finger, or anything else, into the young man. His "strange," "strong" lust is scopophilically contained and wholly channeled into his sexual activity with a female partner. Certainly polymorphous desire is inscribed here, for to argue that only bodily enactment is a valid indication of sexuality is to limit rather narrowly what can be considered "sexual." But in a narrative about enactments, the fact that physical contact between the two males is missing does, at least, signal an instance of discursive erasure that is telling, for it is wholly unremarked upon, invisible to, the narrator; it is simply not contained within the "any" pleasure that he never lets slip.

Increasingly, mid- to late Victorian discourses of sexuality relegated such polymorphous activity to adolescence, to sexual immaturity. Finding explicit expression finally in Freud's theories of childhood bisexuality (growing out of infantile polymorphousness),[29] the notion of proper sexual orientation replacing immature experimentation began surfacing in the pornography of the 1860s, 70s, and 80s. Above, desire for Daphnis is represented as part of a "swoon," a "strange" state of seeming regression; while it is apparently foundational, "stronger than the lust for women," it is now primarily motivational. As John Addington Symonds makes clear in his memoirs of the middle decades of the nineteenth century, sexual contact between young men was quite common in public schools but, much as today, was rigidly disallowed as they approached maturity.[30] A notion of binarized sexual identity could not accommodate desire for both sexes. Thus in an anonymous pornographic novel from 1866, *The Adventures of a School-Boy*, young male characters comment repeatedly upon each other's "beautiful organs of manhood"[31] and even manipulate each other's genitals, but do not interact with pointedly expressed desire for (rather than just admiration for) each other as they seduce and experiment with young women. Of course orientational seams in the narrative abound; when George, the narrator's friend, is "beating about the bush" (147) with a young woman, the narrator helps them out:

Throwing my arms round the legs of both, I lifted them up and placed them in an advantageous position on the sofa. Then inserting my hand between their bellies, I laid hold of George's fiery weapon, and keeping it directed right upon the proper spot, I told him to thrust away now. This he did with hearty good will. The first thrust he was within the lips, the second he was half way in, and the third he was so fairly engulfed, that I had to let go of my hold, and withdraw my hand, so as to admit of their perfect conjunction. (147)

Interesting here, of course, is the fact that the narrator "has to" let go of his hold to allow of their "perfect conjunction," does not necessarily "want to" let go of his hold. Yet clear as well is the implicit assumption that there are "proper" slots for "fiery weapons," though even concerning this notion we find some indecision. A bit later in the narrative, as the boys increase their amorous activities, George declares that "he must try what he could do to re-animate" the lethargic sexual organ of his friend:

He therefore made me kneel in front of him across Maria's head, ... and as he proceeded with his lascivious course of heaves in and out of the cavity of his charmer, he took the point of my weapon in his mouth. With one hand he tickled Eliza's wanton gap with such address and vigour as to cause her to shed tears of joy. With the other he pressed and fondled the somewhat relaxed pillar of my sensitive member, making as much of it as possible enter his mouth and closing his lips upon it with a most delicious suction. (59)

This activity effectively readies the narrator for intercourse with Eliza; it is represented as friendly "renovative" behavior that is precursive to the privileged "final encounter." While the four principal characters fondle and caress each other indiscriminately, they always end up in a heterosexual coupling that is represented as the only proper, final mechanism for orgasm, whatever fluid freeplay is engaged in beforehand. Something like "bisexuality" is a state through which one passes. A male mouth may be unanxiously celebrated as an effective aphrodisiac or sexual aid, but it is only a temporary stop before one's real destination.

By twentieth-century pornographic standards, such a degree of freeplay is almost unheard of—yet it was increasingly, ideologically delimited. As identificatory discourses concerning sexuality solidified, so too did narrow conceptions of proper and improper forms of sexual performance, even for the sexually "liberated" (clearly, one is never "liberated" from discourse). Thus in the pages of two pornographic periodicals from the era, *The Pearl* (1879–80) and *The Oyster* (1884–89), we still find some uncertainty about what is and is not an identity-producing action, yet binarized notions of sexual identity also continue to surface and exert irresistible influence. In "Sub-Umbra, or Sport among the She-Noodles," from *The Pearl*, the two main male characters rub and suck each other with relative abandon: "We handled each other in an ecstasy of delight, which ended in our throwing off all our clothes, and having a mutual fuck between our thighs on the bed; we spent in rapture, and after a long dalliance he entered into my plans, and we determined to have a lark with the girls as soon as we could get a chance."[32] Such activity is portrayed unanxiously, though it is also clearly precursive to the seduction of women. However, another story from *The Pearl*, "Lady Pokingham, or They All Do It," indicates a more discernibly, binarily demarcated notion of identity, with the main female character discovering that her husband (who has never vaginally penetrated her) in fact *strongly* prefers men; in a key scene, she spies on him having oral and anal sex with two youths, one of whom says to the other, "I love you warmer, hotter than ever I could the prettiest girl in the world."[33] When she rushes in and joins the plainly "homosexual" orgy, her husband exclaims "Damned Hellish Bitch!" Though he seems to enjoy the unrestrained activity, he dies within forty-eight hours, overcome perhaps by the lasciviousness of the scene, but perhaps by her intrusion upon it.

Here it comes!

Thus Victorian pornography signals, indeed implicitly participates in, a process of retheorization, pointing toward the conceptualization of an implicitly accepted "natural" homosexual identity for some and a more legitimate, socially accepted "natural" heterosexual identity for others. In "Memoranda from Mr. P." from near the end of the run of *The Pearl*, the narrator tells of his erotic adventures with his landlady, as well as those of his friend, Mr. Reddie, with the landlady's son: "Mrs. Glover was decidedly more to my taste than the boy. So I made assiduous courtship of her on my own account, for Mr. Reddie couldn't even bear for a woman to touch him."[34] While the narrator retains something of the old libertine identity, engaging in sexual antics with both the mother and son, Mr. Reddie does not, violently repudiating all contact with women's bodies. Thus it is not inappropriate for a modern-day commentator on *The Oyster* to call it "a firmly heterosexual publication,"[35] for by the mid- to late 1880s, the freeplay even of the previous decade was noticeably sequestered. "My Early Days," which in its first sentence sets itself up as a sequel to "Lady Pokingham," does indeed build upon that story's assertion of identity. After two young men, Terence and Teddy, engage in a round of mutual masturbation, Terence sighs, "Ah well . . . I enjoyed that but I am sure it is not as satisfying as the real thing."[36] Such acts are now clearly distinguished as adolescent experimentation or makeshift activity until the here explicitly identified "real thing" appears. In the story it does appear, and male/male contact is wholly erased. Yet polymorphous desire is barely channeled into the new sexual binary. On one occasion, Terence and his friend Cecil have sex with the same young woman, one vaginally and the other anally, a scene not uncommon in twentieth-century porn films. The narrator writes, "I could feel my prick rubbing against his with only the thin divisional membrane between them. It was all so exciting that we both spent quickly."[37] They clearly enjoy the sensation of contact with another man, but only when mediated through the "thin divisional membrane" provided by the anal/genital wall of the woman. It may be thin, but it is a wall that now rigidly determines sexual orientation, separating men from identity-undermining contact with each other and providing the divisionary mechanism through which heterosexuality is constructed and maintained. For the men involved, her "membrane" *is* heterosexuality; both men's penises only touch the flesh of a woman, even as they revel in sensations that the term "bisexual" may or may not describe appropriately. The young woman plays only a mediatory role, rendering desire between men nonthreatening and embodying the division between the homosocial and the homosexual.

essaying

If the body of the woman is thereby used to define sexual identity and proper formations of desire, and in a fashion that seems thoroughly beyond the self-awareness of the parties involved, one other significant text from the era indicates that such usages may be consciontiously reflected upon, but remain powerful, even inescapable, nevertheless. *My Secret Life* (1888), the anonymous, but apparently factual, autobiographical account of one man's lifetime of erotic explorations is fascinating, not only for its astonishing array of graphic sexual scenes, but also for its sophisticated narratorial commentary and atypical trajectory. *My Secret Life* depicts a concerted attempt to reclaim a previous state of libertinism, to recover what we might call the "prediscursive." While texts of the era increasingly portray same-sex erotic activity as a poor substitute for the "real thing" and relegate it to adolescent behavior, the narrator of *My Secret Life* attempts to move in the opposite direction, beginning in resolutely "heterosexual" activity, but proceeding to a self-conscious attempt to widen his sexuality, one that often tests the limits of how desire can be retheorized and manipulated. Spanning the middle and late decades of the nineteenth century, the text reveals polymorphous perversity to be a difficult state to achieve, given the ways that discursive norms determine bodily responses.

As an erotic adventurer, the narrator comes to question why society attempts to regulate what one does with one's body, as he challenges, first in theory, social proscriptions on sexual contact between members of the same sex:

> Why may a man and woman handle each other's privates, and yet it be wrong for a man to feel another's prick, or a woman to feel another's cunt? Every one in each sex has at one period of their lives done so, and why should not any society of association of people indulge in these innocent, tho sensual, amusements if they like in private. What is there in their doing so that is disgraceful? It is prejudice of education alone which teaches that it is.[38]

This he states not once but several times, and in relatively sophisticated terms: "There can be no more harm in a man feeling another's prick, nor in a woman feeling another's cunt, than there is in their shaking hands. —At one time or other all have had these sexual handlings of others, yet a dislike to myself about this sexual whim still lingers. Such is the result of early teaching and prejudices" (378).

The narrator actively repudiates and attempts to free himself from such "prejudices." Yet even given his well-thought-out theoretical base and desire to transgress perimeters of sexual identity, he quickly encounters the power that discourse has, the ways bodily sensations and responses are substantially beyond conscious control. After having experimented with oral sex with another man, the narrator feels guilty and ashamed, attributes such reactions to "prejudices and false education," yet cannot feel easy about what he has done "spite of my philosophy that any sexual enjoyment is permissible" (395). He only rouses himself to further experimentation by manipulating language and categories, by deciding that the other man involved "is clearly not a sodomite" (395), a use of the term corresponding to a twentieth-century designation of "homosexual." Aberrational sodomy is no longer a discursive possibility, for the narrator's "conditional" homosexual activity must be contained within a larger rubric of anxiously insisted-upon heterosexuality. Bisexuality has no place in such a binary.

silence

Even as discursive norms substantially control the narrator, language often fails him; certainly his inability to describe his sensations and categorize his range of desires is palpable throughout. "Novelty stimulates desire" (398), he claims, and adds "My libidinosity increased by indulging it" (399), yet that claim to widening is not consistently reflected in ensuing activity, for "After I sucked him that night, I never repeated it but once" (400); in an orgy scene, he does so on the spur of the moment, but then repudiates it forever. He is particularly afraid of the woman involved seeing him indulge himself thus, though she seems utterly at ease about such erotic play and even suggests anal sex between the men; the narrator claims he is revolted, for "such an intention had never once entered my head, had never even occurred to me" (405). When soon thereafter he does try it, as the active partner, he has a violent physical reaction: "I had an ineffable disgust at him and myself—a terrible fear—a loathing—I could scarcely be in the room with him—could have kicked him. He said, 'You've made me bleed.' At that I nearly vomited" (409). While engaging in the anal sex, he writes that he was filled with a "fierce . . . baudiness" (408), that his "brain whirled with strange desire" (406), yet also disclaims such, saying it was an act "in which I had no pleasure—have no recollection of physical pleasure—and which only dwells in my mind with disgust, tho it is against my philosophy even to think I had done wrong" (409). His libertine philosophy simply cannot be reconciled with powerful social regulations on the use of the body; years later, when he lets a young man attempt to bugger him, he gives up: "'Pull it out,' I cried. —Out it came . . . and there it ended. —I did not feel pleased with myself at all. —What is the good of my philosophy?" (568). Inside of a late-Victorian discursive context, the narrator cannot successfully recreate another. While he does continue to have some sexual activity with men and women together, the woman's mediatory role remains necessary for his peace of mind. Despite earnest experimentation and direct challenges to oppressive discourses of sexuality, his "bisexual" pleasure for most of the narrative is scopophilic, not unlike that of the twentieth-century "heterosexual" viewer of visual pornography involving men and women. While it is clear throughout the text of *My Secret Life* that the parameters of sexual desire cannot be fully articulated, described, explained, given the language available to them/us, it is equally apparent that desire has been powerfully and thoroughly complicated by the binary of hetero- and homosexuality.

A successful essay

> I know that I was born a sodomite, the fault is my constitution's,
> not mine own.

> Had I committed a crime against nature when my own nature found
> peace and happiness thereby?
>
> —Wilde, *Teleny*[39]

As numerous commentators have noted, Oscar Wilde, his life, writings, and trial provided a turning point in the discourse on homo- and heterosexuality, a bursting into explicitness of many of the undercurrents surrounding the hierarchized binary of sexual orientation that had been developing for decades. Linda Dowling has argued that "the 1890s represented a cultural space within which may be glimpsed the major themes of a subsequent twentieth-century struggle for homosexual tolerance and civil rights." Wilde, in particular, she argues, "deploys a new and powerful vocabulary of personal identity, a language of mind, sensibility, and emotion, of inward and intellectual relations."[40] Ed Cohen has focused specifically on Wilde's (probably coauthored) pornographic novel *Teleny* as striking a blow for freedom, providing a potent "depiction of male homoerotic desire and practice [that] insists on not only the possibility but the naturalness of same-sex eroticism."[41] So it does, but at what a price and through what inherently limiting discursive mechanisms? Certainly Wilde portrays the naturalness of homosexual desire, but unlike Sade, only by rendering male/female contact for the men involved unnatural and horrific. In the new binary of hetero- and homosexuality, the former claiming the status of the natural and the latter using the same terminology to disrupt the other's claim, bisexuality is actively repudiated, erased; *it* is the remaining unnatural state, one of indecision, messy in-betweenness, unspeakability.

Don't essay this!

In the quotations above and in other passages, *Teleny*'s narrator, Des Grieux, musters powerful arguments against a society that condemns male/male sexual contact. Yet to do so, the narrator, indeed the novel, must rely upon a notion of fixed, even biological, sexual identity (predicated now on an "either/or"ness rigidly enforced) that stands in stark contrast to earlier constructions of a fluid libertine identity. To help validate the "naturalness" of Des Grieux and Teleny's sexual activity, the novel portrays heterosexual contact as horrific. Women are described repeatedly as "loathsome," and the representations of their bodies and desires are indeed designed to revolt. Des Grieux's first detailed description of a woman is of his adolescent sweetheart urinating and farting. He later visits a brothel, a den of "harpies," as he puts it, in which the women are demonized, their bodies portrayed monstrously: "[O]pening her legs as she did so, she took my head between her fat, clammy hands. . . . I saw the black mass of hair part itself; two huge dark lips first appeared, then opened, and within those bulgy lips—which inside had the colour and the look of stale butcher's meat—I saw something like the tip of a dog's penis when in a state of erection, protrude itself towards my lips." Later in this scene, filled with acts of regurgitation, one prostitute even dies after projectile-vomiting a stream of blood, for "the cadaverous wretch had in a fit of lubricity broken a blood vessel."[42] Such is the tenor of the entire novel, which lingers over a rape, two scenes of incestuous desire, and other incidents that allow heterosexuality to be summarily denounced. Cohen claims that "[i]n affirming the naturalness of Des Grieux's homoerotic experience, this new joyous possibility undermines the monovocalizing strategies of the bourgeois heterosexual culture used to ensure the reproduction of its dominance and thus opens up the possibility of representing a plurality of male sexualities."[43] Well, the "plurality" here is exactly two: unlike previous representations of multiple expressions of desire between men, as well as men and women, in pairs and groups, *Teleny* participates in and reflects a narrowing of the discourse on sexuality that still affects our reading of the novel over one hundred years later. It is thoroughly caught up in the binaries of its own and our day.

Near(ly) the end of essaying . . .

While not all post-Wildean pornography participated in the same mechanism of validation (for few were intent upon celebrating a homosexual identity position as "natural"), one does find a uniformity in expressions of clear and fixed sexual orientations. In *Maudie*, published in the first decade of the twentieth century, the author introduces the character "Claude Lestrange, a romantic poet, sodomitically inclined." Near the end of the narrative, Lestrange finally "display[s] his *true* nature" by rushing upon a young man and penetrating him. Another character announces summarily "You're a bugger, sir; a God-damned bugger, and you ought to have an umbrella stuck up your arse, and opened inside, sir. Isn't a *cunt* good enough for you?"[44] The text does not explicitly endorse this violent overreaction but clearly is complicit with a notion of binarized sexual identity in which same-sex contact is thoroughly revolting for heterosexuals and vice versa. In *Maudie*'s sequel, *Pleasure-*

Bound Afloat, a similarly oriented Lord Reggie discovers his own true nature with a young man, whose "dainty face had more fascination for him . . . than any woman's." Only in a culminating scene is there a remnant of polymorphous activity: the anonymous ship's captain, who is conducting a cruise for the hypererotic, participates in an orgy in which he fondles a boy's penis and lets the boy "thrust a finger, moistened by the juice of life that had already escaped from Maudie, into that aperture which was not designed by nature to receive."[45] His own design is clear; the scene ends with a resolutely heterosexual summary copulation. Nevertheless, one cannot help but find noteworthy the playful, though proscribed, fingering of one man by another in the midst of an otherwise heterosexual orgy.

Indeed, such remnants are few and far between. Twentieth-century pornography, for the most part, had been rigidly dichotomized into heterosexual and homosexual categories, hardly disrupted by the numerous sexist, pseudolesbian scenes that are designed to arouse heterosexual men. Even in twentieth-century nonpornographic novels written to awaken social tolerance, such as *Maurice* (written 1914) and *The Well of Loneliness* (1928), we find individuals who *could* be represented as positively, sexually polymorphous but who are instead villainized for their lack of commitment to a narrow notion of identity. Clive in *Maurice* and Mary in *Well* are portrayed as cowards, doomed to unhappiness, because they are unwilling to accept their "true" natures. Such is equally the case in Waugh's *Brideshead Revisited* (1945), in which bisexuality is only a phase through which one passes on the way to a healthy heterosexuality or a pathological homosexuality, and Baldwin's *Giovanni's Room* (1956), where bisexuality itself, if not moved beyond, becomes pathological and personally disastrous. Such (as some have termed them) "biphobic" representations are discussed at length in other essays in this collection.[46] Despite the summary pronouncement of Foucault and the recovery of Wilde as a positive identity-producing individual and discursive nexus, it is clear that polyvalence has its limits, that there are degrees to which silence can be productive, for through the overwhelming monovalence of binary paradigms in our culture, the in-between, the "fence-sitter" becomes an easily erasable anomaly or, alternately, a particularly convenient scapegoat in either/or-based projects of political validation, repudiation, and redress.

another essay

SIN-A-MATIC
psychotropic queer experience
pulsating * gyrating * techno * industrial[47]

Yet the in-betweens did not, have not, wholly disappeared; life and the complexities of desire do not partition themselves always and neatly into the reductive binaries of sociomedical discourse. While Freud's designation of bisexuality as an inherently regressive state, unstable and immature, has held enormous sway, it has also provided a meager basis for a polyvalent conception of identity centered on a repudiation of adult, i.e., traditional, norms. Lillian Faderman, in *Odd Girls and Twilight Lovers*, has charted the "fashionableness" of bisexuality during the 1920s.[48] Certainly 1960s and 70s popular and sexual liberationist culture "allowed" bisexuality as an exotic potential for rebellious, androgynous figures such as David Bowie, Elton John, Joan Baez, and Janis Joplin, as Marjorie Garber has traced in *Vice Versa*. Yet the discourse surrounding, describing, bisexuality has always been caught up in binaries that have undercut its legitimacy: AC/DC, "swinging," and "going both ways" are all metaphors that indicate two poles, are all determined by the discourse of either/or. The tenuousness and ineffectiveness of such discursive experimentations are certainly signaled by the virulence of the backlash against sexual nonconformity during the 1930s, 40s, and 50s, and during the Reagan/Bush era; it is clear that the underlying binary of hetero- and homosexuality was never seriously challenged. In fact, given the political and social necessity of precisely defined programs for civil rights, centered on narrow notions of identity politics, the discourse of binarism has been given even greater currency, has become even more engrained in our vocabulary of inherence, and even biological inheritance. As other essays in this collection explore at length, academic "queer" theorists are themselves, for the most part, still caught up in the same paradigms, the same epistemological bases for theorization and configuration.[49]

Yet popular culture is again providing some disruption and may well be outstripping academic musings in a dramatic fashion. Michael Stipe of the band REM refuses to discuss his sexuality, claiming that the language available to him is inadequate, that current identities are too narrow.[50] An equally compelling, and for me personally exhilarating, example is provided by the advent during the 1990s of "queer" nightclubs, which have relatively little to do with theorized notions of "queerness" except in their putting into action the fluidity that many claim, though rarely realize, for queer theory. As an example, SIN-A-MATIC in West Hollywood, California provides a basis for hope among those who value disruption, as well as a productive site for discursive leverage. Created in 1991, SIN-A-MATIC, along with Club Fuck!, Club Vice, and a few other similarly provocative venues, has as its title-encoded base the desire to recover a prior notion of sexual fluidity, a validation of a quasi-libertinism that encompasses plural sexualities.[51] Its title's evocation of the machine-drive points as well in another direction: a functioning beyond consciousness. Associated with the sexual ambiguity of technoindustrial recording figures like Trent Reznor in Nine Inch Nails and bands like Marilyn Manson, the Revolting Cocks, and KMFDM, such dance clubs revel in the polymorphously perverse. Projected video montages incorporate sexually ambiguous images from popular culture (such as the fetishism of advertising and the incestuous potentials provided by scenes from *The Brady Bunch* and *The Partridge Family*) interspliced with "hard core" pornography ranging from foot worship (which again provides a basis for de-gendering sexual object choices: both sexes have feet) to a proliferation of possible genital sexual contacts, never lingering on one identity base for more than a few seconds. Thus one finds that the queer postmodern, as this could be termed, is actually a toying with the sodomitically premodern.[52]

Such clubs are hardly "outside" of a discourse of binarized orientational identity, yet singles, couples, triples, and other combinations of individuals on the multi-ethnic, age-mixed dance floor do circulate with surprising fluidity and ambiguity, in various states of undress and/or costuming. "Sin" as a stance for connection, as a repudiation of narrow notions of identity, as a collective designation for all non-normative sexualities and erotic potentials, becomes a unifying construct against totalizing, rigid demarcations of desire. Not surprisingly, the Marquis de Sade is a figure often invoked by queer dance-club patrons. While he was horrifically sexist and classist (a fact too often overlooked by those iconizing him), he does provide a rallying point from "before" hetero- and homosexuality, a reveler in a notion of "sodomy" that embraces tactile pleasures with fewer restrictions on the biological sex of the potential partners in "sin." While the AIDS crisis means that sexual machinery has taken on an even greater level of complexity, queer dance-club patrons find in their queerness a potential for polymorphous expression and relative erotic free play that is even castigated in the otherwise tolerant environs of West Hollywood, a substantially gay city surrounded by the multicultural metropolis of Los Angeles. "I want to know precisely who [orientationally] I am dancing with!" exclaimed a gay friend of mine who declined my invitation to join me at SIN-A-MATIC. I, along with many others, do not.

Have we come full circle? Of course not. Binaries of race, class, age, and sexual orientation continue to dominate our lives. Yet on the shelves of adult video stores, "bisexual" pornography has been appearing widely for over ten years, disrupting the otherwise hermetic categories of "gay" and "straight." Even in "heterosexual" porn videos, odd, potentially destabilizing activity is noticeable and proliferating. What can one make of *Guys Who Suck Their Own Cocks,* a recent video that intersplices heterosexual orgy scenes with images of men fellating themselves and ejaculating into their own mouths, or *Girls Who Screw Guys in the Ass* (a title that is, uh, self-explanatory)? The designation "straight" does not adequately contain such activity.[53] "Queer" has the potential for doing so, and the next few years will show us if movement beyond the "straight"-jacket (so to speak) of binary orientation is possible, or if the discourses of mutually exclusive, and socially enforced, hetero- and homosexuality will continue to dominate lives and imperfectly (though substantially) regulate expressions of desire, as it erases the inconvenient, the messy, the polymorphously perverse.

essay ends

Notes

1. Michel Foucault, *The History of Sexuality,* vol. 1, trans. Robert Hurley (New York: Vintage, 1980), 43.
2. See Alan Sinfield, *The Wilde Century: Effeminacy, Oscar Wilde, and the Queer Moment* (New York: Columbia University Press, 1994), esp. chapters 1 and 2.
3. Raymond Williams, *Marxism and Literature* (Oxford and New York: Oxford University Press, 1977), 123.
4. Foucault, *The History of Sexuality,* 27.
5. For an overview of the work of early sexologists, including those named, see David F. Greenberg, *The Construction of Homosexuality* (Chicago: University of Chicago Press, 1988), esp. chapter 9, and David M. Halperin, *One Hundred Years of Homosexuality* (New York: Routledge, 1990), esp. chapter 1.
6. John D'Emilio, "Capitalism and Gay Identity," in *The Lesbian and Gay Studies Reader,* ed. Henry Abelove, Michele Barale, and David Halperin (New York: Routledge, 1993), 471.
7. See Williams, *Marxism and Literature* and D'Emilio, "Capitalism and Gay Identity." Certainly, as Sinfield discovers, the polymorphously perverse libertine became the target of new middle-class ideologies that vehemently repudiated notions of aristocratic privilege and nervously condemned nonreproductive forms of sexuality. And as Louis Crompton has traced, the perverse Lord Byron became a scapegoat of sorts, his story signaling an increasing and anxious demarcation of identity that attempted to enforce uniform heterosexuality and behaviors that met the needs of an industrializing western world; *Byron and Greek Love: Homophobia in 19th-Century England* (Berkeley: University of California Press, 1985).
8. These slippery, unstable binaries are discussed at length in my book *Fixing Patriarchy: Feminism and Mid-Victorian Male Novelists* (New York University

Press, 1996); they include zero-sum-based definitions and configurations of gender, class, and nationality that replaced older notions of "fixed," natural hierarchy.

9.   Michel Foucault, *The History of Sexuality*, vol. 2, trans. Robert Hurley (New York: Vintage, 1985), 187.

10. Janet E. Halley, "The Construction of Heterosexuality," in *Fear of a Queer Planet*, ed. Michael Warner (Minneapolis: University of Minnesota Press, 1993), 82–102. The quotation is from Foucault, *The History of Sexuality*, vol. 1, 101.

11. For a useful overview of the history behind the last term, see James G. Turner, "The Properties of Libertinism," in *'Tis Nature's Fault: Unauthorized Sexuality during the Enlightenment*, ed. Robert Parks Maccubbin (Cambridge: Cambridge University Press, 1987). That factor of privilege encompassed hierarchies of class, race, and gender; the libertine identity was an upper-class *male* identity. The representation of transgressive sexualities for women in literature written by men is clearly filtered through an ideology of proprietorship, so that prostitution is the primary vehicle for portraying sexual noncomformity and the enactment of desire uncontained by sanctioned social arrangements. Even when this is not the case, such as in the anonymous pornographic novel *Eveline* (New York: Blue Moon Books, 1987 [1840]), an "identity" does not appear to be enacted; Eveline appears to be the "exception" whose licentiousness startles the men with whom she has contact.

12. Joan W. Scott, "The Evidence of Experience," in *The Lesbian and Gay Studies Reader*, 408.

13. Martin S. Weinberg, Colin J. Williams, and Douglas W. Pryor's recent overview of bisexual psychologies and practices, *Dual Attraction* (New York: Oxford University Press, 1994), suggests that sexual desire is quite fluid and that sexual identity can change dramatically over time. See esp. chapter 21.

14. Nature/nurture . . . whatever. And for my purposes here, eroticism/pornography . . . whatever; I have neither the space nor inclination to address the terminology debate. Sexually graphic material constitutes a body of rarely discussed cultural, artifactual material that can offer us many insights. Mid- to late Victorian pornography was sexist and classist, showing and celebrating desire that was certainly piqued by, and probably predicated on, unequal power relationships. And among its many horrors, by twentieth-century standards, is contact between adults and children. That, of course, is not dismissable with a simple "whatever," but cannot be adequately analyzed in the following pages. I can only hope that this essay will engender other critiques of these and similarly troubled, troubling issues.

   For a differently focused, but in many ways complementary, discussion, see Marjorie Garber's *Vice Versa : Bisexuality and the Eroticism of Everyday Life* (New York: Simon and Schuster, 1995). Her discussion of Victorian life and love in chapter 13 is particularly well supported.

15. Marquis de Sade, *The 120 Days of Sodom and Other Writings*, trans. Austryn Wainhouse and Richard Seaver (New York: Grove Weidenfeld, 1966), 281, 320, 445. All further references will appear in the text above.

16. Sinfield, *The Wilde Century*, 41.

17. G. S. Rousseau, *Perilous Enlightenment* (Manchester: Manchester University Press, 1991), 142.

18. Randolf Trumbach, "Sodomitical Subcultures, Sodomitical Roles, and the Gender Revolution of the Eighteenth Century: The Recent Historiography," in *'Tis Nature's Fault*, 117.

19. John Cleland, *Fanny Hill or Memoirs of a Woman of Pleasure*, ed. Peter Wagner (London: Penguin, 1985), 178, 192.

20. Michel Delon, "The Priest, the Philosopher, and Homosexuality in Enlightenment France," trans. Nelly Stephane, in *'Tis Nature's Fault,* 126. See also, in the same volume, G. S. Rousseau, "The Pursuit of Homosexuality in the Eighteenth Century: 'Utterly Confused Category' and/or Rich Repository" for further discussion and documentation of the "bisexuality" of the libertine identity.

21. Trumbach, "Sodomitical Subcultures," 117.

22. Foucault, *The History of Sexuality*, vol. 2, 190.

23. Peter Cryle, *Geometry in the Boudoir: Configurations of French Erotic Narrative* (Ithaca: Cornell University Press, 1994), see esp. chapter 6.

24. Donald McCormick, *Erotic Literature: A Connoisseur's Guide* (New York: Continuum Press, 1992), 59.

25. Steven Marcus, *The Other Victorians: A Study of Sexuality and Pornography in Mid-Nineteenth-Century England* (New York: Basic Books, 1964), 286.

26. See esp. his very fine first chapter.

27. This work was probably written by Captain Edward Sellon, a renowned Victorian bon vivant; for more details concerning its history, see the introduction to the Grove Press edition, *The New Epicurean & The Adventures of a School-Boy* (New York: Grove Press, 1984).

28. *New Epicurean*, both quotations p. 61.

29. See Sigmund Freud, *Three Essays on the Theory of Sexuality*, trans. James Strachey (New York: Basic Books, 1962), esp. the second essay, "Infantile Sexuality."

30. John Addington Symonds, *The Memoirs of John Addington Symonds*, ed. Phyllis Grosskurth (Chicago: University of Chicago Press, 1984); see esp. his fifth chapter.

31. *The New Epicurean & The Adventures of a School-Boy*, 128. All further references will appear in the text above.

32. *The Pearl: A Journal of Facetive and Voluptuous Reading*, London, 1879–80 (rept. New York: Grove Press, 1968), 42.

33. *The Pearl*, 388.

34. *The Pearl*, 598.

35. *The Oyster II: Further Selections of Victorian Erotica* (New York: Carroll and Graf, 1989), 6.

36. *The Oyster III: More Selections from Victorian Classics* (New York: Carroll and Graf, 1989), 23.

37. *The Oyster III*, 73.

38. *My Secret Life* (New York: Blue Moon Books, 1988 [1888]), 286. All further references will appear in the text above. For information concerning the history of this startling text and some compelling reasons for considering it factual , see *The Other Victorians*, chapters 3 and 4.

39. Oscar Wilde and others, *Teleny* (London: GMP, 1986 [1893]), 70, 130.

40. Linda Dowling, *Hellenism and Homosexuality in Victorian Oxford* (Ithaca: Cornell University Press, 1994), 27, 2.

41. Ed Cohen, "Writing Gone Wilde: Homoerotic Desire in the Closet of Representation," *PMLA* 102.5 (1987): 805.

42. Wilde et al., *Teleny*, 63, 67.

43. Cohen, "Writing Gone Wilde," 805.

44. *Pleasure Bound: Two Erotic Novels* (New York: Blue Moon Books, 1987 [1908]), 3, 89–90 (first quotation, my emphasis).

45. *Pleasure Bound*, 216, 229, 232.

46. See especially the other essays in this section for literary representations of "bisexualities." As Yukman, Carlston, and Knopf argue, bisexuals have been scapegoated in the transmission of AIDS between the homosexual and heterosexual communities, have been dismissed as "fence-sitters" by both identity groups, and have been generally ignored by academicians. Anyone who peruses recent works in "queer theory" and current collections of essays on "gay and lesbian studies" will note a remarkable lack of attention to bisexuality. Two exceptions, beyond that of Marjorie Garber, are worth noting, however. One is Steven Seidman's superb essay "Identity Politics in a 'Postmodern' Gay Culture: Some Historical and Conceptual Notes," which appears in *Fear of a Queer Planet.* Also commendable is the inclusion of two essays on bisexuality, Clare Hemmings, "Situating the Bisexual Body," and Jo Eadie, "Activating Bisexuality," in *Activating Theory: Lesbian, Gay, Bisexual Politics,* ed. Joseph Bristow and Angelia R. Wilson(London: Lawrence and Wishart, 1993).

47. This is a recognizable "masthead" of SIN-A-MATIC advertisements and flyers. This wonderfully queer dance club is located at 7969 Santa Monica Boulevard in West Hollywood, California and operates on Saturday evenings only. Doors open at 10 P.M., but things don't become interesting until about 11.

48. Lillian Faderman, *Odd Girls and Twilight Lovers: A History of Lesbian Life in Twentieth-Century America* (New York: Columbia University Press, 1991); see esp. her third chapter.

49. For some controversial conclusions regarding the biological bases for binarized sexual orientations, see Simon LeVay, *The Sexual Brain* (Cambridge: MIT Press, 1993). LeVay's methodological problems will be readily apparent and have been questioned widely in the press, in science publications, and in gay and lesbian periodicals. Problems with much contemporary "queer theory" are addressed at length in the theory section of this collection; Alan Sinfield's blind spots are representative of many contemporary literary and cultural critics. Again, Garber is the notable exception; indeed, her discussion of LeVay's work is especially pertinent here. See Garber, *Vice Versa*, 274–75.

50. See Stipe's interviews in *Newsweek* 124.13 (September 26, 1994) and *Rolling Stone* 693 (October 20, 1994).

51. Club Fuck! was raided by the LAPD vice squad in the spring of 1993 and subsequently went out of business. Charges were leveled and later dropped against several patrons for "indecency," which was the result of several women's removing their shirts and one man's, perhaps, showing his penis during a performance art piece. Many patrons interpreted the dramatic raid, with numerous uniformed officers and a hovering helicopter, as harassment against queers and practice for the anticipated unrest (that never materialized) after the second "Rodney King" verdict. I was there

that night and was astounded by the degree of police overreaction. Club Vice appeared a year later at a new venue and promotes itself as the reincarnation of Club Fuck!

52.   "Postmodernism" is, of course, a slippery and controversial term, but a useful one; see Seidman's piece, "Identity Politics," mentioned above. But I would add that Lyotard's "suspicion of the scientistic nature of much theory" describes accurately a potential queer rejection of simplistic sexual binaries; see Jean-François Lyotard, "Answering the Question, What Is Postmodernism?" in *Postmodernism: A Reader*, ed. Thomas Docherty (New York: Columbia University Press, 1993), 25.

53.   The mid-1980s saw a "boom" of sorts in slick, commerical bisexual adult videos with the appearance of titles such as *The Big Switch* (Bistar: 1985) and the *Switch Hitters* series (Intropics) which began in 1986. Raunch/Leisure Time Entertainment is responsible for many of the other interesting, disruptive, quasi-libertine productions, such as *Guys Who Suck Their Own Cocks* (1993) and *Girls Who Screw Guys in the Ass* (1993).

Chapter 5

Loving Dora:
Rereading Freud Through H. D.'s *Her*

Lidia Yukman

> Her poetry and prose, like her
> own psyche, live at the seething
> junctions of opposite forces.
>
> —Louis L. Martz

Few writers have managed to hold open the interval between "opposites" the way H. D. did. Her poetry and prose relentlessly mark the borderline between subject and object, between dreamscape and logic, between categories of sexual difference. Her work falls within a historical moment between 1900 and 1950 in which psychosexual explorations surged, particularly in the work of Sigmund Freud and Havelock Ellis.[1] While H. D.'s novels exhibit formal experiments consistent with modernism, it is her sexual and textual politics that make her unique among modernist writers.[2] In her encounter with psychoanalysis and the "textual self," H. D. came up against many of our contemporary sexual biases and prefigured a whole line of "distinctive impulses of twentieth-century modernity."[3] In particular, *HERmione* (completed in 1927; hereafter HER) explores the "dangerous" borderline of bisexuality.[4]

Freud's most significant work on bisexuality, "Dora: An Analysis of a Case of Hysteria," and H. D.'s novel *HER* are both products of a time period in which the discourses of sexuality and psychoanalysis were being actively theorized.[5] In addition, in each text psychoanalysis suggested the possibility of *reading* the self—psyche as text. The story of Dora and H. D.'s *HER* share several truly exceptional features: both narratives stage a textual version of the splitting and reconstitution of the self, both explore a psychosexual journey in which bisexuality is encountered, and both locate bisexuality at a particular place in language that supports a particular story of the self. Through his "talking cure" Freud wanted Dora to find a position in her own story from which to speak a self. In that story, bisexuality is a problem that Dora must overcome. When H. D. talks, she tells a quite different story, and she needs a different position in language from which to tell it.

In this essay I shall argue that the narrative of "Dora" and the narrative of *HER* each produce different models of bisexuality. In particular I will argue that read against one another, Freud and H. D. provide different bisexual positions in language. Where Freud's "Dora" records a subtext of bisexuality that fits into his story of the Oedipus complex, castration, and repression, H. D.'s novel *HER* produces a model of bisexuality that tells a different story, through a different model of language, to support a different subject position. Specifically, I will be tracing the development of what I am calling a discourse of the interval—a linguistic strategy emphasizing an identity in process through a specifically syntactic refusal to commit to binary oppositions—that highlights a bisexual position.[6] For H. D., the threshold for psychosexual identity and narrative syntax are inseparable.[7] Furthermore, H. D.'s syntax becomes a paradigm for a narrative structure predicated on bisexuality. For this reason it becomes as important to read Freud back through H. D. as it seems to have been to read H. D. through Freud.[8]

text as psyche

Within Freud's story of ego formation, sexuality and language acquisition figure as founding moments for the constitution of the subject. The narrative of the subject's passage through the Oedipus complex and the castration scenario serve as climactic moments of individuation in relation to the phallic signifier. The strongest thematic trope for Freud's narrative, then, is castration.[9]

At a certain stage in ego development, before sexual individuation, all individuals carry bisexual impulses. Freud first posited bisexuality as a phenomenon in which each gender carries a "bit" of the other. While a heterosexual adult can be said to have repressed homosexual desire, a homosexual adult has repressed heterosexual desire. In each case bisexuality must be "resolved." He later pinned down bisexuality as a mark of the uncertainty of sexual division as he developed his theory of the Oedipus complex and castration.[10] This is his "story," and in this story bisexuality figures in a way that supports the narrative of the Oedipus complex, castration, and repression. In his analysis of both Dora and H. D., Freud identified bisexuality as a problem and analyzed it as a fixation brought on by a passage through the Oedipus complex in which the woman fails to transfer her feelings from her mother to her father properly.[11] Homosexual desire in women thus produces the story of a narcissistic fantasy of self-love, or a fantasy of the "ideal, uncastrated, masculine woman" with whom the subject may recreate the mother-child relationship. This, according to Freud, is what happened to both Dora and H. D. to different degrees.[12] In the case of H. D., the bisexuality led to writer's block; in the case of Dora, to symptoms consistent with hysteria. But H. D.'s novel *HER* takes the feminine subject into other stories, narratives predicated on the possibilities opened up through bisexuality and language, rather than limited by them. H. D. prefigures later feminist and poststructuralist critiques of Freud by addressing the pre-Oedipal, the figure of the mother, and the role of language in psychosexual development. Between "Dora" and *HER* a rich dialogue emerges that takes us well beyond prescriptive categories of sexual difference.

While the biographical facts of H. D.'s connection to psychoanalysis and to Freud provide a kind of "architecture" for her novels, their patient/analyst relationship does not account for a fully realized investigation of H. D.'s bisexuality, her textual bisexuality, or, for that matter, the whole significance of bisexuality for Freud or for feminism. Perhaps because bisexuality is still a problem for feminism, feminist criticism on H. D. has tended to box her bisexuality inside her biography. The feminist effort to theorize bisexuality has, to a certain extent, "petered out" as bisexuality continues to be subsumed by an identity politics in which lesbianism is a privileged term.

My discussion here intersects a feminist trajectory in which H. D. has been recuperated, so to speak, from a patriarchal literary tradition. However, my analysis diverges from this trajectory at the level of narrative form. For instance, recent feminist criticism has focused so heavily on the *thematic* links between H. D.'s life and her writing that the *narrative structures* of her novels and their significance to feminist studies, narrative theory, or bisexual theory have been seriously eclipsed. For example, Friedman and DuPlessis state in *Signets: Reading H. D.* that "*HER* can be characterized as a lesbian text because of its critique of heterosexuality and because the marriage plot takes the form of exploring strongly articulated relations between women"(209). Putting aside for the moment the implication that only a lesbian text can critique heterosexuality or challenge an Oedipal narrative trajectory, this characterization only tells part of the story. For *HER* is not an exclusively lesbian text. Rather, in its syntax and in its narrative structure it is a quintessentially bisexual text. Furthermore, it is a novel in which language itself is being tested, as I will show.

In her book *H. D. and Freud: Bisexuality and a Feminist Discourse*, Claire Buck develops a productive argument that H. D.'s bisexuality is an organizing structure of her writing. Buck states that the links between language, sexuality and subjectivity in H. D.'s work are "almost always thematic" (5), staging the way the subject is split by the division of father and mother in Freud's family romance. Buck goes on to suggest that H. D.'s language itself is "fractured" by the family romance, and that H. D.'s subject is often "divided between the maternal and the paternal in its very language" (8). Buck focuses her analysis on the thematic importance of language to H. D.'s representation of the feminine subject, and in the end she comes up with a limited, albeit important, question: What kind of female self does H. D.'s writing produce? My own inquiry departs from this thematic concern in order to focus on a different question: What can the language of H. D.'s text tell us about bisexuality and narrative structure?

bisexuality and writing

For the purposes of this inquiry I am defining bisexuality by means of a poststructuralist account of sexual difference as a linguistic position in which identity is in process, a position already at work in H. D.'s writing. Like Foucault, for example, H. D. tells a story in which the processes of sexuality and subjectivity are indivisible. Like Lacan, H. D. suggests that writing and sexuality are also indivisible. However, H. D.'s model of language and narrative structure also challenge a poststructuralist account. For instance, where Lacanian psychoanalysis deployed a narrative of feminine lack and absence, H. D. tries to write open alternative sexual and subject positions. In this strategy her writing probably comes closest to paralleling the work of Julia Kristeva, who also tries to theorize an opening in the Oedipal model for the maternal, feminine desire and linguistic operations associated with psychosexual development. The important questions concern how H. D.'s models of language, sexuality, and subjectivity differ from poststructuralist accounts and what her language can tell us about bisexuality in particular.

Freud's early accounts of bisexuality in "Dora" (1905), "Hysterical Phantasies and Their Relation to Bisexuality" (1908), and "Fragment of an Analysis of a Case of Hysteria" (1905) all suggest that bisexuality may be found as "bits" of one gender found in the other. For Freud, bisexual impulses were a part of every individual's

development. Homosexual adults resolve bisexual conflicts by repressing heterosexual desire. Within the narrative of the Oedipus complex and castration, bisexuality is an uncertainty, a failure to achieve individuation through sexual difference.
Bisexuality, then, marks a failure to resolve the conflict of double love.[13]

Hélène Cixous's critique of Freud in *The Laugh of the Medusa* breaks open the
definition of bisexuality:

In saying "bisexual, hence neuter" I am referring to the classic conception of bisexuality,
which, squashed under the emblem of castration fear and along with the fantasy of a
"total" being (though composed of two halves), would do away with the difference experienced as an operation incurring loss, as the mark of dreaded sectility. (254)

In place of this bisexuality she offers an "other bisexuality" which "holds on to the
fact of sexual difference, while refusing the fixing of the terms of difference within a
binary opposition."[14] Cixous clearly draws from the linguistic model of Jacques
Derrida in *Writing and Difference,* in which difference is determined by the play of
terms that endlessly displace each other. For Cixous this "other bisexuality" suggests
a subject in continual process: "millions of encounters and transformations of the
same into the other and into the in-between, from which woman takes her forms"
(254). An admittedly tricky definition, Cixous's at least begins to chart the possibilities of a bisexuality that is not predicated on feminine lack or dissolution into an
undifferentiated other.[15]

Claire Buck points out that Cixous's "other bisexuality," while successfully breaking the Freudian/Lacanian frame of woman as lack, can "only operate rhetorically to
destabilize the totalizing concept of bisexuality which she critiques."[16] But H. D. was
wholly involved in establishing a writing identity. Writing was already—before Lacan
and without reference to feminism—a sexually coded activity for her. In Lacanian
terms, speaking subjects must "commit" to one sex or the other. In his model, as in
Freud's, to move back and forth between the sexes implies an "uncertainty" of sexual
identity. But the novel *HER* is quite unique in its insistence on holding open, through
writing, a uniquely bisexual position at the threshold of language.

In H. D.'s *HER* we may find the absence of an empowered, unified, feminine
identity, but in her place we find a dynamic, mobile, *linguistic* position, an interval
within writing in which the refusal to commit to one sex or the other yields to a
"process"—a narrative that emphasizes process and an identity continually in
process—*explicitly and emphatically at the level of narrative language.* This position
can be traced through a kind of "discourse of the interval," a narrative strategy H. D.
developed to engage and challenge the psychosexual models of her period.

In addition, as many critics have noticed about her poetry, the novel *HER* stages a
drama between two kinds of language that H. D. struggled with and against in all her

work.[17] One language is that which has lost its power to mean anything, a language wrecked for the most part by the social trauma of world war. As the social order breaks down, words lose their referents. Thus the crisis in the social world translates into a dead language. The other language is an ideal version in which words and things are once again tethered to one another, sign to referent. In this version, very much alive in H. D.'s poetry and the central feature of the novel *HER*, trees, colors, sounds, people, and words are all a kind of writing. For H. D., "the languages support different versions of the self and sexual difference because the two languages represent opposed ideas of how language operates."[18] But I am interested in how H. D., through her language(s), refuses or resists sexual difference as well.

loving dora, reading her

As the aforementioned critics attest, "If there is one woman who sums up for many what is both fascinating and repellent, most subtle and most bullying in Freud's relationships with women, then that woman is Dora."[19] A "resistance heroine" for Cixous, an exemplary sexual figure for Michel Foucault, Dora has become "a paradigm case for catching patriarchy with its pants down."[20] But the forms that her "resistance" takes are always in the shape of stories. For H. D. Freud represented a certain story or version of sexuality. H. D.'s writing begins to challenge that story at the level of bisexuality and language. Thus, putting the story of bisexuality that Freud constructed up against H. D.'s story gives us a new form of analysis that may yet show us something about bisexuality and narrative language.

Freud's narrative presents a case history divided into three parts: part 1 details the features of Dora's illness; parts 2 and 3 deal more directly with two of Dora's dreams. The analysis of the dreams formed the basis of Freud's account of her bisexuality and hysteric symptoms. Freud's narrative structure is based on a model of ego formation in which the child is located as a symbolic subject with reference to the Oedipus complex, the phallus, and the phallic signifier. Repressed, psychical symptoms surface in this story as threats to a stable subjectivity.

In part 1 we find out how Dora's "plot" merges with Freud's account of psychosexual development. Dora's father originally brought her to Freud in order to cure her of what he considered to be unacceptable behavior, including headaches, fainting, coughing spells, and suicide threats. The mother of the story is largely dismissed as a character, except for her cleanliness obsession. "The single most important point of contact between [Dora] and her mother that Freud was to detect was in their shared preoccupation with the contamination that sexuality entails."[21] Dora's father was beset with a syphilitic history that brought him to Freud initially, and that figures into Dora's understanding of her own sexuality, according to Freud. "Frau K.," as she is recorded in Freud's narrative, was both nurse and lover to Dora's father. Dora became very close with Frau K., taking care of her children and even sharing a bed with her at times. Freud determined that Dora was both jealous of Frau K. and willing to help her conceal the affair with Dora's father. Herr K., on the other hand, developed an infatuation with Dora, and the sexual advances he made toward her at his lakeside villa formed the crisis that Freud would endeavor to interpret. Dora's "disgust" at Herr K.'s advances in turn form the basis for Freud's theories of her repressed desires.

According to Freud, Dora's "symptoms"—including an attack of dyspnea, fainting, coughing, headaches, and her reaction of disgust—were examples of the return of repressed material. Dora became an excellent test case for Freud's theories on feminine hysteria. Freud had a twofold plan: to begin to prove that "sexuality is the key to the problem of psychoneuroses" and to "demonstrate how dream interpretation is woven into the history of a treatment and how it can become the means of filling in amnesias and elucidating symptoms."[22] But Freud was to be confronted with a third problem in Dora's bisexuality.

Freud's first readings centered around Dora's repressed, secret desire for Herr K. Freud navigates through Dora's story toward a theory of repression:

If I may suppose that the scene of the kiss took place in this way, I can arrive at the following derivation for the feelings of disgust. Such feelings seem originally to be a reaction to the smell (and afterwards also to the sight) of excrement. But the genitals can act as a reminder of the excremental functions; and this applies especially to the male member, for that organ performs the function of micturition as well as the sexual function. . . . Thus it happens that disgust becomes one of the means of affective expression in the sphere of sexual life. (47)

Freud goes on to explain in the notes to this section that "the subject of erection" for women "becomes, when repressed, a source of the very frequent cases of avoiding company and of dreading society" (47). For Freud, then, Dora's symptoms fit an Oedipal narrative of a woman's repressed desire, centered on the symbol of the phallus and surfacing as disgust.

If we leave off here, as Cixous pointed out, we leave a story of masculinity intact and feminine subjectivity invisible. The crucial element in this analysis is Dora's disgust; Freud reads her symptoms as expressions of sexual repression. But H. D.'s novel provides a different reading of those symptoms, as I will show, a reading wherein the limits of sexual repression are replaced by the possibilities of a sexuality *in process*. Perhaps the most deeply developed version of a psychosexual subject in process is posited in the work of contemporary theorist Julia Kristeva. I mention

Kristeva here because her revision or extension of Freud/Lacan, like H. D.'s, does not seem to read the limits or borders of subjectivity in quite the same way that they did, even as she engages their models. Rather, Kristeva reads the borders of subjectivity through a corporeal territory (and through the semiotic in terms of signifying processes) in which the subject is always in process, being "generated" or "negated" to different degrees. In this case the subject can never achieve a stable, completely coherent identity. The subject is always being "disrupted" by the signs of its own, unstable borders. Reactions to the abject, or disgust, can thus be read as a "body in revolt."[23] In this reading repression is only part of the story—as Elizabeth Grosz puts it, the abject continually "hovers at the border of the subject's identity, threatening apparent unities and stabilities with disruption and possible dissolution."[24] Dora's disgust would take on different characteristics in this case. As a "subject on trial" and a "subject in process," her symptoms might mark the impossibility of ever reaching a subjectivity that is free from the threat of disruption or dissolution. The question is, Is this a limit driving her toward neurosis or a psychosexual possibility unaccounted for in Freud's story?

Leaving aside for the moment this gap in Freud's story, we move on in his account of Dora to his discovery of her love for a woman, Frau K. It is at this point that Freud revises his analysis to include an attention to bisexuality as a stage of her hysteria. Although Freud thought that loving in two directions was a stage in all psychological development, the refusal to resolve that tension resulted in a "dangerous" bisexuality. Marked by a glaring ambivalence, in summary, Freud's analysis concludes that Dora, stuck in a pre-Oedipal attraction to her mother, overdetermined a fantasy of an idealized woman and fell for Frau K. Freud also determined that these "masculine" feelings are typical of the "unconscious erotic life of hysterical girls" (81), part of a stage of psychosexual development. Now we have the heart of the story for Freud, figured in a conflicted, double love: Dora's first secret was that she desired Herr K.; her second, much deeper secret was that she loved Frau K. Divided by the family romance, Dora tells a story of a subject that is fractured. The problem with this story is that it is predicated on sexual binaries. Freud longed for Dora to continue therapy. Unfortunately for Freud, Dora, like H. D., broke off analysis—and broke down the story—before he would have liked, perhaps leaving her dangerous bisexuality intact. The story of Dora, like H. D.'s novel *HER*, leaves us with neither a "fulfilled" lesbian nor a wandering hysteric. H. D. met a Freudian ambivalence on feminine bisexuality with an alternative version of a bisexual position in language.

The characters and plot of *HER* parallel H. D.'s biography quite literally. The protagonist, Hermione Gart, is H. D. Bert Gart is her older stepbrother and twin self. George Lowndes is Ezra Pound and Fayne Rabb is Frances Gregg.[25] The double, or, as I would argue, triangular, love story that propels *HER* is brought on by the identity crisis which opens the novel. A college dropout, Her returns home to a disappointed father and mother, a fuzzy understanding of self, and an uncertain future. Her's father and brother press a patriarchal family logic and discourse on her: "the mathematical biological intention dropped out Hermione" (4). As DuPlessis and Friedman describe it, "Increasingly she turns to the woman-centered subtexts of the family" (210).

But the fact remains that from the start Her tries to find an identity specifically *between* her mother and father, between masculine and feminine, between patriarchy and the maternal: "What am I between them? I am broken like a nut between two rocks, granite and granite" (81). Both masculine and feminine, paternal and maternal, are "granite" and fixed. As if hypnotized by her father's power and her mother's goddesslike position ("One should sing hymns of worship to her" [81]), Her threatens to "break" into pieces.

Two letters break the thematic confusion that opens the book: one from George Lowndes and one from a classmate inviting Her to have tea and meet Fayne Rabb. Friedman and DuPlessis rightly describe the thematic structure of the novel as being divided into two parts. Part 1 traces Her's relationship to George Lowndes, including her engagement, her acceptance, and her family's initial opposition. Part 2 develops her attraction to Fayne, the break-up with George, the betrayal by Fayne because of her affair with George, and, according to DuPlessis and Friedman, "the final dissolution of both relationships."[26] But the novel does not end with a "final dissolution," and, as I will argue, neither does it conform to a neat, two-part heterosexual/lesbian plot. We must turn to the language of the text at this point, a resistant language, a coded language, a language that stages a refusal of terms predicated on sexual difference.

syntax, sentence, self

The critic Claire Buck identifies in H. D.'s writing the fracturing of language by the family romance. Buck traces what she calls the "poetic and bodily features" of H. D.'s writing to sexual difference. She argues that H. D.'s writing "not only signifies a language of connotation but itself connotes an alternative ordering of sexual difference."[27] In the novel *HER* we find a language marked by continual disruptions in syntax—duplications, subject/object confusions, phonetic overlaps, and metaphoric sound/image plays. Duplication is foregrounded in the novel as a linguistic feature capable of disrupting sequence, sense, and logic—all of which constrain Her thematically as well.

The beginning of the novel can hardly be said to begin except by means of circularity: "Her Gart went round in circles. 'I am Her,' she said to herself; she repeated, 'Her, Her, Her'" (3). Clearly we can identify this kind of syntactic "experimentation" as a representation of "her object status within conventional heterosexuality."[28] In other words, Her is the desired object of George. DuPlessis and Friedman further identify these kinds of sentences as "awkward" when they bump into George Lowndes and "merging" when the story moves toward Fayne Rabb. According to DuPlessis and Friedman, Fayne and Her merge inside sentences such as this: "Her bent forward, face bent toward Her" (217). In other words, these "mirroring moments of syntax[es]" reflect the novel's theme, that Her is moving away from the love of/for a man and toward the love of/for a woman. Within the love story of the former, Her is object; within the love story of the latter, Her is most often read as a "fusion" between subject and object, a sister-love, self-love, or lesbian relationship.

My argument, by contrast, is that Her resists the determining effects of subject or object, man-love or woman-love. If H. D. meant us to read an equation such as Her = Fayne, she would have made certain that we did. Her exists precisely in the tension between categories of textual and sexual difference, actively resisting subject or object status through syntax: "Fayne being me, I was her. Fayne being Her I was Fayne" (210). In addition, Fayne is only one word that Her uses to get to herself. She also uses other words, such as "tree," "AUM," "white," and "bird." Fayne is a word among other words that "beat and formed and unformulated syllables" (25). In other words, Fayne's significance as a word rivals, even challenges, her significance as a dramatic character.

This tension between subject and object marked by the interplay between Fayne and Her, or by the use of the pronoun "her," for example, is a vehicle that lessens—without collapsing—difference. Recalling Cixous's "other bisexuality," the syntax refuses to be fixed by the terms of difference within a binary opposition. In a sentence such as "Her saw Her," or "Her bent forward, face bent toward Her," what is marked is a moment of identification, not dissolution of meaning. Put slightly differently, Her finds identity in *minimal* difference, in words that form a relationship to one another by virtue of sound, syntax, or image connections (in other examples the words "bird," "white," "tree," or, very often, "Fayne"). Which is to say that the syntax marks a refusal to locate identity through a subject/object, masculine/feminine split. But neither is the sentence destroying meaning altogether, since a subject position, albeit in process between Her and Her, or Her and Fayne, is still possible.[29] The syntax marks an identity between subject and object without being fixed by either: a discourse of the interval that subordinates the drama. Can identity form here, or does it remain unformed, a failure of sorts?

As we see, this almost haunting resistance of subject and object is by no means limited to the theme of a double love plot. Biographically and thematically, H. D. "never gave up her search for 'the-man-who-would-understand,'" even as she continued to develop woman as a symbol.[30] Her position as a bisexual woman, an identity in process, as I am arguing, is also always operating at the level of narrative language in syntactic disruptions that deform the narrative drama. For example, the ability of language to "name" Her utterly fails in the face of sounds, colors, and the affect of words:

> She met Lillian at the head of the stairs. "Oh my darling. I adore that colour." "Colour?" What Colour was it? A colour wavered about her, automatically chosen from a row of things, new dresses, old dresses made over. The colour was (wasn't it?) green. "This green colour?" "Yes, you are Undine, or better, the mermaid from Hans Andersen." "Yes, I am Undine. Or better, the mermaid from Hans Andersen." Undine long ago was a mermaid, she wanted a voice or she wanted feet. "Oh I remember. You mean I have no feet to stand on?" That is what Lillian means. Lillian is the first to find me out. Lillian has found me out. There is something about Lillian. She knows perfectly well that I don't belong, that there is no use. Eventually I will tell them that there is no use. Lillian has found out that my name is Undine. (112)

Here we have an example in which the plot is tethered neither to George Lowndes nor to Fayne Rabb, so that the thematic implications lose their determinative power. And while this passage could be interpreted as a narrative instance of prioritizing interior monologue over dramatic plot, such a reading would leave the very unique language of this text wholly unaccounted for. It is as if the narrative redirects us to an entirely linguistic threshold. Her slides into the name "Undine" in a smooth transposition as she comes into contact with color, sound, and language. While she appears powerless as a heroine, she is quite dynamic as a word among words and things. The repetition of the words "green," "Undine," "Lillian," "colour," "her," "Her," and "mean" are more than just phonetic overlaps or slant rhymes. They force us to reevaluate the effect of the syntax in this passage. While the characters lose weight, the words gain affect. In a Freudian reading these examples signal textual versions of a return of repressed material. Their presence marks a threat to order, logic, sense, coherence. H. D. pushes on that "threat" and then quite self-consciously represents these syntactic disruptions as utterly necessary for meaning.[31] Like an unfinished phrase, Her is one piece of a sentence that we have to have more of to understand. One cannot know where Her begins or ends, because the syntax keeps Her moving.

The thematic representation of Her's bisexuality is of course her connection to Fayne Rabb. Her's relationship with Fayne is described by Friedman and DuPlessis as "an eroticism that operates out of a self-loving female center."[32] I would substitute an exclusively lesbian identification with a bisexual position. Here again I would like to suggest that we attend to the formal features of the text in order to tease out the nature of that bisexuality. Most striking about Fayne Rabb is that she appears as words which look and sound like her name all through the text: "Mandy," "Farrand forest," "Mrs. de Raub," "Bertrand," and "the Forest of Arden," to name a few examples. Which is to say that Fayne functions as a word in play with other words. George Lowndes is also part of a signifying chain: "agacant," "gawd's own goddamn," "genius," "Georgio," "Georg," and so forth. Her experiences the relationship that words similar to one another have as productive of meaning: "Fayne, Fayne to herself, repeating it. Parallelograms came almost with a click straight and she saw straight" (128). When Fayne appears as her own name, it is in a conversation around her absence:

Fayne with a click for the first time in consciousness, Fayne, for some inconceivable reason, became part of things just then, became real at just that second, part of things just as the clock hand was making that almost perceptible little forward jerk, that cricket-leg jerk that little old clocks do make, toward (what was it?) the XI that preceded the XII, that meant that some hour was near (V? VI?) and that Nellie would soon be pretentiously making her departure. (130)

Her experiences Fayne as a word, as part of a metaphoric motion, "part of things" and sounds, even part of a strange time, a time that moves out of sequentiality. Both clicking forward as it should and out of sequence and questionable, the clock is a model of syntax. The question in Her's mind as she listens to Nellie is much more "how is Fayne written?" than "who is Fayne?" While Nellie describes Fayne's life, her history, with whom she has lived, what she does, in the end all Her wants to know is "Is she like a cloud, exactly?" To which Nellie responds, "She's a sort of reflection of a stormcloud seen in water" (133). On the borderline of language, Fayne is a sign that ruptures and reorders meaning—narrative, sexual—time and time again. Fayne is a word in play, endlessly signifying, marking and erasing. In Derridian terms H. D. has staged "the fact that signification occurs along a chain in which one term displaces another before being itself displaced."[33]

The power that "Fayne" has to shatter order and emphasize affect through language also reorders sexual difference. For instance, in a scene between Her and George, Her fluctuates between images, people, and things. George, whose kisses make Her feel "smudged out," is telling Her how to think. Right in the middle of George's talking, Her thinks:

George had said "Oh rot, what rot is this you're talking." When for a moment she had realized her head—the bit here, the bit there, the way it fitted bit to bit—was two convex mirrors placed back to back. The two convex mirrors placed back to back became one mirror . . . as Fayne Rabb entered. (138)

Within a Lacanian context of psychosexual development, the mirror stage marks a moment of transition in which the infant's ego identifies with an image of its coherence, producing a symbolic identity. When Lacan looks in the mirror, he sees a "map or image of the body which is internalized by the subject and lived as real."[34] When Her looks in the mirror, the mirrors duplicate, merge, and produce Fayne: "The two convex mirrors placed back to back became one mirror . . . as Fayne Rabb entered." But here is where I would like to bring bisexuality, as a possible founding moment rather than as uncertainty, back into the discussion of language. Where in the beginning of the novel Her experiences a troubled speech in which she is a nut stuck between the two rocks of masculine/feminine, maternal/paternal, here, the way things fit "bit to bit," word to word, offers an alternative reading. The word Her to the word Fayne fractures the border between subject and object. A third territory or interval is created that allows for a bisexual self, a self resisting masculine *or* feminine identification by emphasizing how a "bit" of each always displaces the other. After all, Fayne enters following an ellipsis standing in for an omission of words, a gap or silence that is always part of language, as if the reader is being asked to imagine the degree of difference between Her and Fayne rather than to conflate them altogether.

Another strong example of a discourse of the interval predicated on bisexuality occurs in the section of the novel in which Her has a breakdown. It seems clear that Her must pass through this breakdown in order to find an identity. I would extend that reading to include the "crucible" of language through which Her must pass, not in order to forge an autonomous identity based on individuation and difference, but to open a position that resists sexual division yet stakes a claim for identity. Toward the end of the breakdown, Her emerges:

She felt like a star invisible in daylight. Then her thought widened and the tension snapped as swiftly. It's like a violin string. It's like Fayne exactly. When she said Fayne a white hand took Her. Her was held like a star invisible in daylight that suddenly by some shift adjustment of phosphorescent values comes quite clear. Her saw Her as a star shining white against winter daylight. (225)

Her at this point is standing alone on the edge of an ice-covered pond, absolutely unsure if the border of the ice will support her weight, knowing she is going to go across this shatterable membrane, knowing Fayne has betrayed her, knowing, having just been informed, that George no longer desires to marry her. It is a narrative moment in which the dramatic tension focuses on the danger of the ice, the fragility

of the mind, the vulnerability of the heart. But the passage marks a syntactic movement as well. Using Fayne as a linguistic chiasmus, moving through the repetitions of
the words "star," "daylight," "invisible," and "white," "Her saw Her." Clearly the drama
takes a back seat to the syntactic operations here. "Her," "Fayne," and "white" endlessly articulate one another, disrupting the discourse of desire with the discourse of
the interval, resisting oppositional sexual and textual categories. Here, language and
sexuality can be *detected* as indivisible. The sexuality marked here is not exclusively
woman-centered. It is one of many linguistic encounters through which Her projects
a refusal to fix identity, without falling into the abyss of neurosis. The "breakdown"
breaks open language to alternative possibilities for psychosexual identification.

In *The Madwoman in the Attic,* Gilbert and Gubar traced the possible options for
women in the tradition of the romance plot: marriage, insanity, or death. Similarly,
Nancy Miller called attention to the "explicitly phallocentric" model for novel plots
which has rendered ambition and the quest for feminine identity "unreadable." *HER*
in particular represents a direct challenge to the deadening effects on women of the
Oedipal plot. In the end of the novel, Her does not marry a man or merge with a
woman. She does not kill Fayne, she does not kill herself, she does not go mad. The
"breakdown" replaces castration as the pivotal dramatic determinant and offers us
the opportunity to double back on our reading. Castration, as the thematic trope for
Freud's narrative structure, provides a moment of individuation and difference. If
we read the "breakdown" scene as an alternative to the theme of castration, a narrative of subjectivity could surface without sexual difference, not because gender is
dissolved, but because it doesn't stay in one place. From "star" to "daylight" to
"white" to "Her" to "Her" and back again we find a moment of knowing a self as
process. When we trace the operations of language, what emerges is less an issue of
"who" Her (or H. D.) was than "where" she located her subjectivity and sexuality—
in the intervals, disruptions, and processes of writing.

DuPlessis and Friedman identify the joining of homosexual and heterosexual love
plots in the climax of part 2, when Her discovers that Fayne and George have been
involved with each other. What still needs to be analyzed is the possibility that the
text was never organized by the homo/hetero split but rather, by a refusal to submit
or commit to the homo/hetero split of the speaking subject. Similarly, the dramatic
center of *HER* is not limited to the choice between homosexuality and heterosexuality. Instead, a fundamental bisexuality traceable through the linguistic operations of
the text marks both the "heterosexual" and "homosexual" sections of the novel.

When the novel leaves off with the line, "I done left Miss Fayne all alone upstairs
in your little workroom" (234), the thematic implication might be left ambiguous,
but the linguistic implication loads "Fayne" with all kinds of possibilities. Perhaps

we must learn to take H. D. at her word when she says she "is herself the writing." At the border of writing, bisexuality and the discourse of the interval each surface in their indivisible codes.

To return to Dora: how might H. D. read her? It seems clear from her later work that H. D. continued both to engage Freud's account of bisexuality and to challenge it, as if she were unwilling to accept that the limits of language and subjectivity outlined by Freud were not also possibilities. Since H. D. placed an entirely different emphasis on the relationship between words and things, and on sexual and subjective positions recoverable in and through writing, perhaps she would have heard a different voice, seen a different word in Dora. H. D.'s literary journey both paralleled and diverged from Freud's psychoanalytic trajectories. Their narratives, when juxtaposed, force us to turn back to face our own stories of the way we fit or don't fit into models of language and sexuality.

My analysis here keeps pushing on the important question of bisexuality in literature and literary analysis. Much work—literary, social, political—remains to be done if we are to understand bisexuality as a sexual or textual category. For example, much could be learned from asking how H. D.'s novels are different from Virginia Woolf's *Orlando*. A comparative analysis between Gertrude Stein and H. D. might also yield important information concerning bisexuality and lesbian texts, without, as has been the case thus far, subordinating the one to the other. In past and present narratives bisexuality is too often read as an illegitimate feminist category, an impotent lesbian category, and a neutral cultural category. Perhaps bisexuality is seen as "enemy territory" since its inhabitants "trade camps." This need not be the case, however. Clearly bisexual writers have been developing voices for a long time now. In our modern quests to understand and theorize bisexuality, we may take heart from the work of H. D. HER's was a language most able to hold open opposite forces.

Notes

1.   In particular I am referring to Ellis's *Man and Woman* (London: Walter Scott, 1894), *Studies in the Psychology of Sex* (Philadelphia: F. A. Davis, 1905–10), and *Psychology of Sex* (London: William Heinemann, 1946), and Sigmund Freud's *The Interpretation of Dreams* (1900), *Three Essays on the Theory of Sexuality* (1905), "Hysterical Phantasies and Their Relation to Bisexuality (1908), and "Fragment of an Analysis of a Case of Hysteria" (1905), in *The Standard Edition of the Complete Psychological Works of Sigmund Freud*, trans. James Strachey (London: Hogarth, 1953–74).

2.   I am speaking here of the privileging of internal monologue and action over exterior drama and experiments with narrative sequentiality characteristic of modernist novels. H. D. both engages and radically departs from a modernist literary tradition in her novels.

3. In a quite remarkable way H. D.'s novels stage the relationship between self, sexuality, and writing, anticipating many later poststructuralist concerns, including a deconstructionist model of language, a revised psychoanalytic model that addressed the maternal and the female self, and the possibility of the production of a bisexual self out of the discourses of sexuality. Her work both meets and diverges from later theories developed by Lacan, Derrida, Foucault, and Kristeva, among others.

4. In *H. D.: The Career of That Struggle* (Bloomington: Indiana University Press, 1986), Rachel Blau DuPlessis offers a provocative reading of the word "borderline," suggesting that it "implies the porous vulnerable moment of crossing which scrambles differentiation of persons" (58). DuPlessis argues that a whole "borderline aesthetic" permeates all of H. D.'s poetry and prose.

5. I say that because of the huge influence of Freud and Ellis, and, through feminist criticism's recontextualizing of H. D.'s work, the appearance of other novels that confront and cross sexual boundaries to differing degrees, such as Radclyffe Hall's *The Well of Loneliness,* Virginia Woolf's *Orlando,* and Djuna Barnes's *Ladies Almanack* among others.

6. My exploration differs from others, because I shall argue that H. D. locates bisexuality as a position of process at a different place than Freud did in "Dora."

7. On this issue H. D.'s work prefigures the later theories of Jacques Lacan, because they both end up insisting that language and sexuality are indivisible. Lacan locates the constitution of the subject with two other founding moments, the acquisition of language and of sexual difference. H. D.'s novel *Her* both engages and stages some important challenges to Lacan, as I will argue.

8. Much has been made of the fact that H. D. was a patient of Freud's in 1933 and 1934. Her interest in psychoanalysis and sexology are also well documented. But as Friedman and DuPlessis point out, H. D.'s work is not limited to the psychosexual narratives produced out of this period, even if her work engages these narratives.

9. Hélène Cixous and Luce Irigaray have both critiqued Freud's account of bisexuality, uncovering the narrative of the boy's development or an account of masculinity. In a narrative in which castration is the climactic event, bisexuality can only fall within a pre-Oedipal and phallic trajectory. See Cixous's "The Laugh of the Medusa," trans. Keith and Paula Cohen, in *New French Feminisms,* ed. Elaine Marks and Isabelle de Courtivron (New York: Schocken, 1981) and Luce Irigaray's *This Sex Which Is Not One,* trans. Catherine Porter with Carolyn Burke (Ithaca: Cornell University Press, 1985).

10. See Juliet Mitchell's *Psychoanalysis and Feminism* (New York: Vintage, 1974).

11. As H. D. put it, "F. says mine is absolutely FIRST layer, I got stuck at the earliest pre-OE stage, and 'back to the womb' seems to be my only solution. . . . It's all too wonder-making." See DuPlessis, *H. D.: The Career of That Struggle.*

12. While one must be careful not to conflate Dora's analysis with H. D.'s, it is very important to read the *narrative* of bisexuality in "Dora" against the narrative of bisexuality in *HER.*

13. For the feminine subject this crisis results in an overdetermined fantasy of an ideal, uncastrated mother or narcissistic self-love, a stage "stuck" in the pre-Oedipal stage. See *Feminine Sexuality: Jacques Lacan and the Ecole Freudienne,* ed. Juliet Mitchell and Jaqueline Rose (London: Macmillan, 1982).

14. See Claire Buck, *H. D. and Freud: Bisexuality and a Feminist Discourse* (New York: St. Martin's Press, 1991), 84.

15. I am speaking here of a Lacanian version of a subject that is defined by lack, predicated on the subject's positioning in the symbolic order through the "Law of the Father" (or Freud's Oedipus complex).

16. Buck, *H. D. and Freud*, 85.

17. Many feminist critics have analyzed H. D.'s poetry and cataloged the ways in which H. D. makes use of Greek mythology and theories of language differences to uncover alternatives for feminine subjectivity and desire. In particular her long poem *Trilogy* has interested and engaged critics. See Alicia Ostriker, "No Rule or Procedure: The Open Poetics of H. D."; Susan Gubar, "The Echoing Spell of H. D.'s *Trilogy*"; and Albert Gelpi, "Re-Membering the Mother: A Reading of H. D.'s *Trilogy*"—all in *Signets: Reading H. D.*, ed. Susan Stanford Friedman and Rachel Blau DuPlessis (Madison: University of Wisconsin Press, 1990).

18. Buck, *H. D. and Freud*, 49.

19. See Lisa Appignanesi and John Forrester, *Freud's Women* (New York: Basic Books, 1992), 147.

20. Appignanesi and Forrester, *Freud's Women*, 147.

21. Appignanesi and Forrester, *Freud's Women*, 148.

22. Appignanesi and Forrester, *Freud's Women*, 149.

23. Put slightly differently, Kristeva extends Freud's analysis of oral, anal, and genital drives to include the irrepressibility of the abject, a border which is both a necessary condition for subjectivity and the space of the subject's possible dissolution. Kristeva uses the categories of food, waste, and signs of sexual difference and the corporeal territories of mouth, eyes, anus, ears, and genitals to theorize how societies and individuals define themselves by abjecting that which they cannot accept. The body's reactions to the abject result in "visceral" functions such as "retching, vomiting, spasms, choking—in brief, disgust." See Elizabeth Grosz, "The Body of Signification," in *Abjection, Melancholia, and Love: The Work of Julia Kristeva*, ed. John Fletcher and Andrew Benjamin (New York: Routledge, 1990), 89.

24. Fletcher and Benjamin, *Abjection, Melancholia, and Love*, 87.

25. H. D. identified each character in pencil on the typescript.

26. DuPlessis and Friedman, *Signets*, 211.

27. Buck, *H. D. and Freud*, 8.

28. DuPlessis and Friedman, *Signets*, 212.

29. One is reminded of Benveniste's claim that relationships between words and the differences between words generate categories for all meaning. For example, our subject position in language can be traced through an I/you opposition. H. D.'s syntax refuses and perhaps reorders the relationship between words in a far less differentiating moment, where words are alike and a subject position is still possible.

30. See Susan Stanford Friedman, "'I go where I love': An Intertextual Study of H. D. and Adrienne Rich," in *The Lesbian Issue,* ed. Estelle Freedman, Barbara Gelpi, Susan Johnson, and Kathleen Weston (Chicago: University of Chicago Press, 1985), 127.

31. Again this strategy prefigures at the level of language what Kristeva theorized about the subject and society. Which is to say that H. D. exploits the territories of subjectivity and language that surface in later theories of the abject and the semiotic/symbolic processes of language. See Kristeva's *Desire in Language: A Semiotic Approach to Literature and Art,* trans T. Gora, A. Jardine, and L. Roudiez (Oxford: Basil Blackwell, 1980) and *Powers of Horror: An Essay on Abjection,* trans. Leon Roudiez (New York: Columbia University Press, 1982).
32. Friedman and DuPlessis, *Signets,* 216.
33. See Kaja Silverman, *The Subject of Semiotics* (New York: Oxford University Press, 1983), 34, and Jacques Derrida, *Writing and Difference,* trans. Alan Bass (Chicago: University of Chicago Press, 1978).
34. Grosz, "The Body of Signification," 84.

Chapter 6

Bi-nary Bi-sexuality:
Jane Bowles's *Two Serious Ladies*

Marcy Jane Knopf

I n her essay "The Year of the Lustful Lesbian," Arlene Stein struggles to define Susie Bright's passing lesbian identity, which Stein names bisexuality:

> Because bisexuality may call into question the notion of sexual identity as necessarily being fixed, consistent, and either homosexual or heterosexual, it makes some lesbians uneasy. In a society where heterosexuality is the norm and lesbianism is still stigmatized, bisexual boundary crossings often lead to hurt feelings, as when a woman is left by her female lover for a man. Particularly suspect, and confusing, are women like Bright who sleep with men but maintain a lesbian identity, navigating the turbulent waters of two often contending worlds.[1]

I draw attention to Stein's effort to describe the current difficulties of negotiating bisexual identity in twentieth-century culture as a starting point for calling into question the fixity of sexual identity in heterosexual and/or lesbian discourses. Stein's contention that bisexuality disrupts lesbian identity politics still resonates strongly with many lesbians.[2] Stein seeks to broaden the definition of sexual identity in general—specifically, lesbian identity. I especially like Stein's image of "turbulent waters," for water changes depending on different environments or conditions; there is a fluid motion across water's various identities which is akin to bisexual identity. There are many different positions within bisexual and lesbian identity/ies. Karin Quimby theorizes some of those differences within lesbian desire and identity, particularly the problem that exists when lesbians desire women who also sleep with men. She argues that it may be possible to break down binaries and boundaries within lesbian desire by articulating the kinds of differences that exist in many lesbian sexual subjectivities.[3] Calling attention to the differences in experiences every lesbian brings with her to a lesbian relationship—one of which differences can be her desire for sexual intimacy with *both* women *and* men—is one way to deconstruct butch-femme and other dichotomies within a system of lesbian erotics. While I am not arguing that the category of lesbian include bisexuality, I do want to begin by making the claim that there needs to be room to think about different kinds of "queer" subjectivities in as many contexts as possible.[4]

Bi-Definition

First of all, I want to be clear about the various categories and definitions of bisexuality, many of which Jane Bowles illustrates in her novel *Two Serious Ladies*. There are differences between bisexual experiences, bisexual relationships, and bisexual acts, differences which could also be said to characterize heterosexuality and lesbian sexuality. Bisexuality can mean: (1) refusing to desire only a single gender-object-choice; (2) maintaining simultaneous relationships with differently gendered people; and (3) having long-term, monogamous relationships with differently gendered people in some form of partnership, whether a Boston or heterosexual marriage. These arrangements can also be thought of as serial monogamy in some instances. All these pass under the category of bisexuality (under a loose umbrella of "queer"), but they are not all the same *kind* of bisexuality. Susie Bright perceptively makes a case for noncategorized, bisexual subjectivity: "It's preposterous to ask sexual beings to stuff ourselves into the rapidly imploding social categories of straight or gay or bi, as if we could plot our sexual behavior on a contentious, predictable curve."[5] As much as I admire Bright's conviction, experientially I understand that when individuals (or texts) do not fit into categories, they are nevertheless compelled (or forced) to pass in those very communities or categories. Therefore, I believe there is important work to be done to expand—explode even—such categories, in order that other sexual subjectivities might be included in discussions of sexuality and in order to prevent an automatic reinscription of binary thinking.

One of the many "problems" with the invisibility of bisexuality in general is that it has the potential to fit into a "third" space; yet, because bisexuality is not a gender(ed)-object-choice, it does not fit into the hetero-logic of binary opposition, and bisexual women are generally either classified as lesbians or heterosexual. This categorization is rather ironic, because the very word "bisexual," with its prefix "bi," signifies two. Therefore, even on a basic linguistic level it is difficult to escape the hetero-logic of "bi-"nary oppositions: bisexuality reifies the same gesture it undoes. Marjorie Garber attempts to carve out a bisexual "third" space which can be useful in trying to create bisexual subjectivity:

If bisexuality is in fact, as I suspect it to be, not just another sexual orientation but rather a sexuality that undoes sexual orientation as a category, a sexuality that threatens and challenges the easy binaries of straight and gay, queer and "het," and even, through its biological and physiological meanings, the gender categories of male and female, then the search for the meaning of the word "bisexual" offers a different kind of lesson. Rather than naming an invisible, undernoticed minority now finding its place in the sun, "bisexual" turns out to be like bisexuals themselves, everywhere and nowhere. There is, in short, no "really" about it. The question of whether someone was "really" straight or "really" gay misrecognizes the nature of sexuality, which is fluid, not fixed, a narrative that changes over time rather than a fixed identity, however complex. The erotic discovery of bisexuality is the fact that it reveals sexuality to be a process of growth, transformation, and surprise, not a stable and knowable state of being.[6]

Garber argues that sexuality, in general, should become a space where many modes of thinking or being can exist.[7] "Third" usefully encompasses bisexuality in this way, but "thirdness" also gets ignored when it comes to binary logic, especially in the way binary sexuality gets constructed. Still, I do not want to argue that the kind of fluidity bisexuality reveals is always already an unstable, nonmonogamous, counter-hegemonic mode of being.

Bi-Reading

Typically people read from a hetero-logical perspective, which in turn erases bisex-uals' lived experiences and texts.[8] When one reads through the lens of bisexuality, there is a possibility to escape the either/or mentality of the hetero/homosexual bina-ries.[9] The (ignored) specificity of a bisexual subjectivity includes certain erotic plea-sures, emotional and intellectual attachments, as well as personal identity(ies) which differ from hegemonic sexual binaries.[10] Reading Jane Bowles's novel *Two Serious Ladies* teaches us how to read (and decode) bisexuality in a text. Echoing the move-ment of white, privileged protagonists, Miss Christina Goering and Mrs. Freida Copperfield, Bowles's bisexual characters pass between and within both heterosexual and lesbian communities. This passing means that bisexual women are marked sometimes as lesbian and sometimes as heterosexual, but not necessarily as bisexual. The ability to move fluidly either clandestinely (or obviously) between these kinds of "third" spaces allows for common *mis*readings of women's bisexual texts as lesbian. Passing, then, in Bowles's novel exists as a passing *between* communities or identities rather than *as* other subject positions. However, passing between various sexual communities prohibits bisexuality from occupying its own subject position. Since there is no tradition or history of reading bisexually, readers and scholars do not have a way to detect such subjectivities in various texts. When bisexuals pass between communities, bisexual experiences become obliterated by the very act of passing.

Many times reading bisexually invites the reading of one's own personal sexual subjectivity into the text.[11] This position can be vexed, however, when one reads bisexuality in a text which others read as only hetero/homosexual. Further, any kind of passing—be it sexual, class, gendered, national, racial, or other—involves, more often than not, occupying the space of the economically and/or socially privi-leged subjectivity. Typically, bisexual texts fall into a space of exclusion from both "straight" and lesbian communities or canons, because, like people, texts pass in different categories. This is precisely why we should examine the ways in which Bowles writes about bisexuality—something that past readings of her ignore. In the process, I begin to outline a bisexual way of reading.

Bi-Sexual

There is no explicit historical progression of bisexuality, either inside or outside queer theory or historiography; as a result, finding bisexual writers and/or texts is nearly as difficult a task today as in the 1940s, when the white, Jewish, middle-class Bowles published her first novel. Bowles works through the quandary of her bisexu-ality in her semi-autobiographical novel *Two Serious Ladies* and in much of her short fiction, as she searches for a bisexual subjectivity. She constructs a panoply of female desires in order to rebel against traditional concepts of female independence, identity, and binary sexuality. Written between 1938 and 1943, *Two Serious Ladies* negotiates Bowles's own relationships with her husband, Paul Bowles, and Helvetia Perkins (her first long-term woman lover). Like the women in her novel, Bowles thrived on her sometimes simultaneous relationships with men and women. Bowles's biographer, Millicent Dillon, writes about the push and pull to which both Helvetia and Paul subjected Jane and which Jane resisted: "Helvetia, moreover, was trying to force Jane to choose between Paul and herself. Jane would tell Paul this, but would say that of course she would do no such thing. She did tell Paul that Helvetia hated the idea of her coming so often to see him. Yet Jane would not choose."[12] Her refusal to decide embodies and defines her position as a bisexual: she is unwilling to choose between her male and/or female partners. She also tries to negotiate ways that counterhegemonic relationships could exist. In her own marriage, as well as in her novel, Bowles wants to find a way to revolt against compulsory marriages and partnerships, which Lisa Maria Hogeland calls "the politics of Noah's Ark."[13] At the same time, however, Bowles contends with the problem of finding a balance between the desire she and her fictional counterparts feel for people other than their mates and the jealousy they feel when their partners behave similarly.

Bowles originally conceived her manuscript as *Three Serious Ladies* and included three protagonists: Miss Christina Goering, Mrs. Freida Copperfield, and Señora Ramirez.[14] I am particularly interested in the structural changes the original manuscript implies as alternatives to binary thinking, binary sexuality, and hetero-logics. Bowles challenges binary thinking in the original manuscript by exploring the lives of three different sexually liberated women under the veil of a writing style which is reminiscent of nineteenth-century sentimental fiction. The novel constructs characters who are not only independent (regardless of their legal "marital" status) but free sexually and emotionally as they pass between different communities.[15] Working to find her own sexual space without boundaries and with unlimited choices, she navigates through those "turbulent waters," to use Stein's words, in order to map out a way to live and write as a bisexual woman. However, it is still difficult to conceive of such fluidity without considering the possibly instinctive nature of both desire and jealousy. While Bowles writes about and tries to live a life with open relationships she still finds herself dealing with the attractions that she and her fictional selves feel for people outside of their life-long partnerships, as well as the jealousy that seems an inescapable counterpart of any desiring self.[16]

Dillon remarks that Bowles's characters are very much a part of Jane Bowles herself: "Jane is Mrs. Copperfield and she is Miss Goering, and yet she is outside of them in the narrative voice, shaping dialogue and transitions, finding in her gift for language what must be said and not said about sin and salvation, about sensuality and hope and fear."[17] She alternates her three-chapter novel between stories of Miss Goering and Mrs. Copperfield. Typically, literary criticism and reviews characterized Miss Goering as a "spinster" and Mrs. Copperfield as a lesbian, who leaves her husband for Pacifica, a Panamanian prostitute. But what Bowles does with these stereotypes is perhaps so radical that most critics miss what I believe to be her motives. Like Bowles, both serious ladies are attached to another person in a life-long partnership but strive for a way to negotiate living as bisexual beings in "open" relationships.[18]

In her life, Jane Bowles made the gender-object-choices of heterosexual, lesbian, bisexual, and refused them at the same time. Jane Bowles (most often known for her marriage to Paul Bowles, whose writing overshadows hers in the public mind) is often remembered—if remembered at all—as a woman who wrote a *lesbian* novel called *Two Serious Ladies*. When it comes to designating Bowles's sexuality in critical literature, she is either described as lesbian or heterosexual. Not once in her book *A Little Original Sin* does Dillon use the term "bisexual" to describe Bowles.[19] Even though she mentions some ways in which readers can complicate Bowles as a woman and as a writer, Dillon does not name Bowles as "bisexual," even as she describes a life that is indeed quite undeniably bisexual.

According to the logic of the ways in which texts can pass, those which can be read as bisexual are many times read as heterosexual rather than lesbian. An example of this is the way in which the bisexuality of Bowles's characters (many times read as generic sexual promiscuity) is overlooked or misread by viewing Miss Goering as a spinster and Mrs. Copperfield as a "straight"-woman-turned-lesbian, which perpetuates old stereotypes.[20] Because of these ways Bowles's work can be stereotyped and categorized, it is difficult to read her texts as embodying a bisexual position within a literary canon.[21] Bowles's complexities enable a new way of thinking more generally about category definitions in pedagogy and scholarship. However, this is one of the hazards of writing about bisexuality: the way in which it undoes precisely the work it attempts to do—that is, to occupy more than one, even more than two (in that it embodies the "third" space), sexual subject positions.

In describing the Bowles marriage, Marjorie Garber contributes to the unmaking of Bowles's bisexuality even as she seems to be arguing for it. Garber characterizes the Bowles marriage this way: "What is a marriage? In this case a marriage between a bisexual man and a *lesbian* was reinvented so as to last a lifetime."[22] If Garber is trying to make the argument that Jane and Paul Bowles lived a bisexual partnership, then why would she define him as "bisexual" and her as "lesbian"? Garber claims that she is critiquing the invisibility of bisexuality, yet she contributes to it. Lillian Faderman paints a similar picture of Jane and Paul's relationship, one that envisions Bowles as a lesbian who married as a "bisexual compromise." Faderman writes about Bowles specifically in the context of the 1940s in "Butches, Femmes, and Kikis," a section of her study which she devotes to binaries and identity formation in the lesbian community. Yet Faderman does not see the Bowles marriage as a front but as real desire for heterosexual companionship on the part of both Jane and Paul. Faderman's characterization of the Bowles's marriage implies that Jane made a bisexual compromise: "Paul Bowles was bisexual, though Jane seems to have had sexual relationships exclusively with other women. She and her husband agreed to lead separate sexual lives, but she relied on him for stability and community."[23] Faderman cites Bowles's biographer, Millicent Dillon, but I think both leave out some important information. For instance, Jane and Paul did not lead separate sexual lives for the first two years of their marriage. Her long-term relationships with women turned celibate after a period of sexual intimacy as well.[24] Ultimately, Jane's simultaneous interest in both men and women, on both a physical, emotional, and intellectual level, offers proof that she was indeed bisexual.[25] At the same time, I think Bowles defies such classification, but that is precisely my point: bisexuality is a place mentally, emotionally, physically that does not fit into any one mold— perhaps, ultimately, not even the category of bisexual. Still, one of the difficulties with this theory of a fluid "third" space of bisexuality is that when one puts it into practice, there are often either jealousies (because of the sequestering of desire) that result from the fluidity between relationships, or an inability to maintain long-term monogamous relationships. Bisexuality for Bowles and her characters is a constant negotiation among selves: the lesbian, heterosexual, and bisexual selves.[26]

Bi-Textual

By creating three different female protagonists (in her original manuscript), all of whom engage in some form of life-partnership, Bowles explores ways in which women try to arrange a space in which they are able to commit to a first partner on an emotional and intellectual level while also exploring their sexuality in relationships outside their primary partnership. Miss Goering is not a spinster; rather, she is a woman committed to a Boston marriage with her white lover, Miss Lucy Gamelon. Understanding their relationship as a Boston marriage is important not only within the narrative's plot but in Bowles's nineteenth-century sentimental fiction narrative style.[27]

When Miss Gamelon first appears in the novel, and in Miss Goering's life, Miss Goering's maid announces the arrival of a female visitor. Upon her entrance Miss Goering says to her new friend, "I was thinking about you all last night. . . . It's a funny thing. I always thought I should meet you. My cousin used to tell me how queer you were. I think, though, that you can make friends more quickly with queer people. Or else you don't make friends with them at all—one way or the other. Many of my authors were very queer."[28]

I find this conversation about "queer"ness very interesting. Although the use of "queer" as an inclusive and positive way to describe one's sexual subjectivity is a relatively contemporary practice, Bowles hints at a similar meaning. While in one sense this use of "queer" connotes that they are both societal outcasts, it also gives the impression that, given their desire to see one another and their concern for one another, "queer" indicates a definition along lines of desire as well. In the course of this conversation Miss Goering invites Miss Gamelon to live with her. There is a sense of urgency in this invitation; Miss Goering wants Miss Gamelon to move in immediately—not even to go to her former home to gather her belongings. Miss Goering's attraction to Miss Gamelon is not exclusively sexual; it is also emotional and intellectual. Miss Goering's initial rationale behind asking Miss Gamelon to move in with her may stem from a sexual desire, but other elements of this relationship are equally important. When Miss Gamelon retires early that evening, "Miss Goering took her leave reluctantly. She had been prepared to talk half the night" (13). Miss Goering's desire for Miss Gamelon is for a companion—a partner—with whom she can share her home, life, and sex.

What Miss Goering does not realize is that by having Miss Gamelon move in with her she changes the nature of their relationship from her own perspective. Bowles does not write an explicit narrative of sexual relations between the two women, but she does characterize their relationship in the same vein as a Boston marriage. "Do you enjoy our little life?" she asks Miss Gamelon one evening. "I'm always content," replies Miss Gamelon, "because I know what to take and what to leave, but you are always at the mercy" (14). Their union is supportive, but for Miss Goering this begins a pattern in which she grows tired of her domesticated relationships and seeks her sexual outlets elsewhere. The first of Miss Goering's affairs is with Arnold, a man she meets at a party who almost instantly falls in love with her. After Miss Goering begins her relationship with Arnold (and later with Arnold's father as well, who is equally taken with her), neither relationship is necessarily marked as sexual, but desire exists in each coupling. As a result, tension arises between Miss Gamelon and Miss Goering.

In order to simultaneously carry on relationships, or move between relationships with Arnold, Arnold's father, and Miss Gamelon, Miss Goering attempts to cater to the needs and desires of all three interested parties. In this vein Miss Goering occupies the space of the stereotypical bisexual who cannot be in a monogamous relationship. Miss Goering tells Arnold that she is devoted to his father: "'Well, I hope that the fact that you're devoted to him,' said Arnold, 'won't interfere with our friendship, because I have decided to see quite a bit of you, providing of course that it is agreeable to you that I do'" (30). Miss Goering reveals her interest in intimacy with Arnold and his father only to irritate Miss Gamelon even further. Arnold identifies Miss Gamelon as "Miss Goering's companion" but is unaware that the nature of their relationship is that of a Boston marriage. Miss Gamelon ironically responds to his questioning of her relationship with Goering by saying, "Do you think it's lovely? . . . That's very interesting indeed" (31). Miss Gamelon finds Arnold's characterization of their relationship interesting because she knows he is unaware of the nature of her life-partnership with Miss Goering.

His inability to know that Miss Gamelon and Miss Goering are life-partners enables Miss Goering to play both sides of the fence, living as a promiscuous bisexual woman.

Bowles parallels the narrative of Miss Goering and Miss Gamelon with that of a seemingly heterosexually married couple, Mr. and Mrs. Copperfield, who vacation in Panama. By alternating chapters between these two "couples" Bowles plays with assumptions, proving that neither relationship is as it seems. Mrs. Copperfield is largely concerned with preserving her own self—with her own happiness—a goal which Bowles's other characters share: "Mrs. Copperfield's sole object in life was to be happy" (40). For Mrs. Copperfield, this kind of self-preserving pursuit of happiness includes pleasures of the flesh. Like Miss Goering, Mrs. Copperfield feels committed to her marriage with Mr. Copperfield, but only insofar as she can engage in relationships outside that union; and, in pursuit of this end, Mrs. Copperfield winds up hurting others. Upon their arrival in Panama, a prostitute makes advances toward her, caresses her, and tries to coax her into meeting her in a bar. Though Mrs. Copperfield is walking down the street with her husband, the prostitute says to her, "You come along with me, darling, and you'll have the happiest time you've ever had before. I'll be your type" (41). Mrs. Copperfield asks for some time away from Mr. Copperfield so she can be alone with this young Panamanian prostitute. She and the prostitute walk off together. "I love to be free," Mrs. Copperfield says to the woman after he has left. "Shall we go into your little room? I've been admiring it through the window ..." (43). While Mrs. Copperfield does not have sex with her, she does give the prostitute the dollar she asks for and succeeds in annoying Mr. Copperfield, though he seems used to her taking such liberties in their marriage.

Following this first escapade, Mrs. Copperfield meets Pacifica, another Panamanian prostitute, who approaches Mrs. Copperfield while Mr. Copperfield is at her side. Pacifica assumes, at first, that Mrs. Copperfield is unavailable to her because she is married. When Mr. Copperfield retires for the evening, Mrs. Copperfield stays behind to spend her first evening with Pacifica. Pacifica undresses in front of Mrs. Copperfield and reveals to her, "I like women very much. I like women sometimes better than men." Mrs. Copperfield responds by sharing, "I was once in love with an older woman" (49). Pacifica and Mrs. Copperfield spend their siesta together disclosing feelings about attractions and their own bisexuality, though they do not name it as such. As Pacifica says to Mrs. Copperfield, "You like things which are not what other people like, don't you? I would like to have this experience of loving an older woman. I think that is sweet, but I really am always in love with some man" (50). Mrs. Copperfield does like "other" people and "other" experiences. Mrs. Copperfield's desire for Pacifica is not only desire for a woman but a desire for a woman of color.

Unlike her position when she is with Mr. Copperfield, when Mrs. Copperfield is with Pacifica she is in a position of power. With Pacifica, Mrs. Copperfield passes from a marginal to a dominant position in an intimate relationship. As a white tourist—and sexual colonialist—Mrs. Copperfield participates in the consumption of a variety of goods and people.[29] Mrs. Copperfield's relationship to her landscape and social context changes as she moves from being a privileged "wife" to a sexual colonizer and consumer of "native" prostitutes. A (post)colonialist reading of this travel narrative would argue that, given these circumstances, there cannot be anything but an unequal distribution of power in Mrs. Copperfield and Pacifica's relationship.[30] Mrs. Copperfield's exoticized desire for Pacifica, given the power dynamics in their relationship, is problematic and complex. Bowles does not offer any commentary on the uneasy power relations of these two women; rather, both women fall asleep, holding hands and feeling "very peaceful," which implies that on some level they have come to terms with their differences and similarities. "Very peaceful" is suspect, revealing the ways in which Bowles glosses over the complexity of the colonialist aspects of their relationship. Mrs. Copperfield may feel content, but Pacifica doesn't have the opportunity to voice her opinion. Pacifica may, in fact, also have bisexual desires, but they are not a possibility for her because she *has* to be "in love with some man" or merely "be with some man" in order to make a living as a prostitute.[31] This conversation is particularly significant, because it is the one time in the novel when characters reveal the multiple and unequal desires which are not only sexual but also deeply complicated by race and class.

On the most basic level, Mr. Copperfield has difficulty accepting the way Mrs. Copperfield passes between their marriage and her relationships with women. When he wants to take Mrs. Copperfield on a day trip into the jungle, she worries that she will not return in time to meet Pacifica and her other new friend, Mrs. Quill. In a fit of jealousy over his wife's imminent evening engagement he says: "You aren't really considering *them*, are you? . . . After all, Freida!" (63). As in previous conversations, Mr. Copperfield refuses to talk about his wife's bisexuality and her consequent infidelity. At the same time, Mr. Copperfield's disgust at his wife's sexual object-choices is grounded in his own racism and classism: he is disturbed that Mrs. Copperfield chooses to spend her time with working-class women of color rather than with him. While Mrs. Copperfield might enjoy, on some level, a sensation of power in her relationship with Pacifica, she also gets to exercise control over Mr. Copperfield by not allowing him to run her life and choose her erotic partners. Ignoring Mrs. Copperfield's infidelity and not discussing it further indicates just how threatened Mr. Copperfield is not only by her bisexuality but also by the way she mingles with Panamanians—particularly with prostitutes. Still, Mrs. Copperfield continues to pass between marginal and dominant worlds (between heterosexual and lesbian, between upper-class white tourists and Panamanian prostitutes) in her efforts to negotiate a way in which she can exist as a person who has strong attractions to "native others." Her liaison with Pacifica allows Mrs. Copperfield a position of power in which she can pass between communities and relationships, and ultimately, despite her husband's objections, she continues the affair.

In what functions as a very steamy baptismal scene, Pacifica and Mrs. Copperfield have their first sexual experience together in the ocean. They are both naked in the ocean waters; Pacifica holds Mrs. Copperfield as she teaches her to swim, after which Mrs. Copperfield revels in the memory:

She was trembling and exhausted as one is after a love experience. She looked up at Pacifica, who noticed that her eyes were more luminous and softer than she had ever seen them before. "You should go in the water more," said Pacifica; "you stay in the house too much." (98)

Upon her return to the hotel, Mr. Copperfield asks her about her swim. When Mrs. Copperfield responds by telling her husband that she and Pacifica swam naked, he characteristically discontinues questioning her. Mr. Copperfield's frustration with his wife's new relationship is colored by his own inability to make her focus her desires solely upon him. His jealousy over her growing relationship with Pacifica heats up after this swim, as he learns that she prefers the sensuality and company of Pacifica to his. Moreover, Mr. Copperfield's jealousy is so strong that he cannot understand that Mrs. Copperfield wants to be with Pacifica partly because she wants to experience her own undomesticated sexuality, which is possible with the Panamanian prostitute. Mr. Copperfield becomes exasperated with his wife, which he exhibits by his inability to articulate any name for Pacifica aside from "them." Mrs. Copperfield, like Miss Goering, may grow tired of stagnant, domesticated liaisons. She also wants to experience Pacifica sexually as an exotic partner in contrast to her boring, bourgeois marriage partner.

Mrs. Copperfield and Pacifica's sensual swim mirrors an earlier episode in the novel between Miss Goering and her childhood friend Mary. Bowles begins the novel with Miss Goering's childhood, one that some critics view as being particularly preoccupied with religion and salvation. While this is certainly accurate, there is much more going on in Miss Goering's childhood than simply a preoccupation with religion. This religious passion functions as a safe displacement of homoerotic passion—a common trope, especially in sentimental fiction, where sexual desire must be veiled. Miss Goering's attraction to salvation is directly connected to her desire for her sister Sophie's friend Mary. Mary is forbidden fruit for Miss Goering, as Sophie wants Mary all to herself; and, just as Mr. Copperfield becomes jealous of his wife's affairs, Sophie is jealous of Mary's relationship with Miss Goering: "It was Christina's desire to have Mary to herself of an afternoon. One very sunny afternoon Sophie went inside for her piano lesson, and Mary remained seated on the grass. Christina, who had seen this from not far away, ran into the house, her heart beating with excitement. She took off her shoes and stockings and remained in a short white underslip." (4–5) In her undergarment Miss Goering does a sun-worshiping dance for Mary, her excitement and sexual desire propelling her through her preoccupation with sin and salvation. Sophie becomes jealous when she finds Miss Goering and Mary together on the lawn. Miss Goering and Sophie fight over Mary in what seems to be typical sibling rivalry. However, for Miss Goering, this fight over Mary goes beyond any kind of "traditional" sisterly argument. When Sophie is out one day, Miss Goering takes advantage of having Mary all to herself. Miss Goering makes Mary take off all her clothes to play a game which she calls "I forgive you for all your sins." When Mary asks whether the game is fun, Miss Goering tells her, "It's not for fun that we play it, but because it's necessary to play it" (6), a statement that anticipates Miss Goering's later rationalization for entering into various sexual relationships. In what turns out to be another baptismal scene, Miss Goering takes Mary out to the woods and washes away her sins in muddy water. Miss Goering layers mud around Mary's body and then washes her off while begging that she be cleansed from all her sins—a scene that conveys a double meaning. The element of forbiddenness that surrounds their day in the woods thinly veils the sexual component of Miss Goering's desires. As Bowles says of her at the beginning of this scene, "Christina wasn't yet sure what she was going to do, but she was very much excited" (6). The excitement and desire during the interaction between these two girls contributes to a suggestive beginning to the novel's characterization of Miss Goering's and Mrs. Copperfield's openly bisexual adult lives. Bowles brings Christianity and sexuality together to suggest the ways in which monotheistic, monotruth metaphysical spaces tend to lean toward monogamous, exclusive spaces for desire and recognizing desire. By placing sin, salvation, and sexual desire in the same context, Bowles disrupts the notion that there cannot be fluidity across those lines of thought and desire. From the beginning of the narrative Bowles chronicles two women who are misfits and who attempt to pass in and out of relationships and communities. As both child and adult, Miss Goering is a woman who is not liked, for people do not understand her. Miss Goering deviates from her society—sexually and religiously—and explores the incessant overlap between the two forces.

The jealousy between Miss Goering and her sister Sophie over Mary is similar to the jealousy between Miss Goering and Miss Gamelon. Miss Goering, like Mrs.

Copperfield, has difficulty sustaining passionate feelings in a domesticated relationship. Miss Goering seeks relationships with men and women outside of her Boston marriage, beginning with Arnold and his father. However, once Arnold moves in with Miss Gamelon and Miss Goering, Miss Goering loses her desire for him and begins the excursions on which she hopes to find a new person who can satisfy her desires. Arnold's father begs her not to go—or at least to take him with her—but she explains to him, echoing her earlier conversation with Mary, "It is not for fun that I am going . . . but because it is necessary to do so" (124). The repetition of this statement connects Miss Goering's fascinations with religion, salvation, travel, and sexual desire. On a train trip to Long Island Miss Goering notices a woman seated across from her, whom she looks at "with interest" and who tries furiously to avoid her eye. Miss Goering, on the other hand, attempts to carry on a conversation with her, with the idea of picking her up. The woman succeeds in brushing Miss Goering off by lying to her. A little confused as to why she would lie, Goering responds by assuring her, "I am a lady like yourself" (128). Knowing that Miss Goering is interested in her sexually, the woman grows hysterical and calls the conductor over to talk to Miss Goering. The conductor says to Miss Goering, "You can't talk to anyone on these here trains . . . unless you know them" (128). He asks Miss Goering not to "molest" any passengers again. On this train Miss Goering tries to pass for a bourgeois, heterosexual woman, but to the woman on the train, she appears to be a working-class lesbian. Here, Miss Goering becomes the marginal outcast, the one who is detested rather than desired.

Once Miss Goering arrives on the island, she explores the streets and bars and gazes at the people as a tourist, though she is in her own country. She meets Andrew McLane, who asks her to go to his apartment with him. She eventually moves in with Andy for eight days and explores a new relationship, one that intrigues her largely *because* it is new and adventuresome. In her travels, she, like Mrs. Copperfield, enjoys not only exploring new places but also new relationships, and sex with new bodies. On a trip home she tries to explain her desires to Arnold, as he inquires about her travels:

"I don't know why you find it so interesting and intellectual to seek out a new city," said Arnold, cupping his chin in his hand and looking at her fixedly.

"Because I believe the hardest thing for me to do is really move from one thing to another, partly," said Miss Goering.

"Spiritually," said Arnold, trying to speak in a more sociable tone, "spiritually I'm constantly making little journeys and changing my nature every six months."

"I don't believe it for a minute," said Miss Goering.

"No, no, it is true. Also, I can tell you that I think it is absolute nonsense to move physically from one place to another. All places are more or less alike." (158)

Miss Goering has difficulty subscribing to such beliefs. For her, sexuality is something that she can only truly take pleasure in when passing in communities other than her own. She loses any desire she once had for Arnold, his father, and Miss Gamelon because of their cohabitation, and, eventually, her eight-day escapade with Andy also becomes tiresome.

Another aspect of Miss Goering's loss of desire for Miss Gamelon and Andy is related to Bowles's critique of bourgeois values and lifestyles. When her relationships begin to resemble a settled, domesticated, bourgeois life, Miss Goering loses interest. Part of Miss Goering's attraction to Andy is his working-class life. Once he reforms himself, which coincides with the domestication of their relationship, Miss Goering loses interest. Arnold characterizes Miss Goering's fascination with working-class culture as an intellectual—and voyeuristic—attraction. Miss Goering is a tourist, like Mrs. Copperfield, when she meets Andy. And, like Mrs. Copperfield, Miss Goering's desire for Andy, who works as a slumlord, is rooted in her ability to occupy a position of power and privilege over him. Many of Bowles's characters travel to other places to seek positions of power and experience desires through their power over "others." This dynamic may reflect Bowles's own position as a white, privileged woman; nevertheless, it represents a complicated web of erotic relationships that are inseparable from the politics of power.

One way Bowles plays with stereotypes is to invoke them and then redefine them. Bowles does this with her depiction of women in her novel, particularly prostitutes. Without conventions for thinking about or defining bisexuality, Bowles runs through the gamut of ways in which sexual women are described. In Pacifica, Bowles creates a bisexual woman who thrives not only on money (she needs tourist dollars to support herself) but also on her bisexual desire.[32] Miss Goering too (often characterized as a spinster) is mistaken for a prostitute on the island where she has her affair with Andy. Frank, who desires Miss Goering, assumes she works as a prostitute:

"You work as a prostitute, after a fashion, don't you?"

Miss Goering laughed. "Heavens!" she said. "I certainly never thought I looked like a prostitute merely because I have red hair; perhaps like a derelict or an escaped lunatic, but never a prostitute!"

"You don't look like no derelict or escaped lunatic to me. You look like a prostitute, and that's what you are. I don't mean a real small-time prostitute. I mean a medium one."

"Well, I don't object to prostitutes, but really I assure you I am no such thing."

"I don't believe you." (185)

Typically, the labels of prostitute and lesbian keep "unruly" women like Miss Goering in line. This conflation of naming is a mistake which speaks to Bowles's use of sexual unconventionality itself throughout the novel. By naming women prostitutes, either accurately or by mistake, Bowles disrupts class boundaries. Miss Goering leaves Andy to pursue an affair with Frank. Angry and jealous, Andy threatens to disgrace Miss Goering and "put her to shame." By this time in her life, and in the narrative, this threat does not disturb Miss Goering in the least. She realizes that she needs to find ways to negotiate relationships on her own terms, to find out how she fits into various kinds of relationships sexually, emotionally, and intellectually. As she says to Andy on her departure, "Oh, Andy . . . you make me sound so dreadful! I am merely working out something for myself" (188).

When Mrs. Copperfield tries to negotiate her bisexuality within her lesbian and heterosexual relationships, she too must find a way to help the people she lives among understand. Mr. Copperfield eventually becomes so jealous of his wife's growing attentiveness toward Pacifica that he feels compelled to write a letter to her in which he appeals to her: "You must give up the search for those symbols which only serve to hide its face from you. You will have the illusion that they are disparate and manifold but they are always the same. If you are only interested in a bearable life, perhaps this letter does not concern you. For God's sake, a ship leaving port is still a wonderful thing to see" (111). Mr. Copperfield, though perhaps unknowingly, sees the difficulty of Mrs. Copperfield's boundary crossings. The fluidity across relationships that Mrs. Copperfield seeks is disparate, manifold, and the same. He realizes that any attempt to have a "bearable life" will involve making choices about her desires—choices which Mrs. Copperfield fundamentally does not want to make. Even though Mrs. Copperfield does not live with her husband, she also does not want to leave him. Neither Mr. nor Mrs. Copperfield are interested in divorce or any other end to their marriage. But both partners are equally distraught over Mrs. Copperfield's inability to commit to either her lover or her husband. As she embarks on this new trip to explore her bisexuality, she must map it out as if she were the first person ever to explore such a state of being.[33] This is new territory for the Copperfields, for Miss Goering, for Miss Gamelon, and for Jane and Paul Bowles; these are continual problems for bisexuals living and writing today.

The narrative concludes by bringing Miss Goering and Mrs. Copperfield together. Mrs. Copperfield brings Pacifica back to New York with her as a "souvenir" from her travels abroad, and together they meet Miss Goering. Mrs. Copperfield tells Miss Goering that she cannot go anywhere without Pacifica: "I am completely satisfied and contented" (196). Mrs. Copperfield tells her friend that without Pacifica she would "go completely to pieces" (197). This going to pieces exemplifies, for me, the ways in which bisexuality is read—still a place in which it is difficult, yet somehow mandatory, to pass between heterosexual and lesbian relationships, between positions of marginal and dominant.

Temporality becomes an important issue in reading bisexuality, especially since most readers distinguish the sexual orientation of characters in novels based upon the desires or relationships at the end of a text—rather than looking at the fluctuations and variations of desire throughout the novel. For example, Mrs. Copperfield is with Pacifica in the last scene of the novel, but this scenario does not imply that she is necessarily a lesbian; such a reading discounts the agency Mrs. Copperfield has shown in choosing her "other" desires or relationships at other junctions in the novel. Bowles, who at the time of writing this novel begins to learn how to live by passing between two often contending worlds, between male and female partners, sums it up best by describing bisexuality as fragmented, or in her own words, "in pieces."

Bi-Theory

Bowles projects society's typical perception of bisexuality in *Two Serious Ladies*: it is shocking because of certain societal codes of morality. That is, in hegemonic, heterosexual, "normal" society, bisexuals are perceived as exotic; there is a seemingly innate curiosity attached to the notion that what bisexuals do between the sheets is different from one's own (hetero)sexual practices. Even Jane's family had difficulty accepting the publication of her novel: "Helvetia didn't approve of the book, Paul remembers. She thought it was too obviously lesbian. So did Jane's family and Paul's family. 'It was very much looked down on by both families.'"[34] Even her lover and bisexual husband did not or could not find a name for Miss Goering and Mrs. Copperfield's bisexual relationships, nor a place where their lovers or partners could accept the book outside the "name" of lesbian.

This conflict prevails in Bowles's work and life and resonates with the experiences of many bisexuals today. Especially for those who are coupled, the choice is not one of either/or but of both/and. The "problem" is wanting to occupy many sexual subject positions, but not being able to, wanting to occupy a wide open "third" or "queer" space, but being bound to a system of compulsory binary sexuality. Bowles, like bisexuals in the 1990s, endured such codes. As much as she desired a "third" or "queer" space that would accept her different sexual subjectivities—that did not rely on binary sexuality or provoke jealousy—Bowles was still burdened with the notion that she must choose one partner, or one gender-object-choice. I do not believe that Bowles married because of such societal constraints; clearly, she had strong feelings of emotional, intellectual, and physical love for Paul. But she did not know how to exist bisexually. Throughout her life she constantly tried to negotiate a space for her bisexuality. Not surprisingly, then, literary critics and theorists still find it difficult to locate the sexual subjectivity of writers like Bowles.

That Bowles writes about women who are interested in people other than their life-partners invokes the stereotype that bisexuals are promiscuous, that they cannot commit to just one person. By thinking through her relationships with Helvetia Perkins and Paul Bowles, she also calls into question the very idea of "the norm"—that pairing off into any kind of dyadic couple is "natural." Bowles's honesty in portraying a fluid movement between relationships, between sincere emotional, physical, and intellectual ties to a variety of people, demonstrates just how unnatural—and mentally damaging—such hetero-logics can be. Hetero-logics can contribute to instinctive jealous reactions that lead one to make either/or choices about relationships. Bisexuality still is assumed to imply nonmonogamy—sometimes accompanied by jealous partners—which Bowles illustrates in her characterizations of Miss Goering and Mrs. Copperfield. Bowles creates bisexual subjectivities in her protagonists that contend with jealousy, love triangles, colonialism, and unequal power relations. In the novel the complexities of a fluid bisexual identity are contingent upon a movement from varied power positions. Ultimately, Mrs. Copperfield and Miss Goering's fluid bisexual identities do not conclude just because the novel ends. Readers who choose to see sexual desire as contingent upon temporality will misread Bowles's novel. Reading bisexually means not assuming an either/or conclusion at the end of this text; Bowles's characters move between partners too fluidly in this narrative to allow for a reading of binary sexuality or desire.

Bowles defies categorization by creating characters who cannot be pinpointed accurately as either lesbian or heterosexual. In her novel she breaks down boundaries and crosses lines by redefining sexual subjectivities and categories—by calling into question the very notion that such classifications "naturally" exist. While Bowles breaks new ground in her critiques of compulsory binary sexuality, she also employs dangerous narrative strategies in *Two Serious Ladies*. The voyeuristic and imperialistic desire of Miss Goering and Mrs. Copperfield inscribes sexual colonialism which makes contemporary readings of her novel complex. The racial and class privilege Bowles brings to her writing makes her bold assertion of nonmonogamy and bisexuality vexed, at best. However, rereading and reclaiming Bowles is an important first step in beginning to read bisexually: to read and reread beyond dualistic hierarchies of binary desire. Reading Bowles offers a possibility for reading bisexually which does not collapse racial and class differences but instead requires readers to work through such complexities in their reading practices. With recent (post)colonial and "queer" theory in mind, a new intersection of two politically important disciplines—both of which address previously ignored subjects—can emerge from a critical reading of Bowles.

Notes

I would like to thank several people who helped me work through drafts of this article: Kate McCullough, Jay Clayton, Maria Pramaggiore, Charles Spinosa, Andy Lakritz, and Donald Hall for their supportive commentary on early drafts; Beth Swanson, Tonya Laubach, and Lisa Hogeland for their never-ending stream of helpful feedback; and my inspirational grandma, Marian Gibbons.

1. Arlene Stein, "The Year of the Lustful Lesbian," *Sisters, Sexperts, Queers: Beyond the Lesbian Nation*, ed. Arlene Stein (New York: Penguin, 1993), 29. Stein does not call Bright bisexual in this passage but does imply that there is confusion precisely because Bright chooses to name herself lesbian while continuing to sleep with men.

2. A recent example of the difficult boundaries bisexuals are forced to cross can be seen in the film *Go Fish,* when a group of lesbians from her community confront Daria because they feel betrayed by her sleeping with a man. Daria also (problematically) identifies herself as a "lesbian who sleeps with men" rather than as a bisexual. *Go Fish,* directed by Rose Troche, Samuel Goldwyn and Islet Productions, 1994.

3. Karin Quimby, "*She Must Be Seeing Things* Differently: The Limits of Butch/Femme," in *Lesbian Erotics*, ed. Karla Jay (New York: New York University Press, 1995), 183–95.

4. I should make it clear from the outset that in this paper I am only interested in exploring female bisexuality. Male bisexuality brings to it an entirely different set of questions which I do not have space to explore here.

5. Susie Bright, "Blindsexual," in *Sexual Reality: A Virtual Sex World Reader* (San Francisco: Cleis Press, 1992), 152.

6. Marjorie Garber, *Vice Versa: Bisexuality and the Eroticism of Everyday Life* (New York: Simon and Schuster, 1995), 65–66.

7. Eve Kosofsky Sedgwick brought some complicating notions of bisexuality and gender-object-choice to my attention in the e-mail Queer Studies Listserv. In one of her infamous lists she warns about the dangers of exclusion within the political concept of bisexuality:

   I should add that in a discursive context that WASN'T so radically structured already around gender-of-object-choice, the concept of bisexuality could work very differently: instead of seeming to add the finishing touch to a totalizing vision of human sexuality/gender, it could function as one sexually dissident self-description among many others, some of which would and some of which would not feature gender-of-object-choice. Chubbies and chasers, tops and bottoms and femmes and butches of various gender identifications if any, bears and smoothies, masturbators and fantasists, ****-queens and ****-hags and ****-divas of many sorts, word people and music people and picture people and number people, penetration people and cutaneous-contact people, sober folk and delirium-seeking folk, people who 'do' identity and people who 'do' identification, muscle people and inner children, people for whom public space is sexy and people for whom private space is, couples-oriented people and singletons or group-oriented people, and . . . and . . . and . . .

Eve Kosofsky Sedgwick, "Bi," posted to QSTUDY-L@UBVM.cc.buffalo.edu., 17 August 1994.

8. My discussion of reading bisexually is indebted to Alexander Doty's discussion of what it means to do "queer" readings: "Of course, an important consideration in all this formal and informal queer cultural work is the intersection of cultural history and the personal history of the reader. It is in this intersection that queers have mapped out the complex and diverse space of their interactions with mass culture." Alexander Doty, *Making Things Perfectly Queer: Interpreting Mass Culture* (Minneapolis: University of Minnesota Press, 1993), 21.

9. I realize that this rhetoric about reading bisexually might work against the difficulty critics have reading Jane Bowles as bisexual, but this is part of the problem. There is no tradition of reading texts bisexually, and often it becomes politically necessary for writers like Bowles to be "claimed" or read as lesbian. I hope that my reading of Bowles as bisexual will open up yet another space for discussion and inclusion within the larger framework of "queer" studies.

10. I do not want to argue here for a kind of identity politics that supports the view that only those who identify with a particular subject position can read and understand or claim certain texts. Rather, I am suggesting that because of the fluid nature of bisexuality it has been difficult for some people, including those identified as bisexuals, to read a bisexual text without trying to think of it within current hegemonic terms. I would argue that this is one reason that there are very few texts which can be talked about and identified as bisexual. What is inherently different in reading as a bisexual (but similar to other kinds of boundary-crossing identities, such as those that are racially or ethnically mixed) is that one is often acutely aware of the ways in which bisexuality crosses boundaries.

11. My own experience as a bisexual woman is a constant negotiation between heterosexual and lesbian relationships and communities. Men tend to see bisexuality as a turn-on and women tend to find it a turn-off. As a result I often feel forced to play the "game" of passing, depending on which community or relationship I am in. Moreover, because of heterosexist assumptions that the world is entirely heterosexual, I most often embody the dangerous position of privilege as a heterosexual woman, or at least the world at large perceives me that way. Kate Bornstein offers a very smart and witty discussion of her own (both dangerous and pleasurable) experiences of passing as a transgendered person in *Gender Outlaw: On Men, Women, and the Rest of Us* (New York: Routledge, 1994).

12. Millicent Dillon, *A Little Original Sin: The Life and Works of Jane Bowles* (New York: Anchor Books, 1990), 117.

13. Lisa Maria Hogeland, "Fear of Feminism," *Ms.* 5.3 (November/December 1994): 18–21.

14. Dillon notes that the manuscript originally contained material which can now be read as three separate short stories: "A Guatemalan Idyll," "A Day in the Open," and "Señorita Córdoba." Jane cut these sections from the manuscript at Paul's suggestion. See Dillon, *A Little Original Sin*, 107. It is interesting to think about how these

stories would fit into the already fragmented manuscript of *Two Serious Ladies*. The stories as they stand now reveal Bowles's continuing exploration of female sexuality; in them she plays with the stereotype of the female temptress. They appear in Jane Bowles, *Everything Is Nice: The Collected Stories* (London: Virago Press, 1989). Also see *The Portable Paul and Jane Bowles*, ed. Millicent Dillon (New York: Penguin, 1994).

15. In her 1978 introduction to the novel, Francine du Plessix Gray characterizes Bowles's characters as asexual spinsters. Gray notes: "Mrs. Bowles' acerbic genius for the *outré* does not leave it any grounds for comparison with Radclyffe Hall's sentimental tale [*The Well of Loneliness*]. Neither are her heroines' precipitous declines caused by any preference for lesbianism, for they seem as asexual as they are independent and nomadic, turning to the flesh as a symbol of independence without appearing to enjoy one moment of it." It is precisely this kind of thinking that leads bisexuality to fall into a space of exclusion, since there is no history of reading bisexual relationships in literature.

16. I want to be clear here that this jealousy is not inherently different from jealousy people might experience in exclusively hetero- or homosexual relationships. However, I do think that bisexuality automatically evokes the threat of uncommitted relationships, which often leads to hurt feelings. The way Bowles sets up the relationship between Mr. and Mrs. Copperfield as a parallel to Miss Gamelon and Miss Goering makes room for the possibility of exploring bisexuality. Paul says of his wife that "she was always worried about choice," be it choices for sexuality, identity, or work. Dillon, *A Little Original Sin*, 119. Dillon reveals that both Helvetia and Paul had to contend with Jane's promiscuity and their accompanying jealousy: "Helvetia had reason to be jealous of Jane. During the time that Jane was with Helvetia—as well as before and after—Jane apparently had many brief affairs with other women." Dillon, *A Little Original Sin*, 126. The choices Jane Bowles was most interested in were ones that deviated from the "norm." Her own nonmonogamous marriage and other partnerships, such as the ones she translates into her novel, are a way for her to discover what variations on "traditional" marriages or unions would look like. Still, regardless of Jane's, Paul's, or Helvetia's desires, all three had to contend with jealousy. The push and pull of desire and jealousy are a force that bisexuals and their lovers especially have difficulty escaping. But the passion bisexual women feel for both male and female bodies is not so strong that it keeps bisexuals from living in a monogamous relationship; many can and do. Living and writing about the complexities and difficulties of bisexuality, though, is still largely unmarked territory. Jane Bowles was aware that she could not choose between her attractions to Helvetia and to Paul, attractions that were, in both cases, emotional, physical, and intellectual.

17. Dillon, *A Little Original Sin*, 104.

18. I do not see bisexual relationships as necessarily open. I do, however, think that a nonmonogamous, open relationship is the kind of bisexual subjectivity Bowles attempts to construct in *Two Serious Ladies*.

19. In fact, in most of her work on Bowles, Dillon categorizes her as either heterosexual or lesbian (depending on which of her relationships is under discussion) but does not complicate that binary opposition by talking about Bowles as specifically

bisexual. This is most significant since Jane Bowles is largely remembered as Paul
Bowles's wife rather than as a person or writer in her own right. Her marriage overshadows not only her work but her other relationships, most notably with women.

20.   In his article "Jane Bowles' Other World," Andrew Lakritz reads Bowles's *Two
Serious Ladies* as an exploration of the radical nature of Christina Goering as a
spinster and attempts to deconstruct other female stereotypes in *Two Serious
Ladies*. Bowles defies such stereotypes and characterizations in her depiction of
Goering, who chooses not to marry so that she may lead a sexually, socially, and
economically free life. Andrew Lakritz, "Jane Bowles' Other World," in *Old Maids to
Radical Spinsters: Unmarried Women in the Twentieth-Century Novel*, ed. Laura L.
Doan (Urbana: University of Illinois Press, 1991), 213–234.

21.   I realize that in terms of pedagogy and scholarship it is problematic to break down
binaries to the extent that there is no way to classify a writer like Bowles because
she fits everywhere and nowhere at the same time. That is, by further problematizing her writing and not placing it within a "working" literary canon, Bowles's
exclusion from any canon is further perpetuated.

22.   Garber, *Vice Versa*, 407; emphasis mine.

23.   Lillian Faderman, *Odd Girls and Twilight Lovers: A History of Lesbian Life in
Twentieth-Century America* (New York: Penguin, 1992), 177. I am intrigued by the
fact that Faderman includes the Bowleses under her section which discusses kikis.
Kikis are lesbians who switch between butch and femme subject positions—but I
think the suggestion of other kinds of switching, (i.e., from male to female partners)
might be implied merely by including the Bowleses at this juncture in Faderman's
study. It should also be noted that in her introduction to her remarkable compila-
tion of lesbian literature, Faderman reconsiders Jane Bowles as a bisexual, not as a
lesbian in a bisexual compromise. See Lillian Faderman, *Chloe plus Olivia: An
Anthology of Lesbian Literature from the Seventeenth Century to the Present* (New
York: Viking, 1994).

24.   Jane and Paul married in February 1938, and Jane decided to cease having sexual
relations with him in the spring of 1940. Later that summer she met her first long-
term woman lover, Helvetia Perkins. After two years she and Perkins no longer had
sexual relations, although they were still attached. The same pattern appeared in
Jane's relationship with Cherifa, her other long-term lesbian lover. It is not clear
from her biography whether it was Jane or her partner who broke off sexual relations in either of these relationships. See Dillon, *A Little Original Sin*, 80, 274.

25.   In fact, when they first met in 1937, Jane and Paul discussed their desires to only
live nonmonogamous and bisexual lives: "They talked of their affairs. He had had
affairs with men and women, she only with women. They talked of marriage, of
their ideal of a marriage, and agreed that no marriage was any good unless both
partners were free." Dillon, *A Little Original Sin*, 43. Unfortunately, Paul had more
difficulty than Jane in practicing their original plan, and both Jane and Paul
became jealous when one partner went off with another lover. There was no way to
escape the hurt feelings that accompany such a state of freedom. Dillon reveals that
when Paul began his relationship with Ahmed Yacoubi, Jane became jealous and
hurt: "Though Jane and Paul had long ago chosen to have separate sexual lives,
Jane was not prepared for either the intensity or duration of Paul's relationship

with Ahmed. Ahmed Yacoubi wants it made clear that his relationship to Paul was not a sexual one. But what was important to Jane was the intensity of Paul's feeling for Ahmed and of his involvement in his creative work. Even now she did not speak of her jealousy to Paul directly." Dillon, *A Little Original Sin,* 223.

26. In some ways this is reminiscent of Radclyffe Hall's notion of "three selves." See Radclyffe Hall, *The Well of Loneliness* (New York: Anchor Books, 1990).

27. "Boston marriage" was a term "used in late nineteenth-century New England to describe a long-term monogamous relationship between two otherwise unmarried women." Lillian Faderman, *Surpassing the Love of Men: Romantic Friendship and Love between Women from the Renaissance to the Present* (New York: Morrow, 1981), 190. I apply this term to Miss Goering and Miss Gamelon's relationship for two reasons. Bowles writes in a style reminiscent of nineteenth-century sentimental fiction. While she does write a sexually explicit narrative, she does not provide detailed bedroom scenes. By bringing Miss Gamelon and Miss Goering together as life-partners in a kind of Boston marriage, Bowles parallels Miss Goering with Mrs. Copperfield. This move shows that bisexuals can have lifelong supportive partnerships with men or women and still wish to digress sexually at one time or another. Also, the implicit model of the Boston marriage further complicates any notion of Goering or Gamelon as spinsters, because they are attached in a committed union to one another.

28. Jane Bowles, *Two Serious Ladies* (London: Virago Press, 1979), 11. Future references will be made parenthetically within the text.

29. Both Jane and Paul Bowles's writing is heavily problematic in its representations of colonialist relationships and colonialism in general. For a study of tourist culture, see Dean MacCannell, *Empty Meeting Grounds: The Tourist Papers* (New York: Routledge, 1992). To my knowledge there are no studies, at this point in time, that deal with the intersection of (post)colonialism and sexuality (let alone queer sexuality). However, there is one anthology that deals with sexuality and national identity. *Nationalisms and Sexualities,* ed. Andrew Parker, Mary Russo, Doris Sommer, and Patricia Yaeger (New York: Routledge, 1992). Some of the essays in this collection deal with (post)colonialism as well.

30. Gayatri Chakravorty Spivak offers a Marxist critique of capitalism and the ways in which workers, like Pacifica, are ignored and silenced:

The invocation of *the* worker's struggle is baleful in its very innocence; it is incapable of dealing with global capitalism: the subject-production of worker and unemployed within nation-state ideologies in its Center; the increasing subtraction of the working class in the Periphery from the realization of surplus value and thus from 'humanistic' training in consumerism; and the large-scale presence of paracapitalist labor as well as heterogeneous structural status of agriculture in the Periphery.

See Gayatri Chakravorty Spivak, "Can the Subaltern Speak?" in *Marxism and the Interpretation of Culture,* ed. Cary Nelson and Lawrence Grossberg (Urbana: University of Illinois Press, 1988), 272.

31. See Sara Mills, *Discourses of Difference: An Analysis of Women's Travel Writing and Colonialism* (New York: Routledge, 1992). Mills offers a critique of the colonialist

nature of tourism, dwelling especially on the writings of white women who travel and record their experiences with "native others."

32.　Interestingly, Mrs. Copperfield's relationship with Pacifica seems to anticipate Jane's relationship with Cherifa, who was interested in Jane sexually, personally, and emotionally but who, according to Dillon, also extorted money from her throughout most of their time together: "For years Paul had warned Jane that Cherifa was stealing money." Dillon, *A Little Original Sin*, 395. Like Mrs. Copperfield's relationship with Pacifica, the desire between Jane and Cherifa was troubled by complicated issues of race and class differences. Cherifa was a working-class Moroccan woman who was primarily dependent upon Jane for money, so Dillon's claim that Cherifa "stole" money from Jane is highly problematic in and of itself, regardless of the sexual-colonialist aspect of their relationship.

33.　Paul Bowles works through these issues of bisexuality, jealousy, and desire in his story "Call at Corazón," in *The Delicate Prey and Other Stories* (New York: Random House, 1950).

34.　Dillon, *A Little Original Sin*, 111.

Chapter 7

Versatile Interests: Reading Bisexuality in *The Friendly Young Ladies*

Erin G. Carlston

"Your sister's interests seem remarkably versatile."
"Yes, Leo's interested in all sorts of queer things."
—Mary Renault, *The Friendly Young Ladies*

$\mathbf{I}$n this essay, I will read Mary Renault's 1944 novel *The Friendly Young Ladies* (first published in the U.S. as *The Middle Mist*) not, as it has usually been inter-preted, as a story of failed lesbian love, but as a theorization of bisexuality that chal-lenges the dominant medical and literary discourses on homosexuality in its time.[1] The novel—in which a woman, Leo Lane, eventually leaves her lover Helen for a man, Joe—seems to stage what Terry Castle has named the classic "dysphoric" lesbian plot.[2] But at the same time, the text undermines that plot by indicating that lesbianism, far from being a temporary phase *en route* to heterosexuality, may be the final and most satisfying choice in a life of fully realized bisexuality.

I should note that I use "bisexuality" here as Renault does, to refer both to object choice and, as was more common in the 1940s, to gender identity. The two concepts had become firmly associated by the time Renault wrote *The Friendly Young Ladies*, so that same-sex object choice was thought usually to result from a gender identity "inverted" by congenital defect or psychological disorder. Part of Renault's project in this novel is to untwine the two, and then to disassociate both from any simplistic theory of physiological or psychological causality. In *The Friendly Young Ladies*, Renault suggests instead that both gender identity and object choice are fluid and unstable constructs which may change throughout a lifetime.

In so doing, she rewrites the implicitly homophobic narrative underlying discourses on (bi)sexuality in both her time and ours, a narrative governed by the belief that heterosexuality is so irresistibly hegemonic that anyone who *can* "choose" heterosexual relations *will*, always, and for the rest of her life. By insisting on the versatility of sexual identity and desire, Renault does not trivialize same-sex relations nor privilege a heterosexist account of normative sexual development; on the contrary, she challenges our assumption that there must be a fatal teleology to Leo's foray into heterosexuality. The end of the book, she implies, does not have to be the end of the story.

* * *

Terry Castle, who has written one of the few critical analyses of *The Friendly Young Ladies*, claims that the lesbian text "is likely to stand in a satirical, inverted or parodic relationship to more famous novels of the past—which is to say that it will exhibit an ambition to displace the so-called canonical works which have preceded it" (90). And *The Friendly Young Ladies* does self-consciously insert itself into a tradition of literary treatments of lesbianism, implicitly alluding to texts like James's *The Bostonians* and Proust's *Remembrance of Things Past*. (Its original packaging, considerably less highbrow than the text, also helped to associate it with contemporary pulp fiction; I have in my possession a 1945 paperback edition of *The Middle Mist*, its lurid cover and titillating blurb clearly identifying it with innumerable lesbian-themed dime novels of the era.)

Its crucial points of literary reference are, however, as Renault herself reveals in the afterword to the 1984 Pantheon edition, Radclyffe Hall's *The Well of Loneliness* and Compton Mackenzie's *Extraordinary Women*, both published in 1928. *The Friendly Young Ladies* certainly stands in parodic and inverted relationship to the canonical lesbian text of the twentieth century, *The Well*, which it explicitly recalls in plot structure, specific allusions, and references to medical models. And, like *Extraordinary Women*, *The Friendly Young Ladies* is a comedy of manners, deftly using satire to challenge both Hall's acceptance of the theory of "congenitalism" and Freudian theories that posit lesbianism as an immature stage of psychosexual development.

It must be acknowledged from the outset that *Friendly Young Ladies* is a "versatile" text that eludes monovalent interpretations of its political import. Radclyffe Hall's earnest polemic and adherence to the realist conventions of the nineteenth-century novel demanded—and got—serious attention to, if not always sympathy for, her subject. In contrast, Renault's novel, like Mackenzie's, can seem, as Castle claims, "evasive" in its treatment of sexuality; the bisexual text is apparently as untrustworthy in its indeterminacy as "the unfair, unaccountable sitter-on-the-fence," the bisexual woman (Renault, *The Friendly Young Ladies*, 142). Just as it is difficult to categorize the bisexual's versatile interests, to know exactly where she stands or what she wants, so it is difficult to "pin down" the point of Renault's ironic prose, hard always to know what and who is being mocked. Certainly the comedic genre permits us to take its subject matter lightly if we wish; lesbianism, in both *Extraordinary Women* and *The Friendly Young Ladies*, can be dismissed as a comic diversion by the (heterosexist) reader sufficiently determined to do so.

Furthermore, such a reading of *The Friendly Young Ladies* may seem to be encouraged by the centrality in the text of images of water and boats, especially the houseboat Leo and Helen live in: the river, and the boats on it, are constantly in flux, unstable, impermanent. Boats can be taken as a symbol of the insularity and instability of the homosexual relationship; the houseboat is always in danger of sinking, for example, so the bilge has to be pumped out constantly. Or again, there is the scene in which Leo sets out to seduce Norah, the girlfriend of a young medical student who has been toying with the affections of her younger sister Elsie. Renault writes that after an evening of flirtation, during which Leo triumphantly carries Norah off in a canoe, "Norah found that, as after a moderate indulgence in champagne, little remained behind except a general impression that one had been unusually witty and charming, together with a feeling of light-hearted sophistication and no harm done. And indeed, anything that happens in a light canoe, even when moored, must needs be moderate enough" (197). Is lesbianism, then, merely a token of "light-hearted sophistication," one of the water sports in which these bisexual bohemians indulge—in moderation—until they can return to the terra firma of heterosexuality? Certainly the conclusion, when Leo abandons the houseboat, under which the piles are giving way, for Joe's "perfectly solid" island home, encourages such a reading.

But the text also allows, and indeed points the way to, alternative readings. In particular, its satirical inversion of elements from *The Well* makes same-sex relationships look far more appealing, especially in comparison to heterosexual ones, than does Hall's novel. Like *The Well*, for example, *The Friendly Young Ladies* opens with the portrait of a marriage, the Lanes'; in contrast to Hall's idealization of Sir Philip and Anna Gordon's marriage, however, *The Friendly Young Ladies* offers a scathing depiction of an acutely dysfunctional nuclear family. In *The Well*, it is the strange child, Stephen, who troubles her parents' marital bliss; in *The Friendly Young Ladies*, it is the parents who make their children's lives unbearable.

The Lanes loathe each other and are well on their way to destroying their daughter Elsie's physical and mental health by using her as a pawn in their domestic cold war. The elder daughter, Leo, has fled the family ten years before the action of the novel begins, escaping to what Mr. Lane cryptically calls the "*demi-monde*," much to Elsie's mystification. Finally, unable to tolerate the misery of life at home, Elsie runs away as well and goes in search of her sister, whom she finds living, not with A Man, as she had supposed, but with a lovely young woman. From the moment Elsie arrives on the houseboat, the harmony of Leo and Helen's relationship is explicitly compared to the discord of the Lanes'. There is, for example, a strong emphasis on the reciprocity of Leo and Helen's domestic arrangements; in contrast to the rigid division of space and labor in the Lanes' marriage, Leo and Helen share both a bed and the household chores. Furthermore, they rarely quarrel:

Leo and Helen talked, in the loose disjointed way that arises between people each of whom knows that the other will have picked up the meaning before the sentence is half finished. The very fact that [Elsie] could not follow half they said was curiously soothing; no explanations hammered home, no patient re-statements, no trembling verge of exasperation; only a kind of lazy shorthand.... Down in the midst of the boat were voices, soft and intermittent, which did not argue or contend, like the voices at home, but went on, evenly and mysteriously, and ceased, and began again. (66, 71)

Some readers may complain of the apparent lack of commitment between Leo and Helen, whose relationship seems to be casually nonmonogamous as well as, finally, unstable. But the flexibility of their attachment must be read against the contempt with which marital "commitment" is treated in the text. Marriage is depicted as a stifling, oppressive relation of hostility and frustration, the unhappy result of the fantasies of romance on which Mrs. Lane and Elsie feed. When Helen says to the medical student, Peter Bracknell, "Anyone would think, to hear you talk, that we were a married couple," she is not trivializing her relation with Leo but contrasting it with the constricting bonds of marriage. "I keep telling you," she says in the same paragraph, "we live together because we enjoy it" (218). Marriage, it seems, is incompatible with pleasure.

Indeed, heterosexual relations in general are treated with derision in the novel. Besides the Lanes, we have the example of Peter and Norah, whose relationship consists of manipulative patronization on his part and quiet resentment on hers. Leo's and Helen's flirtations or affairs with men, furthermore, are obviously a trivial amusement to them, so unthreatening that they laughingly compare notes after dates with other people. And watching a stage version of *Façade*, Leo thinks to herself that the Dago "epitomized what seemed to her the more comic aspects of the heterosexual scene" (210). This is, incidentally, the only time a word denoting sexual preference is ever used in the text. Renault thus calls attention to *heterosexuality* as the oddity, the other that must be named because it is not, like the relationship between Leo and Helen, taken for granted. ("Has something rather unusual struck you about us?" Helen asks Leo. "Not for several years," she retorts [146].)

Of all the central heterosexual figures in the novel, only Joe and his lover are portrayed with respect, and this is precisely because their relation is *not* a domesticated or conventional one. When Helen asks Leo why the two have not married, Leo responds, "Ask him, why don't you? It could be that he picked a woman who isn't half-witted" (134). Whereas Hall portrays a world of happy heterosexuals from which Stephen Gordon is cruelly excluded, Renault attacks institutionalized heterosexuality, asking whether anyone not "half-witted" would really aspire to such a peculiar state. In this context, the emphasis on water and boat imagery in her text can be interpreted positively, as an indication that good relationships are always fluid, versatile, in contrast to the fixed conventionality associated in the novel with urban living and heterosexual marriage.

Renault also takes on another of Radclyffe Hall's sacred cows, the medical establishment, which Renault embodies in the pompous and shortsighted character of Peter Bracknell. In the course of the novel Peter rehearses most of the prevailing theories of homosexuality of the day, pointing up their fatuousness by his own. Whether mouthing the theories of proponents of "congenitalism," like Hall's mentor Havelock Ellis, or of Freudian psychoanalysts, Peter and the medical authority he represents are always made to look ridiculous—as when he thinks, in response to a comment of Leo's, "Boathook. Drowning. He knew his Freud. A highly significant choice of symbols and, obviously, unconscious. The first thing was to crack this defensive shell, and then the possibilities were really fruitful. A forgiving, understanding warmth irradiated him" (176).

Peter believes that he can, like Basil in *The Bostonians* or Martin in *The Well*, intervene in and "cure" the lesbian relation between Leo and Helen and sets about to seduce them both in turn. But, unhappily for Peter, both Helen and Leo persistently refuse images of themselves as afflicted or pathological, baffling his well-meaning attempts to diagnose and treat them. And the reader's faith, though not Peter's, in the efficacy of his medical and amorous skills is soon dampened by Helen and Leo's sardonic amusement at his efforts. As a further jab at his presumptuousness, moreover, Leo seduces his girlfriend much more successfully than he seduces hers, suggesting that lesbianism is perhaps rather more attractive, and heterosexuality less, than Henry James or Radclyffe Hall would have allowed.

Peter's self-righteous faith in his own normality—and superiority—typifies the oppressiveness of a medical discourse that defines the "healthy" as the "average." If comical, this discourse can also be genuinely dangerous; some of the objects of Peter's attentions, less savvy than Leo and Helen, have been really harmed by his meddling. The medical model in which he places such faith is, after all, a fiction: Helen eventually says to him in exasperation, "I think you must have read a lot of novels, or something. People don't live that way." "The way people live," her lesbian relationship, is, on the other hand, a fact; one of the "facts of life" that Helen and Joe, certainly the healthiest characters in the novel, accept with tranquillity and that everyone else is at such pains to avoid.

Elsie, for example, thinks of "the facts of life" as "frightful," "appalling," "the horrible secret" (10). It is made very clear that fear of sexuality, both hetero- *and* homosexual, is a major factor in the (mal)functioning of the Lane family. Mrs. Lane warns Elsie constantly of "the threat of rape and seduction," especially by women (11). Later, Elsie's attempts to read Shakespeare founder when she encounters his bi-erotic sonnets; her inability to countenance bisexuality is characteristic of the refusal of reality associated with the Lanes' naive and repressive attitudes toward sexuality (184).

Furthermore, Leo, the lavender sheep of the Lane family, has simply inverted their horror of (homo)sexuality in her crippling fear of heterosexual relations and of her own, female, body, participating in the same unhealthy repression of sexual realities in which her family engages. When she is too embarrassed to admit to Joe that she is feeling unwell because of her period, for example, she overexerts herself and gets really ill. Putting her to bed, Helen snaps at her, "It isn't 1890.... I don't know what you've noticed in [Joe's] books, or his conversation either, to make you think his mother didn't instruct him in the facts of life," and Leo sulkily replies, "There are times ... when the facts of life strike me as so damned silly I stop believing in them" (117).

Renault appears to treat gender inversion or dysphoria unsympathetically here, as an unhealthy evasion of reality: Leo's refusal to accommodate the facts of her female body is literally making her sick. Leo conforms, to a certain extent, to the conventional depiction of the "third sex," the stereotype of the congenital female invert as a man trapped in a woman's body, and hence almost inevitably troubled and confused. Only in Leo's friendship with Joe is she temporarily free of the dissonance between boyish psyche and female body: with Joe, Leo finds "the company of her kind; freely and simply, without the destructive bias of sexual attraction or rejection, he let her be what her mind had made her and her body refused" (164).

Yet Renault's depiction of inversion is ambiguous: if Leo's refusal of femaleness is problematic, for example, her tomboyishness is also charming and seductive, to other women, to some men, and—dare I say—to the reader.[3] Like Stephen Gordon, Leo has the slim-hipped body of a boy, but her body is eroticized in Renault's text in a way Stephen's is not in *The Well*, its supple sensuality constantly emphasized. Furthermore, Renault complicates the notion of inversion as a physical condition fixed by congenital predisposition. Leo bears less resemblance to the monstrous invert of the medical imagination, in fact, than to the fascinating androgyne of the classical imagination.

She has, for instance, the ability to switch gender identities at will; it would be unimaginable for Stephen Gordon, or Rory Freemantle in *Extraordinary Women,* to appear in a convincingly sexy "female manifestation," as Leo does when she puts on a dress and high heels for a party. For Leo, assuming female gender is neither instinctive habit nor an unnatural impossibility, but rather a conscious acting out of one aspect of her identity; as she tells Elsie, "It's me . . . up to a point" (123; my ellipses). When Elsie asks her to put the dress back on to impress Peter, on the other hand, Leo is incredulous; she stages her femininity entirely for her own entertainment and only when the fancy takes her. "It's all right for a minute," she says. "I soon get bored with it" (130).

Leo is equally self-conscious, we note, when presenting herself as a butch; when she sets out to seduce Norah, her tailored costume and masculine mannerisms are even more deliberately theatrical than the red frock she dons as a femme. Whether playing the mannish woman or the femme fatale, Leo treats gendered roles as stage acts. Renault thus moves the question of gender identity out of the realm of biology, and into the realm of the theatrical, the performative. If a "born invert"—Leo has been a tomboy since early childhood—she has nonetheless learned to play an enchantingly wide range of variations on the theme of gender, and this is an essential part of her depth and appeal as a character.

It would seem to be implied, then, that Leo's real problem is not that she is an invert. Instead, it is repeatedly suggested that Leo is deeply conflicted about men, attracted to them but terrified of having sexual relations with them. Leo's body is scarred, like Stephen Gordon's. But where Stephen's scar is the mark of Cain, the symptom of an immutable physical difference that sets her apart from society, Leo's signals her psychic wounds, the sexual fear of men that apparently has resulted from a traumatic sexual initiation and that remains "something one hasn't got the guts to face" (95).

That women turn to lesbianism after traumatic experiences with men is of course a particularly noxious cliché. But it is not Renault's point; she makes that much quite clear by putting this theory in the benighted Peter's mouth, and then having Helen shoot it down, as we will see in a moment. If we acknowledge that one can be sexually attracted to members of both sexes, then we do not have to assume that Leo's sexual conflicts with men have anything to do with her desire for women. It is true that her ambivalence about men *affects* her relationship with Helen (which is not the same thing as causing it), because until she has dealt with her contrary feelings about heterosexual relations, she will not know whether her lesbianism is a kind of avoidance strategy or a genuine preference. Helen reflects that being involved with Leo is "like keeping a wild bird that loves you because it's got a broken wing. If the wing knits up, then you know; one way or another. That would be something real, one could bear that. But to watch this trying and falling down again, each time it's as bad as before, it hurts both ways" (255).

In order to heal her "broken wing," her psychic wounds, it is implied that Leo needs to come to terms with both sides of her dual nature: not necessarily to "become heterosexual," but to embrace the full range of roles available to her in the theater of gender, to explore her interests "in all sorts of queer things." If Renault had been able to carry through with this line to the novel's end, *The Friendly Young Ladies* would stand as a truly remarkable defense of bisexuality. Instead, however, she seems to back away from this rich and subtle treatment of sexuality at *The Friendly Young Ladies's* conclusion. When Leo's relationship with Joe becomes sexual, object choice and gender identity are suddenly reconflated, and heterosexual desire made mysteriously incompatible with both inverted gender identity and same-sex attraction. For no obvious reason, Leo's sexual attraction to Joe kills both the boy Leo was and "his" relationship with the woman "he" loved.

Castle offers one reading of this puzzling finale, arguing that Renault is enacting the "spectralizing" gesture that, in Castle's analysis, signals the "recognition through negation" that has characterized Western culture's reaction to female homosexuality since the Enlightenment (60). The ghost of Leo's boyhood, floating rather melodramatically about the ceiling of Joe's house, points (back) at the unnamed sexual intimacy between Leo and Helen, acknowledged only in the moment that it is replaced by the far more concretely described physical passion between Leo and Joe. Castle writes, with considerable justice, that "[e]ncircled by her male lover, blocked off from her own narrative past, Leo the lesbian becomes Leo the ghost: incapable of speech ... incapable of protest, incapable of retrieving an otherwise sophisticated novel from its own surprisingly crushing final banality" (42; my ellipses).

It is less as an emendation of Castle's reading than as a supplement to it that I wish to point out that there is another erotic configuration yet more spectral, more erased by Leo's final capitulation, than female homosexuality. The term that remains entirely unnamed in the text's shifting triangles is that of *male* homosexuality, the erotic bond that must be suppressed in order to enable both Leo and Joe's homo*social* camaraderie and their hetero*sexual* passion.

Eve Sedgwick has argued in *Between Men* that, in the conventionally triangulated plot of Western fiction, shared erotic interest in a woman is a pretext for the affective male bond; the female term is necessary to mediate what might otherwise become a sexual relation between two men.[4] Castle reformulates Sedgwick's paradigm to argue that in the lesbian counterplot, it is the male term between two women that must "drop out" in order to enable the female homoerotic relationship.

Not surprisingly, *The Friendly Young Ladies*, with its multiple, shifting and bisexual erotic triangulations, seems to put both of these paradigms into play; men "come between" women, but women also "come between" men. Peter intervenes between Helen and Leo; Leo intervenes between Peter and Norah; Elsie blunders unwittingly through a number of triangles. Leo also becomes an object of desire for both Peter and Joe, who only meet because of their common interest in her. But rather than developing a homosocial bond, the men dislike each other intensely, their sexual desire for Leo intensified—in Joe's case, precipitated—by their mutual jealousy. In the end, just before Joe seduces Leo, in the garden where she has been kissing Peter goodnight, she *does* in fact "drop out" of the triangle and Joe's line of vision, leaving Peter as the only object, not of Joe's desire, but of his hostility. Or rather, in a scene where violence and desire become interchangeable terms, Leo and Peter also become interchangeable objects of an aggressiveness that embraces both emotions. Watching Peter retreat down the path, Joe thinks, "It could take only a moment or two to catch him up and knock him into the river; and, during the moment of his disappearance, Leo, standing between, scarcely existed for Joe except as the most evident obstacle to this. Then, suddenly, Peter was gone, and there was only Leo to see" (236).

With Leo thus substituted for Peter as the sole object of Joe's furious/desiring gaze, Joe takes the obvious course of action: he beds her. But if Peter, as original object of Joe's passion (for violence), posed an implicit threat to his heterosexuality, as Sedgwick's theory suggests, then Leo is hardly a safer object choice; for Leo, as we well know by this point in the text, is, psychically, a boy. Earlier in the novel, Helen asks Leo why she hasn't slept with Joe, with whom she is obviously so comfortable. Shocked, Leo says of the idea that "It's—it's indecent." What is indecent, apparently, is the specter of male homosexuality that would haunt any erotic relation between Joe and Leo in her "male manifestation." Just before seducing Leo, Joe thinks with regret that she has been "a good friend, too, as straight as a man" (235). If Leo remains "as straight as a man"—an invert—then Joe cannot go to bed with her and remain "as straight as a man" himself. To safeguard Joe's heterosexuality, Leo must become a woman, a role into which she has literally to be beaten: the two chase each other through the water until Joe punches Leo in the jaw to stop her from struggling and drowning.

It is Leo, then, instead of Peter, who gets knocked into the river; the passionate violence that—when directed toward Peter—threatened to emasculate Joe instead emasculates Leo. She wakes after a night in Joe's arms emotionally troubled, sexually sated—and severely bruised. The "crushing banality" of this scene lies less, perhaps, in the heterosexual romance itself than in the fact that that romance seems to be defined in the most retrograde terms, as an essentially sadomasochistic relation of masculine domination and feminine submissiveness. It does not lessen the distastefulness of this episode to claim that the point here is less about *making* Leo straight than about *keeping* Joe straight; indeed, one has come to depend on the other.

While deploring this conclusion—Renault herself acknowledged "the silliness of the ending" in her afterword—we can speculate, as one always must, about the influence that considerations of audience, fear of censorship, or personal ambivalence may have had over the author's decision to end the novel in this way.[5] More importantly, we should also acknowledge that numerous ambiguities in the text indicate a degree of authorial uncertainty about the desirability of Leo's final transformation.

When Elsie is reading Shakespeare, for example, she finds a scrap of paper on which Leo has copied part of Sonnet 144 (185). Only the couplet is quoted, but the reader is likely to know that this poem, which obviously reflects Leo's struggles with her own bisexuality, describes the conflict between the poet's "good," male angel and his "bad," female angel; the angels represent both male and female lovers of the poet and masculine and feminine aspects of his own person. The couplet that Leo copies out concludes, "Yet this I ne'er shall know, but live in doubt,/Till my bad angel fire my good one out," anticipating the novel's conclusion and suggesting that, if Leo's feminine persona is her "bad angel," then its final triumph is not necessarily cause for celebration.

More subjectively, one could also assert that Leo seems a much more attractive character, as well as a more convincing one, before she turns from boy into woman. Arguably, the real "ghost" at the novel's end is not Leo the lesbian but Leo the heterosexual: she may overcome her gender dysphoria, but rather than becoming a powerful femme like Helen, or an elegant switch, as she was in her previous appearance in female drag, she turns into a spectral, hollow-eyed, nervous wreck. Heterosexuality, it seems, is hazardous to Leo's health; it is difficult to believe we are intended to think that this haggard wraith is an improvement on the charming and sensuous tomboy. But then the new Leo is scarcely fleshed out at all, as the novel ends within a couple of pages after her transformation. It is as if her creator lost (sexual) interest in her after turning her into a nominally heterosexual woman and quickly abandoned her, unable to sustain any further examination of such a lackluster creature.

Finally, we ought to be cautious about reading the novel's ending in the conventional and antilesbian terms that structure the heterosexist masterplot of novels like *The Bostonians*. As I have already suggested, the most obvious reductive and homophobic reactions to female bisexuality are voiced by Peter long before Leo sleeps with Joe, which is surely a signal to the reader not to interpret their affair in the same terms. It is Peter, for example, who muses about Leo, "Eccentricity in women always boiled down to the same thing. She wanted a man" (222). Yet Leo does *not* want "a" man; she certainly does not want Peter. She falls in love with a particular man who, unlike Peter, treats both her relationship with Helen and her gender identity with great respect. Even after the author has apparently killed off Leo's masculine persona (and, implicitly, her lesbianism), Joe still takes them very seriously—and Joe is, as Renault admits in the afterword, the smartest person in the novel. It is Joe, in fact, who leaves us with the narrative's "final word" about the complexity and richness of sexuality, suggesting that Leo's gender switch may not be, and perhaps should not be, permanent: "I can't tell how much he [her male side] means to you," Joe writes to Leo. "Perhaps, ultimately, he is you, and has the immortal part of you in his keeping. Only you can know, and even you may not be sure. It is the fashion to find in such things a casual product of cells and environment, or a disorder to be cured. I think their roots may go as deep as the soul" (275).

Joe's letter, and Leo's reaction to it, actually leave us in some doubt as to whether she will really accompany him to Arizona. After all, the last image we are given is not that of Leo flinging herself happily into Joe's arms but of Leo weeping alone over one of Helen's fragrantly scented dresses. Castle points to the possibility, however improbable, of a "euphoric" resolution to a novel by Sylvia Townsend Warner, arguing that even the realist lesbian text "forfeits plausibility" by the very terms of its subversively unlikely existence (88). Can we not, then, stretch our imaginations to embrace the possibility that Leo stays? Perhaps, we might conjecture, Renault did not show us Leo leaving with Joe because she could not quite bring herself to depict a "happy ending" that wasn't one; the most she could do was gesture in the direction of conventionality, and leave the lesbian reader to imagine the improbable, but far more interesting, alternatives.

All of these points underline ambiguities in the text that allow us to read against the grain of the ending. But there is one explicit theme that, throughout the text, consistently controverts an antilesbian reading of *The Friendly Young Ladies*. Helen's example provides a counterplot that continually interrupts the novel's apparently dysphoric narrative by making it clear that, for the bisexual, heterosexuality can be "just a phase" to be explored on the way to lesbian fulfillment. Helen's importance is subtly suggested to the reader in the passage, early in the novel, where Leo tries to explain to Elsie why she ran away from home and how she is living now. Elsie finally asks, stupidly, who Helen is. "You can't have been listening," Leo says to her in frustration. "That was really the whole point of the story" (89). It is the character of Helen, Renault implies, and not Leo's affair with Joe, that will be "the whole point of the story"; Helen is the pivotal point around which a "bisexual reading" of Renault's novel turns.

Medical models of homosexuality have never been able to account for the woman with a "normal" or non-inverted gender identity but same-sex or inverted object choice. In medical discourse of the 1930s and 40s, it was generally assumed that such a woman had fallen into lesbianism *faute de mieux* or as the result of some trauma with men, and that given the opportunity she would prefer heterosexual relations. Mary in *The Well* is of course one such "normal" woman, but dysphoric lesbian plots are full of them, from Verena Tarrant in *The Bostonians*, to Judith in Rosamund Lehmann's *Dusty Answer*, to Olivia in Dorothy Bussy's *Olivia*—all "feminine" or "non-inverted" women who, after passing through their fascination with or passion for a born invert, return to normalcy, usually leaving their inverted lover doomed to loneliness and/or death.

Renault alone breaks with this gloomy tradition. It is obviously highly significant that it is Leo, the "invert," who leaves with a man and Helen, the "normal" woman, who wishes to stay in the lesbian relationship: Leo, who in another novel would have been congenitally destined for deviance, needs to explore heterosexual relations, whereas Helen, though attracted and attractive to men, freely chooses to love a woman. When Peter trots out the theory that, as a non-inverted woman in a lesbian relationship, Helen must be reacting to some sexual trauma, she responds that—unlike Leo—she has no particular aversion to men or marriage but simply is not interested:

"I suppose I shouldn't ask," [Peter] said, "what has happened to make you afraid of marriage?"

"You can ask if you like. But I'm not afraid of it, so there isn't much point."

"You're young," he said. "You're very pretty; you're domesticated, I imagine, and, forgive my mentioning it, normally sexed. You may want to marry some day; what then?"

"Well, if I wanted to, I should, I suppose." (218)

Anxious to disabuse Peter of his bizarre idea that she must have been wounded by a previous love affair, Helen then goes on to explain to him that living with a man can be oppressive without being traumatic. This is perhaps Renault's most politically radical moment. She attacks the assumption that sexual attraction to men is the only prerequisite for a commitment to heterosexuality, proposing that a woman who is bisexual in her object choice may nonetheless find that women take care of each other, communicate honestly with one another, and nurture each other's work and creativity, whereas men do not do so in their relationships with women. As Helen describes the difficulties of a previous heterosexual affair, we are reminded of the numerous scenes in *The Friendly Young Ladies* depicting the reciprocity of Leo and Helen's relationship, their mutual caretaking: Leo doing Helen's mending, because Helen has been doing hers; Helen teaching Leo to cook; Helen nursing Leo during her period just as, she tells Peter, Leo nurses her. In contrast, her male lover, while very satisfactory in bed,

was just a cad to live with. Things like wanting all the space for his own work and not leaving me any room for mine. Or time. I don't think he liked, really, seeing work at all. I was better at it than he was, that might have been one reason why. Between women, you see, an issue like that is bound to come out straightforwardly, but a man can cover it up for ages. And then, he thought I ought to like his friends but he needn't like mine. If I had a cold or a headache or wasn't feeling bright for the usual sort of reasons, he just used to go out; it never occurred to him to do anything else. Leo isn't any more domesticated than most men, but she isn't above filling you a hot-water bottle and fussing you up a bit. (219)

Helen, then, is completely comfortable with female gender identity and heterosexual desire, but after exploring heterosexuality, has chosen lesbianism for the simple reason that she prefers it, finding it both comfortable and liberating in a way that relations with men are not. In Helen's mind, it is the very fact that she is bisexual in her object choice that guarantees her commitment to Leo; unlike Leo, she is not afraid of sex with men, not fighting some kind of internal battle with her gender identity whose outcome is still uncertain. Having investigated her options, she knows what she wants. "She can be certain of me," Helen muses, "because I'm free. I've gone where I chose, and had what I fancied, and I'm here *because this is better*" (255; my emphasis).

A few pages later, as Helen begins to realize that she is losing Leo, she thinks, "I got all this over before we met each other; if not, I might have been the one" (269). The implication is clearly that "all this," experimentation with heterosexual relations, can be a phase, something to be gotten over; sexual versatility does not have to signal an inevitable progression toward heterosexuality. Helen points the way to the narrative possibilities that lie beyond the text: once Leo has "got all this over," explored a female gender identity and heterosexual object choice, she may well, like Helen, return to lesbianism. Whatever we think of the theory that Leo needs to pursue relations with men in order to progress toward health and wholeness, in light of the portrayal of Helen it is difficult to avoid the inference that the most felicitous conclusion to that process is to end up a radiantly happy, healthy, bisexual lesbian.

The reader who isn't "listening" to the story, who is too focused on *The Friendly Young Ladies*'s ending, may miss the startling point of Helen's presence in the novel. In the history of queer literature, there was no precedent for a character who is fully and unconflictedly bisexual in her object choice and who, with every possibility of returning to "normalcy," cheerfully opts for lesbianism instead, because she prefers it. Those who would consign Renault's text too quickly to the dustheap of "antilesbian lesbian novels" must hesitate when confronted with Helen: who else before the advent of gay liberation dared to say, so explicitly and assuredly, "*this is better*"?

* * *

Both heterosexual and lesbian feminist literary criticism, like heterosexual and lesbian cultures more generally, have usually assumed both that mature sexuality is monovalent, and that once someone's essential gender identity and object choice are established, or revealed, they remain fixed for life. Oddly, lesbian-feminist theory has also tended to share in the heterosexist assumption that heterosexuality is so much more attractive than homosexuality that the bisexual will always, finally, be drawn to straightness; only those with no choice, this argument goes, would choose lesbianism. In these accounts, bisexuality can only represent either an immature stage of sexual development, or a temporary flirtation with deviance; in either case, sexual versatility must eventually be resolved in one direction or the other, whether in life or in books. Thus, in the canonical plots of sexual development, a woman must either move away from unhappy heterosexuality to discover and affirm her essential and immutable lesbianism or give up lesbianism forever to embrace heterosexual normality.

But people, as Helen says, don't live that way. Sexuality can be infinitely more complicated, more flexible, and less categorizable than such theories allow. And accepting that bisexuality of both gender identity and object choice really exists, not as a phase or as an affectation but as an expression of the richness and variability of desire, allows us to approach literary texts with a fresh perspective. The woman who desires men but chooses life with a woman does not have to be tortured, indecisive, and confused; she may be one of the sanest, most self-assured characters in the text. And the lesbian who also comes to love a man, or men, is not necessarily signaling a permanent renunciation of same-sex relations. Reading *The Friendly Young Ladies* as a bisexual text, then, permits us to reinterpret its troubling conclusion and to understand the novel as a powerful, as well as powerfully funny, affirmation of love between women.

* * *

Notes

I would like to thank Terry Castle for the lively discussions that originally inspired this essay, and Marjorie Rosen for her intelligent and insightful help in shaping it.

1. Mary Renault, *The Friendly Young Ladies*, orig. pub. 1944 (New York: Pantheon Books, 1984). The exchange quoted above is on 203.

2. Terry Castle, *The Apparitional Lesbian: Female Homosexuality and Modern Culture* (New York: Columbia University Press, 1993), 85.

3. An interesting, if unscientific, illustration of this point was provided by lesbian and bisexual women students in a course I once taught on the lesbian novel; they enthusiastically judged Leo and Helen the *sexiest* heroines in twentieth century lesbian literature.

4. Eve Kosofsky Sedgwick, *Between Men: English Literature and Male Homosocial Desire* (New York: Columbia University Press, 1985).

5. Given that Renault spent her life with another woman, we may ask, as Castle does, why she never described that experience in her fiction. Castle suggests "that she never attained . . . imaginative freedom . . . regarding female same-sex love," implicitly attributing *The Friendly Young Ladies'* conclusion to internalized homophobia on Renault's part (Castle, 42). She finds further evidence for this in the fact that Renault preferred the "evasive" Mackenzie to Radclyffe Hall. Yet we might equally well ask why Hall painted an almost unmitigatedly gloomy picture of lesbian life when the evidence is that her own lesbian relationships were perfectly happy. The answer has to do, no doubt, with the fact that Renault and Hall had different goals in writing these works and different points to make with them, and that neither text is simply a fictional translation of its author's life. (I would also add, in Renault's defense, that she is probably not the only lesbian ever to have found Mackenzie's campy good humor more relevant to her own experience than Hall's morose self-pity.)

Chapter 8

Invisible Sissy: The Politics of Masculinity in African American Bisexual Narrative

Traci Carroll

After the Egyptian and Indian, the Greek and Roman, the Teuton and Mongolian, the Negro is a sort of seventh son, born with a veil, and gifted with second-sight in this American world—a world which yields him no true self-consciousness, but only lets him see himself through the revelation of the other world. It is a peculiar sensation, this double-consciousness, this sense of always looking at one's self through the eyes of others, of measuring one's soul by the tape of a world that looks on in amused contempt and pity. One ever feels his two-ness—an American, a Negro; two souls, two thoughts, two unreconciled strivings; two warring ideals in one dark body, whose dogged strength alone keeps it from being torn asunder.

—W. E. B. Du Bois

Now even though I hate labels, I still consider myself bisexual. A sexual mulatto.

—E. Lynn Harris

By entitling his first novel *Invisible Life*, E. Lynn Harris invokes Ellison's *Invisible Man* as a metaphor for the African American writer's task of reclaiming manhood, figured in both Du Bois and Ellison as coming out of invisibility and finding a way to see and fully recognize oneself. The metaphor of invisibility recalls the Du Boisian bind of seeing oneself as a refracted image but never as a fully self-present subject.[1] As the political obstacle perhaps most frequently claimed by bisexuals, invisibility is also an important term in Harris's exploration of sexual identity. By filtering bisexual experience through the generic conventions of the passing novel, Harris's novels expand the definition of masculinity to include bisexual practice at the same time that they explore the difficulties of defining bisexuality as a mode of sexual and political identification. The concept of passing links African American and gay literary traditions through their common reliance upon the notion of a fundamental, unitary identity, a truth whose denial offers myriad social benefits at the cost of political compromise and constant fear of exposure. Harris refers to a spiritual of the same name in the title of his second novel, *Just As I Am*, in order to suggest how the internal tension in bisexual identity creates generic challenges for the passing novel, precisely because bisexuality complicates the prospect of full self-definition and self-knowledge: the bisexual subject can never know when he is and is not passing, what it means to be "just as I am." Harris's citation of a spiritual also signals his efforts to reconcile his sexual practice with his faith. The phrase "just as I am" invites a comparison between sin and bisexual identity as two states of being that may be seen as either essential or volitional. If, as the lyrics contend, God will "welcome, pardon, cleanse, relieve" the penitent, "just as I am," two possibilities follow: either one is a born sinner, constantly confronting "fightings, fears within, without" as a result of the sinner's fallen nature, or one consciously pursues sin as an act of will.[2] The contradiction Harris finds at the heart of Christianity emblematizes for him the way bisexuality eludes the distinction between an inherent, immanent sexual identity and one that is willfully chosen and rechosen with every sexual act.

Harris's emphasis on therapy and psychological healing in his second novel also parallels this dynamic of sin and forgiveness. The healing narrative that takes over *Just As I Am* addresses the processes of coming out, unearthing past traumas, and ultimately admitting and accepting one's emotional vulnerability. But Harris's exploration of bisexuality and his focus on formative experiences of racial consciousness raise difficulties for a traditional psychoanalytic model of repression.[3] The concept of repressed sexual desire for the same or the opposite sex, desire that is repressed because it creates conflict or discomfort in the subject's understanding of his sexual identity, does not seem applicable to the experience of Raymond, Harris's bisexual protagonist. In addition to questioning the utility of a repression model in theorizing bisexuality, Harris's emphasis on psychological healing as a work of achieving collective racial self-awareness offers an indirect critique of discourses like psychoanalysis that rely upon a binary opposition, however subtly articulated, between conscious and unconscious. The psychoanalytic tendency toward aligning the unconscious with what is true, what is to be revealed in therapy, reproduces the very dynamic of truth and deception posed by the notion of repression and by narratives of racial and sexual passing. As a sexual identity, bisexuality's constitutive characteristic is that it always obliges one to pass. The "riddle of bisexuality," as Harris articulates it, shows that psychoanalytic approaches to healing tend to fall back upon an inevitable monosexual essentialism which seems built into Freud's concept of the unconscious.[4] Despite Freud's elliptical remark that childhood bisexuality makes it "more difficult to describe . . . intelligibly" the relationship between the object-choices of the id and the identifications of the ego, the emphasis on the Oedipal drama lends a somewhat deterministic quality to psychoanalytic readings which does not accommodate very comfortably the self-contradictory narrative possibilities posed by bisexuality.[5]

Although both Freud and Shoshana Felman have more to say about male heterosexual identity than about bisexuality, their phrase "the riddle of bisexuality" certainly provides an apt image for talking about bisexuality in Harris's novels. Bisexuality is a riddle, an identity riddled with inconsistency. The problem (or the freedom) of bisexuality, as the paired book jackets of Harris's two novels suggest, is that it frustrates many of our common ways of talking about sexuality and identity politics. Bisexuality suggests an ontological status that can never be seen in its totality, because monosexuals tend to filter the isolated sexual practices through utterly bifurcated narratives of heterosexual or homosexual integrity and identity. Harris's epigraph to *Invisible Life*, "Walks like a duck, quacks like a duck, must be a duck. . . . But then again, it might not be a duck . . .," is a metaphor for the riddle of the subject who passes, either racially or sexually. Though not a direct citation, Harris's inscrutable duck uncannily recalls Wittgenstein's perplexing drawing of the duck-rabbit, which thwarts any attempt to distinguish between latent and manifest narrative content: the duck-rabbit is neither a duck nor a rabbit, yet both at the same time, depending upon one's context and perspective. Harris's epigraph, mirrored in the covers of *Invisible Life* and *Just As I Am*, questions the notion of a sexual or racial identity that is consistent with itself and whose coherence can be immediately apprehended through its signifying practices.[6]

The jackets of Harris's novels emblematize a correspondence between racial and sexual signification and passing. The cover of *Invisible Life*, photographed in an appropriately blurry soft-focus, features a light-skinned African American man looking off into the distance, standing between a dark-skinned woman and a dark-skinned man: the woman enacts a sexual claim on the central figure by clasping her hands around his shoulders and gazing defiantly at her male rival, who looks on with hurt and resentment in his eyes. The jacket of *Just As I Am* pictures the obverse scenario, with a slight difference: the protagonist now returns the embrace with another man, and a woman walks away from them, looking over her shoulder with a resigned expression. The novels' covers foreshadow the way light skin functions metaphorically throughout both novels to signify sexual ambiguity, and they highlight Harris's tendency to associate dark skin with stable, knowable sexual identity, particularly with traditional heterosexual masculinity.

The use of color to represent a variable or uncertain identity places Harris's work in a long-standing tradition of racial passing novels, as do other stylistic features: a straightforward narrative style with heavy emphasis on plot, the narrator's middle-class subject position, the lure of personal success in exchange for passing, and a focus on one's duty to the race. At the outset of *Invisible Life*, Harris's protagonist, Raymond, reverses one of the main conventions of nineteenth-century passing narratives such as Frances Ellen Watkins Harper's *Iola Leroy*, Pauline E. Hopkins's *Contending Forces*, and Charles Waddell Chesnutt's "The Wife of His Youth," which emphasize the mulatto's duty to maintain allegiance to a black identity instead of passing for white. The introduction of sexual passing into a narrative structure about racial passing creates radically contradictory social pressures. So, paradoxically, Raymond sees it as his duty to pass: he feels that in order to be truly black, he must pass as straight. Raymond initially represents bi men as a threat to straight African American women and to the black family, the cause of generational rifts between African American men, and the instigators of a sexual tension that forecloses real emotional intimacy between male friends.

Harris's construction of this sense of duty shifts by the end of the second novel, however, as sexual passing begins to threaten the survival of the race. It precisely becomes Raymond's duty to "out" variations of African American sexual identity and to reconstruct family values in order to save the race—and black male youth in particular—from AIDS and homophobia, which threaten to destroy and divide the African American community. The reference to gays as "the children" by Kyle, the novel's central gay character, redefines family and also sets up the possibility of an alternate reading of Oedipal dynamics (*JAIA*, 90). The process of coming out, whereby the declaration of sexual identity and the retrieval of past memories create individual and collective well-being, accelerates in Harris's novels and eventually becomes quite generalized. By the end of *Just As I Am*, confessions made during therapy and about therapy subsume both the coming out and the passing narratives. Cumulative efforts at recalling a pain whose explanation exhausts the powers of both psychoanalytic and political discourses forge their own kind of therapeutic discourse about African American identity and self-knowledge. Homophobia is represented in the psychiatrist's office as a threat to the race; overcoming it promotes healing and wholeness, values often espoused in black feminist theory but generally dismissed as illusory and naive by psychoanalytic and poststructuralist theory.[7]

Initially, Harris's protagonist casts bisexuality as a threat to heterosexual African American women and, by extension, to the black family. When a straight friend dies of AIDS after contracting HIV from a closeted bisexual lover, Raymond confesses: "I was overcome with a tremendous amount of guilt regarding Candace's death. I was part of a secret society that was endangering black women like Candace to protect our secret desires. Would this have happened if society had allowed Kelvin and I to live a life free from ridicule? Was it our fault for hiding behind these women to protect our futures and reputations? . . . Many of us passed in and out of their worlds" (*IL*, 253–54). *Passing* begins to take on multiple meanings in this context; Harris uses the passing novel to suggest that instead of passing *for* an identity that is inauthentic, one might pass *between* identities, "in and out" of equally genuine subject positions.[8] Harris's narrative also implies a more concrete and dangerous meaning of passing as transmission; the overdetermined social act of passing can be one of deadly deception. The location of closeted bisexual men as the contagion bringing HIV into the heterosexual community pervades Harris's reformulation of passing: by passing as straight, bi men may inadvertently pass HIV to their female partners.[9]

Invisible Life's main female character, Nicole, vows to have no more to do with black bi men after she experiences Raymond's intentional deception; she interprets his actions as "part of a calculated plan, like a conspiracy against black women" (*IL*, 194). At the same time, Raymond views his sexuality as a betrayal of black manhood, represented by his father, whom he sees as "the last of a dying breed. A strong, confident, self-made, proud black man" (*IL*, 88). The rhetoric of extinction here also situates Harris's novels in the context of a perceived crisis in black masculinity in journalistic and social science discourse, commonly described in terms of a breakdown of the black family and a lack of role models for African American boys. Curiously, though, Raymond sees in the cause of his betrayal the potential not only for his own redemption but for a surplus effect of racial rejuvenation as well. Raymond displaces his attempt at retrieving and repairing his emotional relationship with his father by striving to find more emotionally satisfying ways of relating to his male lovers that extend beyond simple sexual attraction. Moreover, Raymond's effort to restore a failed intimacy with his own father suggests possibilities for African American father and son in a more general, metaphorical sense; by the end of *Just As I Am*, Harris offers bisexual male identity as a crucial intervention in a collective emotional crisis for young black men.

Exerting pressure against this utopian bisexual potential, however, is the personal risk Raymond takes in making his life visible in a largely homophobic southern black community. According to Raymond, this process of self-revelation generates fear for black bisexuals "of rejection from their own community, if not from their immediate family, then certainly from the African-American family as a whole" (*JAIA*, 221).[10] Harris responds to a potentially hostile environment by reinscribing gay and bisexual men into a version of family values that allows them sexual expression but still demands a stereotypically butch male emotional stoicism. Raymond sums up this butch aesthetic in his conviction that he must suppress his emotional response to the sight of a friend who is dying of AIDS: "I had to be a man. I had to stay strong!" (*JAIA*, 282). Harris inserts an odd twist in this articulation of dispassionate manhood by crediting gay black men with the most complete development of emotionally restrained, butch masculinity: "Life in the black gay community was not for the weak or the weary. It was not for sissies" (*IL*, 50). Recuperating gay identity and emptying out the meaning of "sissy" as a term of insult ironically require recourse to traditional values of masculine stoicism. Harris's title, *Invisible Life*, by echoing Ellison's, registers his concern with the idea of manliness, and his effort to redefine black masculinity forges a thematic link between his work and that of writers as diverse as Ellison, Amiri Baraka, and Eldridge Cleaver. Like his predecessors, Harris emphasizes the importance of personal politics in his construction of masculinity, but instead of basing his definition of black manhood on a fiercely defensive heterosexuality, Harris proposes quite the opposite: since the emotional fortitude of gay men surpasses that of straight men, the only real men are the "sissies."

Harris develops this tactic of redefining manliness and family relatively late in his novels, however, and this reformulation of masculinity requires sacrifice and mourning. The death of Kyle, Harris's central gay character, has salvific value for the novels' gay and bi characters and seems to infuse their sexual identities with a masculine essence; according to Raymond, Kyle "was a man in the real sense of the word" (*JAIA*, 270). Kyle's emotional reserve and his insistence that his friends suppress their tears in his presence, both throughout his illness and at his funeral, secure his claim to manliness, but his desire to find his father before dying is also critical to Harris's account of African American manhood (*JAIA*, 206). Kyle's search for his father remarkably reconstructs efforts in nineteenth-century passing novels such as *Iola Leroy* to reconfigure the family after emancipation; here the disproportionate impact of AIDS on American racial minorities figures as a major epoch in black history.[11] Harris also emphasizes the political effectiveness of the family metaphor for forging African American solidarity through Kyle's use of the term "family" in reference to gay people; tellingly, the first time Kyle uses the term to refer to two lesbian friends he has to explain this meaning of "family" to Raymond (*JAIA*, 258). Raymond's own image of black male bisexuality as "the silent frat" also invokes the metaphor of brotherhood to establish a political resonance between marginalized sexual identities and black fraternities (*JAIA*, 13).[12]

Raymond arrives at this understanding of family only after a reexamination of his initial conviction that families are composed exclusively of heterosexuals and that an openly gay or bisexual identity conflicts with the racial responsibility to be a "real" man.[13] A consistent sense of racial accountability and solidarity also remains central to Raymond's rethinking of family and manhood. This feature of Harris's writing places it more squarely in the tradition of passing novels, and it marks a departure from gay black writers such as April Sinclair and James Baldwin, whose novels suggest that gay life is one of the few spaces in which racial parity is possible. In Sinclair's coming out novel *Coffee Will Make You Black*, her protagonist, Stevie, recalls feeling a sudden confusion and alienation from the women in her family when her friendship with a white teacher is called into question. After she is told by her grandmother that "the only black women and white women who can be friends are hookers and bulldaggers," Stevie realizes that she must demonstrate heterosexual exclusivity in order to retain her racial identity in the eyes of her female relations.[14] Instead, she crosses a symbolic racial boundary by finding comfort in a racially inclusive homoerotic social space. Lee Edelman similarly reads Baldwin's *Another Country* as a scenario in which same-sex relationships potentially reconstruct race relations. In Edelman's account, the unconscious and the anus function as destabilizing zones that overthrow the phallus and the ego, creating an authentic, intersubjective version of black manhood. The experience of mutual penetration creates for Baldwin's characters "the possibility of a male identity no longer dependent for its self-constitution on phobic exclusion" and thus "disarticulate[s] the coercive 'wholeness' of an identity based on fantasmic identification with a part."[15] Raymond's distaste for white men, however, as well as his phallocentric eroticism, complicate Edelman's suggestion that anal intercourse poses a consistent challenge to the racist deployment of the phallus.

In marked contrast to Edelman's account of homoeroticism, Raymond values precisely the scopic economy authorized by the phallus, claiming that "the feeling of reaching simultaneous orgasm with a man and seeing it . . . was magic" (*IL*, 230–31). This emphasis on the male orgasm as a visual sign of male potency and desire is not surprising given Harris's use of rhetoric from Ellison (and thus indirectly from Du Bois) about seeing and being seen. The relationship between race, masculine identity, and the ability to see another person and see oneself properly creates an intensely phallic power dynamic in Harris's discussion of sexuality. In

Harris's erotics, the constitution and contradiction of black manhood are very much caught up in this "fantasmic identification" with the phallus, because that identification authorizes the powers of seeing and being seen. At times, Raymond associates gay life with a daunting hypervisibility; the sincerity and openness of Kyle's life, for example, takes on for Raymond an almost pornographic quality because it is "all out there for the world to see" (*IL*, 221). It seems hardly coincidental that the displaced and proactive shame Raymond experiences after his first experience with a man is the shame of being seen, of being the mute object of his community's disapprobation for acts that would symbolize for them not only personal weakness—he would be seen as a "punk"—but a racial failure as well. Raymond confesses to the reader, "I thought about the humiliation my parents and fraternity would feel," and decides to barter full sexual visibility and self-presence for his community's approval, resigning himself to the fact that "[t]hat part of my life would just have to remain invisible" (*IL*, 19, 224).

Even after Raymond comes out to his father and gains some degree of acceptance from his family, he still feels compelled to be circumspect, to suppress any visible indications of his desire for men: "My father knows that I like men but I don't think he wants to see me being affectionate with a man in his presence" (*JAIA*, 289). The anxieties about self-presence and ego integrity that are condensed in the image of the phallus also resonate in Raymond's accounts of emotional interactions with men. Early in his experience with men, Raymond associates same-sex love with an emasculating effeminacy that threatens psychic integrity; he reins in the feelings he has for a male lover that generate a "fear of losing one's self," a fear which he considers to be "a man thing with me" (*IL*, 219). Raymond's father concisely establishes a tie between the threat of dissolution, symbolized by penetration, and the historical emasculation of African American men when he articulates his bewilderment at hearing that his son is bisexual. His question, "Isn't it tough enough being a black man?" is accompanied by a fear of personal diminishment through penetration: "You didn't let them sc—" (*IL*, 246). Raymond's father chokes on his question in order to deny the imagined scene of his son's penetration; his halted utterance speaks to his investment in maintaining the phallus as the signifier of both impenetrability and masculine identity.

Raymond strives to keep his desire for men invisible so that he can maintain social visibility as an African American man. This self-contradictory position, however, complicates the central axiom in passing literature that what one passes *as* is inauthentic, a self-betrayal and a racial betrayal that will eventually be exposed. Bisexuality shakes the essentialist ground of passing literature because it seems to admit the possibility of an unintentional and perhaps inevitable kind of passing that is not motivated by a desire to deceive oneself or others, yet is often associated with a duplicitous intentionality. An identity that defines itself not as a subject position but as a movement *between* positions suggests that what one appears to be is always a sincere expression of one's sexual identity; there is no true, essential, or repressed identity to be exposed or contradicted. Throughout the course of the two novels, Raymond seems to be sorting out the ethical difference between intentional and unintentional bisexual passing. Raymond initially considers himself "blessed" in his ability to "pass in and out of the heterosexual world" (*IL*, 262). Harris's experiment with honest passing ends, however, as his protagonist discovers political entailments to passing that go far beyond the potential for self-delusion. A male lover's homophobic insults, the suicide of a young man in Raymond's former fraternity, his younger brother's developing homophobia, and the trauma of coming out to his parents lead Raymond to politicize his bisexuality and to emphasize the importance of coming out.

Harris not only argues for the importance of coming out as a ritual that clarifies bisexuality's inherent disjunction between the manifest appearance of a fixed sexual identity and a latent ontology of diverse sexuality but also suggests a collective therapeutic value of coming out. Harris combines coming out dynamics with the conventions of the passing novel and emphasizes psychological healing, raising questions about the conspicuous scarcity, and (in)appropriateness, of psychoanalytic approaches to African American literature. Harris resolves questions of sexual and racial identity through a teleological narrative about therapy, exemplifying what Hortense Spillers has characterized as a need in African Americanist discourse for something like Freud that isn't Freud. As Spillers argues, the institution of slavery provides "one of the richest displays of the psychoanalytic dimensions of culture before the science of European psychoanalysis takes hold," yet the process of "dispossession as the loss of gender" enacted by slavery and its historical legacy has made a grotesque of psychoanalytic categories for African Americans, creating a theoretical bind.[16]

Just as Spillers's "Mama's Baby, Papa's Maybe" makes it clear that we cannot approach matters of gender through a traditional Freudian discourse uninflected by race, contemporary African American writers such as Harris and Randall Kenan tease us into considering both the necessity and the impossibility of psychoanalytic readings of their own works. Kenan's narrator in "Cornsilk," a story about incest, attests to the pull of something both seductive and ridiculous in the psychoanalytic critique of African American literature when he coyly claims that his story "sounds Freudian; but it is not Freudian, not Freudian in its intent, though perhaps in its execution."[17] It is no accident that narratives of incest and passing have often coincided in novels about race; both plots revolve around the uncanny and its play between sameness and difference, the familiar and the unfamiliar.[18] Harris, Spillers, and Kenan all point to the possibility that psychoanalysis, given the complex history of white displacements and projections of sexuality onto black bodies, also appears as an uncanny simulacrum when applied to African American literature, a way of reading that can seem precisely on the mark and all wrong at the same time.

Through his concern with defining bisexuality, Harris questions what I would argue to be the foundational and thus the most troublesome psychoanalytic binary for African Americanist discourse—conscious/unconscious—and translates it into an idiom more accommodating to African American and bisexual experience. Because the category of the unconscious can be so easily deployed to dismiss or deflate the importance of interpretations with a more political or historical focus, psychoanalytic theory often meets with skepticism among African Americanists. The possibility of latent narrative content threatens any highly politicized discourse with the suggestion that, because we cannot fully know what we are doing, we perhaps should not trust the normative convictions on which we base our conscious political goals. This radically depoliticizing current in psychoanalysis requires that any theorization of the unconscious, in order to be of use to African Americanist criticism, develop a more sophisticated historical and social analysis of the way psychoanalytic principles are constructed. Judith Butler locates as one shortcoming of psychoanalytic feminism the assumption "not only that sexual difference is more fundamental [than racial difference], but that there is a relationship called 'sexual difference' that is itself unmarked by race."[19] Harris's emphasis on individual self-awareness and collective healing in his novels also suggests the extent to which many theories of sexual difference are determined by epistemologies that tend to separate what we can know of ourselves from what we cannot, creating as their effect a Du Boisian sense of sexual and racial double consciousness.

Du Bois's articulation of double consciousness provides an illuminating contemporary commentary on the Freudian impulse toward institutionalizing self-knowledge. Regardless of what many consider to be its essentialist bent, Du Bois's 1903 pronouncement still remains a frequently invoked model for talking about African American subjectivity. The disjunction between racial and national identity in Du Bois's concept of double consciousness bears a remarkable similarity to the binary opposition between consciousness and the unconscious in psychoanalytic thought, yet it also deconstructs Freud by redrawing the imagined line of self-fracture.[20] The poles of "twoness" for Du Bois, "American" and "Negro," function as conscious and unconscious, blackness being the repository of a barely glimpsed truth about oneself whose complete access is prohibited or limited by racism.

Du Bois's difference from Freud lies in his suggestion that a white, nationalist principle of consciousness has performed a historical operation on a formerly self-present black consciousness, forcing it into a position of self-unknowability.[21]

Du Bois's depiction of an historical theft from African consciousness by a self-present, self-knowing white American consciousness helps to clarify the considerable resistance to psychoanalysis in African Americanist theory. Michel de Certeau has also remarked at length on the colonizing drive of the kind of theoretical knowledge represented by psychoanalysis, a system of knowledge which requires a definition of its object as basically unself-conscious:

Freudian psychoanalysis provides a particularly interesting version of this secluded knowledge lacking both expressive procedures (it has no language of its own) and legitimate proprietor (it has no subject of its own). Everything works on a postulate that its effects have caused to be taken for a reality: there is knowledge, but it is unconscious; reciprocally, it is the unconscious that knows. Patients' stories and Freudian case histories (*Krankengeschichte*) narrate the knowledge at length. Moreover, since Freud, every psychoanalyst has learned from his experience that "people already know everything" that he, in his position of being the one who is "supposed to know," can or might be able to allow them to articulate.[22]

According to the psychoanalytic model, one knows that there is self-knowledge, but one cannot retrieve or express it except through submission to the social conventions of that therapeutic discourse, which presents that knowledge as something the expert has sounded from the depths, his gift to the would-be knower, that which is "allowed." The discourse of psychoanalysis as a theoretical institution thus relies heavily on a mode of interaction which perpetuates the type of double consciousness outlined by Du Bois.

Harris's depiction of bisexual identity intimates an intricate and crucial relationship between Du Boisian double consciousness and the depth hermeneutic built into psychoanalysis. By playing images of sexual and racial passing off one another, Harris frustrates the notion of a fixed, stable sexual identity. Instead of presenting passing as a repression or denial of true racial identity, Harris reconstructs passing as an inevitable effect or unintended by-product of bisexuality. Bi writing and theory are especially apropos to Du Bois's historical and theoretical dilemma, because the prospect of continual, inadvertent passing challenges the depth hermeneutic that underwrites both psychoanalytic understandings of consciousness and the identity politics of a great deal of African American and queer theory. In Harris's novels sexual passing displaces its historical referent, racial passing, and carries the weight of its ontological difficulty; many bi characters pass as straight, and at times they also pass as gay.[23] Raymond reiterates the sense of racial placeless-ness often associated with the tragic mulatto subject of passing narratives as diverse as Harper's *Iola Leroy*, James Weldon Johnson's *Autobiography of an Ex-Colored Man*, Nella Larsen's *Passing*, Jessie Faucet's *Plum Bun*, and William Faulkner's *Light In August*. Harris's protagonist, however, experiences his sense of displacement on the level of sexual identity, as he asserts, "I didn't feel comfortable in a totally gay environment or in a totally straight environment" (*JAIA*, 4). More self-consciously, Raymond signals his literary kinship with the protagonists of previous African American passing novels by collapsing together experiences of racially and sexually ambiguous identity: "Now even though I hate labels, I still consider myself bisexual. A sexual mulatto" (*JAIA*, 4).

Attempts on the part of Raymond and other characters to learn the meaning of racial solidarity in a sexually diverse culture ultimately drive Harris's plots, but this strand of racial essentialism appears in dizzying double focus with a critique of gender essentialism. Fears of committing a racial betrayal and shifting hierarchies of racial betrayal coexist uneasily with a gradually unfolding suggestion that there is no teleology of racial or sexual identity to be revealed or preserved. Unlike a traditional passing novel or coming out narrative, in which the performance of white or straight identity can appear only as a false step in one's development or as treacherous false consciousness, Harris's novels initially offer bisexuality as a state of being in which one is always passing and one is never passing, because all possi-bilities for sexual identification are viable and conscious at once. Felman has suggested that bisexuality disrupts "the smooth functioning of the very institution of representation," and Harris's works show how bisexuality throws the very idea of sexual identity into question by challenging the assumption of a correspondence between signifying sexual practice and signified sexual identity (55).

Diana Fuss describes the difficulty underlying struggles of identification like Raymond's as a conflict between a conviction that modes of self-identification constantly shift and the fear that relinquishing a concrete notion of identity destroys the basis for a politics.[24] Edelman also shows how Du Bois grapples with this tension between essentialism and fluidity, which he ultimately resolves in favor of essentialism. Du Bois posits true (heterosexual) black manhood, ever elusive in a racist society, as the invisible referent of double consciousness. Although Harris's novels rigorously rework the codes of black masculinity, they ultimately reproduce this Du Boisian essentialism. In fact, it seems that many of the theoretical critiques of essentialist thought perhaps unintentionally end up producing another, more elusive and thus more persuasive type of essentialism in their analyses. By invoking the destabilizing effect of the unconscious, theorists such as Fuss, Butler, and

Edelman perpetuate a subtle essentialism which is masked by an asserted commitment to a poststructuralist critique. Many psychoanalytic readings unfortunately seem to engage in a bit of intellectual legerdemain that ends up reinstating essence in the form of the unconscious; these readings characteristically posit, sometimes in a tone of marked exasperation or condescension, the unconscious as a site of ultimate meaning accessible only to the theorist.[25] Fuss's assertion, for example, that "[t]he problem with basing political identities on identity politics is that identity politics rarely takes into account the subversive and destabilizing potential of the Unconscious" rhetorically positions the unconscious so that it denies any claim of self-awareness on the part of those about whom she speaks (104–5). Similarly, Butler's defense of Lacanian feminism against materialist challenges on the grounds that "these criticisms neglect the critical dimension of the unconscious which, as a site of repressed sexuality, reemerges within the discourse of the subject as the very impossibility of its coherence" discounts the possibility of maintaining one's politics and examining one's individual psychology at the same time.[26] Butler's reference to meanings created in moments of strategic essentialism "that always exceed the purposes for which they are intended" also suggests a moment of naiveté in political identification.[27] There is a troubling ease in the way formulations like these, their claims that the unconscious, slippery and inaccessible to all but the theorist, is the remedy for the false consciousness of politics, neglect to interrogate the history of a racially inflected discourse about the unconscious and self-knowability.[28]

Harris's depiction of African American bisexual experience speaks to a tendency in psychoanalysis toward a racially charged mystification of self-awareness and to the possibility of bisexuality as an identity that knows its own unconscious. The relative inattention to bisexuality in queer theory also suggests how bi identity creates complications for theorists who define gender as the effect of its iteration.[29] Because bisexuality has no referent behavior that exists in "a relation of entailment" to it and no spatial rhetoric of community for its enactment, it deconstructs gender in a more thoroughgoing way than many of the practices, such as drag and butch-femme, cited by queer theorists for their destabilizing potential.[30] Because the language of gender play and subversion offers only very limited analytical possibilities for examining a sexual identity that is defined by its own internal self-contradiction, theories of practice and their relation to identity may be more immediately applicable to bisexuality.[31] Harris addresses the difficulty of assessing the meaning of isolated sexual practices in a definition of sexual identity. As Kelvin, Raymond's first male lover, reminds Raymond: "you know one time doesn't make you gay" (*IL*, 27). Kelvin's statement raises vexing questions for gender theorists: How many times *does* it take to make you gay? Is gender identity simply a process of experiential accretion? By what calculus can we distinguish a monosexual person who occasionally has sexual relations with members of the same or opposite sex from a bisexual person? Is sexual identity cumulative, an additive process in which the sum of past actions adds up to the "being" of gay or bi? Or does one operate out of a reserve of sexual identity, a fund of certainty that can sustain endless withdrawal and self-contradictory practice? Must one practice a sexual identity at all in order to inhabit that identity?

Raymond's own self-acceptance later in *Just As I Am* is still fraught with confusing, self-contradictory statements that raise similar questions: "All I know is it feels right for me. A part of me. It's just who I am" (271). Bisexuality seems both to force and to elude clarity, asking whether sexual identity is fractional, a "part" of someone, or constitutive, "who I am," or a kind of psychic space one drifts hazily into, something that "feels right." Such questions illustrate the relative convenience and attractiveness of collapsing practice with identity in recent gender theory, and they point out queer theory's shortcomings for addressing the bisexual issues raised in Harris's novels. The experience of Harris's protagonist suggests that enacting bisexual identity implies a nonrepression of sexuality, a recuperated form of double consciousness whose binary oscillation differs from the dynamics of sexual repression that purportedly maintain the integrity of homosexual and heterosexual identity. As Harris's novels suggest, bisexual practice and bisexual identity are two different agendas. The association of bi practice with gender play and destabilized subject positions perhaps authorizes its claim to theoretical sophistication, but more importantly, for Harris, irresponsible bisexual practice represents both the possibility of racial betrayal by passing along HIV and a relinquishing of the opportunity for self-examination and self-definition. Insofar as sexual identity can never fully subtend racial identity for Harris, the "saga of the tragic sexual mulatto" requires an alternative telos to the revelation plots typical of the passing novel, the coming out narrative, and the psychoanalytic repression plot (*JAIA*, 146).

Although Harris begins his novels by recuperating passing as a necessary and inadvertent aspect of bisexual identity, he later examines the ethical entailments of passing as calculated deception. The main turning point in Harris's treatment of passing focuses on Basil, Raymond's homophobic male lover. Basil sees his sexual involvement with Raymond as a firmly delimited set of practices that do not in any way complicate his heterosexual identity. Basil's absolute distinction between practice and identity is summed up in his response to one of Raymond's attempts at deflecting his advances: "When I reminded him that he wasn't gay or bisexual he remarked, 'I know but I wouldn't mind kicking it with you'" (*JAIA*, 86). Once Raymond accepts gay practice as compatible with African American identity, theorizing the distinction between bisexual practice and bisexual identity becomes a more insistent concern for him, and Basil's attitudes begin to appear more self-interested, cavalier, and opportunistic.[32] The ramifications of Basil's internalized homophobia register for Raymond during a forced confinement in Basil's closet, during which he hears him make love with a girlfriend who unexpectedly arrives. By calling up the history of African American captivity with this image, Harris makes literal the metaphor of the closet and suggests its double resonance for gay African Americans. Raymond emerges from Basil's closet free and politicized, leaving behind a heteronormative and potentially treacherous bi practice for a politically engaged bi identity. Raymond's new identity politics finally displace his earlier suspicion, reinforced by the homophobic assumption that gays choose their identity out of perversity and by the biphobic characterization of bi men as "confused boys," that bisexuality is either obstinately volitional or a transitional state leading to gay self-awareness (*IL*, 43). The seemingly epiphanic nature of the closet incident, however, should not obscure the process of accretion that enables Raymond to see the event as a turning point. It is not that Raymond *becomes* bisexual at that moment, but that he reaches a critical experiential mass, claiming bisexual identity as a precipitate of former practices that were polarized by their seemingly predetermined attachment to gay or straight identity.

By the end of *Just As I Am*, Harris completely rejects intentionally deceptive passing and redefines African American identity as necessarily inclusive of gay and bi sexuality. As he learns that sexual passing has dangerous implications, he begins, paradoxically, to represent the notion of bisexuality as a fixed quality of his personality by associating it with an imperfectly mobile, fundamentally unshifting racial signification: "[M]y sexual orientation was not a belief or choice, but a fact of my birth. And just like the color of my skin and eyes, these things could not be changed, at least not permanently" (*JAIA*, 1). As Harris turns back to an ontology of sexual and racial identity, one reconstructed and defined by a principle of oscillation, a sense of unforgiving responsibility regarding sexual practice and identity develops in his novels: sex diverges into hard work and self-indulgent expenditure, depending upon its impact on racial politics.

With his rejection of passing as a dangerous, if not deadly, play of sexual signification, Raymond turns to the hard work of engendering bi masculinity. In stark contrast to queer theorists and performers who stress the representation of gender as play, Harris asserts a butch work ethic that is consistent with his stoic emotional aesthetic. Work first appears in Harris's novels as the exercise of a dormant heterosexual capacity; one must work heterosexuality like a muscle to keep it supple. As Raymond finds gay practice more engaging, he begins to fear that his heterosexual desire will fall into latency unless it is periodically called up for recognition. Early in *Invisible Life*, Raymond believes he must conserve his heterosexual potential not only to preserve the integrity of his own ego but as a piece of work that enacts racial solidarity. Raymond's experiences with other men interfere with his heterosexual pleasure and create a psychological distance from straight sex that turns it into a kind of work: "I tried to determine the difference between making love with a woman and with a man. While I had enjoyed this night of passion with Sela, I wondered if I had been too methodical in my lovemaking or if I had allowed myself to just let go as I had done so many times before with male partners. Was making love to a woman now work instead of enjoyment for me?" (*IL*, 110). Raymond is prey to a persistent fear—condensed in the question "Could I even get it up?"—that he can inadvertently unman himself by neglecting the heterosexual faculty (*IL*, 100).

As Raymond becomes more reconciled to his bisexuality, however, his sense of work shifts. Instead of proving his straight capacity, he expresses an ethical concern with the kind of disinterested assessment of potential lovers he associates with bisexuality; when a female coworker asks him to dinner, he accepts, as a test of his new faith in the potential held out by his identity: "I want to prove to myself that I can be attracted to a person no matter what their physical wrapping" (*JAIA*, 329).[33] While this formulation does indulge a problematic suggestion of bisexual objectivity, it also suggests the extent to which Raymond has decathected from the idea of an attraction to women as heterosexual capacity, fetishized as the cherished and uncertain ability to "get it up." The protagonist's psychological work of self-examination and self-acceptance does not end here, however. Although the site of Raymond's work shifts from his own psychic interiority to his external world, the work of elaborating bisexual identity remains racially inflected in its various forms. The hard emotional work of coming out, the work of nursing friends with AIDS, the political work of organizing a minority AIDS foundation, and the work of theorizing bisexual identity displace Raymond's earlier preoccupation with his career as an attorney and the work of maintaining heterosexual potential. Accessing and exteriorizing what is presumed to be unconscious also turns out to be work that subsumes all other labors for Raymond and the other characters: recalling and releasing pain become agonizing and necessary work in Harris's aesthetics of manly emotional stoicism.

Since bisexuality implies its own nonteleology, Harris substitutes the teleology of a therapeutic discourse that allows him to reconfigure the conventional romantic love narrative. Harris appropriates and, to use Butler's term, "queers" the traditional comic ending: everyone gets married or paired off, all the gay and bi characters come out—except Basil, who marries anyway, under the ominous cloud of deception—and everyone is politically active.[34] All the major characters must undergo some type of coming out process before their marriage, however; coming out operates as a clarifying ritual in which one claims self-knowledge and forges collective racial healing before entering into the contract of partnership. Kyle's protracted illness and salvific death, which remarkably recall the deaths of both Eva and Tom in *Uncle Tom's Cabin*, establish the need for grief and mourning, confession and self-acceptance. The Kyle subplot institutes an economy of sentiment that inspires in Harris's characters a potentially effusive grief that they must hold at bay until they can integrate it with a painful process of self-examination that speaks to a work of undisclosed collective mourning. This emotional work presses the limits of the butch emotional aesthetic epitomized by Kyle, who insists on no tears in his presence or at his funeral and who "was so strong that way, never letting anybody know how he really felt" (*JAIA*, 222). Harris calls for an excruciatingly delicate emotional balancing act: one must examine one's pain, but the man who shows emotion in the process, makes his pain visible, is a sissy and, as such, invisible.

Even African American women are called upon to be real men in this regard. As Nicole recounts a story to her therapist about white girls smearing shit on a dress she is to wear in a beauty pageant and pinning a racist note on it, she recalls being told by her mother that if she cries in front of them, they win. Nicole can only tell this story and release her pain in front of her therapist, who allows her to cry and not lose. The admission of knowing intellectually that this incident is based on the white girls' ignorance and fear, yet still being hurt by it, is compounded for Nicole by the interdiction on an expression of the pain that would make it visible. Nicole's eventual emotional release constitutes a variant of coming out and solidifies the importance in Harris's novels of believing in self-knowledge. After Nicole's confession of shame, Nicole's African American therapist comments that most of her patients are also black, suggesting a logic of requisite African American self-revelation that militates against the traditional psychoanalytic theory of the unconscious.

Harris signals his awareness of the racial inflection of psychoanalytic epistemology in Raymond's curious account of his criteria for selecting a therapist. Raymond claims he chose a white female doctor because "I was convinced that a white male doctor wouldn't understand my problems, a black non-gay male doctor certainly wouldn't, and a black female doctor would probably be judgmental" (*JAIA*, 281). Besides discounting the availability of a gay black doctor, Raymond locates a presumably sympathetic emotional orientation, "understanding," in female consciousness, but limits a nonaccusatory, disinterested objectivity to white women. Such a depiction seems at odds with Harris's project of rescuing African American self-consciousness from a traditionally white "watching agency," as Butler calls the superego, that represents multiple social norms.[35] The watching eye of the white therapist recalls the Du Boisian eye, measuring the souls of black folk against its tape. But the institution of therapy in Harris's novels does not exist as an end in itself, an enterprise whose theoretical integrity is primary. Harris's therapists fulfill a transitional role, preparing characters for their self-sustaining interactions in an envisioned African American family. Harris undercuts the authority of Raymond's therapist by focusing the narrative eye on her at times, describing her laughter at one of Raymond's jokes as "one of the first times I ever recalled her showing so much of herself" (*JAIA*, 329). Harris manages to instrumentalize the institution of therapy and to sever its associations with a voyeuristic white principle of full self-consciousness that denies self-knowledge for African Americans.

Harris must resolve yet another problem signified by his characters' entrance into therapy, however: the sense that one's emotional machismo has failed. Raymond shares some of Nicole's shame and constructs a kind of therapy closet when he speculates: "Perhaps she (Nicole) was like me and didn't want anyone to know she was seeing a therapist" (*JAIA*, 281). Nicole also frames her delayed disclosure to a friend that she has been seeing a therapist as a confession: "I was ashamed. You're only the second person I've told. You know how people are about things like that" (*JAIA*, 295). A proliferation of confessional utterances winds up the novel: Nicole casts Ray's revelation that he is in therapy as a confession, and after another gay friend tearfully comes out to Nicole, she sees her confession as a moment of intimate self-revelation: "Exposing your true self to a friend is a wrenching experience that most people will never endure" (*JAIA*, 316). Harris's characters can only discharge the residual shame of seeking therapy by moving the structure of therapeutic confession into their personal lives and dispensing with the therapist for a partner who will fulfill the same role. Nicole's therapist, for example, is delighted to learn that she is no longer necessary to Nicole because Nicole is going to be married. When Raymond falls in love he also reclaims a sense of authenticity and self-presence, the conviction that the unconscious, figured here as the heart, is accessible: "I'm finally living a life that wouldn't piss God or His newest angel off. I'm listening to my heart again" (*JAIA*, 368).

Learning to heal oneself by listening for the heart's voice both resolves the novels' questions, adopted from Ellison and Du Bois, about the possibility of learning to see and to know oneself, and offers a teleology that includes in its sweep both a monosexual romantic love plot and a consideration of bisexuality's inherent nonteleology. In an oblique reference to *The Color Purple*, Harris reformulates Alice Walker's account of what "pisses God off" as a breach of identity politics. Kyle remarks: "I think God just gets mad with us when we get down here and try to be something we're not. I really think that pisses Him off" (*JAIA,* 247). By appropriating the judging eye of God, Harris claims an unlimited self-presence and fullness of subjectivity that eclipses theoretical claims to the unconscious as the ultimate fund of meaning. Harris's butch epistemological slant leads him to emphasize the pragmatic, enabling value of essentialist fictions of self-identity and self-presence in the name of racial responsibility. The labyrinthine connections between racial and sexual identity, aesthetics and epistemology, and practice and theory in Harris's novels defy an either/ or logic by both suggesting the need for a psychoanalytic approach to African American literature and also, perhaps, exemplifying its impossibility.

Notes

1. In his poem "Object Lessons" Essex Hemphill complicates the dynamic of seeing and being seen in another way by exploring what he calls the "desire to be object," "the feeling of being pleasure." Hemphill defines his desire according to his ability to designate and to occupy the positions of subject and object: "I appropriated this context." *Ceremonies: Prose and Poetry* (New York: Plume, 1992), 69.

2. Charlotte Elliot and William B. Bradbury, "Just As I Am," in *Heavenly Highway Hymns: A Choice Collection of Gospel Songs, Both Old and New, Suitable for Religious Work and Worship,* ed. Luther G. Presley (Dallas: Stamps-Baxter Music and Printing, 1956), 124.

3. In Frederick Crews's critique of psychoanalysis in "Victims of Repressed Memory," *New York Review of Books* 61.20 (1 December 1993), an essay otherwise permeated by a bizarre masculine hysteria, he insightfully questions whether "[t]he content of our repressions is preponderantly sexual in nature" (56). Harris implicitly raises a similar question, suggesting that the concerns expressed in African American writing and theory might require a different notion altogether of the unconscious, one that addresses the role of repressing and recalling memories that are crucial in the formation of racial rather than sexual identity.

4. Shoshana Felman, *What Does a Woman Want? Reading and Sexual Difference* (Baltimore: Johns Hopkins University Press, 1993), 120.

5. Felman, *What Does a Woman Want,* 221. Marjorie Garber's reading of Freud in *Vice Versa: Bisexuality and the Eroticism of Everyday Life* (New York: Simon and Schuster, 1995) provocatively suggests that a theory of human bisexuality is the latent repressed content of Freud's life work: "Bisexuality remained for Freud throughout his career a key problem—perhaps *the* key problem, both in theory and in practice" (193). Garber's adherence to such a dynamic of repressed desire, however, does not account for the psychological dynamics that self-defined bisexuals experience in their relations with others, and it tends to flatten out bisexuality into a universally available, titillating "sexual postmodernism" that is enabled by consumerism, fashion, and fan culture. Garber's thesis suggests that bisexuality and the heterosexual unconscious are in fact the same thing: "[W]e edit out and rationalize away many of the erotic moments in our lives because they do not conform

to our outward assessment of ourselves. Call this repression or sublimation or (what is one of its least salubrious defense mechanisms) homophobia; by whatever name, it is a refusal to acknowledge the place of desire" (232). The vocabulary of repression, refusal, and defense mechanism may help describe the way in which people who identify themselves as heterosexual manage their same-sex erotic attachments, but as an explanatory framework for addressing bisexual identity, the model of repression seems to beg the question.

6. Ludwig Wittgenstein, *Philosophical Investigations*, trans. G. E. M. Anscombe (New York: Macmillan, 1968). The drawing of the figure which looks like both a duck and a rabbit, but not at the same time, allows Wittgenstein to "distinguish between the 'continuous seeing' of an aspect and the 'dawning' of an aspect" (194). Wittgenstein's emphasis on new uses of language enacting their own theories, which must "dawn" on the user, parallels Harris's efforts to theorize a sexual identity that can only become visible, can only "dawn" on someone, as the cumulative result of a sequence of isolated practices that enact it. E. Lynn Harris, *Invisible Life* (New York: Anchor Books, 1994), hereafter cited as *IL*. E. Lynn Harris, *Just As I Am* (New York: Doubleday, 1994), hereafter cited as *JAIA*.

7. In her book on African American women's autobiography, *Black Women Writing Autobiography: A Tradition within a Tradition* (Philadelphia: Temple University Press, 1989), Joanne M. Braxton cites the genre's potential for "restoration and self-healing" (11). bell hooks, in *Talking Back: Thinking Feminist, Thinking Black* (Boston: South End Press, 1989), also speculates in writing her autobiography that "I had become attached to the wounds and sorrows of my childhood, that I held to them in a manner that blocked my efforts to be self-realized, whole, to be healed" (155–56). As a counterexample, in "Woman Skin Deep: Feminism and the Postcolonial Condition," *Critical Inquiry* 18 (Summer 1992), Sara Suleri has no patience with critics like hooks who rely heavily on a rhetoric of wholeness and fragmentation, which she characterizes as a "banality of easy dichotomies," implying "a complete absence of intellectual exchange" (764). Suleri describes the essentialism she sees in hooks as an embarrassingly anti-intellectual claim that "personal narrative is the only salve to the rude abrasions that Western feminist theory has inflicted on the body of ethnicity" and expresses her respect for critics who apply their theoretical virtuosity to the abrasions inflicted by law (764). But Suleri does not address the difficulty posed by essentialism even for the most rigorous of critics, such as Hortense Spillers, who in "Mama's Baby, Papa's Maybe: An American Grammar Book," *Diacritics* 17.2 (Summer 1987), similarly speaks of a racially inflected "estrangement and 'disremembering' that require many years to heal" (76).

8. In this case, male bisexuality functions as femininity does in Felman's account of female bisexuality. In *What Does a Woman Want*, Felman's reading of Balzac's bisexual character Paquita (whose racial ambiguity, incidentally, is suggested by recurring references to her "golden eyes") argues that "the signifier 'femininity' . . . is precisely constituted in *ambiguity*, it signifies itself in the uncanny space *between two signs, between* the institutions of masculinity and femininity" (55).

9. The ascription to bisexuals of HIV's spread into the heterosexual and lesbian communities seems to rest on the common equation of bisexuality with promiscuity

and indiscriminacy, the notion that dual desire derives from a grotesque overabundance of desire or a maniacally generalized desire to have sex with "anything that moves." This assumption of bisexual indiscriminacy leads to the idea that bisexuals practice their sexuality in a more dishonest and irresponsible fashion than do heterosexuals and homosexuals and are thus more likely to *pass* HIV along than those with a monosexual identity.

10.   In her essay "Homophobia in Black Communities," in *Talking Back: Thinking Feminist, Thinking Black,* bell hooks addresses the complicated intersection between heterosexual privilege and notions of African American community.

11.   The novels of Pauline Hopkins, particularly *Of One Blood* and *Hagar's Daughter,* also focus on the revelation of family ties across racial lines. The distinction between intentional and unintentional racial passing, however, which underpins these writers' moral commentaries on passing, becomes both more important and more difficult to ascertain in Harris's novels.

12.   For a history of African American fraternities, see Wilson Jeremiah Moses's *The Golden Age of Black Nationalism, 1850–1925* (New York: Oxford University Press, 1978).

13.   Another strand of Harris's narrative, however, figures heterosexual betrayal as a racial abandonment: when Kelvin, Raymond's first lover, cuts off communication, Raymond learns he hasn't heard from him because "rumor had it that he was dating a blonde Tri Delta, and because Kelvin was so good-looking, all the black girls on campus were furious" (*IL,* 42). The insult of Kelvin's involvement with a white woman follows upon the injury of his heterosexual abandonment and establishes Raymond's identification with straight African American women.

14.   April Sinclair, *Coffee Will Make You Black* (New York: Hyperion, 1994), 210.

15.   Lee Edelman, *Homographesis: Essays in Gay Literary and Cultural History* (New York: Routledge, 1994), 70–71. It also seems to me that Edelman makes a problematic association between anal penetration and male homosexual subjectivity. In what ways, if any, would heterosexual or lesbian anal penetration complicate psychological investments in the phallus?

16.   Spillers, "Mama's Baby, Papa's Maybe," 77.

17.   Randal Kenan, *Let the Dead Bury the Dead* (New York: Harcourt Brace, 1992), 92.

18.   Mary Dearborn's *Pocahantas' Daughters* (New York: Oxford University Press, 1986) elaborates on this connection between the themes of passing and incest in nineteenth-century narratives about race.

19.   Judith Butler, *Bodies That Matter: On the Discursive Limits of "Sex"* (New York: Routledge, 1993), 181.

20.   In "Du Bois' 'Double Consciousness': Race and Gender in Progressive Era American Thought," *Studies in American Political Development* 6 (Spring 1992), Adolph Reed, Jr. has persuasively argued that Du Bois's statement has been subject to myriad ahistorical modes of "interpretive distortion" (114). I may not be able to escape a similar charge here, but my interest is in looking at why Du Bois' formulation has been appropriated in this particular way and how African Americanists have used it to occupy a perceived lack in subjectivity theory.

21.   Du Bois's description of double consciousness in *The Souls of Black Folk* (Chicago: McClurg, 1903) sounds almost physiological. The intensity of the psychological

bind registers as sensuous experience in Du Bois's description, a "peculiar sensation," which corresponds closely with Terry Eagleton's account of Freud's aesthetic understanding of bodily drives in *The Ideology of the Aesthetic* (Cambridge, Mass.: Basil Blackwell, 1990): "a mighty warring of somatic forces," which the ego strives to construct as a "solidity" (265–66). Eagleton describes Freud's model of unconscious desire in a way that uncannily reproduces Du Bois's image of "two warring ideals" that are experienced as a "sensation." There is, however, an important exception: no ego, however precariously self-divided, emerges in Du Bois's account to manage these forces. In Du Bois's rewriting of racial consciousness, it appears that racism has severely confused several basic Freudian categories: the id appears as incompletely somaticized "warring ideals" that are not so much psychologically managed as physically endured by bodily force, a "dogged strength," which stands in for the ego and prevents a violent psychic dismemberment.

22.   Michel de Certeau, *The Practice of Everyday Life*, trans. Steven Rendall (Berkeley: University of California Press, 1984), 71.

23.   Passing as gay often protects bisexuals from being repeatedly subjected to a biphobic gay perfection narrative in which their mode of identification is dismissed as a mere stage in one's development as a fully self-present gay subject, but Harris focuses more intently on the dangers of passing as straight.

24.   Diana Fuss, *Essentially Speaking: Feminism, Nature, and Difference* (New York: Routledge, 1989), 104.

25.   In his study of Hawthorne, *The Province of Piety: Moral History in Hawthorne's Early Tales* (Cambridge: Harvard University Press, 1984), Michael Colacurcio provides an example of this rhetorical gesture remarkable for its clarity of structure. In his reading of Hawthorne's tales, Colacurcio suggests a connection between a critical aesthetic of suspicion (the unconscious shows how most people don't know what they're doing), a self-interpellation into the rationalist epistemological discourse of theory (but since I can see that they don't know, I must know what I'm doing), and a self-defensive posture (don't confuse me with people who don't know what they're doing): "Edifying or not, the process of maturation has a logic of its own. The Unconscious has a reason which the political commitments and even the family sentiments do not know. And it has wrecked more than one enlightened critical system" (132). The ineffable unknowability of the unconscious, like a post-Christian God whose presence is glimpsed only in fleeting, intellectually transcendent moments, seems to inspire in the theorist a reflexive awe in readings like this one. The tone of such references to the unconscious, more than the content of the argument, suggests that the categorical interrogation of the unconscious would amount to a type of theoretical heresy, or at least a gross intellectual philistinism. Terry Eagleton makes a similar critical move in an aesthetic register when he defines unconscious desire as an aesthetic experience of the sublime: "Desire is itself sublime, finally defeating all representation: there is a substrate in the unconscious which cannot be symbolized" (265). God, beauty, power, desire, and chemical process: all these reflect back on one another in the unconscious and enable the theorist to define it according to the needs of his argument.

26.   Judith Butler, *Gender Trouble: Feminism and the Subversion of Identity* (New York: Routledge, 1990), 28.

27.   Butler, *Gender Trouble*, 4.
28.   I hasten to emphasize here the difference between Butler's assertions in *Gender Trouble* and her more careful account of the racialization of discourses about sexuality in *Bodies That Matter*, to which this essay is certainly indebted. I remain fundamentally skeptical, however, of applying the categories conscious/unconscious in African Americanist criticism without a rethinking that more closely examines the essentializing potential of the unconscious as a category.
    The dangerous facility which I find in a great deal of psychoanalytic reading seems to stem from an assumption that psychoanalytic discourse derives from a more scientific, and thus a more indisputable, set of paradigms than many other critical approaches. Freud's own anxiety regarding the conceptual status of psychoanalysis shows up in his predilection for terms derived from chemistry, such as *sublimation, condensation, precipitate,* and *displacement,* and it surfaces as well in his conclusion to his lecture "The Ego and the Id," in *A General Selection from the Works of Sigmund Freud,* ed. John Rickman (Garden City, N.Y.: Doubleday, 1957), which, coincidentally, advances and retracts a theory of childhood bisexuality: "Psychoanalysis is not, in my opinion, in a position to create a *Weltanschauung* of its own. It has no need to do so, for it is a branch of science, and can subscribe to the scientific *Weltanschauung*" (234). An embittered and embattled Freud more pointedly argues for the scientific legitimacy of psychoanalysis in the preface to his "New Introductory Lectures on Psychoanalysis" and attributes resistance to psychoanalysis to popular anti-intellectualism:

In no other field of scientific work would it be necessary to insist upon the modesty of one's claims. In every other subject this is taken for granted; the public expect nothing else. No reader of a work on astronomy would feel disappointed and contemptuous of that science, if he were shown the point at which our knowledge of the universe melts into obscurity. Only in psychology is it otherwise; here the constitutional incapacity of men for scientific research comes into full view. It looks as though people did not expect from psychology progress in knowledge, but some other kind of satisfaction; every unsolved problem, every acknowledged uncertainty is turned into a ground of complaint against it. Anyone who loves the science of the mind must accept these hardships. (xvii)

The historical connections between rationalist scientific discourse and the ideologies of racism and progress suggest, however, that it is *precisely* "some other kind of satisfaction" that many historically disempowered groups of people have sought, and that the systematized but coercive "love" offered by institutions has failed to provide "satisfying" ways of being and knowing.
    Freud's theoretical piggybacking on the institution of science, however eloquently qualified, creates what Pierre Bourdieu describes in *Language and Symbolic Power,* ed. John B. Thompson, trans. Gino Raymond and Matthew Adamson (Cambridge: Harvard University Press, 1991) as a "miracle produced by acts of institution." Such a miracle is simultaneously "a kind of curse," because it infuses certain speech acts with the power of law and dismisses others utterly, based on the degree of the speaker's ability to ally himself with institutional power

(126). This miracle-curse continues to haunt both adherents and detractors of Freud with an offer of institutional legitimacy that contravenes and mystifies its correlative threat of existential insignificance, a threat warded off only by such "rites of institution" (126).

For example, Shoshana Felman does distance herself from the totalizing, uncritically rationalist apology that Juliet Mitchell makes for psychoanalysis, but she ultimately abandons her own misgivings regarding the scientific status of psychoanalysis. Felman implicitly cites Lacan's coy, evasive remarks as her own account of the cultural capital held by psychoanalysis:

> To suggest, however, that psychoanalysis is not—or may not be—a simple science, is by no means to disqualify the truth inherent in its theory or the efficiency proceeding from its practice. "Psychoanalysis," says Lacan, "has to be taken seriously, even though it is not a science. It is not a science because—as Karl Popper has amply demonstrated—it is irrefutable. It is a *practice*. . . . All the same, psychoanalysis has consequences." (70)

Felman channels the institutional power of Lacan's voice in her citation; Lacan's remark becomes Felman's own and strangely reverberates without commentary at the end of a section that critiques the methods many theorists have used to uncritically perpetuate the power of psychoanalysis.

Even vehement critics of Freud, such as Frederick Crews, fall into similar patterns of institutional defense. Crews dismisses Ellen Bass and Laura Davis's *The Courage to Heal*, a book on the recovery of repressed memories of sexual abuse, on the grounds that its authors are "radical feminists who lacked any background in psychology" (49). His critique follows more from a kind of institutional panic than from a questioning of Freudian categories. Crews fears that the discourse of psychoanalysis is becoming popularized and intellectually degraded by practices, such as body work, dream work, trance work, and past life regression, that smack of mysticism (50). Crews's enterprise bears a striking resemblance to Felman's, in the sense that both seem motivated by a desire to preserve the integrity of psychoanalysis as a theoretical institution. Felman defends it from feminist critiques, while Crews tries to rescue it from those he sees as twentieth-century witch doctors who have reduced the theory of repressed memory into a "demonology" that infects the practice of psychoanalysis and potentially discredits legitimate claims of sexual abuse (57). By fortifying the boundaries of psychoanalysis, Crews and Felman preserve a system of thinking that derives its legitimacy from a scientific rhetoric that denies our ability to read and to know ourselves and withholds self-knowledge from nonexperts.

29. Judith Butler's *Gender Trouble* and Carol-Anne Tyler's "Boys Will Be Girls: The Politics of Gay Drag," in *Inside/Out: Lesbian Theories, Gay Theories*, ed. Diana Fuss (New York: Routledge, 1991), are particularly well-argued examples of this theory of gender as performance.

30. Michael Warner's introduction to *Fear of a Queer Planet: Queer Politics and Social Theory* (Minneapolis: University of Minnesota Press, 1993) questions the notion of a gay community, "because much of gay and lesbian history has to do with

noncommunity, and because dispersal rather than localization continues to be definitive of queer self-understanding ('We Are Everywhere')" (xxv). It seems, however, that gays and lesbians much more readily find themselves in a local subculture that provides some sort of challenge to heteronormative culture than do bisexuals, for whom community would have to offer a symbolic challenge to any form of monosexuality.

31.   See, for example, Pierre Bourdieu's *Outline of a Theory of Practice,* trans. Richard Nice (Cambridge: Cambridge University Press, 1972) and *Distinction: A Social Critique of the Judgement of Taste,* trans. Richard Nice (Cambridge: Harvard University Press, 1984), as well as de Certeau's *The Practice of Everyday Life* .

32.   I am aware of the theoretical problems posed by my use of the phrase "gay practice" as a sort of theoretical default mode in reference to sex between same-sex partners. The elaboration of a vocabulary that can account for the relationships between sexual practices and sexual identities remains one of the main challenges facing bi theory.

33.   The claim to objectivity among some bisexuals and bi theorists, or at least to a greater degree of distance than that which gay or straight people can claim, deserves deeper inspection here. As an example of what Lisa Orlando calls the "utopian potential" of bisexual election in "Loving Whom We Choose," in *Bi Any Other Name: Bisexual People Speak Out.,* ed. Loraine Hutchins and Lani Ka'ahumanu (Boston: Alyson, 1991), see Rebecca Shuster's "Bisexuality and the Quest for Principled Loving," in *Closer to Home: Bisexuality and Feminism,* ed. Elizabeth Reba Weise (Seattle: Seal Press, 1992). Orlando's essay presents a more complicated view of the notion of free bisexual choice.

34.   Butler, *Bodies That Matter,* 176.

35.   Butler, *Bodies That Matter,* 182.

Part Three

Biopia:
Perspectives on
Bisexual Visual Culture

Chapter 9

Biopia: Bisexuality and the Crisis of Visibility in a Queer Symbolic

Brian Loftus

"As the eye, such the object."

—William Blake

The language of sex speaks with two tongues simultaneously. For while andro-centric heterosexuality is the implied and stabilizing referent of the sexual system, its terms engage in a symptomatic double speak. Gayle Rubin points out the cultural conflation of biological sex and sexuality through gender and documents this epistemological collapse in the normative slippage between two forms of the word "sex":

[T]he word "sex" has two very different meanings. It means gender and gender identity, as in "the female sex" or "the male sex." But sex also refers to sexual activity, lust, intercourse, and arousal, as in "to have sex." This semantic merging reflects a cultural assumption that sexuality is reducible to sexual intercourse and that it is a function of the relations between women and men. The cultural fusion of gender with sexuality has given rise to the idea that a theory of sexuality may be derived directly out of a theory of gender.[1]

The critique of this monolithic structure of sexuality, which articulates itself only through a conflation of biological sex, cultural gender, and sexual practice, reveals

207

the category of bisexuality to be a contradiction in terms, insofar as the word attempts to wed the concept of multiple desire to a single and stable sexuality or sexual identity. According to Rubin's model of sexual identity as a culturally reified point of intersection between competing definitions of sexuality, the inherent contradiction of bisexuality is itself doubled. The form "to have sex" precludes the plurality of bisexual activity, since in this arrangement sex acts can only be identified as homosexual or heterosexual; bisexual identity is at once fragmented and dispersed between these two exclusive categories of identity. Likewise, the noun form violently binds the plural and fluid bodies of bisexual desire to a homogenized subject. This subject, fit into the system strictly as male or female instead projects difference onto the distinctly gendered object of h/er desire and is thus accounted for by the binary dominant fiction in terms of the same, denying the possibility of sexual difference. (I use "h/er" as a singular rather than a dual pronoun that designates both the English "her" and the German "er" for "he.") That is, this fiction insists that sexual difference remain coextensive with and confined to gender difference. Ironically, sexual difference thus defined guarantees a heterosexual reading of the subject, regardless of desire or practice.

In light of this semantic slippage surrounding sex and the identities sex pretends to structure, I would like to make clear that what I am examining here is not the category of bisexuality as a descriptive foundation of identity. While many theorists or activists seek to consolidate bisexual identity in historical, political, and psychoanalytic contexts, I prefer to push this conception of bisexuality further, to see it not as a term describing a subject but rather as a semiotic tension—a contradiction, a multiplication, and at times even a trope—within the field of sexuality that constitutes the subject in various and inconstant ways. Accordingly, I use the term bisexuality to describe many configurations of sexuality beyond the conventional definition based on object choice. Since I take as my primary topics of this essay the male homosexual, the visible body, and the heterosexist presumptions of culture, most of my references to bisexuality will designate the composite sexuality of a queer male in a social system which infers, indeed imposes, sexuality from the visible markings of biological sex. Bisexuality, then, describes the coincidence of two presumed distinct sexualities in the same subject, while also signifying a disruption or inconstancy along the sex/gender/sexuality chain that assumes sexuality and gender role from biological sex and relates the three definitionally.

Though I recognize the political utility of an identity-based conception of sexuality both to identify points of oppression and to provide points from which to mobilize, what I hope to show here is that the concept of bisexuality is fundamentally unsuitable to signify identity as such, since the plurality of bisexuality—defined by two nonidentical sexualities—explodes the very terms of identity—sameness, stability—that it seeks to inhabit. By abandoning such strategic essentialism I do not mean to deny its political usages, but rather to prevent identities from emerging simply within the terms of their own oppression and to uncover more fully the hegemonic standards and forces which produce such identities.

What this argument attempts is an interrogation of the natural link between sex and sexuality by exploiting the notion of bisexuality to challenge heterosexuality as a viable identity and to show it instead as an ideological consequence of masculine privilege. Using the male homosexual as a crisis point of an androcentric symbolic order, my inquiry falls into three main sections. First I will examine the mechanics of vision as it surveys the physical body, revealing the eye not as a benign descriptive force but rather as an ideologically constitutive function. Since psychoanalysis depends to a large degree on bodily sight to configure sexual positions and their corresponding conditions of difference and desire, this section will map out the intersections, dependencies, and potential points of subversion in the relationship between psychoanalysis and phallocentrism. Next, I will look at how the male homosexual appears as the paradoxical figure of both excess and absence in this system, since his desire frustrates the visually determined and gender-distinct terms of sexuality. Finally, I will look to the modes of camp and the strategic demands of passing to offer possible, though problematic, modes in which to de-sign the body—to render discrete, and at times oppositional, the conflated terms of body and desire which define sex.

Eve Sedgwick insists that ideology and discursive practice position the subject within the logic of the chiasmus: "in order for . . . ideology to be truly invisible, the narrative is necessarily chiasmic in structure: that is, . . . the subject of the beginning of the narrative is different from the subject at the end, and . . . the two subjects cross each other in a rhetorical figure that conceals their discontinuity."[2] Indeed, for the visible sexual subject to emerge, contradictions along the rigid and naturalized sex/gender/sexuality axes must be rendered invisible. This is achieved not only in the crossings between noun and verb forms of "sex" and their implied doubles of gender and sexuality but also in the metonymic association of the category of gender with sameness and the category of sexuality with an expression of difference between gender. In the first case, gender is governed by the logic of the sameness since gender identity is conferred by identification with and the denial of difference between a group of sexed bodies. The chiasmus is formed by the fiction which equates biological sex and gender but which cross-references sexual practice with gender by defining sexuality as a necessary condition of gender, as "a function between men and women."[3] Thus, to be male is to be masculine, but masculinity itself is experienced in its sexual relation with femininity. The second case, wherein sexuality is configured through gender difference, falls into the same contradictory progress from same to different. For here, the difference of (hetero)sexuality necessitates a coherence of gender based on biological sex by defining both gender and sex as that which desires a generically different object. Since the "rhetorical figure that conceals their discontinuity" in this doubled chiasmus of sex/gender/sexuality is the literal figure of the body, those desires which do not conform to the social narrative are overwritten and still classified as "the same" by virtue of the visible and justifying term of the physical body. In consequence, the conventional definition of bisexuality as desire for both genders, just like homosexual desire, cannot exist as such within this system, since any sexual identity is determined and limited by the sexual marking of the physical body. Instead, bisexuality, as the coincidence of two sexualities within the same subject, is produced by and marks the ideological displacement or repression of "deviant" sexuality by the heterosexually understood body.

To theorize or speak of *a* category of bisexuality, then, is to replicate the very ideological mechanisms that have produced the term in order to limit desire and sexual expression to socially recognized and policed bodily divisions. Instead, one must conceive of *bisexualities* produced through the tensions, contradictions, and intersections of the cultural oppositions which delimit sexuality: male/female, masculine/feminine, and hetero/homosexual. As in the case above, when invisible desire contradicts the "normative vision"[4] which can only read the body in terms of heterosexual gender difference, a doubled sexual position is produced. For while vision is always subjective, the social eye and the mechanics of binocular vision repress the possibility of such subjective multiplicity, insisting instead upon resolution and predetermined recognition. Sight never allows "pure access to a single object; vision is always multiple, adjacent to and overlapping with other objects, desires, and vectors"[5] and bespeaks "an account of a body with an innate capacity, one might even say a transcendental faculty, to misperceive—of an eye that renders differences equivalent."[6] Just so does culture refuse and displace resistant desire with the fiction of "natural vision"[7] and occlude sexuality with its visible and naturalized signifier: the body. Simply put, sex is the category which produces the intelligible body, and this sexed body in turn determines sexuality. Since, in our phallocratic culture, power is accorded and difference relationally derived by means of the always already gendered and heterosexually marked and understood body, the potential contradiction between body and desire, power and oppression, stands to challenge the very structure of the symbolic order. While for lesbians, this disjunction produces a condition that Kate Davy describes as "doubly missing"[8]—her exclusion from culture as lesbian is already inscribed in the fundamental oppression and social absence guaranteed by the insistence of her sexual marking as woman—for gay men the conflict between desire and gender is contradictory instead of compounding.

Here, I would like to interrogate the dependence of (hetero)sexual categories and cultural power on vision in terms of this "transcendental faculty to misperceive." In the case of the cultural opposition between masculinity and homosexual desire, I call this structure *biopia*, which is the necessary semiotic production of a category of bisexuality by compulsory heterosexuality's assumption and suppression of homosexuality in the space of visual indistinction between the two. This term describes the ideology of *méconnaissance* by which the straight culture refuses to "see" sexual difference except through gender. Sexual difference is thus reduced to and stipulated as the binary categories of biological sex that justify and naturalize heterosexuality. But this limitation of sexuality to a function of difference between genders ontologically precludes homosexual or bisexual subjects. By establishing the structures and functions of biopia in the oppression of queer males, and by identifying bisexuality as a semiotic consequence of this displacement, heterosexual masculine privilege emerges not as a stable or natural arrangement but rather as one that depends upon the alternative sexualities it effaces.

The queer male, by virtue of his "both at once" status of male and homosexual, occupies a doubled sexual position.[9] For while the fiction of heterosexual masculine privilege irrevocably generated by his sexed body positions him in opposition to his oppressed homosexual desire, this opposition constructs a categorical trope of bisexuality to mediate between the queer's paradoxes of inside/outside, same/different, and hetero/homosexual, which all originate in the crises of visible distinction. Bisexuality thus stands as both an interpellative metaphor by which the standard binary oppositions and structures of heterosexuality are constructed, and as an inherently disruptive and repressed fiction which collapses the very distinctions it was invoked to produce. For while the demand for heterosexuality eclipses homosexual desire, it is itself displaced by this tension between sexualities, this bisexuality it incurs. Although the ways in which bisexuality functions to augment heterosexuality inevitably suppress homosexuality by a strict reading of the body within a heterosexual script ordered by the parameters of gender, I would like to focus on the possibilities of a queer symbolic grounded on this indeterminate paradox instead of on binary opposition, in order to re-vision the trope of bisexuality as a frustration of hegemonic categories rather than as a normative consequence of compulsory heterosexuality. By examining the visual bias used to reinforce gender stability, masculine privilege, and heterosexuality itself, as well as the potential semiotic designing of the body and the "violent dialectic" of camp as site and praxis of this disruption,[10] I would like to redouble the contradiction of bisexuality, to envision the subject and the trope itself as "both at once."

Sights of Sexual (In)Difference

Most feminist psychoanalytic and semiotic criticism of the past twenty years, along with more recent cultural and subaltern studies, have identified the Lacanian symbolic order not only as a system of phallocratic binary valuation but also as a function of interpellation profoundly dependent upon the visual to render its categories intelligible and operable. The subject is constructed by, to borrow a metaphor from Virginia Woolf, "the perpetual solicitation of the eye."[11] Within this scopic economy, difference must at once be displayed and disguised, the dispossessed term operating as a visual signifier of difference or dependence in relation to phallic centrality, but one which can only be located at the margins and articulated as a blind spot. Sex, for instance, is assumed from the presence/absence of the penis, while sexuality only exists as it is articulated by and through this marker. In *Essentially Speaking: Feminism, Nature, and Difference*, Diana Fuss has charged that "most anti-essentialists . . . are hesitant to discuss the body at all for fear of sounding essentializing,"[12] since physical/biological categories stand as the strongest essentializing forces. However, recent constructionist theories attempt to explain the mechanisms and ideologies of vision which naturalize the bodily surface. These destabilizations of the most basic tool of "natural" sexual division represent, perhaps, the most powerful critique of essentialism. I would like to exploit these constructionist readings to examine how psychoanalytic theories of subject formation and sexuality treat vision, purposely or inconsistently, and to explicate how this tradition allows a discourse of sexuality not dominated by the body.

Though Lacan himself does not supply the most direct or convincing feminist or antihomophobic arguments, I ground my analyses of vision, sex, and hegemony in the theory of the cultural gaze he puts forth in both "The Split Between the Eye and the Gaze" and "The Mirror Stage as the Formative Function of the I." In these essays, Lacan identifies sight and the field of vision not as a tabula rasa but as secondary to a "something prior to [the] eye," an ideological substratum which informs and shapes what is seen:[13] "the regulation of form . . . is governed, not only by the subject's eye, but by his expectations."[14] The mirror stage is the point at which the child is interpellated into the symbolic by means of a (mis)recognition of "alienating identity," of self as other;[15] the eye and the I are conflated in the moment of tautological vision which takes the self as the external object and teaches the nascent subject to see through a process of reflection. Since "the mirror image would seem to be the threshold of the visible world,"[16] what is seen is always already a repetition of culturally conditioned forms and meanings, and the subject is formed through the body's subjection to the gaze. The suppressed conflict between self and visual image is "the dialectic that will henceforth link the I to socially elaborated situations"[17] and will link, too, I would argue, the eye with the demands of culture. The gaze frames the legible sign of the visible body through a pre-scripted cultural fiction of regulated sexuality that works as a prescribed corrective lens. In this context, I would first like to make visible, as it were, how gender difference, masculine privilege, and heterosexuality are stabilized through the visual bias and naturalization of the body in Freud's "Femininity," to show how this valorization of these categories is itself a re-vision, and then to visualize this symbolic sexual system disrupted by the coincidence of presence and absence, lack and excess, in the structure of biopia. In accordance with Lacan, then, we can say of the gaze, "not only does it look, it also shows,"[18] and what it shows are the ideologies of the eye.

Although Freud's account of gender difference purports to be based on a model of bisexuality, his terms and assumptions actually refuse the sexual difference they depend upon by installing heterosexuality as the normative assumption and telos of his argument. In "Femininity," Freud virtually announces Lacan's notion of a "something prior to [the] eye" with his assessment of sexuality: "enough can be seen in the children if one knows how to look."[19] Indeed, in Freud's delineation of feminine sexual development, the visible plays an unquestioned and primary role. For Freud identifies the site/sight of the penis as the catalyst and basis of feminine sexual development. It is both the primary and stable term of a narrative of sexuality which otherwise posits motility, metamorphosis, shifts, and, explicitly, bisexuality—though his vision of bisexuality emerges merely as a temporal marker to authorize and secure a heterosexual narrative. The priority of the penis begins with its assumed cross-gender meaning; just like the boy, the girl begins sexual experience in a phallic phase in which sexual pleasure is derived from the clitoris, turned under the normative gaze of Freud into a virtual though "small penis."[20] To solidify his claim that the penis is the source of all sexuality, he boldly posits anatomical similarity as the first of his "indications of bisexuality":[21] "the little girl is a little man."[22] However, sight of the male genitals introduces the categories of difference and lack as the girl compares her own "inadequate" genitals to the male's. This "reading" of the body initiates the castration complex. Freud's formulation of the girl's response to the castration complex is itself normative; the fiction of lack assigned to the girl on the basis of vision is subjected to revision. By supplying a narrative of lack and devaluation attached not to the girl's response to the sight of the male genitals but to the adult woman in her relation to men, Freud indicates that this woman-as-lack structure is in fact produced by the cultural gaze and the heterosexual script which devalues woman: "This means, therefore, that as a result of the discovery of women's lack of a penis they are debased in value for girls just as they are for boys and perhaps later for men."[23]

While the lesbian is accounted for in this narrative within the "doubly missing" model Davy maps out—she is simultaneously barred from adult sexuality, devalued as lacking mother "in the practices of homosexuals, who play the parts of mother and baby,"[24] while her concomitant marking as child guarantees her inevitable identification with the lack Freud assigns to the little girl—this evaluative lack is figured in terms of contradiction. For not only has Freud identified the devaluation of woman with the larger workings of culture, but he offers, in "Femininity," a competing narrative which presents woman not as absence or lack but, conversely, in terms of excess. For, according to Freud, the girl's recognition of self as lack institutes a series of metamorphoses which figures her growth, in "comparison with what happens with boys" as "more difficult and more complicated," an excessive model of development through which the little girl must accommodate her sexuality to her relation to the penis.[25] The "two extra tasks" that the girl must undergo in order to reach sexual maturity are the change of erotic object from the mother to the father and the change of erotogenic zone from phallic clitoris to the vagina.[26] Thus, this biased bodily reading, informed by the always already devalued woman, leads Freud to formulate the second of his "indications of bisexuality": the categorical evolution from masculine to feminine (as opposed to the earlier homologous erotic structures). Bisexuality in Freud, then, is constructed to signify both excess and lack and to produce and reconfirm masculine priority and heterosexual paradigms of sexuality. Since he describes as bisexual the movement toward femininity, while suppressing the possibility of feminine desire in the male, bisexuality functions as a trope here, standing in for masculine priority, compulsory heterosexuality, and feminine instability and marginality simultaneously.

Judith Butler, however, offers to destabilize this trope by exposing its motivating terms. First, when Freud conceives of bisexuality as anatomical similarity, he continually uses the penis as the basis of comparison: the girl's clitoris is a "small penis," and her sexual pleasure is coded within a "phallic phase."[27] In her reading of "On Narcissism," Butler adumbrates Freud's strategic reliance on the penis as a repressed strategy of substitution masking as priority. In "On Narcissism," Freud compares narcissism to the self-involvement of pain, employing the example of a toothache, subsequently likened to diseased organs, which then gives way to a direct metaphor of organic excitement: "the genital organ in a state of excitation" is "the familiar prototype of an organ sensitive to pain, in some way changed and yet not diseased in the ordinary sense."[28] Shortly thereafter, Freud paradoxically contends: "certain other areas of the body—the erotogenic zones—may act as substitutes for the genitals and behave analogously to them."[29] Butler identifies the chiasmus between penis/organ and prototype/substitution: "The collapse of substitutions performed by these genitals is, however, reversed and erased. . . . [T]he erotogenic zones are said to act as substitutes *for* the genitals. In the latter case, it seems that these self-same genitals—the result or effect of a set of substitutions—are that for which other body parts act as substitutes."[30] The penis then is never a stable base of reference but merely a metaphor of originality, a figure of the "prototype," which arises at the end of a chain of substitute metaphors and then pretends to a position of stability in order to empower further substitutions. The moment of unmediated bodily sight as the basis of femininity and heterosexuality is itself mediated by this Freudian inter-text to reveal the original recognition of presence and lack, as well as their associated sexes, male and female, as symbolic and substitutive metaphor.

The point I wish to make by comparing Butler's analysis of "On Narcissism" with Freud's vision of femininity is that the role of vision turned upon the body to determine gender and sexuality is in fact never primary or determinate. Instead, the workings of the eye are conditioned by the ideological categories afforded by the narratives of phallocentric heterosexuality, which vision naturalizes as effects of the visually motivated trope of bisexuality. Butler in fact supports my contention that bisexuality works as a semiotic tool to naturalize heterosexuality as sexuality in general. Though Freud conceives of bisexuality as an evolutionary phenomenon culminating in, if not producing, heterosexuality, Butler brings to light the prior categories of heterosexuality which not only structure the "primary bisexuality" of which heterosexuality is an effect but also demonstrate how Freud precludes the very possibility of homosexual desire necessary for bisexuality.

The conceptualization of bisexuality in terms of dispositions, feminine and masculine, which have heterosexual aims as their intentional correlates, suggest that for Freud bisexuality is the coincidence of two heterosexual desires within a single psyche. The masculine disposition is, in effect, never oriented toward the father as an object of sexual love, and neither is the feminine disposition oriented toward the mother (the young girl may be so oriented, but this is before she has renounced that "masculine" side of her dispositional nature). In repudiating the mother as an object of sexual love, the girl of necessity repudiates her masculinity and, paradoxically, "fixes" her femininity as a consequence. Hence, within Freud's thesis of primary bisexuality, there is no homosexuality, and only opposites attract.[31]

In this frame bisexuality cannot be read but as a substitute category for heterosexuality, used to valorize the categories of visual sexual difference as it represses homosexuality and the possibility of sexual difference outside of the clear distinction between presence/absence of the phallus. This logic of substitution threatens to destabilize the narrative it empowers. For since heterosexual development depends upon the trope of bisexuality to mask its inconsistency between gender and desire (as manifested, for instance, in the girl's "masculine phase" accounting for her desire for the mother), this masking function offers to intercede in the subject's first encounters with vision and heterosexuality to unfix biological sex from sexuality at the moment of their supposed conjunction.

Indeed, just as Freud misread the girl's body, attributing to it a "small penis," thus destabilizing the visible body to secure normative heterosexuality, so does the postphallic logic of castration serve to "correct" bodily misreading to guarantee heterosexuality, paradoxically out of supposed homosexuality. Because the primal scene occurs before the child has recognized sexual difference as phallic presence or lack, s/he cannot understand the scene through gender difference but rather views the sex act as one between two subjects, both of whom bear the phallus. In this indeterminacy, vision reveals itself as susceptible to both imaginary desire in the perceived multiplication of phallic possession and as a potentially subversive, rather than normative, construct of heterosexuality. For in the latter case, not only is the category of biological sex which renders (hetero)sexuality intelligible circulated by the very mechanism of vision that should stabilize and confirm it, but this biopic moment also institutes a fundamental substitution at the first conjunction of sexuality and sight: homosexuality displaces heterosexuality. Lee Edelman suggests in his article "Seeing Things: Representation, the Scene of Surveillance, and the Spectacle of Gay Male Sex" that the imagined profusion of the penis demands that "the primal scene specifically takes shape as a sodomitical scene,"[32] "one in which the supposition of homosexuality is embedded."[33] However, Edelman argues, this disturbance of the rigid heterosexual paradigm that allows the child to recognize and identify with deconstructed, indeterminate gender roles, and thus with alternative arrangements of sexuality beyond those structured by gender difference, is suppressed by the heterosexual association of castration with vision. By introducing the possibility and threat of castration as equivalent to, and even defining, gender difference through bodily sight, the binary and mutually defining categories of heterosexuality revise the narrative of the imagined sodomitical scene. Coupling the "supposition of homosexuality" with the threat of castration, the sexual plurality and possible identification offered by the primal scene are retrospectively suppressed. The child is thus fixed to a gender role structured around the opposition of presence and lack and held there by the threat of erasure, of being subject to castration and defined by lack. This movement that defines gender distinction—the movement from the imaginary doubled position and possession of the penis to the symbolic threat of castration—is at best an ironic guarantor of heterosexuality, since it constructs its categories only by threatening to discard the very mark of sexual difference.

If the penis is represented by psychoanalytic models in impossible positions—present where it is absent and both reifying and renouncing the body—the body itself cannot be described in any actual sense by these moments of seeing. Instead, vision constitutes the seen body as it constitutes the seeing subject, interpellating both into a heterosexual model. With this recognition, we can now identify discourses of sexuality based not on the body they construct as their referent per se, but upon the visually apprehended body which serves as a conditioned signifier. Biopia represents this point of intersection between the body and the eye and describes the constituting effects through which a queer body is made to pass. At the same time, biopia puts this heterosexualization into crisis by the very instability of both the signifier (the body) and the trope (bisexuality) that are needed to secure the surface terms of biological sex and to confirm these terms as defining sexuality. At this point, I would like to look at the queer male subject configured and refigured in this system as he is caught in a web of competing signs and positions, sexual markings and potential erasures.

Of Subjects and Optics

This visual bias, which founds and polices categories of sex ensures, even as it wavers, that homosexual desire remains invisible and that any claim to identity must be made through heterosexual terms and an erasure of the queer self. But it is within this contradictory logic of visibility and determination, sexual marking and revision, that biopia comes to work as a destabilizing force. If heterosexual ideology works in hierarchical contradiction here to mark the sexual subject only in relation to the primary erasure and absence of castration and through its necessary recognition, then the place of the male in the system of sexual marking is caught in competing models. For while Monique Wittig sees the woman as the sole, marked sex and argues that the male passes as the unmarked and presumed universal, Luce Irigaray sees the primacy of the male as the ground for marking all sexual figures: woman in this system of "hom(m)osexuality" is merely negatively marked as "not-man."[34] Though seemingly contradictory, both of these models make the same point. What is at stake in a system of sexual marking is the establishment of hierarchy and the distribution of power. That men are simultaneously, or (as Sedgwick would have it) chiasmically, viewed as marked and unmarked, sexed and unsexed, suggests the masculine gender as the site of ideological production and the male body as its visible point of coherence and crisis. Eve Sedgwick's notion of the homosocial adumbrates this situation, as she sees power, position, and property exchanged "between men" through the cultural devaluation of woman. This contradictory discourse of power, then, insists on a heterosexual order while it promotes a sexual misreading; the only mark of sexuality in this system is gender. To be male in culture is to be in power and heterosexually positioned in relation to woman. Ironically, then, Sedgwick's concept of homosocial desire, whereby power, position, and recognition is passed between and defined by men, precludes the visibility of homosexuality. It is this problem of competing categories of sex and power within the paradox of the in/visibility of sexual difference among men that I would like to map out on the body of the male homosexual.

Eve Kosofsky Sedgwick again guides my methodology here as she stresses that it is important for queer theory to recognize the potentials of inverse power relations in every subject position, to see the oppressor within the oppressed: "We aren't yet used to asking as antihomophobic readers how a variety of forms of oppression intertwine systemically with each other; and especially how the person who is disabled through one set of oppressions may by the same positioning be enabled through others."[35] Here again, it is the coimplication of compulsory heterosexuality and its dominant fiction of visible difference which create the fundamental paradox, the biopia, of male homosexuality, what Diana Fuss, borrowing from Irigaray, terms its "both at once" status.[36] For as men, male homosexuals are heirs to the phallic privileges of the sociosymbolic—"they are oppressing"[37]—but as fags they fall outside of culture. While my later investigations into the potential of the de-signed body and camp to work as models for breaking down this biopic stratification of the subject, I would first like to articulate more fully the paradox of the queer's "bisexual" position within and without heterosexuality.

This inside/out positioning that Fuss identifies quickly breaks down into a crisis of "ocular proof." For the symbolic order is established by a series of visual distinctions which are successively hierarchized around the categories of possession/lack, homogeneity/difference, and self/other. Lacking the visual cues of difference that other indices of oppression carry on the surface of the body (or on its metonymic surface), the male homosexual can only be mis/recognized by the appropriating social eye as the self-identical possessor of the phallus; his visible body continually displaces the invisible desire that it fails to signify. In this movement, the normative criterion of gender not only reveals itself as irrevocably attached to and substituting for the category of heterosexuality; it also establishes anatomical sex as the primary site of difference. Thus, if compulsory heterosexuality understands and interpellates the queer subject within its terms of visible distinction, the queer self is marked by his own erasure, the fiction of heterosexual masculine privilege positions him in opposition to his desire. Jonathan Dollimore identifies this opposition between visible phallic possession and invisible queer sexuality, "the opposition masculine/

homosexual," as a construction of the heterosexual contract and an elaborate displacement along the axes of gender difference, "a conflation of two classic binaries (masculine/feminine; hetero/homosexual)."[38] However, as the collapse of sexuality into gender difference erases the latter binary (hetero/homo, or the possibility of difference on a register of sexuality) in the terms of heterosexual presumption, same-sex desire—as it confounds the assumed, privileged, and structuring gender-as-difference demand—threatens in turn to reduce the binary logic of the symbolic order into a mere articulation of the same, an imaginary inability to distinguish self from other, subject from object, or to formulate the fiction of gender from the recognition of penis and castration. According to this logic of conflation, appropriation, and phallo-visual privilege, the queer subject is in a position of doubled erasure; he must position himself in a heterosexist cultural order which not only conceals him but also is menaced by his terms of desire. This collapse is prevented, however, by the guarantee of biopia, whereby the power of same-sex desire to destroy the categories of heterosexuality is repressed by the trope of bisexuality. In this case, bisexuality negotiates between the surface sign of the body and the unsignified desire of the subject to keep conventional sexual distinctions intact and to understand the subject within them. While this function of biopia serves to bolster the heterosexual system, it is important to see that it also preserves queer desire, though in a suppressed position, preventing the subject from falling into an erased position outside of any symbolic structure. Unless a queer symbolic is to remain coextensive with and limited to the imploding Lacanian symbolic of the phallic self-identical male, it must take as its primary structuring term this very crisis of biopic in/visibility that at once marks and erases his sexual difference.

Monique Wittig casts this theoretical model and the terms of its border-blurring subject, constantly under threat of overlay or obliteration, into an optic metaphor:

If I try to look at the dotted line that delineates the bulk of the social contract, it moves, it shifts, and sometimes it produces something visible, and sometimes it disappears altogether. It looks like the Möbius strip. Now I see this, now I see something quite different. But this Möbius strip is fake, because only one aspect of the optical effect appears distinctly and massively, and that is heterosexuality. Homosexuality appears like a ghost only dimly and sometimes not at all.[39]

According to the "between the lines" terms of the social contract, then, this "ghostly" homosexual subject manifests and marks himself "only dimly" in the contradictory spaces of excess and absence which are both ultimately rendered invisible through cultural erasure and the function of biopia.

Let me first present the absent subject. As detailed above, the radical invisibility of the queer self is ensured by the symbolic prerequisite of heterosexuality and the regulating system of validation and punishment which enforces its conditions. The demand "to pass" coerces the subject to announce his identity in a denial and displacement of erotic difference sutured over with the dominant fiction of the heterosexual paradigm; he masks his desire by mimicking the desire of the other and appropriates validated social roles and manners to gain a place within instead of without the cultural system. Simply put, the need to pass, to erase the markings of homosexuality in the interests of social validation, mobility, and security, guarantees a radical absence and invisibility as the basis of subjectivity. Thus, by virtue of the blind spot of erotic difference, homosexuality is under constant threat of submersion, reinscription, and erasure by the enveloping and appropriating dominant culture whenever the subject's queerness is not excessively performed or his coming out manically repeated. It is by this default positional marking of invisibility that the superculture ransoms as straight, same, and self-identical all that visibly accords, all that passes.

However, in this guise of invisibility, the dichotomy of excess and absence begins to collapse in terms of queer performativity and the simultaneous demands of biopia. For just as Foucault's repressive hypothesis sees an excess of sexual signs and discourse emerging from the very censorship of sexuality—"[T]his was not a plain and simple imposition of silence. Rather, it was a new regime of discourses. . . . [T]hings were said in a different way"[40]—we must consider the absent markings of sexuality demanded in passing, not as a simple absence, but as an elaborate semiotic construction of layered and self-erasing markings (straight drag) and so conceive of the queer subject as a subversively sedimentary and plural self. This excess of identity, the "both at once" access and guise of the gay masquerade, identifies its mechanism of visibility. To be recognized as queer means to appear only in excess of eclipsing cultural demands, desires, and restrictions, an act of naming that occurs largely through the overt displays of pornography, camp, drag, activism, or a continual announcement of identity in the mandated redundancies and reenactments of coming out.

Quite simply, coming out must necessarily be repeated, because the body, unable to register sexual difference, refuses to signify homosexuality and reinscribes the subject at the moment of his silence. This enforced passing at the level of the body is oppressive, silencing homosexual desire, yet it also has a subversive potential, since it activates the mechanics of biopia and the trope of bisexuality. The subject in this configuration moves from the margins of excess (in his stratified, straight-upon-gay physicality) and absence (in his suppression) to the more central, illusory position of full subject by virtue of this passing. And though this subject position is achieved strictly by means of an erasure and displacement, the necessary category of bisexuality produced in the disjunction of homosexual erasure and heterosexual presence stands as a marker of this hegemonic operation. But the problem of the body remains. If the body is the single sign of sexuality and this body and the sexuality it signals is always straight, it is only through contradiction that bisexuality as the subversive marker of suppression is embodied or manifest. Accordingly, revising the stable and material terms of the physical body, I suggest that perhaps this embodied figure is itself essentially figural, emerging as the overt mark of contradiction saturating the discourse of sexuality from biology to desire, body to bed.

If coming out stands as an explicit distinction between heterosexuality and homosexuality, the categorical contradictions, the play between excess and absence invoked to police and control this emergent subject position, attest to a figural inscription of bisexuality that marks the tension between homosexuality and its continued reinscription by the body. Since the queer self has been rendered visible only in excess of legal, reproductive, and representative social structures, he is a subject historically constituted in moments of transgression or border defiance. Coming out stands at once as an act of excess, defying the established borders of culture, and as a transgression of the law of the visible, contradicting the law of the body and disconnecting biological sex from (hetero)sexuality. Coming out, Act Up's queer reformulation of Descartes (I am out, therefore I am), is a discursively rather than visibly constructed act of excess and is especially vulnerable to cultural attack, for it is constructed only within the symbolic categories established by compulsory heterosexuality. Judith Butler articulates this cultural function of "performative contradiction" which renders the excessive and the visible always already invisible:

This presumptive heterosexuality . . . functions within discourse to communicate a threat: "'you-will-be-straight-or-you-will-not-be.'" Women, lesbians, and gay men . . . cannot assume the position of the speaking subject within the linguistic system of compulsory heterosexuality. To speak within the system is to be deprived of the possibility of speech; hence, to speak at all in that context is a performative contradiction, the linguistic assertion of a self that cannot "be" within the language that asserts it.[41]

Once the extradiscursive act of coming out is performed, a swift social and institutional machinery of erasure and contradiction comes into play to punish the transgressor, to erase and reinscribe the breaching subject within the terms of his very emergence.

In the following narrative, Eve Sedgwick demonstrates, in the context of legal decisions, this paradoxical space of transgression and erasure which surrounds the possibility of coming out and public visibility:

In Montgomery County, Maryland, in 1973, an eighth-grade earth science teacher named Acanfora was transferred to a nonteaching position by the Board of Education when they learned he was gay. When Acanfora spoke to news media, such as "60 Minutes" and the Public Broadcasting System, about his situation, he was refused a new contract entirely. Acanfora sued. The federal district court that first heard his case supported the action and rationale of the Board of Education, holding that Acanfora's recourse to the media had brought undue attention to himself and his sexuality, to a degree that would be deleterious to the educational process. The Fourth Circuit Court of Appeals disagreed. They considered Acanfora's public disclosures to be protected speech under the First Amendment. Although they overruled the lower court's rationale, however, the appellate court affirmed its decision not to allow Acanfora to return to teaching. Indeed, they denied his standing to bring the suit in the first place, on the grounds that he had failed to note on his original employment application that he had been, in college, an officer of a student homophile organization—a notation that would, as school officials admitted in court, have prevented his ever being hired. The rationale for keeping Acanfora out of his classroom was thus no longer that he had disclosed too much about his homosexuality, but quite the opposite, that he had not disclosed enough.[42]

Sedgwick goes on to show that the queer subject is rendered invisible not only by his sentence to cultural absence but also by virtue of an excessive "disclosure at once compulsory and forbidden": "The most obvious fact about this history of judicial formulations is that it codifies an excruciating system of double binds, systematically oppressing gay people, identities, and acts by undermining through contradictory constraints on discourse the grounds of their very being."[43] The queer subject is culturally negated in the crossfire of competing terms and dictates, which deny any ontology of a queer subjectivity and render invisible the most primary moment of self-distinction, "I am," thus conflating subversive categories of excess with the default fiction of absence. This move of cultural eclipse and purgation, this constructed lack, not only renders the queer invisible, outside, and absent, but functions as an "excess of significance"[44]—the burden of all sexuality, Rubin claims— that reinforces and actually produces the very cultural space that excludes it. Diana Fuss adumbrates this necessary relational dependence of "the same" upon the excluded different: "The homo in relation to the hetero ... operates as an indispensable interior exclusion—an outside which is inside interiority making the articulation of the latter possible, a transgression of the border which is necessary to constitute the border as such."[45]

Indeed, "the homo in relation to the hetero," figured here in terms of contradiction—interior/exclusion, transgression/containment, subversion/perpetuation— marks the place and function of the trope of bisexuality. It is by means of this very trope, which engages the terms of contradiction defining bisexuality and biopia, that the homosexual is not completely overwritten or dropped out of this relation by the chiasmic logic of heterosexuality. If the body is always the motivating figure of such relations, then the structure of biopia has forced the physical form to embody contradiction instead of naturalizing it.

The De-Signed Body

The trope of bisexuality as a by-product of straight demands and the exclusion of homosexual desire attests that, indeed, "[e]very outside is also an alongside."[46] A queer symbolic, then, must visualize as its immediate terms those which in fact mediate and confound the exclusionary categories and borders of the heterosexual system by multiplying and amplifying the play of contradiction and difference which constitutes the border itself. The body as the failed sign of desire, with its assumed borders and natural categories, should serve as the primary point from which to produce this narrative of ambiguity. To a large degree, the Lacanian symbolic order presumes as its structuring term the physical body, which is, in fact, always already symbolically mediated. For it is from this primary sign that such fundamental distinctions as self/other, male/female, and presence/absence emerge. In turn, these hierarchized binaries produce desire in their identification of lack. However, as the queer crisis of biopia has shown, the body does not produce the condition of desire for the homosexual male, but rather opposes it. Homosexual desire, quite simply, threatens to throw the binary distinctions generated by the body into unitary distinction, as the eroticized body refuses the condition of absence necessary for the symbolic tension of privilege and lack from which desire emerges. From where, then, does homosexual desire emerge? Perhaps it is the body itself that the homosexual properly lacks, and it is thus the sign of desire.

The possibilities for a queer symbolic that doesn't explode the very terms of its organization must depend upon and exploit the principle of contradiction and coexistence instead of the symbolic's principle of distinction. Difference is thus conceived not as an external descriptive category of identity but as an internal, coexistent, and contradictory force constituting identity. The task is, then, to locate "differences within identity" rather than to locate them "outside identity, in the spaces between identities"[47] in the fiction encouraged by a symbolically mediated and conditioned body masking as primary and physical. Accordingly, the body cannot produce signs for a queer symbolic but must appear only at the end of a complex signifying chain which discursively constructs the lacking body, much in the way that the Lacanian symbolic order supplies the absent phallus. It is the narrative of this bodily construction that a queer symbolic engages. Harold Beaver identifies the realm of "Homosexual Signs" as one guided by "the multiplication of signs"

(105) and "the urge to interpret."[48] These two conditions demand not only a refusal of the physical body as a unitary and stable signifier (in favor of the contradictory mandate of multiplying and interpreting the sign) but also a multiplication and account of the symbolic order as a "duplicate culture" itself, composed of "constantly interrupted and overlapping roles."[49]

In this light, the concept of a queer symbolic is also a move to queer, or to render different in itself, the coercive, self-recognizing symbolic order. In order for difference to be dispersed within and throughout this system, the contradictions and conflations produced by the cultural order's dependence upon the physical body as a natural anchor must be dealt with theoretically and these paradoxes then turned on the body itself. Lacan de-signs the body, driving a wedge between body and signifier, when he distinguishes the penis from the phallus and separates the symbol from the body.

Like Sedgwick's chiasmic model of gender and sexual definitions[50] and Edelman's identification of castration and phallic lack as a corrective lens to the phantasmatic dispersion and plurality of the phallus in the primal scene, Lacan, in "The Signification of the Phallus," begins with and insists upon antinomy: "There is an antinomy . . . that is internal to the assumption by man of his sex: why must he assume the attributes of that sex only through a threat—the threat, indeed, of their privation?"[51] In this view, then, the sexed body is only naturalized under threat of collapse or dismemberment, a condition that should serve to denaturalize the process, since phallic privilege is produced by display of phallic absence. However, in this system, phallic possession is equated with full presence. Lacan argues for the conflation of genital attribute and phallic privilege: "these relations will turn around a 'to be' and a 'to have,' which, by referring to a signifier, the phallus, have the opposed effect, on the one hand, of giving reality to the subject in this signifier, and, on the other, of derealizing the relations of the signified."[52] Thus the phallus as signifier sexes the body and masks its own status as signifier, "derealizing" its relation in "the comedy" of what Lacan calls "a 'to seem,'" which reinforces possession as it displaces it.[53]

But this seeming wholeness, the seamless conjunction of body-gender-sexuality is impossible, since it is achieved by an alien and alienating signifier ("it speaks in the Other").[54] Lacan, in fact, identifies the phallus not as an "imaginary effect," "object," or "organ," which would reify wholeness and identity, but as a signifier that conflates difference: "it is the signifier intended to designate as a whole the effects of the signified."[55] It is the "effects" which masquerade as and are opposed to wholeness that mark "[man's] relation as a subject to the signifier"[56] and stand as a range of denaturalizing forces that the body (subjected to the phallic mark) effaces. The body (and sexual difference) is constituted by the cultural phallic signifier with no relation to the interpellated subject or h/er sex except as it marks h/er, producing difference between the body and the signifier itself. The "effects" of the signified, how the phallus "derealizes" and "conditions ... by its presence as a signifier,"[57] are the mechanics of a "tangibility that has been transformed into a purely visible [and thus symbolic] experience."[58]

For Lacan, the phallus works as a mediating signifier, granting the body the illusion of wholeness through its sexual marking, which in turn positions the body within a hierarchical heterosexuality. It is because of these two conditions—the body as inseparable from its heterosexual coding and the necessity for the distinction between presence and lack to produce desire and the sexed body (a distinction that queer desire frustrates)—that the homosexual may be said to lack a body. Unfortunately, the condition of subjectivity demands a body to signify presence. The homosexual, however, must present a body which, while always already heterosexual, is nonetheless also a failed citation of heterosexuality, marked as it is with the contradiction of bisexuality.

If the sexed body is produced by its relation to possession or lack of the phallic signifier, it is necessarily produced discursively. In her *Bodies That Matter*, Judith Butler contends that such discursive production is grounded in a model of citation, which is in itself indebted to a failing process of repetition:

As a sedimented effect of a reiterative or ritual practice, sex acquires its naturalized effect, and, yet, it is also by virtue of this reiteration that gaps and fissures are opened up as the constitutive instabilities in such constructions, as that which escapes or exceeds the norm, as that which cannot be wholly defined or fixed by the repetitive labor of that norm. This instability is the deconstituting possibility in the very process of repetition, the power that undoes the very effects by which "sex" is stabilized, the possibility to put the consolidation of the norms of "sex" into a potentially productive crisis.[59]

Butler uses this notion of "constitutive instabilities" to undermine the possibilities of citation, repetition, or natural primacy, by showing how such operations imply the impossibilities of the very terms from which they logically proceed. In terms of the sex/gender/sexuality chain, sexuality's citation of gender and gender's citation of the body actually reproduce the body as an unstable or lacking original. Through this strategy, Butler at once exposes the ideology of the natural sex/gender conflation and locates the production of this ideology in the process of repetition this ideology demands:

There is no "proper" gender, a gender proper to one sex rather than another, which is in some sense that sex's cultural property. Where that notion of the "proper" operates, it is always and only improperly installed as the effect of a compulsory system.... [A]ll gendering is a kind of impersonation and approximation. If this is true, it seems, there is no original or primary gender ... gender is a kind of imitation for which there is no original; in fact, it is a kind of imitation that produces the very notion of the original as an effect and consequence of the imitation itself.[60]

Perhaps the most radical consequence of Butler's philosophy here is the hierarchical reversal it effects between origin and product. For if culture assumes the body as the natural origin for gender, and gender as the origin of sexuality, Butler's model suggests, "it may now be necessary fully to invert and displace that operation of thought."[61] In this system, then, the body is not the primary signifier from which cultural roles, and thus sexual practices, emerge, but rather the body is produced by "a compulsory performance of sex"[62] which makes coherent the binary distinctions of gender and, finally, sex and naturalizes the symbolic and discursive consequence of body as immediate cause.

Though this body produced in accordance with the demands of heterosexuality stands as a lack to the homosexual, the situation is disruptive to heterosexuality as well. For when sexual difference is registered culturally at the level of the body, and homosexual desire can only manifest itself through a heterosexually marked body, this heterosexuality is put into crisis by the consequent trope of bisexuality belying the authority of sexual marking. The pressure of this crisis initiates a cultural attempt to discern and re-mark the border. In terms of homosexuality, the constitutive trope of bisexuality and the mechanics of biopia are challenged by the heterosexual order, as the homosexual's body is subjected to intense narrative to position as physically different what sex/gender marks as the same. For in order to preserve the body as the anchor of the heterosexual order of sex, difference in sexuality must be occasioned by a prior difference on the sexed and sexing body.

Lee Edelman identifies this mandated visibility of homosexuality on the surface of the body as "homographesis" and explicitly links this paradigm of vision and sexuality with the imperative of representation, difference, and the symbolic order itself. For while "the cultural production of homosexual identity in terms of an 'indiscreet anatomy' ... testifies to the cultural imperative to produce, for the purposes of ideological regulation, a putative difference within that group of male bodies that would otherwise count as 'the same,'" "it becomes both possible and necessary to posit the marker of 'homosexual difference' in terms of visual representation—in precisely those terms that psychoanalysis defines as central to the process whereby anatomical distinctions register and so become meaningful in the symbolic order of sexuality."[63] Thus while "homographesis" defines this normative "designing" of the homosexual body to signal sexual difference within the realm of sexed indistinction, it also reveals a concomitant "de-signing" of the body, a throwing into radical doubt the naturalized significance of the body:

The graphesis, the cultural inscription, of homosexual possibilities, by deconstructing the binary logic of sexual difference on which symbolic identity is based, effectively disrupts the cognitive stability that the visual perception of "sameness" and "difference" would otherwise serve to anchor. Insisting on a second order of visually registered sexual difference, homographesis both responds to and redoubles an anxiety about the coherence of those identities for the solidification of which it is initially called forth.[64]

The visual *méconnaissance* of biopia, then, finds as its symbolic consequence the representational system of homographesis, which insists upon submitting the male body to sexual marking while it also makes visible this signification of the body to render the hom(m)o-sexual bisexual, as one ironically coexisting in two categories of sexual "identity." This distinction of the homosexual from the heterosexual at the level of the body fails to be complete, however, and the trope of bisexuality is preserved, since the body itself is produced by and signals heterosexuality.

Camp/Sights: The Politics of Surface

While heterosexist culture attempts to construct a homosexual body different from conventionally sexed and seen bodies, and while this process inevitably fails, homosexual desire also demands the production of a viable body. This concern for body building, if you will, to authorize queer desire and subjectivity is the concern of camp. Camp announces the category of the heterosexual body as a legitimate site but through the crisis of display and the invisibility of desire exposes it not as a naturalized identity but rather as a sign. Ironically, this display of the body to signify difference actually works to announce the ideological process of marking this body as different. For the homosexual male, overt display of the body works to de-sign the biopic mechanics of cultural vision and to proclaim through hyperbolized and sexualized display his difference from the naturalized heterosexual male. With his emphasis on "image," D. A. Miller argues that it is precisely through the body's status as sign that this de-signing articulates itself: "the so-called gym-body of gay male culture ... displays its muscle primarily in terms of an *image* openly appealing to, and deliberately courting the possibility of being shivered by, someone else's desire. Even the most macho gay image tends to modify cultural fantasy about the male body."[65] This display as de-signing structure both invokes (without repressing) the strategic trope of bisexuality—as the visible sexual category of male is multiplied and two distinct sexualities are produced, the hyperbolized gay and naturalized straight—and names the camp moment in its insistent play between presentation and representation of cultural codes. As a mode of expression and symbolic organization, camp offers at once to differentiate the queer self from the demanded heterosexual role and to function within the authorized terms of negation of the patriarchal symbolic by rendering the body itself both-at-once instead of forcing sexuality to inhabit the position of ambivalence, threatened by displacement.

The distinguished homosexual body is thus a body of signs. Paradoxically, in terms of a queer symbolic's mode of coincidence, the first task of a homosexual discourse must be differentiation and distinction. However, this distinction, as Butler points out, is made through the mode of imperfect citation. If camp is defined in part through its insistence upon semiotic production and difference, this difference is ironically produced through a co-option of culturally reified structures. At its most basic, camp produces difference through its refusal to accept the surface signs it adopts as anything but surface. This alienation, distinction, and multiplica-tion of cultural positions is accomplished by camp's "unceasing production of signs" and the concurrent "call to interpretation that it issues"[66] and works to de-sign socially imposed identities. For with the self-consciousness, artifice and parody that define the camp moment, the subject in its drama is flaunted as a social act; the codes of culture, its props. The "camper," whom Beaver calls the "prodigious consumer of signs,"[67] exploits the plurality of his visible/invisible status in the biopia of a heterosexist culture of competing and mutually erasing codes and roles not only to render visible the social script but to illustrate as well the ideologically neutralized space between the self and the cultural stage. He simultaneously produces and performs symbolic codes precisely to show these normative signs and compulsory categories at work through a strategy of hyperbolized repetition. In a manically insistent and repetitive catalog of camp and masquerade theory, which itself seems to mimic and perform what it reports, Carol-Anne Tyler succinctly outlines the mechanisms and consequences of camp, here in the context of drag and genderfuck:

> To be a mimic, according to Irigaray, is to "assume the . . . role deliberately . . . so as to make 'visible,' by an effect of playful repetition, what was supposed to remain invis-ible. . . ." To play the feminine is to "speak" it ironically, to italicize it, in Nancy Miller's words; to hyperbolize it, in Mary Ann Doane's words; or to parody it, as Mary Russo and Linda Kauffman describe it. In . . . camp, one "does" ideology in order to undo it, producing knowledge about it: that gender and the heterosexual orientation presumed to anchor it are unnatural and even oppressive.[68]

What allows the camp aesthetic to escape cultural policing and censorship is its invisibility, for what it makes visible, by engaging, are the always already visible contours of cultural surface, a naturalized blind spot. But by working within the terms of culture, to return to an earlier argument, camp must erase itself as it speaks; the bisexually perverse potential of indeterminacy is neutralized by its repe-tition of the codes that repress it. Tyler worries that since camp takes as its ideals the models of heterosexuality associated with the white middle class, it becomes indistinguishable from straight culture's oppressive ideologies. Butler, in an argument presented earlier, sees the reinscription of the subversive subject in the oppression inherent in the language s/he must speak: "Discourse becomes oppressive when it requires that the speaking subject, in order to speak, participate in the very terms of that oppression."[69] Even the discursively produced queer body of camp is continually under threat of submersion by the heterosexuality of the very body it borrows. Yet Butler's deconstruction of original and imitation—whereby both terms infect each other to enact on the one hand the impossibility of origin and, on the other, a function of failed repetition—empowers a double reading. For, within the logic of camp even this erasure is foregrounded and troped; the invisible made visible. In camp's insistence upon self-consciously displaying coercive codes, David Bergman suggests that "the apparent emptying of self-expression is most conspicuous."[70] This evacuation of self threatens not only to mimic the erasure of the queer self by the same social marks it examines but also, in consequence, to reduce camp itself to a self-emptying category, since it negates all agency. However, this surface self-negation is the truly subversive potential of camp. For since it is the very rendered-visible surface of culture with which it constructs the self-consciously seeing and seen subject, any movement toward evacuation is necessarily performed on the surface and not on the fiction of depth these categories imply. Thus, the heterosexual body camp flaunts by either contradicting or hyperbolizing gender, through drag or parody, respectively, is displayed as a representation, since body and gender are dissociated by these strategies of contradiction or exaggeration. This image is itself redoubled; the camp body presents itself as purely semiotic—a representation of the representation that the body signifying sex already is.

This metarepresentational quality of the "homosexual" body distinguishes it from the body played straight. This body's semiotic and fluid status gains stability only through circulation and further signification and thus undermines the naturalized materiality, fixity, and sexuality of the visibly read heterosexual body. The point is not to build a literal body, an impossible task, but rather that in the construction of a figural homosexual body, the notion of a stable, material, heterosexual body is deconstructed. If biopia describes a demand to read the body in one way only, through the category of heterosexuality, the contradictions and disturbances that it marks conversely demand a succession of readings and re-visions. Camp's politics of surface interrogates and multiplies sexual signifiers and reveals a body that does not mean in one simple way but, rather, cannot stop meaning.[71]

While the trope of bisexuality and the mechanics of biopia, as outlined here, have been used to construct relational difference and hierarchical oppression, they have been repressed simultaneously by the ideological contradiction and suppression of the chiasmic fiction that there is "one point around which everything can be placed in order; this point exists and it is unique."[72] Although our sexual system constructs the sexed body as this point of intelligibility, coherence, and naturalization, this argument has shown the body itself to be anything but unique and has, in fact, questioned its condition of existence per se. Instead, the body itself stands as a symptom of metonymic infection, conditioned by the sexual categories and symbolic systems it pretends to ground. The body's claim to identity is riddled through with theoretical crossings as well, since its various cultural categories themselves compete for political primacy and the myth of identity gives way to a multiplicity of possible identities. Judith Butler articulates the various points of view from which to read the body and situate identity: "[T]heories of . . . identity that elaborate predicates of color, sexuality, ethnicity, class, and ablebodiedness invariably close with an embarrassed 'etc.' at the end of the list. Through this horizontal trajectory of adjectives, these positions strive to encompass a situated subject, but invariably fail to be complete."[73] Not only does this multiple potential render any association of the body and identity impossible, but it also invokes the mechanics of cultural vision into narratives of intersections, interruptions, (mis)recognitions, sanctions, and suppressions, of which sex is only one. The structures of (in)visibility and hegemony producing the trope of bisexuality and the semiotics of biopia reveal the physically read subject as a palimpsest whose body not only imprints upon and displaces metaphysical possibilities for identity but is in turn written over by social fictions. While these cultural imperatives have only a metonymic relation with the culturally naturalized body, their effects work to conflate any disjunction. It is this disjunction that a politics of surface, or camp's bisexual, biopic layerings, interrogate. A queer symbolic predicated on an unstable dependence of the visible upon what it represses designates the mirrored and multiplying border as the site of contest for definitional control and thus cultural positioning. Nothing less is at stake than disrupting and rendering visible the inequity of culture's blinding equation of an eye for an I.

Notes

1. Gayle S. Rubin, "Thinking Sex: Notes for a Radical Theory of the Politics of Sexuality," in *The Lesbian and Gay Studies Reader*, ed. Henry Abelove, Michèle Aina Barale, and David M. Halperin (New York: Routledge, 1993), 32.
2. Eve Kosofsky Sedgwick, *Between Men: English Literature and Male Homosocial Desire* (New York: Columbia University Press, 1985), 15.
3. Rubin, "Thinking Sex," 32.
4. Jonathan Crary, *Techniques of the Observer: On Vision and Modernity in the Nineteenth Century* (Cambridge: MIT Press, 1993), 16.
5. Crary, *Techniques of the Observer*, 20.

6. Crary, *Techniques of the Observer*, 90.

7. Crary, *Techniques of the Observer*, 26.

8. Kate Davy, "Fe/Male Impersonation," in *The Politics and Poetics of Camp*, ed. Moe Meyer (New York: Routledge, 1994), 142.

9. Diana Fuss, *Essentially Speaking: Feminism, Nature and Difference* (New York: Routledge, 1989), 46.

10. David Bergman, *Gaiety Transfigured: Gay Self-Representation in American Literature* (Madison: University of Wisconsin Press, 1991), 43.

11. Virginia Woolf, *The Waves* (New York: Harcourt, Brace, Jovanovich, 1931), 157.

12. Fuss, *Essentially Speaking*, 50.

13. Jacques Lacan, "The Split between the Eye and the Gaze," in *The Four Fundamental Concepts of Psychoanalysis*, trans. Alan Sheridan (New York: W. W. Norton, 1977), 72.

14. Lacan, "The Split between the Eye and the Gaze," 71.

15. Jacques Lacan, "The Mirror Stage as Formative of the Function of the I as revealed in Psychoanalytic Experience," in *Écrits*, trans. Alan Sheridan (New York: W. W. Norton, 1977), 4.

16. Lacan, "The Mirror Stage," 3.

17. Lacan, "The Mirror Stage," 5.

18. Lacan, "The Split between the Eye and the Gaze," 75.

19. Sigmund Freud, "Femininity," in *New Introductory Lectures on Psycho-Analysis*, trans. and ed. James Strachey (New York: W. W. Norton, 1933), 150.

20. Freud, "Femininity," 146.

21. Freud, "Femininity," 141.

22. Freud, "Femininity," 146.

23. Freud, "Femininity," 157.

24. Freud, "Femininity," 161.

25. Freud, "Femininity," 145.

26. Freud, "Femininity," 145.

27. Freud, "Femininity," 146.

28. Sigmund Freud, "On Narcissism: An Introduction," in *The Standard Edition of the Complete Psychological Works of Sigmund Freud*, vol. 14, trans. James Strachey (London: Hogarth Press, 1925), 84.

29. Freud, "On Narcissism," 84.

30. Judith Butler, *Bodies That Matter: On the Discursive Limits of "Sex"* (New York: Routledge, 1993), 60.

31. Judith Butler, *Gender Trouble: Feminism and the Subversion of Identity* (New York: Routledge, 1990), 62.

32. Lee Edelman, "Seeing Things: Representation, the Scene of Surveillance, and the Spectacle of Gay Male Sex," in *Inside/Out: Lesbian Theories, Gay Theories*, ed. Diana Fuss (New York: Routledge, 1991), 101.

33. Edelman, "Seeing Things," 94.

34. Luce Irigaray, *This Sex Which Is Not One*, trans. Catherine Porter and Carolyn Burke (Ithaca: Cornell University Press, 1985), 172.

35. Eve Kosofsky Sedgwick, *Epistemology of the Closet* (Los Angeles: University of California Press, 1990), 32.

36. Fuss, *Essentially Speaking*, 46.

37. Fuss, *Essentially Speaking*, 46.

38. Jonathan Dollimore, "Homophobia and Sexual Difference," *Oxford Literary Review* 8.1–2 (1986): 5.

39. Monique Wittig, *The Straight Mind and Other Essays* (New York: Harvester/ Wheatsheaf, 1992), 40.

40. Michel Foucault, *The History of Sexuality: An Introduction*, vol. 1, trans. Robert Hurly (New York: Vintage Books, 1978), 27.

41. Butler, *Gender Trouble*, 116.

42. Sedgwick, *Epistemology*, 69.

43. Sedgwick, *Epistemology*, 70.

44. Rubin, "Thinking Sex," 11.

45. Diana Fuss, "Inside/Out," in *Inside/Out: Lesbian Theories, Gay Theories*, ed. Diana Fuss (New York: Routledge, 1991), 3.

46. Fuss, "Inside/Out," 5.

47. Fuss, *Essentially Speaking*, 103.

48. Harold Beaver, "Homosexual Signs (*In Memory of Roland Barthes*)," *Critical Inquiry* 8 (Autumn 1981): 104–5.

49. Beaver, "Homosexual Signs," 104.

50. Sedgwick, *Epistemology*, 87–89.

51. Jacques Lacan, "The Signification of the Phallus," in *Écrits*, trans. Alan Sheridan (New York: W. W. Norton, 1977), 281.

52. Lacan, "The Signification of the Phallus," 289.

53. Lacan, "The Signification of the Phallus," 289.

54. Lacan, "The Signification of the Phallus," 285.

55. Lacan, "The Signification of the Phallus," 285.

56. Lacan, "The Signification of the Phallus," 287.

57. Lacan, "The Signification of the Phallus," 285.

58. Crary, *Techniques of the Observer*, 124.

59. Butler, *Bodies That Matter*, 10.

60. Judith Butler, "Imitation and Gender Insubordination," in *Inside/Out: Lesbian Theories, Gay Theories*, ed. Diana Fuss (New York: Routledge, 1991), 21.

61. Butler, "Imitation," 29.

62. Butler, "Imitation," 29.

63. Lee Edelman, *Homographesis: Essays in Gay Literary and Cultural Theory* (New York: Routledge, 1994), 10–11.

64. Edelman, *Homographesis*, 12.

65. D. A. Miller, *Bringing Out Roland Barthes* (Los Angeles: University of California Press, 1992), 31.

66. Beaver, "Homosexual Signs," 105–6.

67. Beaver, "Homosexual Signs," 105.

68. Carol-Anne Tyler, "Boys Will Be Girls: The Politics of Gay Drag," in *Inside/Out: Lesbian Theories, Gay Theories*, ed. Diana Fuss (New York: Routledge, 1991), 53. In this passage, Tyler quotes from Irigaray, *This Sex Which Is Not One*, 76; Nancy Miller, "Emphasis Added: Plots and Plausibilities in Women's Fiction," *PMLA* 96 (1981): 38; Mary Ann Doane, "Film and the Masquerade—Theorising the Female Spectator," *Screen* 23.3–4 (1982): 82; Mary Russo, "Female Grotesques: Carnival

and Theory," in *Feminist Studies/Critical Studies*, ed. Teresa de Lauretis (Bloomington: Indiana University Press, 1986), 217, 224; and Linda Kauffman, *Discourses of Desire: Gender, Genre, and Epistolary Fictions* (Ithaca: Cornell University Press, 1986), 294–95, 298.

69. Butler, *Gender Trouble*, 116.
70. Bergman, *Gaiety Transfigured*, 105.
71. I am indebted to Greg Bredbeck and his 1990 course on Shakespearean metadrama at the University of California, Riverside, for this model of incomplete and resignifying signification. This was formative to my thinking, because it introduced a performative alternative to the usual stance of the oppressed's exclusion from language and the symbolic. In this model, the symbolically refused not only demands symbolic presence but hyperbolically motivates symbolization to the point of collapse. By impelling unending signification, the symbolic other forces signification itself to approach self-reflexivity, in that the chain of signification documents its own inadequacy. One meaning replaces another, qualifying not the subject but its own inadequacy to represent the subject. Greg used Shakespeare, specifically Cleopatra's body and pronoun reference in the sonnets, to make his point; I use the literally figurative body. I hope he approves my appropriation.
72. Crary, *Techniques of the Observer*, 51.
73. Butler, *Gender Trouble*, 143.

Chapter 10

Rough Trade:
Sexual Taxonomy in Postwar America

Chris Cagle

> **Rough trade:** An uncultured, roughly dressed and spoken man picked up by a homosexual, or such men generically. See **trade.**
>
> **Trade:** Generic for male prostitutes to homosexuals, or for heterosexuals to whom homosexuals prostitute themselves, the existence or direction of any exchange of money being irrelevant. **Do for trade:** To have homosexual relations with a hetero-sexual male (prostitute or otherwise), usually referring to fellating him, the object usually being interpolated into the idiom, as, e.g., to do him for trade. **Trade** may be used as a predicate nominative in referring to a single person generically, e.g., "He is trade," such a person also being called a piece of trade.
>
> —Gershon Legman, "The Language of Homosexuality"[1]

Resisting categorization of human sexuality has been one emerging goal of bisexual theory and politics. Recent bisexual theory is caught between seeing bisexuality as another category of sexual identity and seeing it as a challenge to sexist, heterosexist, and monosexual divisions of human sexuality and gender. In the mass media, too, the rhetoric of category-blurring has become popularized, and even *Newsweek*'s biphobic July 1995 cover story on bisexuality talks about the new sexual "fluidity" on campuses. Still, it remains underexamined why bi-sexual theory finds categorization per se so central a concern or why the confusion, blurring, or mediation of sexual categories is seen as good, politically worthwhile, or radical.

Marjorie Garber has observed that the issue of categorization is more than the problem of fitting bisexuals into a schema. "There are also taxonomies of bisexuality itself," she notes, listing the various types of bisexuality writers have named.[2] This essay uses one specific bisexual category to suggest limitations of a blurred-boundaries understanding of bisexuality: the trade man, or the heterosexually identified, homoerotically inclined man. His example is instructive because (1) the trade should represent that very breakdown of categorization; (2) the appearance of representations of the trade man coincides historically with changes in social scientific concerns about sexual "behavior" and "identity" as separate and chartable facets of human sexuality; and (3) this coincidence immediately poses questions about the relation between identity position and political agency, a topic underexamined in relation to bisexuality. Consequently, I seek to sketch a historiography of bisexuality after World War II. To this end, I will examine the discourse of social science in the postwar years to assess how the trade emerges at a historical moment of crisis around sexual categorization, and I will read this crisis in one of the cultural products (films) of postwar America. Such an examination, I contend, will challenge continuum and spatial models of bisexuality and suggest other methodologies available to bisexual theory.

Sex and Science: The Kinsey Report Revisited

The years immediately following World War II in the United States have been a central period of interest to many gay historians and queer theorists.[3] Most eminently, these years witnessed an apex in the development, escalation, and propagation of homophobic rhetoric and state-sponsored repressive measures, aided and emblematized by McCarthyism's conflation of Communism and homosexuality. At the same time, gay subcultures were, in most American cities (large and small), just beginning to emerge as sizable, distinct, and self-conscious.[4] Thus, for these historians and theorists, the 1940s and 50s explain and emblematize the current demonizing of gays and lesbians and at the same time serve as the historical background out of which the gay liberation movement arose. However, more than just these easily marked social developments, the 1940s and 1950s saw an emergence and proliferation of new ways of categorizing human sexuality, and at the heart of these emerging taxonomies was an increasing faith in the separability of sexual behavior and sexual identity.

Monosexual gay historiography itself has repeatedly divided sexual "behavior" and "identity" within a theoretical framework that flatly ignores bisexuals. I would argue that John D'Emilio is not far from the sentiment of many monosexual gay historians and thinkers (nor from that of many bisexuals) when he states, "The distinction between behavior and identity is critical to an understanding of contemporary gay male and lesbian life."[5] D'Emilio then points to Jeffrey Weeks's argument for a historical consideration of gay identity: "Homosexuality has existed throughout history," writes Weeks. "But what have varied enormously are the ways in which various societies have regarded homosexuality, the meanings they have attached to it, and how those who were engaged in homosexual activity viewed themselves. . . . As a starting point we have to distinguish between homosexual behaviour, which is universal, and a homosexual identity, which is historically specific—and a comparatively recent phenomenon."[6] Weeks's division of homosexuality into a universal behavior and a historically specific identity supports the tendency of many gay historians to argue for a constructionist position while still having recourse to a universal "homosexual" behavior, identifiable throughout history.

The problems this division poses for the bisexual theorist are striking. First, any attempt to launch a pre-identity, behavior-centered approach to history writing will inevitably collapse most "bisexual" behavior into the exclusive domains of "heterosexual" and "homosexual" behaviors, as we can see in the way that Weeks (like D'Emilio, Adam, and Katz) emphasizes "homosexual" history, behavior, and identity. Second, the emergences of bisexual identities do not necessarily coincide historically with those of monosexual identities. Third, Weeks's claim that homosexual behavior is universal ignores the monosexual presumption of that "universal": Ford and Beach's ethnographic study suggests that exclusive, i.e., monosexual, same-sex behavior is rare, even nonexistent, in many non-Western societies.[7]

Yet the problems surfacing with current monosexual histories are more than that of the historian's bad faith or monosexual presumptions. Rather, a move away from Weeks's "homosexual" project to a more bisexual or bi-inclusive one highlights a more central problem with these historians' identity/behavior model: its failure to consider the historical context of the very analytical vocabulary it employs. In particular, its assumptions about sexual behavior and identity follow directly from Kinsey's Report on male sexuality and its conceptual paradigms.[8] Highlighting the continuity between Kinsey's assumptions and present-day historical and theoretical models will help develop a bisexual historiography, because (1) Kinsey's methodology abruptly denaturalized terms like *homosexual, heterosexual,* and *bisexual,* terms which have become continually *re*naturalized in the process of writing a (monosexual) identity-based history; (2) the report signals a schism between sexual identity and behavior, a division that implicates any history of "bisexuality" before the development of an affirmative bisexual "identity"; and (3) Kinsey's seven-point scale of sexuality has influenced, even instigated, so many attempts to theorize bisexuality.

The Kinsey Report shocked the American public by demonstrating how wide the gap between sexual behavior and professed sexual identity really was. Particularly at issue were Kinsey's findings on homosexuality, which based results on individuals' sexual experience, not on self-categorizations. As Jeffrey Escoffier notes, "Moral outrage and a great deal of professional hypocrisy greeted the report, but few Americans remained immune to a new awareness of the gap between public attitudes toward sexual behavior and daily sexual activities."[9] Many others, too, have noted the moral outrage and change in attitudes that the Report has provoked to date. On the other hand, the crisis in sexual taxonomy that it represents has been far less discussed.

In his 1948 essay "Sex and Science: The Kinsey Report," cultural critic Lionel Trilling attacks Kinsey for following a mechanistic, "superstructural" approach to sexuality research, thereby ignoring the individual's own appraisal of his sexuality.[10] In Trilling's assessment, the Report repeats the kind of mistake Marx made when he tried to analyze society scientifically and in terms of pure quantity, without regard to the psychological dimension of social life. This "radical materialism," as Escoffier calls it,[11] allows Kinsey to reveal the gap between values and behavior by insisting on the primacy of quantitative research (number and frequency of orgasms, frequency of psychic and emotional experiences, etc.). While Escoffier values Kinsey's materialist approach to sexuality as opposed to Trilling and others' homophobia, he ends up criticizing Kinsey on the very grounds of his materialism: "Kinsey's emphasis on acts and the number of orgasms ideologically closed off his analysis from its political and historical meaning. If his synchronic analysis of sexual outlets obscured the emergence of 'sexual revolution,' his ontology of acts obscured the emergence of political subjects—such as youth, women, and homosexuals—who would make the postwar sexual revolution."[12] Much of Escoffier's critique is well founded; Kinsey's act-based methodology does fail to consider historical change and context adequately.[13] Further, as Trilling would argue, the Report does not fully state the correlation between numerical analyses of sexual behavior and their intended social effect.

Still, Escoffier's unreserved privileging of identity politics as the point of reference for understanding the Kinsey Report is limiting. A behavior-focused study of sexuality may not aid in one political task, say, providing an adequate narrative of the rise of urban gay subcultures, but it may be a necessary tool in another, for instance, assessing sexual transmission patterns of HIV. By emphasizing the postwar sexual revolution, Escoffier closes off consideration of the new sexual taxonomy to those not falling under the rubrics of the monosexually defined gay and homophile movements. Furthermore, the use these homophile and gay liberation movements have made of the data in the Kinsey Report (e.g., the frequent adoption of "one in ten" as a slogan) suggests that their identity-based politics and the behavior-based results of the Report are not as separate as Escoffier might suggest.

For these reasons, the quantifiable and even mappable split between sexual identity and sexual behavior (which often is accepted as obvious) needs to be examined as relatively recent in the categorization of human sexuality. Reading the trade man as a bisexual figure resists the monosexism and identity/behavior split, which work in tandem. For the trade fails to qualify either as a straight man, on account of his same-sex behavior, or as a gay man, on account of his straight identity. Any analysis which denies the importance of behavior collapses the trade man into a straight man, and any which denies the importance of identity collapses him into a gay or bisexual man.

As thorny an issue as his classification can be, it seems easier nonetheless to read the trade as trade than to question the very vocabulary of taxonomy. To say the trade "represents" the intersection of identity and behavior is to make the trade man the one who is representing. It seems important, therefore, to examine the linguistic slippage between transitive and intransitive valences of "represent" or between person-based and category-based meanings of "trade" or "bisexual." One way to accomplish this task is to turn away from social science and toward cultural representations of the trade.

Film Noir and the Transference of Guilt: *The Case of* Strangers on a Train

In keeping with a dual focus on "official" and subcultural rhetorics of deviant sexuality, I would like to highlight works from two particular genres of film that came to prominence around the early forties: film noir and the narrative experimental film. Specifically, I am concerned with the appearance of the trade man in two contemporaneous films, Alfred Hitchcock's *Strangers on a Train* (1950) and Kenneth Anger's *Fireworks* (1947). These two films are remarkably similar in their use of a common pickup scenario, the lighting of a cigarette, and their inclusion of a trade character. I would like to examine the iconography and characterization that comprise each film's representation of the trade man and to understand these representations in the context of postwar changes in sexual taxonomy.

One recurring thesis in studies of postwar cinema is that film noir portrays and signals an underbelly of insecurity in postwar American culture. The genre not only uses its dark, high contrast and overly shadowed aesthetic to convey the corruption, danger, and crime of modern urban life but also, following the lead of *romans noirs* and other popular fiction of the period, develops a variety of cinematic codes to depict sexually deviant characters and subcultures and makes such representations central to its "dark" vision. Bisexuality, homosexuality, incest, and pornography began to appear in its narratives, and, increasingly, sexual dissidents were major characters, even protagonists. Also, films noirs complicate the formerly undisturbed heterosexual coupling, and often their narratives end in deception, distrust, separation, or unceremonious death.[14] However, because the motion picture industry's Hays Code was still in effect, screenwriters and filmmakers had to get around prohibitions against any explicit reference to "homosexuality or sexual perversion." The two most popular ways of coding dissident sexualities were character typing through iconography and self-conscious narrative subtext, often Freudian in nature. Both the first and last of the original cycle of films noirs—*Maltese Falcon* (John Huston, 1940) and *Touch of Evil* (Orson Welles, 1955)—provided audiences a look at homosexuals: a fastidious queen and a butch lesbian gang leader, respectively. Meanwhile the popularization of psychoanalytic vocabulary and concepts in Hollywood (especially following Hitchcock's 1945 film *Spellbound*) allowed *White Heat* (Raoul Walsh, 1949) to turn the story of a mother-fixated gangster into a Freudian parable of homosexual desire.

Though generally not a textbook example of noir, like *Maltese Falcon* or *White Heat*, *Strangers on a Train* nonetheless enacts the disruption of the heterosexual couple in its noirish suspense narrative. Furthermore, the film relies on both iconography and Freudian narrative to depict nonstraight sexuality. Without regard to these two elements, the plot seems fairly straightforward: Guy Haines (Farley Granger) is a tennis celebrity and aspiring politician who is accosted on a D.C.-bound train by a stranger, Bruno Anthony (Robert Walker), who proposes a plan to exchange murders. Bruno will kill Guy's wife, Miriam (who is unwilling to divorce him and thus poses an obstacle to Guy's profitable marriage to Ann Morton, a senator's daughter), and in return, Guy is to murder Bruno's father. Guy declares the proposal insane but leaves behind his lighter, which Bruno takes as a sign of agreement to the plan. Miriam is murdered, and Guy finds himself in the classic "transference of guilt" scenario; he can neither kill Bruno's father (for that would get him convicted of two murders) nor ignore Bruno's demands (for Bruno has the incriminating lighter).

However, the film's iconography and Freudian subtext have led many to read the narrative as one of same-sex seduction. Robert Walker portrays Bruno as an effeminate and flamboyant man whose soft-spokenness turns into psychotic rage at a moment's notice. He is characterized as suspiciously close to his mother (who gives

Bruno a showy tie and, at one point, a manicure) and unhealthily resentful of his father. For his part, Guy Haines exhibits the full signs of projection that mark the paranoid subject, and psychoanalytic criticism often reads the double as the sign of repressed or latent homosexuality.[15] Throughout much of the narrative's development, the relation between the two men seems to overshadow any romantic connection between Guy and Ann Morton, which comes across as stifled. Like other films noirs, furthermore, *Strangers on a Train* points to a larger context of escalating homophobia that conflated un-Americanism with nonheterosexual behaviors and identities.

In Robert J. Corber's cogent reading of the film, Guy's narrative is an allegory of blackmail that speaks to a postwar crisis of doubt, fed by the Kinsey Report, as to whether homosexuals could be recognized on sight. As Corber notes, several narrative motifs resonate with McCarthyite fag-baiting rhetoric. Most apparently, Bruno falls easily into the pattern of the gay villain recurring in many of Hitchcock's films;[16] the paranoia with which the fairly effete and harmless Bruno becomes the incarnation of evil by the film's end evokes the paranoid rhetoric of anti-Communism. Also, Bruno's infiltration into the shadows of every Washington, D.C. monument and his blackmail of Guy speak to many Americans' fear of Communist or un-American infiltration through the blackmail-susceptible position of the "homosexual." Ironically, Corber argues, the Kinsey Report, credited with loosening up American morals, in fact "exacerbate[d] the emergent heterosexual panic."[17] On the one hand, the Report emphasized the apparent masculine normalcy of many gay men and only fed into the paranoia over blackmail and security among, for instance, members of the U.S. Senate.[18] On the other, Kinsey's insistence that sexual identities were fluid and that same-sex desire was an innate physiological capability fed fears that gays could seduce and corrupt even the best of men and governments. Corber argues that the paranoiac crisis of *Strangers* lies in the instability of Guy Haines's straight identity, an instability brought to the fore by the Report's assertion of the widespread and undetected prevalence of gay sex.

Corber does examine Lionel Trilling's attack on the Report yet does not apply his analysis to the film nor reinterpret the text in light of Trilling's disdain for the behavior-based analysis. The film, however, does allow for a fruitful reconsideration. For at the same time that its narrative of blackmail suggests a homosexual panic, Guy Haines's panic erupts from a destabilized identity and transferred guilt. Guy's attempt to distance himself from his sexual connection to Bruno (the meeting with the stranger on the train) catches him up in paranoia as he attempts to assert his innocence. Within the psychological realm of the film, the question of guilt for Miriam's murder becomes synonymous with the question of the "guilt" for same-sex activity.

Hitchcock's famed "transference of guilt" assumes more than tangential importance, then, in assessing the film's attempt to police dissident sexualities. As discussed by Rohmer and Chabrol, transference of guilt is more or less a moral quandary: the morally sound protagonist finds himself implicated suddenly in a hostile moral universe.[19] In this view, *Strangers* is about the unpeaceful coexistence and symbiosis of good and evil. Slavoj Zizek, however, summarizes the concept in more semiotic terms:

In Hitchcock's films, murder is never simply an affair between a murderer and his victim; murder always implies a third party, a reference to a third person—the murderer kills *for* this third person, his act is inscribed in the framework of a symbolic exchange with him. For this reason, this third person finds himself charged with guilt, although he does not know anything or, more precisely, refuses to know anything of the way he is implicated in the affair. . . . At any moment, the idyllic texture of the everyday course of events can disintegrate, not because some iniquitous violence erupts from under the surface of social rules (according to the common notion that, beneath the civilized mask, we are all savages and murderers), but because all of a sudden—as a result of unexpected changes in the symbolic texture of intersubjective relations—what was a moment ago permitted by the rules becomes an abhorrent vice, although the act in its immediate, physical reality remains the same.[20]

The crisis that gay sex presents in *Strangers* is in one way just the converse of the situation Zizek describes: that orgasm that once was an abhorrent vice is, after the Kinsey Report, an experience common to 38 percent of white American men. On the other hand, the reality of same-sex behavior is far from immediate and physical and appears in the film only by implication, resting mostly on the subcultural iconography of the lighter.[21] With the emergence of widespread urban gay subcultures after World War II, Guy Haines's very act of lighting Bruno Antony's cigarette or of leaving his lighter behind on the train could no longer remain simply an innocent act but necessarily entered a deviant framework of symbolic exchange.[22] This symbolic exchange is not merely the textual "crisscross"[23] of the film but more broadly derives its meaning from the context of subcultural codes. Specifically, the lighter is a well-known prop of the pickup, yet the importance of the lighter to same-sex cruising etiquette remains unnoticed by the critics of *Strangers*. One can see in court cases of the early 1950s that police vice officers knew the codes of the pickup while the court acted as if such codes did not exist. The D.C. Court of Appeals case *Dyson v. United States* provides an excellent example of such a scenario.[24] The appellant had been arrested and convicted when trying to pick up an undercover officer. The ruling reads, "A police officer assigned to the morals division of the Metropolitan Police Department testified that shortly after midnight on October 10, 1952, he was approached by defendant, who asked the officer to light his cigarette. The officer handed him a book of matches, and after defendant had lit the cigarette and returned the matches, 'he placed his left hand on my privates and squeezed them.'" In its decision, the court focused on the D.C. Code's definition of assault: "A man who takes improper liberties with the person of another man without the latter's consent is guilty of assault, unless man so fondled is himself a deviate and responds favorably to the approach."[25] This cryptic definition of assault does not understand consent to be evident and further defines it as a common sexual deviance, so that differing sexual identities (particularly of entrapping police officers) can be further evidence of some violation of "consent." However, never did the judges consider that the light was, for many nonstraight men (and many vice officers interested in entrapment), itself coded consent as unmistakable as spoken consent.

With knowledge of this cruising etiquette, the conversation between the strangers on a train takes on a new meaning. Bruno is not simply asking Guy to light his cigarette (a later scene in which a stranger on the train asks Bruno to give him a light suggests that he probably carries around matches) but is in essence cruising him, even if the Hays Code would not let him follow up with anything more explicit. Guy readily obliges with the light and soon is fascinated by this stranger who a minute before was prying into his personal life. Yet much as the judges in *Dyson* ignored gay codes in considering sexual consent, present-day critics of the film ignore the implications of consent the shared light denotes.[26]

At the same time, theorists, critics, and historians tend to ignore the specter of bisexuality that informs the crisis of sexual taxonomy. Not only did the court in the *Dyson* case emphasize the clause in the D.C. Code which denied nonstraights protection from assault ("perversion" being construed as "consent"), it failed to consider that the officer's straight identity might not preclude same-sex desire.[27] Thus, the ruling's division between normal authority and perverse criminality rests on a panic over bisexuality predicated upon the systematic assumption of monosexuality. Corber's reading of *Strangers*, and many gay histories of postwar homophobia, perpetuate a similar mistransposition of such panic over bisexuality onto an opposition of homosexual versus heterosexual politics. For Corber, Kinsey's findings have bearing on the film because they destabilized the notion of visible sexual identity: anyone could be gay (including the straight-acting Guy Haines or the straight-acting Farley Granger) and one would never know it. Corber notes the slippages of sexual identity which result from this destabilization (slippages which so readily emerge when one tries to discuss the character of Guy Haines), yet he does not consider that the crisis of the homosexual as infiltrator may be in fact a crisis of the bisexual. After all, the panic arises not simply because a gay man passes as straight, but further, because he may have sex with men while in a sexual, romantic, or marital relationship with a woman.

In this light, the consistency with which critics either (1) read Guy Haines as either a gay character or a straight character or (2) like Corber, vacillate between the two, seems to suggest a monosexual presumption. A more cogent reading would be to see Guy as quintessential trade, carrying on relations with men (as well as with women) but identifying himself as entirely heterosexual. Critics have been able to read Guy as a gay character or alternately, as a straight one, only by leaving out certain information. But more to the point, they leave out this information in order to read *through* the confused and confusing (from a monosexual perspective, at least) category of the trade man.

Fireworks *and the Duplicitous Trade*

Strangers exemplifies a postwar panic over bisexuality, yet Hollywood cinema of the period provides little insight into the developing sexual subcultures or their representations of the trade man. I would like, therefore, to turn to one gay-authored experimental film, Kenneth Anger's *Fireworks*. Made just three years before *Strangers* and one year before the publication of the Kinsey Report in 1948, *Fireworks* gives an explicit view of the emerging subcultural representations of the trade man. The film works out of the intersecting social contexts of the gay and film cultures in Los Angeles. As much a representative of experimental narrative filmmaking in the style of Maya Deren as a reworking of film noir scenarios of violence and desire, as much a politicized celebration of gay culture and identity as a work sharing visual and narrative codes with gay pornography, the film's take on the trade is not merely ambivalent, but multivalent.

The narrative motifs of cruising and homophobic violence in *Fireworks* resemble those in *Strangers on a Train*. As with the conversation between the two strangers on a train, the act of cruising, in particular of asking for a light, forms a central strand of the film's narrative. After waking from a dream-filled sleep, Anger's character goes out into the night through a door marked "Gents" and spots a sailor in a bar. He holds up a cigarette and asks for a light, and the man responds by slapping Anger. He then, in another shot, offers him a light. Later, a group of sailors carrying chains chase Anger's character down and brutally beat him. A semen-like liquid pours down on his face, suggesting sadomasochistic fantasy as well as criticism of these "straight-identified" men who get off on beating up queers with whom they themselves have sex. The film ends with Anger in bed with a muscular man, presumably a sailor, though the man's face is scratched out of the emulsion.

Most criticism of *Fireworks* focuses on the subjective, erotic qualities of the film. P. Adams Sitney, for instance, cites Anger's film as "a pure example of the psycho-dramatic trance film: the film-maker himself plays out a drama of psychological revelation. . . . It is truly remarkable that a seventeen-year-old film-maker could make so intense an analysis of himself at a time when any allusion to homosexuality was taboo in the American cinema."[28] As remarkable as Anger's work may be, it emerged within a particular social and historical context, one which saw not only the development of an urban gay subculture but also the burgeoning of independent 16mm cinema, including prominent examples of gay-authored cinema: the films of Anger, Curtis Harrington, Gregory Markopoulos, and, arguably, Willard Maas. Richard Dyer, in *Now You See It*, one of the few histories of lesbian and gay films to situate these cultural productions systematically within a broader historical context, focuses on the importance of Los Angeles with its "particular mix . . . of developed gay and film (in and outside Hollywood) cultures" in the launching of gay filmmaking.[29] Los Angeles, in fact, would serve as the site of the beginning of homophile organization, with the foundation in 1950 of the Mattachine Society and the publication in 1953 of *One*.[30]

Bisexuality was a hotly contested topic in these homophile organizations, and in the pages of *One* exchanges would sometimes flare over the role of the bisexual in gay culture. One 1953 article, entitled "The Homosexual Culture," flatly refuses to read the bisexual as other than a participant in homosexual culture: "As for . . . bisexuals, thousands of them participate in the homosexual culture, and they are, to all intents, homosexuals, an occasional heterosexual affair notwithstanding. Some predominantly homosexual individuals may have occasional heterosexual relations. This scarcely makes them heterosexual as long as they are *basically* homosexual in thought, desire, orientation and culture."[31] In another issue, one bisexual wrote a letter, denying the possibility of a bisexual identity: "I am a bisexual. And the years have taught me . . . [t]hat I cannot stay a bisexual if I am to find any measure of happiness at all." The author ends the letter in an exhortation to assume a monosexual identity: "So for goodness sakes, if you are a bisexual, jump off that rail and cast your lot with either the heterosexuals or the homosexuals. This is one time when half-and-half doesn't mean you are the cream of the crop. It just means you are confused—let's face it!"[32] I have suggested how a bisexual panic underlies the paranoia of *Strangers*; here, a similar bisexual panic is in operation in the production of a "gay" identity.

Los Angeles offered, in addition, a strong queer subculture, in which two institutions were especially important: gay porn photography and film. Dyer notes, "Two of the first regular photographic studios producing male physique studies and running a mail order service supplying them were Bruce of Los Angeles and the Athletic Model Guild (AMG), both of which started in the early forties."[33] Both in terms of narrative and visual style, Anger eroticizes the trade man in a manner that shares certain codes with gay porn. When Anger is cruising the navy man in the bar, the sailor takes off his shirt and begins to model his body. As with the introductory shots of the sleeping Anger, side lighting further eroticizes the spectacle of the flexing biceps and pecs, and the resulting visual style shares much with the physique photography of the AMG. However, unlike Anger's sleeping body, this actor's body, decidedly more muscular, is aware of the camera's attention and is in fact posing for the viewer. Anger then holds up a cigarette, suggesting the need of a light. The sailor responds by slapping him down to the ground. The film then switches back to the original room, with a fire in its fireplace, as the sailor lights Anger's cigarette with a twig from the fireplace. Does the rough trade reject Anger's advances, or does he accept them, as the second playing out of the light scenario would suggest? Neither is clearly the correct story, or, more precisely, both are. Not only does the first scenario portray the trade man as violent, but his violent rejection itself signifies him as "straight," especially with the asymmetrical visual portrayal of him and Anger; unlike the easily read queerness of Anger (with his wet dream and the pictures he sorts through), the sailor's sexuality is ambivalent.

Fireworks uses certain motifs that recur in gay porn, most obviously the straight-identifying man and the sailor of the urban underworld. Dyer interprets this appropriation in a reclamation of gay identity: "Soldiers and sailors were no longer straight-identified men seen from afar by gay-identified men, they were gay—or at any rate sometimes queer or homosexual—themselves."[34] Indeed, the military and especially the navy were instrumental in the development of subcultural identities,[35] yet the sailors in Anger's film fit the type of the rough trade and violently reject the protagonist's advances. The eroticism of the straight-identifying sailor pervades Anger's film works precisely through the vacillation between the trade's unavailability and availability; the sailors are eroticized because they embody a seemingly straight masculinity but at the same time can be "had" and "done for trade."

Here the trade's defining erotic qualities stem from a paradox of identity that one can read as either nominal—expecting from the trade man a proclamation of straightness regardless of sexual intentions—or economic, valuing the straight-identified man for his simultaneous availability and unavailability or scarcity. This paradox continues today, with debates in gay periodicals over the political correctness of gay pornography's trade stars: some gays denigrate representations of the trade man as encouraging self-hatred among gay men; others attest to the entrenched cultural stubbornness and economic power of such representations or revel in fantasies of doing the inaccessible straight man. Of course, these debates have remained safely out of view of the "legitimate" press and thrive mostly in porn magazine forums, where heated exchanges will often arise. One such forum in the porn mag *Manshots*, for example, includes two letters attacking porn makers for using trade stars, with one "Matthew" saying, "I find if a 'straight' man is unwilling to even touch a dick, let alone participate in any form of safe sex, then he should be considered straight and left alone." The editors took a somewhat more generous view of the trade: "Matthew's points are well taken, but perhaps a bit too dismissive regarding the trade men of porn. By presenting themselves as being 'straight,' these actors lend themselves to a sort of sexual intrigue by which many viewers are captivated. The trade performer fuels a special kind of fantasy—that even the most heterosexual man can, under the right circumstances, be had, and that a self-proclaimed 'straight' man such as [porn actor] Rex Chandler is only expressing hidden feelings under the guise of performing."[36]

Although the author of these comments seems confident in his response, the disjuncture between identity- and behavior-based categorizations of sexuality becomes dizzying upon examination. Is "under the guise of performing" redundant? Is the self-proclamation of straightness, in Chandler's case, a performance or the guise of performance? Does Chandler's identity lie with his proclamation or with his hidden feelings? To complicate the situation, such notions of hidden feelings underneath performance are themselves only "a special kind of fantasy." The difficulty these questions pose lie in the relation between positionality and political agency, that is, to what extent being a trade challenges certain categorizations or, alternately, strengthens a certain self-hatred among gay men. As bisexual theory has been fraught with this very same problem, I will turn now to addressing the relationship between continuum and spatial models of bisexuality and the rhetoric of category-blurring.

Bisexual Theory and the Trade Man

Kinsey's notion of the bisexual continuum has helped constitute in many ways a modern conceptualization and political self-awareness of bisexual identity yet has limited at the same time the parameters in which to conceive of "identity." *Sexual Behavior in the Human Male* proposed the paradigm of the seven-point scale of homosexuality, in which exclusive heterosexuality and exclusive homosexuality are poles on a continuum of varied human sexual experiences. According to the study's findings, about half of all white American men could reasonably be described as "bisexual" in one way or another, be it by sex life or fantasy. While Kinsey's study has been influential in shaping the conceptualization of bisexuality, it fails to consider that the idea of "continuum" itself imposes a linear and spatial model onto a human sexuality without innate space or order. First, I will briefly consider how current bi politics challenges Kinsey's notion of the bisexual continuum. Second, I will examine the spatial conceptions of ethical vantage in bisexual theory, particularly as they relate to the trade figure.

Recent historical and theoretical developments challenge our ability to conceive of bisexuality solely in terms of "between" gay and straight or half-homosexual, half-heterosexual. A vocal "new bisexual movement" has called attention to the biphobia and exclusionary propriety of the gay establishment in debates over group names, parade organization, and political strategy. In addition, as activists and theorists drop the rubric "gay" in favor of the antiseparatist inclusivity of "queer," bisexuals and straights posit their own versions of queerness in order to complicate views that see sexuality as an either/or entity.

Further, the AIDS epidemic has problematized the categorization of gay and bisexual men; many straight-identifying men have (often unsafe) sex with other men, and pedagogical strategies of targeting "risk groups" often fail to reach these men outside the gay community. As anthropologists Shirley Lindenbaum and Carole S. Vance have noted, social-science research on sexual behavior has been of little use in understanding the sexual transmission of the HIV virus, because of the conflation of sexual identity and behavior or the privileging of identity-oriented models of research.[37] One of the few empirically oriented studies to consider the theoretical implications of trade men, a study by the Centers for Disease Control of HIV-1 seropositive men donating blood,[38] determines that a high incidence of men who contracted HIV through sex with other men were in fact heterosexually (25 percent of the sample) or bisexually (30 percent of the sample) identifying and often had little contact with gay social networks and safe-sex information. Among black and Hispanic men, the incidence of nonhomosexual identification was even higher (67 percent of the black men and 51 percent of the Hispanic men in the sample). Certainly, the study's limited sample constrains its possibilities for generalization. "Despite these limitations," the study concludes, "this group of non-homosexually identified men represents a population whose behavior is not well understood and who may not have been reached by our current approaches to AIDS education."[39]

Some theorists of bisexuality have begun to challenge the continuum paradigm of sexuality. One notable example—and one of the few bi-queer-theory attempts to date—is an essay by Elisabeth A. Däumer entitled "Queer Ethics; or, the Challenge of Bisexuality to Lesbian Ethics."[40] Däumer, in the interest of problematizing straight, lesbian, and gay political assumptions, touts the queer bisexual as an important, transgressive figure. Imagining such a figure, whom she gives the fictitious name Cloe, she declares, "Neither straight nor gay, Cloe is also not bisexual, at least not in the traditional, still current, sense of the word—pre-genderized, polymorphously perverse, or simply sexually undecided, uncommitted, and hence untrustworthy."[41]

Despite its reading of gender and sexuality as volitional, Däumer's attempt to expand the category of bisexual is laudable for its awareness that the term "bisexual," particularly as it is conceived in the continuum between "heterosexual" and "homosexual," can reinforce a dual conception of sexuality as much as it can challenge it.[42] Also, she lists compelling reasons for assuming a bi-queer perspective to "deconstruct the bipolar framework of gender and sexuality":

1. Because bisexuality occupies an ambiguous position *between* identities, it is able to shed light on the gaps and contradictions of all identity, on what we might call the difference *within* identity. . . .
2. Because of its nonidenticalness, bisexuality exposes the distinctive feature of all politicized sexual identities: the at times radical discontinuities between an individual's sexual acts and affectional choices, on the one hand, and her or his affirmed political identity, on the other.[43]

These claims for bisexuality parallel to some extent my argument for the theoretical examination of the trade man; the trade's ambiguous position encourages a retheorization of other sexual identities. Furthermore, I have focused on the trade because of the interesting discontinuity between his acts and affectional choices and his identity.

However, Däumer makes some slippages between bisexuality and epistemological vantage. Bisexuality (or the trade) as a concept may disrupt monosexual and gendered assumptions, but *being* a bisexual or a trade man does not *necessarily* disrupt (or disrupt in the same way). The trade man is one starting point for unpacking this collapse in bi theory, not because he is between identities but because he is in between the very mappings of identity and behavior. In other words, his interest to the bi or queer theorist may not lie in the threat that his troubling, transgressive, or liminal nature poses to modern binary logic but rather in his emergence at a time when a taxonomic separation of same-sex behavior and homosexual identity helped shape both public and subcultural understandings of sexual identity positions. As bisexuality becomes a political movement and an identity option, bisexual theorists must be aware of an emerging visible disparity between the number of people who identify as bisexual and the number of people whose sexual behavior is bisexual, particularly as the bisexual movement may use Kinsey's behavior-based statistics to attack (monosexual) gay notions of identity.

Ed Cohen exhorts lesbians and gays "not [to] make an identity out of whom we fuck."[44] The trade certainly does not and for this reason poses a "problem" to current straight, gay, and bisexual political practices. If, as Cohen points out, the sexual pleasures of lesbians, gays, and bisexuals are many and varied, the trade man presents a different array of pleasures. How is one to read them? What is one to make of the homophobic rejection implicit in his identity? Certainly, I do not posit the trade man as the only vantage for the examination of identity and sexual behavior; he has far less to say for women's sexualities than men's, and much of his appeal to gay men in, say, pornography, is intimately tied to, though perhaps not synonymous with, the systematic devaluation of both gayness and effeminacy in our society. Nor do I intend to vindicate the trade as "radical" or "transgressive," evaluations which would rely on a fairly naive and unexamined collapse of episte-mological or ethical vantage. I do contend, however, that the trade man can serve as the occasion for critical reexamination of the limits of monosexual identity politics and of the limits of bisexual theory's conceptual vocabulary.

Because it resists the monosexualizing impulse of gay culture, which tries to make either a heterosexual (today's trade) or a gay man (tomorrow's competition) out of these nonhomosexually identifying men, bisexual theory and politics can provide a more inclusive vantage point from which to discuss the trade man; however, one often sees an exclusivity in bi-queer politics' reaction to straight-iden-tifying bisexuals, similar to the exclusivity in the gay movement which marginalized bisexual concerns. Robyn Ochs, a bi activist who organizes the nationwide bisexual network Bi-NET, remarks, "I'm not going to spend my time building a movement for bis who don't identify as queer. If they want their own bisexual movement, they can do it themselves."[45] This statement, which, I venture, echos the sentiment of many bisexuals and gays, demonstrates how the thorny issue of the straight-identi-fying bisexual prevents gays or queer bisexuals from reaching an open and wel-coming consideration of the trade bisexual.

Much as bisexual identity has challenged the exclusivity of monosexual gay politics and theory, so then does trade identity test the inclusive claims of bi-queer politics and theory. Any welcoming consideration of trade sexuality will not be easy, though, for either gays or queer bisexuals: distrust of closeted men in denial, class- and race-bound standards of sexual identity, and the connection of eroticiza-tion of straights with queer self-hatred all keep bisexuals and gays from readily vindicating the trade man. But straight-identifying men comprise a good number of the people who have sex with men and who could benefit from queer activism, and any theoretical engagement with bisexuality that ignores the very historical and political manifestations—and limitations—of the category "bisexual" is not only incomplete, but suspect.

Notes

1.   Gershon Legman, "The Language of Homosexuality," *Sex Variants* (New York: P. B. Hoeber, 1941), quoted in Jonathan Katz, *Gay/Lesbian Almanac: A New Docu-mentary* (New York: Harper and Row, 1983), 571–84.

2.   Marjorie Garber, *Vice Versa: Bisexuality and the Eroticism of Everyday Life* (New York: Simon and Schuster, 1995), 30.

3.   John D'Emilio, *Sexual Politics, Sexual Communities: The Making of a Homosexual Minority in the United States 1940–1970* (Chicago: University of Chicago Press, 1983). Katz, *Gay/ Lesbian Almanac*. Barry D. Adam, *History of the Gay and Lesbian Movement* (Boston: Twayne, 1987). Lee Edelman, "Tearooms and Sympathy, or Epistemology of the Water Closet," in *Nationalism and Sexualities*, ed. Andrew Parker and Mary Russo (New York: Routledge, 1991), 263–84. David Savran, *Communists, Cowboys, and Queers: the Politics of Masculinity in Arthur Miller and Tennessee Williams* (Minneapolis: University of Minnesota Press, 1993). Steven Bruhm, "Blackmailed by Sex: Tennessee Williams and the Economics of Desire, " *Modern Drama* 34, no. 4 (December 1991): 528–37.

4.   While this claim may be and has been disputed, I have relied on the accounts of D'Emilio, in *Sexual Politics, Sexual Communities*, 23–39, and David Comstock in *Violence against Gay Men and Lesbians* (New York: Columbia University Press, 1992), 6–7, among others, in pinning the emergence of urban gay subcultures to World War II and the era immediately following.

5.   John D'Emilio, *Making Trouble: Essays on Gay History, Politics, and the University* (New York: Routledge, 1992), 75.

6.   Jeffrey Weeks, *Coming Out: Homosexual Politics in Britain from the Nineteenth Century to the Present* (London: Quartet, 1977), 3.

7.   Clellan S. Ford and Frank A. Beach, *Patterns of Sexual Behavior* (New York: Harper and Brothers, 1951). Ford and Beach begin their section on "Homosexual Behavior" by noting, "Goethe wrote that homosexuality is as old as humanity itself and can therefore be considered natural, and human history lends his statement the ring of truth" (125). However, just as eager to assert the subordination in importance of same-sex behavior, they conclude, "The cross-cultural and cross-species comparisons presented in this chapter combine to suggest that a biological tendency for inversion of sexual behavior is inherent in most if not all mammals including the human species. At the same time we have seen that homosexual behavior is never the predominant type of sexual activity for adults in any society or in any animal species" (143).

8.   See Alfred C. Kinsey, Wardell B. Pomeroy, and Clyde E. Martin, *Sexual Behavior in the Human Male* (Philadelphia: W. B. Saunders, 1948).

9.   Jeffrey Escoffier, "The Politics of Gay Identity," *Socialist Review* 15, nos. 4–5 (July–October 1985): 122.

10. Lionel Trilling, "Sex and Science: The Kinsey Report," *Partisan Review* 40, no. 4 (April 1948): 460–76, reprinted in *The Liberal Imagination: Essays on Literature and Society* (New York: Viking, 1950), 223–42.

11. Escoffier, "The Politics of Gay Identity," 124.

12. Escoffier, "The Politics of Gay Identity," 126.

13. Though not addressed by Escoffier, this materialism also fails to consider racial differences in sexual norms and behavior. Kinsey was aware of differences in both between white and black populations but hypothesized that these were determined by class, education, or economics. Because the Reports used data only from white populations, and because researchers since have neglected the statistical autonomy

of black sexual practices, this area remains ill researched. One notable exception is Martin S. Weinberg and Colin J. Williams, "Black Sexuality: A Test of Two Theories," *Journal of Sex Research* 25, no.2 (May 1988): 197–218. Unfortunately, this study remains solely concerned with heterosexual behavior.

14. See Richard Dyer's article, "Homosexuality and Film Noir," in *The Matter of Images: Essays on Representation* (New York: Routledge, 1993), 52–72.

15. Otto Rank, *The Double: A Psychoanalytic Study*, trans. and ed. Harry Tucker (Chapel Hill: University of North Carolina, 1971).

16. See Robin Wood's essay "The Murderous Gays: Hitchcock's Homophobia," which itself puts forth an intriguing notion of bisexual authorship and spectatorship. *Hitchcock's Films Revisited* (New York: Columbia University Press, 1989), 336–57.

17. Robert J. Corber, *In the Name of National Security: Hitchcock, Homophobia, and the Political Construction of Gender in Postwar America* (Durham: Duke University Press, 1993), 63; Kinsey, Pomeroy, and Martin, *Sexual Behavior in the Human Male*.

18. Corber, *In the Name of National Security*, 63–64; see also U.S. Senate, 81st Cong., 2d sess., Committee on Expenditures in Executive Departments, *Employment of Homosexuals and Other Sex Perverts in Government* (Washington, D.C., 1950).

19. Eric Rohmer and Claude Chabrol, *Hitchcock: The First Forty-Four Films* (New York: Ungar, 1979), 73–74.

20. Slavoj Zizek, *Looking Awry: Reading Jacques Lacan through Popular Culture* (Cambridge, Mass.: MIT Press, 1991), 74–75.

21. While Hitchcock himself *may* have had little direct contact with these subcultures, he was not the only one working on the film. The presense of Raymond Chandler as screenwriter, for instance, may have shaped the film's representation of the gay pickup more than Hitchcock's Freudian ideas. In his novels Chandler presents Marlowe as generally "in the know" about queers. See *The Big Sleep* (New York: Vintage, 1992), 97–103, in which Marlowe uses the light as an insinuating insult to Geiger's lover.

22. Thus, when Zizek, in *The Sublime Object of Ideology* (London: Verso, 1989), 147, considers the incriminating lighter to be the one object in *Strangers* that is without a double, he ignores the very exchange in which the lighter is situated. It is the object which allows Bruno to murder Miriam—both figuratively, when it signifies Guy's assent to and desire for the act, and literally, when it illuminates Miriam's face so that Bruno can identify her—and becomes the exchange-counterpart of Miriam's murder, emblematized by her spectacles. Both objects, ironically, facilitate sight, and after completing the murder, Bruno gives the glasses to Guy. This object trade is important, for it suggests that the "crisscross" is not only the exchange of murders but also an exchange of Guy's affection (the lighter) for Bruno's services as a killer, which so obviously benefits Guy and only Guy.

23. See Sabrina Barton, "Crisscross: Paranoia and Projection in *Strangers on a Train*," *Camera Obscura* 25–26 (January/May 1991): 75–100.

24. *Dyson v. United States*. 97 A .2d 135. The earlier conviction was affirmed.

25. D.C. Code 1951, § 22–504.

26. See, for example, Donald Spoto, *The Art of Alfred Hitchcock: Fifty Years of His Motion Pictures* (New York: Doubleday, 1992), and Raymond Durgnat, *The Strange*

Case of Alfred Hitchcock, or, the Plain Man's Hitchcock (Cambridge, Mass.: MIT Press, 1974).

27. A refreshing dissent came from Judge Hood, who questioned whether the officer had indeed suffered undue harm: "His belief, or at least hope, was that his action would be favorably received, and nothing in the officer's testimony supports an inference that such action was repugnant to him. The officer was there for the purpose of receiving an advance of this sort because, as he said, 'that is my job.'" Hood went on to criticize the prosecution of a solicitation case under the charge of assault: "He was charged with assault and convicted on proof of homosexuality." For another case which presumes the entrapment officer's monosexual straightness, see *Bicksler v. United States.* 90 A .2d 233.

28. P. Adams Sitney, *Visionary Cinema: The American Avant-Garde*, 2d ed. (New York: Oxford University Press, 1979), 100–101.

29. Richard Dyer, *Now You See It: Studies on Lesbian and Gay Film* (New York: Routledge, 1990), 105.

30. Before the Mattachine, even, Los Angeles was showing signs of political organization around issues of sexuality. D'Emilio cites the Knights of the Clock, a social organization for interracially involved homosexuals, and *Vice Versa*, a magazine for lesbians which began publication in 1947. *Sexual Politics, Sexual Communities*, 32.

31. David L. Freeman, "The Homosexual Culture," *One* 1, no. 5 (May 1953): 10.

32. Geraldine Jackson, "As for Me," *One* 1, no. 1 (January 1953): 16–17.

33. Dyer, *Now You See It*, 114.

34. Dyer, *Now You See It*, 112.

35. D'Emilio, *Sexual Politics, Sexual Communities*, 24–31. Comstock, *Violence against Gay Men and Lesbians*, 6–7.

36. *Manshots* 4, no.1 (October 1991): 6–7.

37. Shirley Lindenbaum, "Anthropology Rediscovers Sex: Introduction," *Social Science and Medicine* 33, no. 8 (1991): 865–66; Carole S. Vance, "Anthropology Rediscovers Sexuality: A Theoretical Comment," *Social Science and Medicine* 33, no. 8 (1991): 875–84.

38. Lynda S. Doll, Lyle R. Petersen, Carol R. White, Eric S. Johnson, John W. Ward, and the Blood Donor Study Group, "Nonhomosexually Identified Men Who Have Sex with Men: A Behavioral Comparison," *Journal of Sex Research* 29, no. 1 (February 1992): 1–14.

39. Doll et al. "Nonhomosexually Identified Men Who Have Sex with Men," 13.

40. Elisabeth A. Däumer, "Queer Ethics; or, The Challenge of Bisexuality to Lesbian Ethics," *Hypatia* 7, no. 4 (Fall 1992): 91–105.

41. Däumer, "Queer Ethics," 92.

42. Däumer, "Queer Ethics," 96.

43. Däumer, "Queer Ethics," 98.

44. Ed Cohen. "Are We (Not) What We Are Becoming? 'Gay,' 'Identity,' 'Gay Studies,' and the Disciplining of Knowledge," in *Engendering Men: The Question of Male Feminist Criticism*, ed. Joseph A. Boone and Michael Cadden (New York: Routledge, 1988), 174.

45. Gabriel Rotello, "Bi Any Means Necessary," *Village Voice* 38, no. 26 (June 30, 1992): 38.

Chapter 11

Framing Contention: Bisexuality Displaced

Mariam Fraser

Between each of us and our sex, the West has placed a never-ending demand for truth: it is up to us to extract the truth of sex, since this truth is beyond its grasp; it is up to sex to tell us our truth, since sex is what holds it in darkness.

—Michel Foucault

In *The History of Sexuality* Foucault argues that sexuality, in contemporary western society, is perceived to be a privileged site of the "truth" of the self.[1] We may believe that our sexuality is repressed, he argues, and that it is in need of "liberation," but the endless proliferation of discourses on and around sexuality— our efforts to reveal our sexuality, to expose it, declare it, and confess it—serves only to bind us all the more tightly into regimes of knowledge and power. Although sexuality does not reside within the self, nor is it inherently expressive of the truth of the self, we nevertheless *perceive* it to be so. "A double petition," Foucault writes, "in that we are compelled to know how things are with it, while it is suspected of knowing how things are with us" (78). Discourses of sexuality, therefore, are *productive* rather than repressive, they produce the self we may know, and they produce sexuality as an essential aspect of that self. For Foucault, sexuality is a "technique" of the self and the self itself an aggregate of the very techniques which we employ to describe it.[2] While sexuality is not the only technique of the self, and although it does not work in isolation from other techniques of the self[3] (for example, sexuality and choice are usually perceived to function together), it does signify an especially dense transfer point of power and knowledge. Would a "self" without sexuality, for example, be understood as a self at all? And what of a sexuality that does not "belong" to, or reside within, a self?

This chapter is based on a study of the relationship between bisexuality and the different techniques by which the textually mediated figure of Simone de Beauvoir is produced as an "intelligible" (stable and coherent) self. When I began this project, I assumed that representations of de Beauvoir would at least sometimes identify her as "bisexual" (that texts on de Beauvoir would call the sexuality they ascribed to her "bisexual"), or that she would perhaps be constituted as such (that it would be possible for the reader to identify de Beauvoir as "bisexual" despite her being represented as either lesbian or heterosexual). The aim, therefore, was to analyze the "kinds" of bisexualities which were produced through the discourses surrounding a celebrated individual. After examining representations of de Beauvoir across three different genres (academic texts, biographies and newspaper articles) however, it seems that de Beauvoir is rarely named or produced as "bisexual."[4] Moreover, it is the very techniques which produce the self of de Beauvoir that also render bisexuality, as a technique of the self, inconceivable. While seeking neither to define de Beauvoir's sexuality nor to define bisexuality, I will illustrate this assertion by exploring representations of de Beauvoir in the British press.[5] These newspaper representations of de Beauvoir make no direct reference to bisexuality. More interestingly, they also disable even the possibility that bisexuality could author the self of de Beauvoir (as heterosexuality and lesbianism are frequently *perceived* to do). Put simply, the representations do not merely neglect to mention bisexuality in the production of de Beauvoir as an individual; they also preclude the very notion of a bisexual self.

This essay is structured by the concept of the "frame," which is drawn from Lynda Nead's study of the female nude.[6] Nead argues that, in western metaphysics, "form (the male) is preferred over matter (the female); mind and spirit are privileged over the body and substance and the only way to give meaning and order to the body in nature is through the imposition of technique and style—to give it a defining frame" (23). For Nead, the concept of "the frame" suggests "a metaphor for the 'staging' of art, both in terms of surrounding the body with style and of marking the limit between art and non-art, that is, obscenity" (25). The naked female body, then, in its "raw" state, is perceived as "matter." Through the imposition of male "artistic" techniques, this matter is tamed, literally framed, and delivered from obscenity: stylization and aestheticization transform the naked female body into "the female nude." This nude conforms to the Aristotelian definition of "beauty" to the extent that it embodies "order and symmetry and definiteness" (Nead, 7).

Like the naked female body, de Beauvoir is subject to a process of stylization that holds her within specific frames of cultural acceptability.[7] She is often photographed, for example, in the act of writing.[8] Pen and paper—the tools of her trade—are on her lap, in her hands, or on the table. Usually, these portraits of de Beauvoir "at work" capture her in a straight-backed and upright position, modestly dressed, with her hair held in a neat bun. Such images reveal a calm and *composed* de Beauvoir—an ordered, orderly, and overwhelmingly well-*maintained* woman. Written representations support this kind of visual image; journalistic reportage chooses to constitute even de Beauvoir's psychic happiness in terms of her passion for writing. "All her life she regarded them [herself and Sartre] as primarily a writing couple. Her image of happiness was a sunny room, with two people in it, both of them writing. And in cafés, bars and hotels, chiefly in and around Saint-Germain-des-Prés this was the pattern of their life together. She was, and acknowledged herself to be, a happy woman" (*Independent on Sunday,* 10 June 1990, 15). The order of mental exercise, the assumed "symmetry" of heterosexuality, and the concrete assurance that an intellectual secures happiness through writing each corresponds to Aristotle's definition of beauty. This is de Beauvoir framed: in a photograph, in a room, in a description. A further parallel with the female nude—and a further result of the process of containment—is that de Beauvoir is situated within the realm of "high culture": her life and work furnish an academic industry, and her books and biographies are reviewed in "quality" broadsheet papers.[9] This "high" cultural interest in de Beauvoir is partnered by a mode of visual representation which positions her at three-quarter angles (as opposed to full frontal), a representation which conforms to the conventions of western art and which, echoing the genre of (white upper-class) family portraits, establishes de Beauvoir in a specific social setting.[10]

Susan Sontag's *On Photography* provides a bridge by which to cross from Nead's "visual" analysis to an analysis of written material.[11] Sontag writes: "[p]hotography is commonly regarded as an instrument for knowing things. When Thoreau said, *'You can't say more than you see,'* he took for granted that sight had pride of place among the senses" (93, my emphasis). Sontag's thesis, that the ubiquity of photography in western society has led to an "aestheticizing of reality" (176), is confirmed in journalese, a style that defers to an assumed "photographic imagination." The written texts not only encourage a static, unchanging perception of de Beauvoir (as in a freeze frame) but are also frequently literal descriptions of photographs:

The photograph on the back jacket [of the book *Letters to Sartre*] stays in the reader's mind. Here is the great philosopher [Sartre], in his knitted shirt buttoned up to the neck: his dear little shirt, as Beauvoir would say. Here is the author of the letters [de Beauvoir], looking frayed, hair knotted in a cleaning lady's scarf. Her glass is empty, Sartre's is half full. So many years of hard thinking, hard loving: so sad they look like an old janitor and his wife, out on a (very modified) spree. (*Independent on Sunday,* 2 February 1992, 30)

Despite this author's long review of de Beauvoir's letters to Sartre, which highlights her relationships with women as well as men, it is the *photograph* that ultimately "speaks the truth" of de Beauvoir and tells the reader what there is to "know" about her: when all is said and done, the ambiguity of the past is dissolved in favor of a representation which (re)figures de Beauvoir as no more than one half of a parochial, "married" couple.[12] Photographs teach us "a new visual code, [they] alter and enlarge our notions of what is worth looking at and what we have a right to observe. They are a grammar and, even more importantly, an ethics of seeing" (Sontag, 3). Thus when de Beauvoir's turban—something of a trademark—came undone at Sartre's funeral, the newspaper emphasized that the "symbolic" moment (de Beauvoir herself coming undone/falling to pieces) was "not missed by photographers" (*Independent on Sunday,* 2 February 1992, 30). Sontag's suggestion that the "whole of a life may be summed up in a momentary appearance" (Sontag, 159) is demonstrated in a flash (of the camera's eye): captured on film, the potent heterosexual image was not merely encapsulated but dramatically magnified.

The style of writing which dominates press reports bears witness to the prioritization of photojournalism in an increasingly spectacular society: the reader is frequently encouraged to "visualize" the written description. "She [de Beauvoir] looked to me frailer and less tall than one might have expected. In her trouser suit and its matching purple turban she was still essentially feminine. Her voice was dry and rapid, her red-nailed hands impatient and restless" (Margaret Crosland, quoted in *Independent on Sunday,* 2 February 1992, 30). This "portrait" of de Beauvoir ("a verbal picture; a graphic description"—*Oxford English Dictionary*) lends itself to the imagination; that is, the reader is prompted "to image" the frail, slight, and (therefore?) "essentially feminine" de Beauvoir. The interchangeability of literary and visual terms—a photographic *grammar*, a literary *portrait*—indicates how thin a line divides the visual from the written: all of the examples above, whatever their medium of expression, indicate to the reader "what is worth looking at" and "what we have a right to observe" (Sontag, 159). In the written representation of de Beauvoir and Sartre in "a sunny room," in the description of a photograph of de Beauvoir and Sartre in a café and of de Beauvoir at Sartre's funeral, the reader is directed to observe de Beauvoir's heterosexuality. And when the *Independent on*

Sunday describes de Beauvoir's "frailty," her clothes and her nails, it is her femininity which is signaled.

Like the distinction between the naked female body and the nude, an "ethics of seeing" constitutes what can and cannot be consumed, what is figured, and what is excluded, from the frame: "the policing of the boundaries of cultural accept-ability is, quite blatantly, a policing of the boundaries of sexual acceptability" (Nead, 95). The very maintenance of frames and boundaries presupposes—even constitutes—a threatening "exterior." Thus the female nude marks not only "the internal limit of art" but also "the external limit of obscenity" (Nead, 25). If the nude represents a figure of unified perfection and "purity"—a coherent and harmonious "whole" which is perceived to reflect a rational self—what lies beyond the frame of representation is, by contrast, that which is fragmented and defiled, "polluted." The following three sections of this essay will explore three disciplinary frames which circumscribe the figure of Simone de Beauvoir. Taken together, they do not form a coherent or unified vision of sexuality and, in some respects, are even mutually exclusive. What they share however, is a resistance to producing bisexuality as a subject of representation. The final section of the chapter will briefly compare the strategies which "frame" de Beauvoir to the "concepts of pollution and rituals of purification" identified by Mary Douglas (quoted in Nead, 31). I will return to the notion of techniques of the self in this section and look at the implications of the "framing" of de Beauvoir, the "rituals of purifica-tion," for bisexuality.

The Paint and Oil of Existentialism

This frame explores how the binding link forged by the press between de Beauvoir and (representations of) "existentialism" effaces bisexuality. Existentialism has two (related) functions here. First, it is perceived to be the raison d'être behind de Beauvoir's many relationships; as such, her "motive" lies not in an active sexual desire for both men and women but rather in her infamous intellectual "pact" with Sartre (that they should have "contingent" affairs while maintaining their "essential" relationship). Second, existentialism serves to attribute to de Beauvoir a certain "masculinity." This is not to suggest that de Beauvoir plays the "man" in her relation-ships with women, but rather that she is assumed to possess characteristics which are conventionally designated "masculine" (voyeurism, lack of emotion) and which consequently position her "outside" the affairs. The effect of this "distancing" is to limit de Beauvoir's perceived investment in her female lovers, so diminishing their role in her sexual biography.

The press representations of de Beauvoir's sexual relationships confirm Nead's contention that: "[t]he evocation of blanket terms such as 'love' and 'human relations' can ... work to hide a range of cultural, sexual and moral norms in a hazy mist of universal consensus" (Nead, 106). De Beauvoir's "pact" with Sartre robs her "contingent" relationships of those features traditionally associated with affairs: spontaneity, romance, and love. Nelson Algren (one of de Beauvoir's "contingent" partners) encapsulates the majority of press opinion in the question "'How can love be contingent? ... Contingent upon what?'" (quoted in the *Financial Times*, 15 August 1987, London Page 12). The virtually legal terminology in which the pact with Sartre is represented suggests that it is the "dry" flavor of the arrangement that warrants disapproval. Thus: "the terms of de Beauvoir's contract with the existential maestro do not seem to have been negotiable" (Algren). What the press must negotiate, therefore, is an expression of sexuality unescorted by "love." To this end, Algren comes to represent the figural enactment of all that is "normal"—and all that is heterosexual. "He [Algren] thought in his naive American way that two people who loved as they did ought to get married and be faithful to one another" (*Financial Times*, 19 January 1991, London Page 14).[13] His belief in marriage and fidelity constitutes "a breath of fresh air amongst the welter of self-justification in the Sartre-Beauvoir circle" (*Financial Times*, 15 August 1987, London Page 12).

If de Beauvoir's pact with Sartre serves to deprive the press of a traditional heterosexual love story, they in turn use this "contract" to deprive her of sexual desire. De Beauvoir is perceived to have affairs because she "want[s] experience more than pleasure" (*Independent on Sunday*, 2 February 1992, 30); she "had several lovers at once—though curiously not always with much pleasure." The "existential experiment which was their [de Beauvoir and Sartre's] long, open 'morganatic' marriage" thereby comes to play a large part in de Beauvoir's (a)sexual biography (*Sunday Telegraph*, 8 December 1991, 116). In particular, this "existential experiment" serves to occlude sexual pleasure. Such an occlusion, contrived by the press, implicitly suggests that while heterosexual pleasure is absolute, any other form of sexual expression requires a motive other than pleasure itself. The *Sunday Times*, for example, suggests that de Beauvoir's "own relations with women were tortured, rarely erotic" (2 August 1987). Although directly acknowledging de Beauvoir's relationships with women, the extract dismisses the "erotic" in favor of the "tortured" (and figures these as mutually exclusive). Within this context, it appears inconceivable that Olga Kosakiewitch, say (as opposed to Nelson Algren), should question the philosophy behind de Beauvoir's contingent affairs or should ask how it is possible for love to be contingent.

"Existentialism" in this first instance, then, bears comparison with the "paint and oil" of "artistic" representation, which, by foregrounding its technique, "inhibits or blocks the immediate sexual gratification" (Nead, 97). Wrought as the motivation behind de Beauvoir's relationships, existentialism "clothes" an otherwise wayward sexuality and transforms her into the equivalent of a nude. Since sexual pleasure alone cannot explain (or justify) de Beauvoir's behavior, it must be entirely forfeited. Without this, the unspeakable issue of "sexual gratification" might bear articulation.

"Asexuality" also features in de Beauvoir's relationship with Sartre, once again as a consequence of existentialism. This relationship is perceived to be "as much cerebral as sexual"; de Beauvoir is aptly quoted as saying that she and Sartre "went to bed, blissfully happy, our heads full of words." In short, "[w]ords were what they [de Beauvoir and Sartre] both lived for until quite late in life. True to their doctrine of 'transparency,' they kept few secrets from each other" (*Sunday Telegraph*, 26 January 1992, 111). De Beauvoir's pleasure is based in the academy, her "marriage" is "a marriage of true minds" (*Guardian*, 16 April 1986). This sexual inflection situates de Beauvoir firmly within the hierarchy of western metaphysics: "her mind" dominates and takes precedence over (and is, by implication, separable from) "her body." An aesthetic stylization which employs "existentialism" as the medium of expression thus signifies "form" as opposed to "matter" and "order" as opposed to the abyss of chaotic substance. Like the representation of de Beauvoir writing, the woman here is contained within a scaffold of scholarship.

This representation of pleasure is "aesthetic" insofar as it is literally "purified of pleasure." To this extent it can be distinguished from venal sensuality: "Legitimate, or high, culture is . . . constituted through the denial of lower, vulgar or venal enjoyment and the assertion of the sublimated, refined and disinterested pleasure. . . . Bourdieu provides us with an example of cultural distinction based on the separation of the aesthetic ('pleasure purified of pleasure') and the venal ('pleasure reduced to the pleasure of the senses')" (Nead, 84). The qualities that "existentialism" defines in this context are the very same as those which constitute the sublimated pleasure of the aesthetic: voyeuristic distance, "objectivity," intellectualism, and cold exploitation. These features, conventionally dubbed "masculine," harness the female nude and produce it as "an extension of the elevated male attributes associated with the mind" (Nead, 14). Thus de Beauvoir "looks" with the eyes of the male: "[s]he and Sartre were incurable voyeurs who specialized in emotional threesomes" (*Sunday Times*, 2 August 1987).

The perceived "voyeurism" motivating these relationships resonates with the *disinterested* pleasure of the aesthetic and therefore suggests a distance between de Beauvoir and her lovers. De Beauvoir, like the masculine spectator, is situated "outside" her relationships: she looks *at* but does not partake *in*. This, then, is the second way in which existentialism is employed to contain the sexuality embodied by de Beauvoir. Positioned as the "male artist"/dry philosopher, she is figured as power "in, as well as under, control" (Nead, 17). The metaphorical gender switch enables not only de Beauvoir's own, now masculinized, body to be "mastered" but also, *through* this body, those of her female lovers as well. Again, existentialism is used to link her sexuality not to desire but to intellectualism. The intellectual experiment, moreover, is even conceived to be something of a *duty*. "De Beauvoir tries to ignore their [her female lovers'] jealous tears and explain away their demands, describing them cold-heartedly, and in intimate detail, to Sartre" (*Sunday Telegraph* , 8 December 1991, 116).

If her lovers are objects in an experimental research project, by extension de Beauvoir must be the objective researcher, a rational self who "acts on" others. "Certainly there is something cold, exploitative in her attitude.... [W]e cannot know how the experimental subjects feel, for theirs are merely contingent lives" (*Independent on Sunday,* 2 February 1992, 30). That it is the *lives* of the "experimental subjects" which are contingent (as opposed, simply, to their relationship with de Beauvoir) indicates that love story and life story are collapsed here: life is (all about) love/sex relationships. This complete contingency additionally situates de Beauvoir in a still more powerful position over her lovers. In the following extract, the roots of de Beauvoir's "cold" attitude are perceived to lie in the existential concept of "inauthenticity": "De Beauvoir has a very chilling habit of describing other people's emotions of jealousy and resentment against herself as 'inauthentic,' even lecturing one girl about it: in existentialist philosophy 'inauthentic' means self-deceiving, or being in bad faith, and that seems to me to describe exactly de Beauvoir's own behaviour in using the term to deny other people's feelings" (*Sunday Telegraph* , 8 December 1991, 116). By valuing "authenticity" (an intellectual concept) over and above "other people's feelings," de Beauvoir sacrifices her own "humanity." Her behavior is "inauthentic," insofar as "inauthenticity" is constituted as a denial of "other people's feelings." That this criticism is rarely leveled at men (indeed, sensitivity to others may be regarded as emasculating), suggests that the masculinization of de Beauvoir cannot be sustained at any great length. In the final analysis, de Beauvoir "is" a woman, and the cost of effacing her femininity in order to account for her sexuality is too high to maintain. The preferred strategy in this example, then, is to constitute intellectualism and emotional responsibility as mutually exclusive: de Beauvoir's femininity, albeit somewhat wayward, is ultimately recuperated, and subsequently her (feminine) behavior is condemned as inauthentic.

In sum, "existentialism" serves as a two-pronged strategy of containment through which the representations of sexuality ascribed to de Beauvoir have been aestheticized (anaesthetized) and purified (sterilized). First, like the application of "art" (on)to the naked female body, de Beauvoir is restrained and styled through the technics of an asexual biography: like the nude, she is confined to the unemotional, controlled, and intellectually reflective arena. Second, representing the "masculine" artist/painter herself, de Beauvoir controls not only her own female body (insofar as it is denied an energetic sexual desire) but also the bodies of her female lovers as well (they are her "objects").

A further implication is that de Beauvoir's relationships with women are not only perceived as specifically *not* pleasurable and *not* erotic but also orchestrated from within the frame of heterosexuality: the relationship with Sartre, itself bound by the intellect, shrouds her liaisons with women. This is demonstrated by the *Independent Weekend* headline which reads: "Letters from a Radical Lover—in which Simone tells her beloved Jean-Paul what she gets up to while he's away" (23 November 1991, 31). The effect here is to render de Beauvoir's relationships with women secondary to her relationship with Sartre: they occur only when he is "away." On Sartre's return (the return of the primary relationship), their importance will presumably be diminished. Since they are constituted as "additional," rather than "central," the "affairs" qualify for neither serious nor independent consideration. They have no inherent value, because their definition lies in something other than themselves: in the first instance, they are experiments in existentialist "authenticity," in the second, they are secondary to the relationship with Sartre. This representation of de Beauvoir, therefore, not only precludes (bi)sexuality but also ensures that heterosexual hegemony is in no way threatened.

Being Bohemian

The second frame explores the consequences for bisexuality of the reputation of de Beauvoir and Sartre, in Britain, as "universal Parisians" (*Times*, 19 April 1986, 9). In this context, representations of de Beauvoir are housed in three adjoining rooms: "French," "intellectual," and "bohemian." This lifestyle exerts such magnificent force over the whole of de Beauvoir's self that bisexuality becomes subsumed within it. Hence, bisexuality is not perceived to be constitutive of the self (as other sexualities, particularly heterosexuality, are); instead, de Beauvoir's sexual behavior is informed by her bohemian milieu. If it had been possible to "separate" this lifestyle from de Beauvoir, the press imply, her "capricious" sexual behavior might also (by her own preference even) have been circumvented. As we shall see, this is confirmed in the final frame.

Representations of de Beauvoir/Paris (for they are collapsed) appear as no more than snapshots in the album of a collective popular imagination. Like a tourist visiting France, the images collected here repeatedly confirm stereotypical British images of French national identity.[14] "Resemblance is a conformity, but to what? To an identity. Now this identity is imprecise, even imaginary, to the point where I can continue to speak of 'likeness' without ever having seen the model. . . . I spontaneously call them 'likenesses' because they conform to what I expect of them."[15] The cumulative effect of these images, found also on book covers and in posters, in films and journals, in novels and in the academy, is that history, "past and present" represents only "a set of anecdotes" (Sontag, 23). Replicated thousands of times over, these images of history do not evolve, but rather remain static and motionless—even "naturalized" (things could never be different)—like a photographic "still." This analysis of the second frame, therefore, uses a "postcard device" in order to capture the flavor of the stylized and aestheticized "souvenirs"—"featherweight portable museums" (Sontag, 68)—offered by British newspapers, from which the reader is free to consume and purchase a history.

1. Postcards from France

The first postcard finds de Beauvoir collapsed with "France." It is the postwar period, and French society is ripe for radical change: "the reader is taken through a story which, however plainly told, cannot fail to fascinate, for it is woven into important aspects of France's 20th-century history, above all with the often tumultuous postwar resettlement of French society" (*Financial Times*, 1 February 1992, London Page 12). The historic moment is dominated by a changing political climate: rebellion is possible and romantic. A sleight of hand positions de Beauvoir both inside and outside this self-reflective period. She offers "insider" information on the events—"Simone de Beauvoir's most successful novel was *Les Mandarins* (1954), a *roman à clef* about Sartre, Camus, herself and other luminaries of the French left-wing after the liberation" (*Times*, 15 April 1986, 18)—and yet she is also central to those events herself: "[T]he prize-winning novel, *Les Mandarins*, explores the postwar Parisian cultural world where they were the joint dominant force. . . . They were closely involved in attempts to start a Left Bank resistance movement during the war, and were at the centre of leftwing postwar political protest" (*Guardian*, 15 April 1986, 1). De Beauvoir is therefore not only imbricated *in* and *with* postwar France but also *creates* postwar France.

A large, front-page photograph in the *Independent Weekend* (23 November 1991) shows de Beauvoir in a typical French boulevard; her youthful face is set against a predictably opaque background, complete with tall "French" buildings and traditional streetlights. The photograph—playing with the paradoxical blend of the naive and the risqué which so frequently represents "the French" to "the British"—is as much of France as it is of de Beauvoir: each defines the other, to the point where they are inseparable. Like written representations, this visual "chronicle" does not "reflect" so much as constitute both de Beauvoir *and* France. The impenetrable link ensures that when de Beauvoir dies, a part of France is perceived to be buried with her: "Vive la Différence / Simone de Beauvoir and the Death of Parisian Left Bank Culture" (*Times*, 19 April 1986, 9). The demure satisfaction intimated by the British press is further confirmed in the *Economist*: "It was one of those times when France stops to look at itself and at the rich literary tradition which its current writers seem unable to top up" (19 April 1986, 100).

Three years later, France's national literary archive acquired the rights to the letters of de Beauvoir and Sartre, which confirmed the British press's view that de Beauvoir is an institution in France's national cultural heritage. In this context, Gilbert Joseph's "wild, vitriolic attack on their [de Beauvoir and Sartre's] Second World War Resistance record" (*Sunday Telegraph*, 26 January 1992, 111) was interpreted in the British newspapers to be an attack on French national identity. The British coverage of the "Parisian response" to the incident not only affirmed that the reporters' perception had been justified (a curiously circular exercise) but also occasioned further nationalistic stereotyping and a trace of badinage: "Paris literary papers have divided over the issue, and few are content to dismiss the matter, as one new year reveller in a Boul' Mich' café did, with a Gallic shrug" (*Financial Times*, 1 February 1992, London Page 12). Gallic shrugs in Gallic cafés proved, to the British, that de Beauvoir and Sartre not only "arouse fierce passions in France" (*Sunday Telegraph*, 26 January 1992, 111) but also, in some measure, define France.

2. Postcards from Paris

This national identity is further collapsed with an "intellectualism" that is perceived to reside in Paris. It also provides an additional vehicle with which to distinguish the "British" from the "French": "You could scour London, look in every café in Soho and never find their like. . . . Britain had academics, journalists, novelists, but professional intellectuals who lived on and off their ideas—Britain in those years had none. Happy days" (*Times*, 19 April 1986, 9). With the merest whisper of relief, the *Times* also suggests that "Bloomsbury can offer no comparison. In their prime Sartre and de Beauvoir were Paris. It was . . . an endless giddy round of thought and writing . . . and, of course, talk, talk, talk. This seriousness about the life of the mind; this was a Gallic trait prized above all." Sartre and de Beauvoir "were Paris" and Parisians are defined by "the life of the mind." This "seriousness," the chief characteristic of present-day France, is seen to be rooted in a long "French" tradition which extends as far back as the Revolution: "When the ancien régime was overthrown, new heads had to be supplied to replace those that had rolled. The philosophes and provincial lawyers who had inspired the revolution thought it natural that those with bonnes notes—the highest marks—should go to the top of the classes. Intelligence maintains a centrality in Paris which, in London, is reserved for sportsmen, princesses and the dead" (*Sunday Times*, 2 August 1987). Despite the ironic tone, de Beauvoir's lifestyle is constituted with the full force of French history behind it. No surprise then, that the press dramatically highlighted de Gaulle's response to requests that he should arrest Sartre (for his role in inciting French workers to rebellion): "On n'arrête pas Voltaire." Not only above law and order, de Beauvoir and Sartre are also beyond politics—a status which crosses even continental boundaries: "they were given what amounted to diplomatic status when they travelled—to Cuba, Russia, China, Czechoslovakia, Hungary" (*Independent on Sunday*, 10 June 1990, 15). This lifestyle, hewn in immense proportions, gives rise to conclusions like that of the *Times*: "Sartre and de Beauvoir begin to appear in retrospect famous for their membership of a celebrated menage as much as for their philosophy and novels. They had achieved, in this age of mass culture, star status on account of their lifestyle" (19 April 1986, 9). The media machine's production of de Beauvoir and Sartre as "stars" not only raises them above law, order, and politics but also distances them from the public at large. Because de Beauvoir is unlike "ordinary" folk, her perceived sexual difference (from the unspoken "norm" of heterosexuality) can be attributed not to individual preference but to her celebrated lifestyle.

3. Postcards from Cafés

Finally, French intellectual identity is also an "inherently" bohemian identity. In a perverse twist of priority, existentialism is even perceived to be the *consequence* of "bohemianism." Construed as "the expression of Sartre's deeply rooted café complex" (*Guardian*, 22 December 1992, 8), existentialism is presented as only a ruse with which to justify the lifestyle: "[T]here is certainly something enviable in so much free-loving, free-loading and free-wheeling. François Mauriac, appalled and fascinated, conceded that unless God existed there was no reason not to want to live their way." In short: "What a winning trick to turn doing what you want into a revolutionary morality!" (*Sunday Times*, 2 August 1987). The marriage of intellectualism and bohemianism, neatly packaged in historical tradition, enables a comparison to be wrought between de Beauvoir and Sartre and the protagonists of *Les liaisons dangereuses*. The passage cited below is critical: in essence the work and sexuality of de Beauvoir and Sartre are judged elitist (and therefore hypocritical), malicious (and therefore unoriginal). The analogy enables both French tradition and high culture to be turned against themselves:

Simone de Beauvoir devoted herself to didactic sedition. She and Jean-Paul Sartre spent their lives sawing high-mindedly at the lofty branch on which their talents had entitled them to sit. It is hardly news that the two of them had an unusual relationship. In fact, it was less 'unique' than a variation on the one to be found in *Les Liaisons Dangereuses*, where a pact binds the 'essential' lovers to disclose to each other the details of their 'contingent' affairs. The existential mandarins were left-wing aristos: Laclos Deux, you might say. (*Sunday Times*, 2 August 1987)

That a viable juxtaposition can be sustained between two fictional characters and de Beauvoir and Sartre confirms the suspicion that they too are no more than fantasy. The analogy is further supported in representations of Sartre's flippant attitude to sex: "In general we make love once, then I wash quickly and I'm at the Café Riche around eleven" (quoted in the *Guardian*, 22 December 1992, 8). Valmont himself could not be more dry.

It is around the ubiquitous "café" that this lifestyle is centered. Photographs frequently show de Beauvoir in a typically Parisian café, replete with brass bar running around the walls (newspapers wedged between them) and the paraphernalia of café snacks (vinegar bottles, sugar, etc.). De Beauvoir and Sartre are also often pictured with the inevitable glass of red wine that accompanies representations of so many café lifestyles. The *Economist*, in an article entitled "Life Is a Café," dispels any doubts the reader might be harboring about the map of Parisian culture: "For France, read Paris: for Paris, the Left Bank. . . . [F]or the Left Bank . . . read Saint-Germaine-des-Prés, and for this bare square mile, read the Café de Flore" (20 October 1984, 103). De Beauvoir herself is portrayed as much concerned with the trappings of this café culture. The *Sunday Telegraph* emphasizes the "list of cafés, titles of films and books, names of people at parties, food, cocktails, money and pretty clothes" and wryly concludes "existential woman seems to be material woman too" (8 December 1991, 116). The cumulative effect of this soap opera cum fairy tale, however ambivalently presented, is that de Beauvoir's relationships with women are rarely highlighted and are usually passed over without comment. Typically, de Beauvoir and Sartre "are often sleeping with the same woman" (*Independent on Sunday*, 2 February 1992, 30). The emphasis lies instead on de Beauvoir and Sartre's "literary reputation, the glorious days of the liberation, existentialism and Saint-Germain-des-Prés, de Beauvoir's *The Second Sex* and her

Prix Goncourt" and finally "their many complex affairs" (*Independent on Sunday*, 10 June 1990, 31).

De Beauvoir's "many complex affairs" merit no individual attention, since they are just one of any number of "glorious events" that took place during her lifetime. Her "rebellion" is additionally perceived to be well past its sell-by date: "if her antics now sometimes seem an adolescent rebellion, only those who remember France in the Thirties can really measure how necessary that rebellion was" (*Sunday Telegraph*, 26 January 1992, 111). Although necessary then, de Beauvoir's frolicking "adolescent antics" represent no more than teenage growing pains on the road to full "adult" maturity. History marches on. De Beauvoir's writing (about her sexual partners): "seem[s] dated, quaint, or innocently self-conscious, 'her emotional naivete,' as Margaret Crosland [one of her biographers] says, 'was nothing short of endearing'" (*Sunday Telegraph*, 26 January 1992). "Endearing"—but not threatening—de Beauvoir's "rebellion" speaks of the past rather than the future. As such, it suffers from a disconcerting "statis of arrest" (Barthes, 91); the only pleasure it provides "passes through the image" (Barthes, 118).

These representations of de Beauvoir create the impression that bisexuality is more a product of history and culture than a *sexuality* that *of itself* contributes to the production of the self. Unlike heterosexuality, bisexuality is not an expression of de Beauvoir *specifically*, so much as an indication of the flavor of the period and the ambiance of the setting in which she happened to be situated. Bisexuality is therefore not merely inspired by this specific time and context but is also confined to it: if bisexuality *has* a history, it is equally imprisoned *in* and by that history.

Heterosexual Scandal

The suspicion that bisexuality is only born of, and confined to, bohemianism is confirmed in the media responses to de Beauvoir's letters to Sartre (published in English in 1991): "[R]eaders may have felt there was little more light to be shed on this very public pair, but it seems they were wrong; in the year of her death, de Beauvoir's letters to Sartre were found in the back of a cupboard and when they were published in French last year they caused a sensation. . . . [H]er letters revealed how partial the disclosures of the past had been" (*Sunday Telegraph*, 8 December 1991, 116). The letters may have come out of the cupboard, but de Beauvoir remained in the closet: although they documented once and for all de Beauvoir's relationships with women as well as men, the coverage these letters received emphasized instead the author's "guilt" regarding her sexual behavior. It was de Beauvoir's anxiety, not bisexuality, that ultimately proved "the scandal": "[T]he horrid truth that emerges from these accounts is that de Beauvoir is at some level sorry. She understands the jealousy she and Sartre have caused; she describes it page after page. She feels remorse.... [S]he feels jealousy herself" (*Sunday Telegraph*, 116). The "truth" of de Beauvoir which emerges from the annals of historical myth is, of course, heterosexual. "For those who have not suspected it already ... Simone de Beauvoir is not Existential Woman, heroine of Bohemia. Not only does she have feet of clay; she has the ruthless and sentimental heart of a bourgeois housewife" (*Sunday Telegraph*, 116).

The effect of representing de Beauvoir as "emotional" returns her first to femininity and then to heterosexuality. The shift of frame from "heroine of Bohemia" to "bourgeois housewife" also erases all notion of bisexuality; even though de Beauvoir was not physically heterosexual, or monogamous, she was still emotionally faithful to Sartre: "through all these [her affairs] and other, briefer 'flings' she remained loyal to Sartre, an unmarried cuckold, a submissive non-wife" (*Sunday Telegraph*, 26 January 1992, 111). As in the first frame (where existentialism constituted the bounds of sexuality), bisexuality is again perceived to stem from de Beauvoir's "primary" relationship and her "pact" with Sartre. Additionally, in both instances, the emphasis on the role of Sartre in de Beauvoir's sexual biography serves to deny her her own agency. This final frame however, moves the figure of de Beauvoir one step nearer to coherent heterosexuality: that her emotions are predominantly those of "guilt" and "remorse" suggests that were an alternative available, de Beauvoir might have taken it. She was not "happy," but she nevertheless "did it" to keep Sartre: "she [de Beauvoir] is constantly trying to manipulate Sartre, and keep her position as number one wife. Significantly, at one particularly threatening time for her, she addresses him as husband" (*Sunday Telegraph*, 8 December 1991, 116).

Using the letters then, commentators inscribe onto de Beauvoir a sexuality that inheres in her *self*, not in existentialism or bohemianism. Imbued with the authoritative weight of autobiographical narrative, this final framing ensures that it is de Beauvoir herself (as opposed to either a philosophy or a lifestyle) who is in "possession" of "her" sexuality: it is de Beauvoir who bears sole emotional responsibility for—as well as, significantly, the ensuing "remorse" over—her actions.[16] Nevertheless, the constitution of de Beauvoir as a sexual protagonist *only* in relation to a heterosexual narrative suggests that she "is" heterosexual.

Pollution and Purification: Implications for Bisexuality

The frames outlined above represent "rituals of purification" insofar as they "clothe" the figure of de Beauvoir in art and halt the "filth and pollution" that would otherwise issue from this body (Mary Douglas, in Nead, 7). However, since the art/obscenity pairing constitutes an (almost) complete system of meaning, the nude (and de Beauvoir)—although frequently conforming to the conventions of art—also threatens risk and instability (Nead, 25): "[A]ll margins are dangerous. If they are pulled this way or that the shape of fundamental experience is altered" (Douglas, in Nead, 33). I should like to add, therefore, lest my own interpretations of the newspapers have imposed a coherence of their own, that these representations of de Beauvoir are not absolutely secure; occasionally, the margins of "respectable" heterosexuality are "pulled" out of shape.

Images of cannibalistic savagery, for example, are employed where de Beauvoir and Sartre's "triangles" are acknowledged: "[De Beauvoir and Sartre's] recently published wartime correspondence reveals devouring egos in which third parties were first swallowed up and then spat out in sexually exploitative tangles of Byzantine complexity" (*Financial Times,* 1 February 1992, London Page 12). In a description that evokes cannibalism, de Beauvoir's "devouring ego" is seen to be "exploitative." Once again, the vehicle of press disapprobation is Nelson Algren; it is his sensibility which has been slighted. "Hell, love-letters should be private. I've been in whorehouses all over the world and the woman always closes the door" (Algren, quoted in the *Independent on Sunday,* 2 February 1992, 30). De Beauvoir is perceived to be worse than a whore, because "even" a whore "closes the door." The metaphor of condemnation, which is both gendered and derogatory, bears comparison with the charges brought against pornographic obscenity: "The crime of pornography is . . . the reintroduction of sex into the public sphere. Pornography makes sex visible; it takes what has become the most profound and private aspect of individual being and transforms it into a public commodity, exposed to the public gaze" (Nead, 100). The exposure of the letters, as in the pornographic scenario, reduces "love" (the private love letters) to "sex" (the whore metaphor). As private intrigue becomes public "common" knowledge, "high" culture (de Beauvoir) is transformed into "low" culture (the whore). The incident with Nelson Algren exemplifies the tension which runs throughout these representations. It also indicates that the "obscene" is unwelcome within the frame of the aesthetic and that (attempted) censorship is a prerequisite to the maintenance of order: "[d]esirable femininity has been constructed specifically in terms of both health and beauty—to be fit for life is to be fit for art" (Nead, 77). In order that de Beauvoir be rendered "fit for life," her relationships with both men and women must be "framed."

This framing requires considerable work on de Beauvoir, or effort, if she is to sustain cultural acceptability (specifically in relation to sexuality). As this essay has demonstrated, in the first frame, de Beauvoir's relationships with women as well as men are acknowledged, but her experience is perceived to occlude sexual pleasure: de Beauvoir's "motive" is grounded in existential experimentation, rather than sexual desire. In the second frame, de Beauvoir's sexuality is seen to be the result of, and have its roots in, the historical period in which she lived and the lifestyle into which she was born: it is the specific combination of a French/intellectual/bohemian identity which produces "bisexuality," but ultimately confines it to "history." In the final frame, bisexuality is displaced in favor of a representation of de Beauvoir as guilty and regretful of her "other" (i.e., nonheterosexual) experiences. Here, her relationships with women are seen as not only contingent upon but also even inspired by Sartre: the figuration of de Beauvoir as self-recriminating, therefore, serves to contain her "other" liaisons firmly within the bounds of heterosexuality itself.

What is significant here, I think, is not merely that the joint force of these three frames ensures that (unconstituted) bisexuality remains beyond the frame of representation. More importantly, these frames represent only *heterosexuality* as though it were an integral part of de Beauvoir's self. This in itself is not unrelated to the concept of the frame. Lynda Nead identifies the Aristotelian definition of "beauty" (with which this essay began) to be part of a larger discourse, where the issue at stake "is the production of a rational coherent subject. In other words, the notion of a unified form [exemplified by the female nude] is integrally bound up with the perception of self, and the construction of individual identity" (Nead, 7). Heterosexuality inheres in de Beauvoir such that she is perceived to be both possessed of it (it belongs to her) and possessed by it (she belongs to it; it is a technique of the self which defines her self). In other words, heterosexuality expresses the truth of de Beauvoir and is linked to her *individuality* insofar as de Beauvoir, *specifically*, "is" heterosexual.

Bisexuality, by contrast, is not a technique which contributes to the production of de Beauvoir's self, because its "roots" are perceived to be *external* to the self. The "source" of bisexuality lies instead in existential philosophy and/or bohemianism. Because bisexuality resides outside of the self (of de Beauvoir), the notion of "bisexuality" as a technique of the self is, in this context, inconceivable. Perhaps the margins at which bisexuality pulls, then, the obscene feature which shatters the integrity of the unified self—what Nead identifies as the "rational coherent subject"—is that it implicitly indicates that not all sexuality necessarily resides *within* an individual self; indeed, sexuality may exceed the individuality ascribed to the self. If, as Foucault argues, "[b]etween each of us and our sex, the West has placed a never-ending demand for truth," then representations of de Beauvoir, in displacing bisexuality, simultaneously destabilize the notion of the self and the location of the truth of the self. Perceived to be "external" to the self, representations of bisexuality call the "ourness" of "our" sex into question.

Notes

Thanks to Jackie Stacey, Lynne Pearce, and Maria Pramaggiore for their helpful comments on earlier drafts of this chapter; a special thanks to Celia Lury.

1. Michel Foucault, *The History of Sexuality, vol. 1* (Harmondsworth, England: Penguin Books, 1990), 77.

2. See Michel Foucault, "Technologies of the Self," in *Technologies of the Self: A Seminar with Michel Foucault,* ed. Luther H. Martin, Huck Gutman, and Patrick H. Hutton (London: Tavistock, 1988).

3. Techniques of the self may also contradict and conflict with each other.

4. The period analyzed covers 1984 to 1994.

5. It is taken as given that the media does not passively reflect sexuality but actively participates in the construction and dissemination of sexual identities.

6. Lynda Nead, *The Female Nude: Art, Obscenity and Sexuality* (London: Routledge, 1993), 2.

7. This is not to suggest that either the naked female body, de Beauvoir, or bisexuality somehow exist prior to, or transcend, cultural framing: instead, all three are constituted through discourse itself. I am using Nead's analysis here, because it enables parallels to be drawn between the processes by which the naked female body is held within the frame of cultural acceptability (stylization and aestheticization, which transform the naked body into a nude) and the ways in which representations of de Beauvoir's sexuality are situated within the bounds of (hetero)sexual (dominant cultural) acceptability.

8. De Beauvoir is compared to other "eccentric" women writers such as Virginia Woolf (*Sunday Telegraph,* 20 December 1992, 11), Dame Edith Sitwell (*Independent on Sunday,* 2 February 1992, 30), George Sand, and Madame de Staël (*Sunday Telegraph,* 26 January 1992, 111). These women are additionally distinguished by their sexuality, over which a question mark might be perceived to hang.

9. I found only one reference to de Beauvoir, a short obituary, in the British tabloids between October 1984 and December 1992.

10. See John Berger, *Ways of Seeing* (London: Penguin Books, 1977) and John Tagg, *The Burden of Representation: Essays on Photographies and Histories* (London: Macmillan, 1988), 37.

11. Susan Sontag, *On Photography* (Harmondsworth, England: Penguin Books, 1979).

12. This "revelatory" capacity of photography—which contributes to an impression of "depth"—is ironic, given that the photograph is composed of an entirely bounded surface from which nothing "emerges."

13. This is the first example of a British newspaper signaling and intensifying national differences: the "naiveté" of the Americans (all Americans?) is situated against the (presumed) "sophistication" of (all?) French relationships. I will consider the press's manipulation of "British" and "French" national identities in more detail below.

14. De Beauvoir's "French" identity does not constitute the "whole" of her self, just as sexuality does not constitute a self.

15. Roland Barthes, *Camera Lucida: Reflections on Photography* (New York: Hill and Wang, 1981), 101–2.

16. That de Beauvoir's "scandalous reputation" is largely rooted in her perceived "guilt" and "self-recrimination" provides an acute demonstration of Foucault's notion of self-surveillance, so familiar to the disciplinary technics of modernity. The criticisms leveled against de Beauvoir might be partially put down to the degree to which she embodies a set of values that provoke serious cultural anxiety (in particular, sexuality and gender). The 1990s have witnessed the language of the 1960s liberation movements (feminism, lesbian and gay liberation, and the civil rights movement)—which spoke of "rights" and "choice"—turned upon itself: the conservative fear that such groups demand "more" than "equality," coupled with the tensions generated by the AIDS "crisis," has inspired a reactive back-to-basics discourse. Thus when representations of de Beauvoir repeatedly constitute her as "at some level sorry" for her actions (*Sunday Telegraph*, 8 December 1991, 116), she is an eerie embodiment of the present social desire to "make amends" and take (a specific kind of) "responsibility."

Chapter 12

Straddling the Screen: Bisexual Spectatorship and Contemporary Narrative Film

Maria Pramaggiore

Bisexual characters have been popping up all over the screen, usually in the midst of romantic triangles, scenarios that highlight the inevitability of choosing between "same" and "opposite" sex desire.[1] In her recent account of the lesbian vampire film in *Vampires and Violets: Lesbians in Film*, Andrea Weiss examines bisexual romantic triangles and argues that "[t]he degree of narrative closure largely determines what meanings the lesbian vampire films can generate, and the extent to which lesbians can find alternative or oppositional meanings. In the conclusion of a typical bisexual triangle film—*Personal Best, The Bostonians*—given an even fight between a heterosexual man and a lesbian, the man will win out every time, thereby restoring the 'natural order.'"[2] The natural order Weiss refers to is, of course, the narratively and socially "natural" resolution heterosexual coupling provides. Weiss's observation is insightful, because it acknowledges that a textual element—the degree of narrative closure—plays a role in generating viewer resistance. In other words, audience members, in this case lesbian spectators, do not produce oppositional readings of films solely on the basis of their sexual identities; the text itself must in some manner invite alternative readings.

Weiss's comments on lesbian vampire films are important in another regard. She mentions the bisexual triangle as a common trope in films that deal with lesbian relationships but considers the triangle only insofar as it functions as an impediment to lesbian desire, as an obstacle that sets the stage for the ultimate and inevitable conflict between a lesbian vampire and a mortal man. By treating the bisexual triangle only as a means through which a lesbian narrative is recuperated by heteronormative coupling, Weiss neglects to examine how bisexual triangles might complicate, rather than enable, hetero- and homosexuality. Thus, she perpetuates the notion of bisexual desire as an intermediate or transitory developmental phase.[3]

In *Making Things Perfectly Queer: Interpreting Mass Culture,* Alexander Doty raises the issue of bisexual triangles in the context of another film genre—the Hollywood musical—and characterizes triangulated erotics as instruments of heterosexual recuperation of gay male sexuality.[4] Gene Kelly's "male trio" musicals, for example, feature two "conventionally sexy" actors who are teamed (tripled?) with a "comic, less attractive buffer who is meant to diffuse the sexual energy generated between the two male leads when they sing and dance together" (11). Another group of Kelly's films—which includes *Singin' In the Rain*—"resort[s] to the more conventional heterosexual(izing) narrative device of using a woman to mediate and diffuse male-male erotics" (11). According to Doty, neither strategy is successful: ultimately the triangulated narratives fail to "fully heterosexualize" Kelly and his male costars (11). Like Weiss, Doty does not explore how the bisexual triangle may be responsible for the narrative's failure to fully heterosexualize these characters and acknowledges in a footnote that he has given rather cursory attention to "specifically bisexual [reading] positions" (105).

The comments of Weiss and Doty regarding the bisexual triangle offer a useful starting point from which to examine contemporary films that feature triangulation and to ask whether they invite specifically bisexual readings. Analyzing triangulation as more than merely a weapon in the heterosexual narrative arsenal offers a more complex understanding of the way films depict sexuality than the "either/or" imperative offered by many feminist, gay, and lesbian analyses of film. Reading contemporary films from the bisexual "fence" involves a reconsideration of both narrative structure and spectatorial identification. The fence is a position from which "same" and "opposite" sex desires of particular characters can be explored rather than viewed as mutually exclusive and is a location from which spectators may be expected to form multiple identifications among variously sexed and gendered characters. Reading from the fence also calls into question the foreclosure of bisexual desire by monosexual, coupled resolutions. As a bisexual spectator, necessarily straddling a screen constructed for heterosexual couples,[5] I question the monosexual imperative that characters within film narratives must and do choose between identification and desire and that spectators must do so in relation to the screen. I therefore seek to eroticize identification as well as to explore the fluidity of desire.[6]

Bisexual reading practices may be invited by recent mainstream films that depict fluid eroticisms and nonheterosexual desires; in other words, these film texts may construct a "fence-sitting" spectator. It is important, therefore, to briefly examine how mainstream studios and independent producers have found representing sexual alternatives a lucrative business practice, and how the new economics of sexual deviance informs the texts produced within this context.

Contemporary Queer Film: Industrial Fences

The historical circumstances which have given rise to explicitly gay and lesbian films are numerous and complex, involving film production, marketing, distribution, viewing practices, research and criticism. Film critic/theorist Robin Wood, for example, identifies the "steadily growing force of the gay liberation movement, no longer content with a plea for tolerance of homosexuals, but in close alliance with radical feminism, calling into question the very construction of sexuality within our culture" as a force motivating his avowedly political perspective.[7] Film scholar-critics such as Vito Russo and Parker Tyler have surveyed the representations of gays and lesbians from the vantage points of politics and aesthetics. Tyler, who in 1973 claimed that "sexual integrity is omnisexed," wanted to "free the sexual body and all its behavior from the straitjacket of conventional ideas that limit them for serious contemplation and cripple them on the open ground of the imagination." In order to do so, he argued that we must consider the "basic genders . . . irrelevant."[8] Mainstream and avant garde films have represented a variety of genders and sexualities since before the feminist and gay liberation movements gained prominence in the early 1970s, yet few popular writers or academics have acknowledged mainstream films' representations of alternatives to heterosexuality prior to the "sexual revolution" of the late 1960s. Criticism in the 1980s and 1990s has only just begun to address celluloid sexualities in a more comprehensive manner, informed by feminist, gay and lesbian film, cultural theory, and political activism.

During the 1980s, partially in response to the AIDS crisis, the popular press and academia have focused attention on the cultural presumption of heterosexuality and its attendant circumscription—political, legal, and cultural—of "deviant" sexualities. "Queer theory," made visible during the late 1980s and early 1990s with the publication of Eve Kosofsky Sedgwick's *Epistemology of the Closet*, is the academic counterpart of the activism outside academia which increased visibility of gay and lesbian political and representational issues.

The "in your face" politics of ACT UP and the widespread commitment to "out-ness" and identity politics have made certain economic opportunities obvious to creators and purveyors of mass culture. As Danae Clark explicates in "Commodity Lesbianism," the capitalist practice of product differentiation and the increased visibility of gays and lesbians have given rise to "gay window advertising" practices.[9] Advertisers and their clients adopt this dual ("both/and") representational strategy in order to make inroads into gay and lesbian markets while not offending "tradi-tional" audiences.

This strategy, double-edged in its conception and execution, is also at work in contemporary cinema. Films that depict alternatives to heterosexuality have found profitable markets, a situation which calls to mind (yet another) fence: that strad-dled by film producers seeking a wider audience than that comprising lesbians, gay men, bisexuals, and transgendered people. The economic imperative of the mass market informs even the most well-intentioned attempts to move beyond compul-sory heterosexuality, however, and subtends recent film narratives that attempt to have their sex both ways. In her review of *Three of Hearts*, for example, Lucy Richer notes that an unconvincing action subplot only serves to further the romance narrative, a structural flaw which "is a sure sign that the film is protesting too much, an over-compensation typical of Hollywood movies which are genuinely trying to work sexual roles into new stories, but are nervous of trampling on too many traditions at once."[10] Independent films with gay, lesbian, and bisexual themes, such as *The Crying Game, Priscilla: Queen of the Desert,* and *The Wedding Banquet* have been successful at the box office, relative to production costs and relative to mainstream products such as *Three of Hearts* and *Threesome* (perhaps because as independents they are able to take more risks), suggesting that their appeal is not limited to gay, lesbian, and bisexual consumers. If Hollywood, and the plethora of independent producers whose work dominates the contemporary film industry, need to "cheat" their representations of homosexualities for mass audi-ence appeal—making them legible to those on both sides of the fence—it may be the case that the ambiguities, doubleness, and "both/and" of bisexual desire are encoded in contemporary films and may, in part, make bisexual reading practices possible and necessary.

Bisexual reading practices, theoretically, need not be limited to spectators who identify as bisexual persons.[11] I share Doty's position in this regard: "[U]nless the text is about queers ... the queerness of most mass cultural texts is less an essen-tial waiting-to-be-discovered property than the result of acts of production or reception. . . . [Q]ueerness [is] a mass culture reception practice that is shared by all sorts of people in varying degrees of consistency and intensity" (xi, 2). I would add, however, that even when texts are "about" queers or queerness, textual elements can repress or express possibilities for bisexual desires, that is, nonsingular desires that may be detached from strict sex and/or gender oppositions. Furthermore, bisexual readings may be available to anyone reading cultural texts, but they are also a specific product of historical and cultural circumstances which authorize these readings.

If reading bisexually is conceived of as a cultural practice that requires for its existence a formal apparatus as well as a readership motivated to perform such readings, then identifying as a bisexual person is neither necessary nor sufficient for reading bisexually. However, an understanding on the part of viewers that bisexual desires and perspectives exist is necessary. That the growth of bisexual visibility during the 1980s and 1990s occurred primarily *within* gay and lesbian movements[12] suggests that gay- and lesbian-themed films are appropriate textual sources for bisexual elements that address spectators on the fence. Paradoxically, because the term "bisexual" historically has been used to denote gay and/or lesbian sexuality as well as bisexuality, the meaning(s) of bisexuality(ies) are subject to both a surplus and a surfeit of visibility, and the films I analyze are no exception. In *The Crying Game*, for example, the bisexual character Jody can be identified as such only after his death. In *Three of Hearts*, Ellen is displaced from her central position in the triangulated narrative by the straight male character's action subplot, and, in *The Hunger*, bisexual desire is conflated with vampirism, a common device for representing lesbian desire in horror films.

The mainstreaming of sexual deviance, including bisexuality, is a double-edged sword; film narratives that treat homosexuality, lesbianism, and bisexuality are subject to certain generic constraints of "normalization." They often reiterate narrative traditions which speak to viewers' investment in monosexuality and make it difficult, although not necessarily impossible, for readers to deviate from the familiar rhetoric of romantic coupling.

Queer Couplings

One narrative tradition that poses problems for alternative representations of sexuality is the device of coupling. Virginia Wexman's recent study of Hollywood cinema points to the ways romantic coupling on screen has both reflected and shaped norms regarding marriage, gender, and sexuality.[13] Conventional coupled romance narratives, whether concerned with gay, lesbian, or heterosexual scenarios, make it difficult to recognize or to imagine bisexuality other than as a developmental stage prior to "mature" monogamous monosexuality.

The three films I discuss reconfigure romantic *triangles* in overtly gay, lesbian, and bisexual terms. In the history of Western representations of love, romance, and sexuality, a triangulated structure of desire, according to literary theorist René Girard, constructs the love object.[14] Eve Sedgwick, examining the implications of male homosociality, concludes that, in English literature, the bonds between male rivals are as strong as those between either man and the female love interest.[15] Marjorie Garber observes that erotic triangles are important to examine in terms of positioning, arguing that erotic desire depends upon one's position within the triangle rather than upon essential gender or sexual identities.[16] She stresses the importance of examining "the connections among the 'other' partners that need articulating" (433). In other words, the rivalry, jealousy, and competition that characterize relations between and among certain characters within a triangle generally are construed as involving only similarity and identification, rather than identification *and* desire. Because the triangle offers the possibility for simultaneous desire and identification among its various positions, regardless of the gender of the figures occupying those positions, triangulation often highlights the both/and quality of bisexual desire.

Moreover, romantic coupling and temporal closure are related narrative structures affecting the possibility of representing desires which are not restricted to "one" sexual object or one "type" of sexual object. Coupling signifies completion, wholeness, and stasis and usually suggests a diachronically stable object choice. Temporality is critical. In order to use a visual medium to render "same" and "opposite" sex desires that are not mutually exclusive, two conditions must obtain: either the film must depict multiple, variously sexed partners in particular scenes, or it must suggest an "oscillation" between partners of both sexes. Clearly, neither of these alternatives has been acceptable politically and/or aesthetically in most gay/lesbian films, many of which seek to validate coming out and the ultimate formation of a homosexual union. Furthermore, chronological narrative structures that assign more weight and import to the conclusion—typical of Hollywood film rather than, say, European art cinema—may be less compatible with bisexual reading strategies, which focus on the episodic quality of a nonteleological temporal continuum across which a number of sexual acts, desires, and identities might be expressed.

I have chosen to examine three films in which bisexuality is explicitly represented and in which triangles are crucial to representing bisexuality.[17] Although films which do not attempt queer representations can be read queerly, as Doty demonstrates, it is equally important to investigate recent feature films which present gay, lesbian, and bisexual persons, relationships, and themes in terms of the ways that those films have expanded, and sometimes simultaneously foreclosed, bisexuality as a sexual identity and practice. If, as I have argued here, temporal and narrative conventions are critical to a bisexual reading practice, then gay and lesbian narratives which reinforce notions of coupling and closure may make a bisexual reading as difficult as, or even more difficult than, a more mainstream Hollywood product which involves some form of triangulation.

In *The Crying Game* (Neil Jordan, 1992), *Three of Hearts* (Yurek Bogayevicz, 1992), and *The Hunger* (Tony Scott, 1986), triangulated relationships express complex relations along and between all vertices. Such triangles can remain unresolved when the films' conclusions offer open-ended possibilities for erotic desires. The "third term" produced within a triangulated context—a position sometimes but not always occupied by a bisexual character—becomes a metaphor for and/or agent of structural instability in heterosexual relations rather than operating as merely an obstacle for heterosexual or homosexual characters to "overcome." In addition, when the temporal structures in these films are more ambivalent, less determining, they further undermine the stability of any form of coupling.

Analyzing these films from a bisexual perspective, I focus on romantic coupling and the treatment of temporality as key structural components which gesture beyond monosexualities. In addition to these formal concerns, I examine whether or not the narrative content resolves the tension between identification and desire created in the context of the bisexual triangle. That resolution, when it assumes the form of an opposition between identification and desire (heterosexuality) or a conflation (homosexuality), gives resonance and permanence to monosexual formations and disallows the continual interplay of identifications and desires across sex and gender that characterizes bisexuality.

The additional theoretical challenge bisexualities pose to film studies concerns not the textual politics of contemporary queer cinema but practices of spectatorship themselves. In other words, bisexual readings, invited by triangulated and temporally fluid narrative patterns, are also contingent upon certain practices of spectatorship that, as of yet, have not been clearly articulated within film theory. Below, I briefly outline how bisexuality has been employed by feminist film theorists, who have developed readings of sexuality in cinema to the greatest extent. In feminist film theory, shifting and imprecise terminology regarding bisexuality—particularly the adoption of a Freudian model of a constitutional bisexuality—clouds attempts to develop more complex and nuanced models of spectatorship.

Fencing the Screen

Bisexual reading practices are dynamic processes involving both textual address and a motivated readership. In theories of film spectatorship, this posited inter-action encompasses the narratives and images projected upon the screen (high-lighted in structural or apparatus approaches) and the audience's activities of and investment in interpreting those images (emphasized in cultural studies and ethno-graphic approaches).[18] Apparatus models present cinema as a seamless ideological machine, whereas reception studies emphasize readings and responses of historical spectators whose activity of watching is assumed to construct the text's meaning, often in opposition to culturally authorized interpretations. Studies of gay and lesbian film spectatorship, of particular relevance here, often rely implicitly on the assumption that gay and lesbian audience members are uniquely willing and able to read against the grain of mainstream texts to rewrite heterosexual endings or to elucidate homoerotic or homosexual elements which the narrative elides or represses.[19]

In their studies of spectatorship, Judith Mayne, Rob Lapsley, and Michael Westlake conclude that "the relation between text and spectator is better com-prehended as a dialectic," arguing that the spectator is both constituted by and constitutes the text.[20] The model of bisexual spectatorship I employ assumes that spectators construct textual meaning, yet also recognizes that a film's narra-tive and visual structures, while not inescapable, must inform viewer positioning. I am speaking from both sides of the screen—the "fence," as it were, in the field of film studies—to argue that both textual address and social-historical circum-stances provide the conditions of possibility for bisexual reading prac-tices. "Fencing" thus refers to my positioning of the film screen in a shifting and indeterminate "both/and" location "in between" social and economic practices of production and reception, not unlike the problematic but sometimes produc-tive positioning of bisexual practices and identities as "in between" hetero-sexuality and homosexuality. The term also refers to the sport of fencing, the dodging and parrying that all spectators continually engage in, working with and against film's representational conventions to produce meaningful readings. Finally, in its most prosaic form, "fencing" refers to unloading stolen property. I embrace the materialist connotations of this definition and connect that extra-market activity to my understanding of bisexual spectatorial pleasure, a pleasure often stolen from conventional monosexual narratives that, sometimes unwittingly, encourage bisexual readings through their deployment of the romantic triangle.[21]

Bisexing Feminist Film Theory

Feminist film theory asks us not only to read films in terms of narrative structures and visual techniques that privilege heterosexuality and heterosexual difference but also to consider how we read films as spectators marked by our sexes and sexualities. Laura Mulvey's "Visual Pleasure and Narrative Cinema" posits a psychoanalytically inflected masculinized spectator as the ideal object of mainstream Hollywood's enunciative apparatus.[22] Mulvey argues that visual and narrative pleasures are predicated on a heterosexual division of labor which both invites the spectator's identification with male characters and appeals to his need to fetishize women's threatening, castrated bodies. Mulvey characterizes the masculine spectator as one who unproblematically identifies with on-screen men but must disavow the threat implied by the on-screen woman's bodily castration. "A male movie star's glamorous characteristics are thus not those of the erotic object of the gaze, but those of the more perfect, more complete, more powerful ideal ego conceived in the original moment of recognition in front of the mirror. . . . But in psychoanalytic terms, the female figure poses a deeper problem . . . her lack of a penis, implying the threat of castration and hence unpleasure" (34–35).

Mulvey's original model of cinema's all-consuming masculine gaze has been criticized for its apparent assumption of passive spectators in thrall to a pervasive patriarchal ideology and for its neglect of the female spectator.[23] Her ability to imagine an oppositional film practice, however,[24] does suggest that spectators, when presented with alternative modes of filmic representation, will meet that challenge with a heightened awareness of the ideological implications of conventional narrative structures. Mulvey's early theories are relevant to bisexual spectatorship because she begins with a psychoanalytic model of heterosexual difference and assumes that male and female spectators' opportunities for identification with opposite-sex characters and desire for same-sex characters are severely circumscribed.

Whereas Mulvey's original thesis endows the cinematic apparatus with the determinative power to satisfy both narcissistic and scopophilic (identificatory and projective, object-oriented) desires of the masculine spectator, she later recognizes that not all spectators comfortably occupy that position. "In-built patterns of pleasure and identification impose masculinity as point-of-view," she continues to argue in "Afterthoughts on 'Visual Pleasure and Narrative Cinema' Inspired by *Duel in the Sun*," but questions "whether the female spectator is carried along , as it were by the scruff of the text, or whether her pleasure can be more deep-rooted and complex."[25] Describing female spectators' pleasure in identifying with active characters (generally, but not exclusively, male) as "an oscillation between 'passive'

femininity and regressive 'masculinity,'" Mulvey relates such trans-sex identification or "transvestism," to women's inability to establish a stable sexual identity
(25–28). This association of an unstable bisexuality with women is based upon
Freud's analysis of women's unsuccessful repression of their phallic, masculine
aspirations; Mulvey here reiterates this "constitutional" model of bisexuality,
based itself upon processes of identification rather than desire. That is to say, bisexuality here is figured as an inability to identify fully with either male or female
characters, rather than as desire for characters of both sexes, regardless of the spectator's sex or gender identity.

Mulvey's notion of women's trans-sex identification practices has been questioned on the grounds that identification involves denying the differences between
the spectator's and the object's bodies. Anne Friedberg notes that "countless films
(with monsters, robots, animals) attest [to the fact that] any body offers an opportunity for identificatory investment."[26] Robin Wood considers identification practices
in relation to horror films, where, he claims, spectators are simultaneously fascinated with and disgusted by the monster, who embodies social taboos, including
homosexuality and bisexuality. Other scholars point to the certainty of spectators'
capacity for multiple identifications across sex, race, and species.[27] These capacities
may indeed be termed bisexual spectatorship practices, as I am using that term, for
they encompass identification and desire—narcissism and scopophilia in Mulvey's
Freudian system—without neatly distinguishing between the two or defining them
as oppositional.

Tania Modleski discusses women's bisexuality and its implications for male characters' identification with women in Hitchcock films, linking bisexuality to mother-
daughter relationships that threaten patriarchal power relations. She implies that

women's bisexual nature, rooted in preoedipality, and her consequent alleged tendency to
overidentify with other women and with texts, is less a problem for women, as Doane
would have it, than it is for patriarchy . . . not only . . . [because] female bisexuality would
make women into competitors for "the male preserve," but far more fundamentally
because it reminds man of his *own* bisexuality (and thus his resemblance to Norman
Bates), a bisexuality that threatens to subvert his "proper" identity, which depends upon
his ability to distance woman and make her his proper-ty.[28]

Here she suggests that bisexuality is not the exclusive property of on-screen women
or female spectators but, nevertheless, is more likely to be repressed by on-screen
and spectatorial subjects who define themselves as male, hinting that part of that
heterosexual male self-definition is based upon the repression of bisexuality. Here,
bisexuality is a metaphor for a masculine/feminine split in the subject that is prob-

lematic for male characters who seek to assert a singular and fully masculine identity. Bisexuality for the man, however, as it is for Mulvey, is a question of identifying with the mother rather than of experiencing identifications with and desires for various others, including men and women, transgendered people, and/or androgynes.

Modleski's notion of bisexuality, importantly, is asymmetrical along the male/female axis and, therefore, is implicated in gendered power relations, including those that may govern spectatorship practices: "[A] discussion of bisexuality as it relates to spectatorship ought, then, to be informed by a knowledge of the way male and female responses are rendered asymmetrical by a patriarchal power structure. As Hitchcock films repeatedly demonstrate, the male subject is greatly threatened by bisexuality, though he is at the same time fascinated by it; and it is the woman who pays for this ambivalence—often with her life itself" (10). In Hitchcock's films, men seek to repress the preoedipal identification with the mother, with dire consequences for women. Male characters project their repressed feminine aspect onto women characters, who do the suffering for both of them, a dynamic Modleski calls a "dialectic of identification and dread" (13).

These discussions of bisexual spectatorship rely almost exclusively upon the notion of identification "across" gender. They do not adequately address the question of the relationship between identification and desire, however. From my perspective on the fence, reading a film bisexually has less to do with aligning one's identity with a particular character (on the basis of male/female sex distinctions or on the basis of activity/passivity) and has more to do with the spectatorial difficulty of clearly distinguishing between wanting to "be" a character (Mulvey's ego-ideal) and wanting to "have" a character (scopophilic, fetishistic, erotic possession through the gaze). Reading bisexually recognizes that culturally imposed binary sex and gender differences do not guarantee the "proper" channeling of ego- or object-driven desire for characters or spectators: any character is a potential ego-ideal as well as a sexual object for other characters and for spectators.

In each of the films I analyze, the characters' struggles between identification and desire do not obey heterosexual codification, which is what distinguishes them from most gay and lesbian characters, for whom objects of identification and of sexual desire often are as easily differentiated as they are for heterosexual characters. The films do not resolve or contain bisexual desires through monosexual recuperation, instead resisting the happily-ever-after resolution of heterosexual or homosexual coupling. The couple's romantic status is either problematized and indefinitely deferred (Fergus-Dil in *The Crying Game*; Sarah-Miriam in *The Hunger*) or displaced by a cross-sex buddy relationship that results from bonding over the same love object (Connie-Joe in *Three of Hearts*). *The Crying Game* and *Three of Hearts* do privilege the couple as unit, but not heterosexuality or homosexuality per se, and they emphasize the ongoing importance of triangulated desire. *The Hunger* more explicitly presents the fluidity of triangulated bisexual desire, perhaps because of its peculiar temporal structure: the "life" expectancy of a vampire.

Desire Deferred: The Crying Game

The Crying Game's central metaphor of fluid identity finds geographical and textual resonance in the water crossings between Ireland and England and in the scorpion and frog fable. This parable about trust and true nature which Jody tells to Fergus, who retells it to Dil in the film's conclusion, underscores the danger of rigid adherence to an essential, unchanging identity. The scorpion destroys itself and the frog because the scorpion is locked into its "natural" role as destroyer. The untrustworthy character of the scorpion also hints at the shifting and duplicitous nature of political and romantic triangles; in this film, being and seeming are often at odds in both political and sexual terms. The environment of political intrigue associated with IRA terrorism resonates with the "hermeneutic of passing"[29] Marjorie Garber identifies in *M. Butterfly*; she observes that *"passing* is what *acting* is, and what *treason* is" (143). The act of passing itself, undertaken at various points by all of the primary characters in the film, introduces triangulation in the sense that triangles are formed among (1) the persona a character adopts; (2) the person he or she "really" is in the text or subtext of the film; and (3) the character or spectator toward whom the performance is directed. Passing in this film is also a practice of fluid identity: characters are engaged in both passing *as* and passing *between*.

The film's romantic triangles are structured by a series of looks, all involving Fergus, the self-sacrificing hero ostensibly at the center of the narrative. Several romantic configurations express Fergus's heterosexual, homosocial, and homoerotic capacities but also complicate his attempt to differentiate between identification and desire. Fergus struggles with his desire to have (Jody) and his desire to be (Jody). In Lacanian terms, these desires—to have and to be—are associated with the phallus, the imaginary signifier par excellence. A bisexual reading of this film recognizes that, in fact, Jody occupies the paradoxically absent center of the film, for it is Jody, a black bisexual man, who occupies the untenable position of the phallus (an object no one can be or have). Clearly, the film's phallic rhetoric is racially inflected, with implications for its representation of masculinity: Fergus holds Jody's penis while the latter urinates, and Fergus, along with spectators, witnesses Dil's unveiling of her/his penis.

Fergus's sexuality is therefore constructed in relation to a black phallus, traditionally a racist signifier of hypermasculinity, whose various manifestations in this film, however, serve to undermine the equation of black male bodies with excessive heterosexual desire.[30]

Throughout the film, Fergus's involvement with actual sex partners (Jude and Dil) is mediated by Jody, whose positioning as a "third term" defines his status as an object of both identification and desire for Fergus. In the opening sequence, Jude entices Jody into a truncated sexual liaison while Fergus watches; until Jody's capture it is unclear whether Fergus is a jealous lover or disapproving onlooker.[31] This first triangle (Jody-Jude-Fergus) emphasizes parallels between Jody and Fergus as well as their competition for Jude: when Jude complains about her role as sexual bait for the black British soldier, for example, she tells Fergus that she was able to carry out the distasteful task because she pretended that Jody was Fergus.

During Jody's incarceration, Jody and Fergus look at the photograph of Dil that Jody carries with him, a moment in which Dil supplants Jude as the object of their sexual interest. As they both look at Jude at the carnival and at Dil in the IRA hideout, Fergus and Jody forge an identification through their gazes. In these instances of visual triangulation, the structure of jealousy and competition tradi-tionally associated with romantic triangles is recast in the more ambiguous terms of the homosocial/sexual relation between Jody and Fergus—also dependent upon gazes. Jody asserts his ability to look despite the fact that he is objectified and dehu-manized by his captors and is the constant object of Fergus's gaze. "You're the hand-some one," Jody tells Fergus, his words muffled by the hood over his face. Frann Michel writes that the connection between Jody and Fergus is "part kinship, part antagonism, part eroticism,"[32] which also suggests their joint resistance to Jude, the increasingly cruel and crude female outsider. The ensuing narrative maintains a delicate balance between Fergus's (homosexual) desire for Jody and his (homoso-cial) desire to be Jody. Despite his growing attachment to Dil, Fergus's identification with Jody does not eclipse his desire for Jody. Fergus's identification with and desire for Jody are evidenced by his dreams of Jody during sex with Dil, his mimicry of the cricket game (Jody's game) he observes from his work site, his desire to take care of Dil, and his decision to disguise Dil in Jody's cricket clothes.

The canted angle and figure placement in the scene where Jody and Fergus look at the photograph literally resituate the vertices of the initial romantic triangle; the camerawork is the visual corollary to the narrative's reconfiguration of romance, as Dil becomes the object of Jody's and Fergus's gazes. Fergus mirrors Dil's place in the photograph; he stands over Jody just as Dil leans over Jody in the photograph. The composition produces a multiplicitous reading of Fergus as identifying with and desiring both Jody and Dil. The figure placement can be read as indicating Fergus's desire to occupy Dil's position in relation to Jody or as foreshadowing Fergus's assumption of Jody's position in relation to Dil.

Yet identifying with and desiring Jody are dangerous propositions, given the difficulty most characters, including Fergus, have in "reading" Jody's various identities "properly." A West Indian from Tottenham, Jody's political, national, and sexual identities are the most fluid of all the characters and the most disturbing in terms of monosexual coherence and narrative closure. Jody stands for the British colonial presence in Ireland, but neither his national nor sexual identity is capable of being recuperated by traditional definitions of race, citizenship, or monosexual orientation. Jody plays cricket and appears to be an assimilated colonial, yet his usurpation of the sport of the colonizer—like the costumes he dons as soldier and cricket player—can be read through Homi Bhabha's concept of mimicry, a "double vision which in disclosing the ambivalence of colonial discourse also disrupts its authority."[33] It is appropriate, then, that Jody's cricket pitch is the "googli," roughly equivalent to a knuckleball in American baseball: his pitches are never what they appear to be. His comments to Fergus about the treatment of black people in England and Ireland—a discussion in which Fergus likens his status as an Irishman to Jody's as a black man—suggest that Jody is well aware of his impossible location in a world demarcated by strict definitions of race and nation. A British subject and soldier, he is nevertheless despised, called a "nigger" in Ireland. This "fenced" national identity—partly British, partly "West Indian"—parallels Jody's sexual ambidexterity, which we learn about only after his death.

We first encounter Jody in the context of a sexual liaison with Jude and as a devoted lover of Dil, whom we are encouraged to assume is a woman. Yet Jody must be described—in retrospect—as neither exclusively heterosexual nor homosexual, but bisexual. He establishes a strong homosocial/sexual bond with Fergus, is involved in a relationship with Dil, a transsexual,[34] and apparently looks forward to a sexual encounter with Jude. The implicit gender ambiguity of Jody's name, as well as Jude's, suggests that both figures pose a challenge to strict categories of gender and sexual identity: Jude through her increasing association with unfeeling "masculine" violence, Jody through his nonexclusive sexual desire. Yet Jody's bisexuality is absent from the film in the present tense—deferred until the unmasking of Dil's penis in a scene which privileges Fergus's visceral and negative reaction.

Jody and Jude are violently eliminated from the ever-shifting romantic triangle, the former in a tragically inevitable "accident" of colonial military might, the latter in an equally inevitable confrontation with Dil that the film constructs as anything but tragic. The blame for Jody's death is displaced onto Jude, whose transformation into a high-tech hit woman and femme fatale makes that displacement seem acceptable. Even dressed in Jody's clothes, Dil is more woman than Jude, because Dil suspects that it takes "tits" and "ass," not violent coercion, to secure the affections of Jody and Fergus. Dil's performance as a woman in this predominantly male environment may thus require the elimination of Jude, the biological woman whose shifting identity nevertheless maintains consistency in terms of her excessive violence. In this film, clothes do not "make the man" or woman, for Jude's transformation is more style than substance.

Fergus less frequently fantasizes about Jody and ultimately assumes his persona as imprisoned storyteller, suggesting that Fergus's identification with Jody has come to overshadow his desire for Jody. Fergus's incarceration prevents his full assumption of Jody's position in relation to Dil, however. The all-male prison environment in which Fergus resides, with its implicit overtones of homosexuality, emphasizes the gender distinction between Fergus and Dil and situates the two as a couple but does not resolve Fergus's sexuality in terms of a "true" hetero- or homosexuality. As Jonathan Romney puts it: "Fergus' revelation is not that he is 'really' homosexual, but that sexuality must adapt to the demands of love in a loveless world."[35]

Thus the narrative skirts both a conventional romantic heterosexual resolution and a gay coming out saga and provides a deferred fantasy of coupling that is detached from monosexuality and remains triangular. Fergus becomes Jody, yet his desire for Jody has not been quelled by the violence that follows in the wake of his makeover of Dil in Jody's image.[36] Fergus becomes Jody, but with a difference; he cannot act on his desire(s) for Dil, for Jody, or for anyone else, a situation that foregrounds certain questions pertaining to the nature of desire when it is not "acted out" in sexual terms. His desire for Jody may be expressed *through* his identification with Jody, not in opposition to it, as a prisoner retelling the frog-scorpion story. The deferral of consummation is manifested in the glass barrier between Fergus and Dil, a visually permeable structure that David Lugowski takes issue with: "The film clearly wants to play against the notion that 'biology is destiny,' and yet the social discourse surrounding Fergus's relationship with Dil is not fully explored. The result is that the film's coda . . . is a little too pat, leaving one to wonder about the significance of the glass barrier between the two men."[37]

This deferral of sexual consummation resists the "happily ever after" formula, a resistance ironically underscored by Lyle Lovett's rendition of "Stand by Your Man," a song which does double duty in describing both Dil's and Fergus's positions. The glass barrier is a transparent body much less fluid and more stringently policed than the Irish sea; yet it stands for the fluid, undecidable third term that structures the film's political and sexual aesthetic. In Fergus's relationship with Dil, that vertex is variously occupied by Jody, by Jude, by Dil's penis, and by the British state. This representational triangularity is, like the film screen itself, a structure in which, fencelike, identification and desire meet but do not cancel each other out.

And Buddy Makes Three: Three of Hearts

In *Three of Hearts,* issues of triangulation and temporality pervade a film about love stories that ultimately displaces romantic love in favor of coupled friendship. The break-up of a relationship between a lesbian and a bisexual woman gives rise to a triangulated relationship among the two women, Connie and Ellen, and Joe, the man Connie hires to break Ellen's heart so that she will return to Connie. Underlying this master plan is the assumption of a symmetrical and oscillating serially monogamous bisexuality (arguably, the least threatening enactment of bisexuality). The plan assumes that Ellen will reject men in general and return to women in general, and Connie in particular, after Joe breaks her heart. Joe and Ellen fall in love, but when Ellen learns that Connie and Joe have conspired against her, she rejects them both.

The relationship between Connie and Ellen ends in the second scene of the film, and their romance is presented only in the past tense, through videos that Connie watches obsessively. This representational device reverses the traditional associations of videotape with immediacy,[38] for although the tapes transmit the spontaneity and intimacy of Connie and Ellen's relationship, their use in the narrative highlights a tearful Connie's obsessive postmortem·inability to relinquish the romance. Douglas Keller observes that the film is "a quasi-lesbian romance for the '90s without any lesbian sex and without any in-depth examination of a lesbian relationship in the '90s."[39] Lucy Richer is more direct on this point: "[t]he film lacks the courage of its convictions, shy to show girls snogging."[40] One may reasonably ask whether the romance itself is lesbian if Ellen is bisexual; often, bisexual women "disappear" when they are sexually involved with women, only to reappear as bisexual when they take up with male lovers.

The temporal structure of the film thus supports the notion of serial bisexual monogamy but gives us the present tense of Joe and Ellen's sexual coupling and Joe and Connie's friendly coupling. The lesbian-bisexual relationship is distinctly relegated to history, while the buddy relationship unfolds in "real time." After their second date, Ellen explains to Joe that she and Connie "used to be a couple." The temporal displacement of the women's relationship clears the way for Ellen's complete immersion in a sexual and romantic relationship with Joe and serves to align viewer sympathy with the "real-time" relationships between Ellen and Joe and, especially, between Connie and Joe.

The film's heart may be in the right place in terms of its attempt to depict a bisexual woman's plight, but the narrative's movement undermines the liberal attempt to embrace all sexual identities. For example, in the scene in which Ellen and her sister discuss Ellen's relationship with Connie, Ellen refuses her sister's reading of the relationship as a manipulation on Connie's part. "I loved Connie and she loved me," she states. Yet Ellen's desires are represented as unstable; her rejection of Connie in the opening of the movie is not attributed to anything specific in their relationship except that she "needs space." Furthermore, she is immediately and completely vulnerable to Joe, who poses as a student in her poetry class at NYU, and his initially bungling attempts at sincerity. The suspense, and, therefore, narrative interest, is carried by Ellen's developing sexual relationship with Joe, because it is unclear whether her desire for him is strong enough to overcome his betrayal. Ellen is most important as the third term which establishes a friendship between Connie and Joe, and Joe assumes the central location in the film as the subplot of his dangerous affiliation with a criminal underworld, and Connie's attempts to help him, takes center stage.

Joe mediates Connie and Ellen's relationship throughout the film. Edmond Grant writes that reducing the women's relationship to "near-subliminal status," is "a disservice to the gay characters, making [the film] simply another nimble variation on the old Hollywood three-way love affair. Which leaves us with the prospect of a movie centered around the third point of the triangle, a dimwitted male prosti-tute."[41] While the triangle involves a lesbian, a bisexual woman, and a straight man, and offers possibilities for sexual multiplicity—for example, a more complicated investigation of Joe's gender and sexuality, given his commodified and objectified status as a prostitute—this film revolves around Joe's heterosexuality and serial monogamy. Joe's buddy relationship with Connie, and his initiation into lesbian culture, develops through bonding activities such as playing pool and brushing their teeth before bed.

The resolution of the film secures the coupling of Joe and Connie as buddies who share a (lost) love object while it rejects any conclusive sexual relationship for Ellen. Thus, the relationship of identification forged between Connie and Joe, and furthered by scenes in which they look at photographs or videos of Ellen is strength-ened by the failure of their relationships with Ellen. The Connie-Joe friendship is minimally tinged with the prospect of sexual desire when Joe demonstrates his supposed talent for seducing "any woman any time." He compliments an extremely vulnerable and appreciative Connie on her appearance in one of their buddied bedroom scenes. That she falls for his performance is meant to suggest that no woman, not even a lesbian, could be immune to the pleasures of his male attention, rather than that Connie might explore her sexuality with a man.

While it might seem that Ellen's departure in the final scene limits the potential for a bisexual reading of, or pleasure in, this film, Ellen's single status at the end of the film, in fact, prevents her joint desires for men and women from collapsing conveniently into a single relationship and, therefore, staves off an implicit reimposition of monosexuality. The coupling in *Three of Hearts*, as in *The Crying Game*, does not secure heterosexuality but instead suggests the importance of a coupled *friendship* over (heterosexual, homosexual, or bisexual) romance. The open-endedness of the conclusion resists the codification of Ellen's sexuality as dependent upon an individual object choice and also resists the overarching celebration of romance to the exclusion of alternative couplings, such as that between Joe and Connie.

Lacking the structural and thematic complexity of *The Crying Game* or the polymorphous perversity of *The Hunger*, *Three of Hearts* nevertheless provides an excellent example of mainstream films that attempt to offer viewers alternatives to heterosexuality and coupling, and thus are capable of calling forth bisexual readings that focus on third terms and temporal fluidity. But ultimately many of these films are less imaginative and subversive than they might be. The relationship between Connie and Joe, for example, is predicated on their shared attraction to Ellen, confirming the stereotypical view of lesbians as heterosexual men in women's bodies. Furthermore, the both/andness of bisexual desire is circumscribed by the rigidly serialized nature of the romantic involvements.

Timeless Sex, Regular Feedings: The Hunger

In Tony Scott's *The Hunger*, the narrative's open-ended temporal organization and refusal of definitive monosexual coupling are manifested in the figure of the vampire through her/his desire for companionship, need for human blood, and status as the undead. In the opening scene, shots alternate between an ape in captivity and the lead singer in a band playing at the gothic-themed nightclub frequented by vampires Miriam Blaylock and her husband, John. This sequence introduces the visual and thematic parallels the film makes between the human and inhuman, parallels which subvert distinctions between human and ape, dead and undead, vampire and victim. Cross-cutting between the singer, intoning "Bela Lugosi's dead . . . undead . . undead" from behind a mesh screen on stage, and the caged ape, the experimental captive of doctors investigating aging, also brings to the foreground the importance of pleasure in identificatory looking and the way in which such looking implies control.

Vision is central to the vampires' hunt: initial close-ups of Miriam and John at the club depict their eyes shrouded in sunglasses as they watch an exhibitionist male-female couple dance. Miriam, John, and their prey—who resemble Miriam and John physically—form a group that is associated with both sexuality and blood-lust. This encounter sets the stage for the film's rendering of the vampires' polymor-phous mesh of desire for and identification with their victims. John and Miriam take the couple home, nonverbally promising seduction, as the editing emphasizes the similarities between Miriam and the woman. In particular, matches on action associate Miriam's gestures with that of the woman: one lights a cigarette, the other takes a drag from her own cigarette; as the woman dances in front of a white screen, Miriam's shadow occupies the blank half of the screen. Furthermore, this anony-mous female victim serves as a visual mediator between the two women protago-nists (Miriam Blaylock and Sarah Roberts). The woman's short red hair and her gesture of running her hands through it foreshadow the hair color and nervous habit of Sarah Roberts, a doctor researching the aging process, who becomes Miriam's lover and victim.

By drawing these parallels, the film raises the question of Miriam's identification with, desire for, and oral incorporation of her victims. Diana Fuss has remarked upon the oral/anal incorporation of the "other" as a trope of gay male sexuality in *The Silence of the Lambs*.[42] In *The Hunger*, oral eroticism and violence suggest the powerful identification between vampire and victim and emphasize the shared bloodlust of Miriam and Susan, who are shown with bloody mouths in several scenes. The counterpart "feeding" shot for John is early on, where his lips are covered in the lipstick of the first female victim, signifying his oral insatiability, sexual ambiguity, and identification with female vampires and victims.[43] The male and female vampires feed on humans of both sexes for physical sustenance; further-more, Miriam chooses certain humans (John, Sarah) to make over into vampire companions. As she injects some of her own blood into their veins, she makes her victim-lovers "a part of her": parts that will never die, but which must eventually age into decrepitude.

Precisely because the vampire companions Miriam creates cannot maintain their vitality forever, she must replace them approximately every two hundred years.[44] But Miriam's choice of companion depends not only upon her sexual desire but also upon her capacity for identification and hopes for companionship. John suspects that Miriam plans to replace him with Alice, the child who comes to their house to play the violin. During his rapid deterioration, John kills young Alice, an easy target for a decaying vampire, thus obliterating by incorporation the triangle formed by Miriam, John, and Alice when the three play music together.

Miriam's previous lovers have been men and women. She seems to have relied upon one primary companion at a time—another example of serial bisexual monogamy—yet also forms triangles, like that between herself, John, and Alice, when she senses the literal need for new blood. Miriam's seduction of Sarah makes her a vampire, arguably one of Miriam's "children" (she has created them),[45] and disrupts Sarah's relationship with her male lover. After having sex with Miriam, Sarah envisions Miriam reflected in a mirror that should be reflecting her male lover, first visually and then physically replacing him with Miriam. Sarah finally kills him for his blood, a reversal of the trend toward coupled heterosexual recuperation Andrea Weiss observes. In other words, although these bisexual triangles eliminate male figures (John and Sarah's boyfriend), paving the way for exclusively lesbian relationships, they also represent dyadic relations, such as that between Sarah and Miriam, as more unstable than triangular structures. Feeding and dyadic stability require the existence *and* annihilation of the third term, as in the opening scene where "seducing" and feeding upon the anonymous couple satiates Miriam and John.

When Sarah learns she has become a vampire, less herself and more Miriam, she attempts to kill herself, and thus to weaken Miriam's power. But Sarah survives, usurping Miriam's position at the film's conclusion as the "matriarchal" vampire. In the final scene, Miriam, who has physically deteriorated because of Sarah's attempted suicide, is confined to a coffin secured with chains and encircled by a fence. Sarah is shown with a young couple, a man and a woman. Although she kisses the young woman, suggesting a preference, there is no clear implication that either must be sacrificed—only that some human(s) ultimately will become Sarah's victim(s) and/or lover(s). In fact, because triangles have been represented as at least as stable, if not more stable than, couplings, and because it is unclear exactly how long vampires live and in what physical condition, the conclusion is unresolved on several counts. The temporal pattern of vampire existence, stretching through the centuries, disrupts linear time measured in human terms, and the final bisexual triangle invites a bisexual reading wherein same and opposite sex desires need not supplant one another but may oscillate over time or coexist simultaneously.

The narrative revolves around the bisexual woman vampire whose couplings with her victim-lovers are secured only by the repeated incorporation of the third term—another victim who is perhaps also a lover. Furthermore, her knowledge that her human-cum-vampire companions must eventually age and deteriorate forces her to look for a third party. Miriam seeks companions for their erotic and identificatory potential; in addition, she must make her lovers over in her own image—make them parts of her—in order to coerce or secure their companionship and her continued existence.

The polymorphous vampire, whose sexual and sensual appetites wed desire and identification, may be the quintessential representational figure of bisexuality in the 1980s and 1990s, evidenced not only by *The Hunger* but also in Anne Rice's vampire chronicles.[46] The vampire's peculiar physiognomy permits an exploration of sexuality beyond gender and sex, because desire becomes an all-pervasive rhythm of sex, blood, and satiation rather than courtship, coupling, and conclusion.

Conclusion?

In these film readings I have attempted to account for the various fences that are critical to theorizing cinematic bisexualities: the fence constructed by writers, directors, and producers who attempt to garner a mass audience and also investigate alternatives to heterosexuality; the fence of spectatorship theory in film studies, which forces a recognition that both sociohistorical events and textual rhetoric inform spectatorship; and the fence of bisexual representation, an ambiguous and often undecidable location where identification meets desire. Rather than focus on whether or not these films represent bisexual men and women in stereotypical ways, I find it more useful to consider what the requirements are for anyone to perform a bisexual reading of narrative films. My conclusions with regard to textual issues are that temporality (whether a final coupling is presented at all or is presented as permanent) and coupling (whether the coexistence of same and opposite sex desire in a single individual can be suggested, or if a final choice reflects a stable monosexual orientation) are key facets of bisexual narrative structure. I have argued that the deployment of triangulation, temporality, and closure is as important to representational politics as are individual characters or sexual stereotyping.

Furthermore, I have argued that reading films bisexually demands a more nuanced approach to the issue of identification, in terms of spectators' and characters' multiple sexual and identificatory investments. In order to perform a bisexual reading, one must relinquish monosexual structures of looking which deem either same or opposite sex characters the appropriate pool from which to draw from for either identification or sexual objectification.

Notes

1. I use the problematic concepts of "same" and "opposite" sex desire, and the coexistence of these desires, as part of my working definition of bisexuality for the purposes of this article. I am aware of the limitations this model imposes on theorizing sexualities "beyond" binary notions of male and female. I am also convinced, however, that contemporary bisexualities are constructed in light of and in spite of cultural practices that define subjects as male and female and normalize heterosexual difference as complementarity. I am suggesting that a male or female or multiply gendered subject may construct her/his/its/their sexual object choice as "both/and" instead of "either/or." This definition of bisexuality departs from the "constitutional" model employed by film critics such as Robin Wood, in *Hollywood From Vietnam to Reagan* (New York: Columbia University Press, 1986) and Dennis Bingham, in *Acting Male: Masculinities in the Films of James Stewart, Jack Nicholson, and Clint Eastwood* (New Brunswick: Rutgers University Press, 1994), which posits that every individual is composed of masculine and feminine aspects.

2. Andrea Weiss, *Vampires and Violets: Lesbians in Film* (New York: Penguin, 1992), 103.

3. Sue George, in *Women and Bisexuality* (London: Scarlet Press, 1993), discusses the frequent characterization of bisexuality as "a dangerous stage" and attributes this formulation to both Freud and Kinsey (28–33). Jay P. Paul too notes the tendency to see bisexuality as a stage. "Bisexuality: Reassessing Our Paradigms of Sexuality," in *Two Lives to Lead: Bisexuality in Men and Women*, ed. Fritz Klein and Timothy Wolf (New York: Harrington Park Press, 1985), 22. Also see Judith Roof's *A Lure of Knowledge: Lesbian Sexuality and Theory* (New York: Columbia University Press, 1991) for a discussion of film pornography and its treatment of lesbian sex as an intermediate location on the path to heterosexuality.

   The bisexual woman in the two examples Weiss cites is positioned as the child in the primal triangle of Freud's family romance: she will attain hetero/monosexuality through the repression of her narcissism/desire for her mother and channel her libido toward her father, her proper heterosexual object. Freud theorized a preoedipal bisexuality that has particular repercussions for women, who must eventually relinquish their desire for the first object, the mother. He also held that there was a conflict between identification and object cathexis, a distinction which I question in my analysis of bisexual spectatorship. I characterize a bisexual viewing practice as one which refuses to "choose" between identification and sexual desire.

4. Alexander Doty, *Making Things Perfectly Queer: Interpreting Mass Culture* (Minneapolis: University of Minnesota Press, 1993).

5. See David Bordwell, Janet Staiger, and Kristin Thompson's *Classical Hollywood Cinema: Film Style and Mode of Production to 1960* (New York: Columbia, 1985), where they discuss the ubiquity of goal-oriented heterosexual love in classical Hollywood cinema. In their nonrandom sample of one hundred films, "ninety-five involved romance in at least one line of action, while eighty-five made that the principal line of action" (16).

6. See Jackie Stacey, _Star-Gazing: Hollywood Cinema and Female Spectatorship_ (New York: Routledge, 1994) and Teresa de Lauretis, _The Practice of Love: Lesbian Sexuality and Perverse Desire_ (Bloomington: Indiana University Press, 1994) for two different viewpoints on the relation between identification and desire in cinema spectatorship. De Lauretis views Stacey's more fluid conceptualization of desire and identification as a problematic de-eroticization of lesbian desire. Stacey remarks that she seeks not to de-eroticize desire but to eroticize identification (29).

7. Wood, _Hollywood from Vietnam to Reagan_, 3.

8. Parker Tyler, _Screening the Sexes: Homosexuality in the Movies_ (New York: Da Capo Press, 1993 [1973]), xxiii, xix, xx.

9. Danae Clark, "Commodity Lesbianism," _Camera Obscura_ 25–26 (Jan./May 1991): 181–201.

10. Lucy Richer, "_Three of Hearts_," _Sight and Sound_ 3 (August 1993): 54.

11. In _Bi Any Other Name: Bisexual People Speak Out_ (Boston: Alyson Publications, 1991), Loraine Hutchins and Lani Ka'ahumanu describe bisexual identity as "individuals of either sex who are attracted to both sexes" (2), and this is the definition of bisexual identity I am using here. I distinguish between bisexual identity and bisexual spectatorship practices: the latter refers to the activity of viewing by spectators, regardless of gender or sexual identity, which acknowledges that same and opposite sex desire are not mutually exclusive.

12. I use these terms intentionally, because, until very recently, queer movements have been organized according to gay and lesbian agendas, despite the presence and work of bisexuals and transgendered people. See Michael du Plessis's "Blatantly Bisexual" in this volume for a discussion of the politics surrounding such naming practices.

    Amanda Udis-Kessler's "Identity/Politics: A History of the Bisexual Movement," presented at "In/Queery/Theory/Deed," University of Iowa, November 18, 1994, provides an excellent account of bisexual activism in relation to gay and lesbian organizing. An earlier version of that paper appears in _Bisexual Politics: Theories, Queries, and Visions_, ed. Naomi Tucker (Binghamton, N.Y.: Haworth Press), 1996.

13. See Virginia Wexman's _Creating the Couple: Love, Marriage, and Hollywood Performance_ (Princeton: Princeton University Press, 1993). Wexman's final chapter, "Destabilization of Gender Norms and Acting as Performance," is ostensibly an account of the breakdown of traditional coupling. It appears in the book's epilogue which is itself entitled "Beyond the Couple." But Wexman's choice of three exemplary films is disappointing. Apparently chosen for their deployment of particular performance styles (improvisational, absurdist, and Brechtian) are Robert Altman's _Nashville_ (1975), David Mamet's _House of Games_ (1987), and Spike Lee's _Do the Right Thing_ (1989), all films that problematize marriage, but not the naturalization of heterosexual coupling.

14. René Girard, _Desire, Deceit, and the Novel: Self and Other in Literary Structure_, trans. Yvonne Freccero (Baltimore: Johns Hopkins University Press, 1990).

15. Eve Kosofsky Sedgwick, _Between Men: English Literature and Male Homosocial Desire_ (New York: Columbia University Press, 1985).

16. Marjorie Garber, _Vice Versa: Bisexuality and the Eroticism of Everyday Life_ (New York: Simon and Schuster, 1995).

17. In *Now You See It: Studies on Lesbian and Gay Film* (London and New York: Routledge, 1990), Richard Dyer discusses gay and lesbian films prior to 1980, a date he admits is somewhat arbitrary (2), and points to the proliferation of gay and lesbian filmmaking since 1980. In that study, he, too, is interested in "the deliberate, overt and owned expression of [gay/lesbian] feelings and perceptions in film" (1).

18. See Judith Mayne's *Cinema and Spectatorship* (New York: Routledge, 1994) for a discussion of models of spectatorship in historical and theoretical perspective.

19. See Elizabeth Ellsworth, "Illicit Pleasures: Feminist Spectators and *Personal Best*," *Wide Angle* 8 (2): 45–56 and Richard Meyer, "Rock Hudson's Body" in *Inside Out: Lesbian Theories, Gay Theories*, ed. Diana Fuss (New York: Routledge, 1991), 259–88 as examples of how spectators, including film critics, read against the grain in terms of film narrative and star persona.

20. Rob Lapsley and Michael Westlake, "From *Casablanca* to *Pretty Woman*: The Politics of Romance," in *Contemporary Film Theory*, ed. Anthony Easthope (London: Longman, 1993), 190–91 and Judith Mayne, *Cinema and Spectatorship*, 43, 76, and chapter 4.

21. I am arguing that triangulation triggers bisexual connotations. Investigating the use of the romantic triangle in films which are not explicitly representing alternatives to monosexuality may also prove fruitful but is beyond the scope of this essay.

22. Laura Mulvey, "Visual Pleasure and Narrative Cinema," in *Issues in Feminist Film Criticism*, ed. Patricia Erens (Bloomington: Indiana University Press, 1990 [1975]), 28–40.

23. See D. N. Rodowick, "The Difficulty of Difference," *Wide Angle* 5 (1): 4–16.

24. Mulvey, "Visual Pleasure," 39.

25. Laura Mulvey, "Afterthoughts on 'Visual Pleasure and Narrative Cinema' Inspired by *Duel in the Sun*," *Psychoanalysis and Cinema*, ed. E. Ann Kaplan (New York: Routledge, 1990), 24–35.

26. Anne Friedberg, "A Denial of Difference: Theories of Cinematic Identification," in *Psychoanalysis and Cinema*, 42.

27. Janet Bergstrom, "Enunication and Sexual Difference (Part One)," *Camera Obscura* 3–4 (Summer 1979): 33–69 and Nick Browne, "The Spectator-in-the-Text: The Rhetoric of Stagecoach," in *Movies and Methods* vol. 2, ed. Bill Nichols (Berkeley: University of California Press, 1985), 458–75. In *Hollywood from Vietnam to Reagan*, Robin Wood discusses bisexuality in the horror film genre in terms of the monster's embodiment of social taboos and the spectator's multiple identifications with both the monster and her/his victims (92).

28. Tania Modleski, *The Women Who Knew Too Much: Hitchcock and Feminist Theory* (New York: Routledge, 1988), 8.

29. Marjorie Garber, "The Occidental Tourist: *M. Butterfly* and the Scandal of Transvestism," in *Nationalisms and Sexualities*, ed. Andrew Parker, Mary Russo, Doris Sommer, and Patricia Yeager (New York: Routledge, 1992), 121–46.

30. The scene in which Jody is beaten by Jude and bleeds from his mouth further suggests that his phallic status is a "both/and" one: the only visible parts of his anatomy are his bleeding lips, a signifier of female genitalia.

31.   Another of the film's implicit ironies is the possibility that Jody has been targeted by the IRA as the soldier most likely to fall into their sexual trap *because* he is a black man.

32.   Frann Michel, "Racial and Sexual Politics in *The Crying Game*," *Cineaste* 20 (1) (1993): 30.

33.   Homi Bhabha, "Of Mimicry and Man: The Ambivalence of Colonial Discourse," *October* 28: 129.

34.   Although biologically a man, a fact which the film foregrounds to the point of the spectacular, Dil dresses and, importantly, lives as a woman, which distinguishes the character from the traditional transvestite. See Marjorie Garber's, *Vested Interests: Cross-Dressing and Cultural Anxiety* (New York: Routledge, 1992), particularly chapter 6, "Breaking the Code: Transvestism and Gay Identity."

35.   Jonathan Romney, "*The Crying Game*," *Sight and Sound* 2 (November 1992): 40.

36.   An ironic reference to Hitchcock's *Vertigo* may be at work here. Fergus is successful at making his "woman" over (into a man), whereas Scottie Ferguson was not (Gavin Elster got there first).

37.   David Lugowski, "Genre Conventions and Visual Style in *The Crying Game*," *Cineaste* 20 (1) (1993): 34.

38.   See, for example, Timothy Shary's "Present Personal Truths: The Alternative Phenomenology of Video in *I've Heard the Mermaids Singing*," *Wide Angle* 15.3 (July 1993): 37–55. Shary argues that video images, when used in a film, call up cultural associations with live news broadcasts, specifically, with the simultaneity of filming and transmitting images that video technology permits and with the medium's ability to capture reality (37–38, 41–42). The association of video with immediacy and real time in *I've Heard the Mermaids Singing* is largely due to Polly's first-person narration and the fact that her video camera can only broadcast live images (46–47), which differs significantly from the use of videotape as visual archive in *Three of Hearts*.

39.   Douglas Keller, "Only Two of Three Hearts Portrayed Convincingly," *Tech* 113 (25) (April 30, 1993): 7.

40.   Richer, "*Three of Hearts*," 54.

41.   Edmond Grant, "*Three of Hearts*," *Films in Review* 44 (July/August 1993): 264.

42.   Diana Fuss, "Monsters of Perversion: Jeffrey Dahmer and *The Silence of the Lambs*," in *Media Spectacles*, ed. Marjorie Garber, Jann Matlock, and Rebecca L. Walkowitz (New York: Routledge, 1993), 181–205.

43.   Certainly Scott's casting of rock star David Bowie in the role of the husband also calls forth associations with bisexuality, because of Bowie's ambiguous sexual persona. The lipstick traces and John's apparent obsession with his appearance create further references to Bowie's "stage" personae. A number of star biographies document Bowie's contradictory public statements about his sexuality, including Peter and Leni Gillman, *Alias David Bowie: A Biography* (New York: Holt, 1987).

44.   This time span is suggested in John's flashbacks to his initial encounter with Miriam, where they are both playing musical instruments in costumes that suggest the late eighteenth or early nineteenth century.

45.   See Barbara Creed's *The Monstrous Feminine: Film, Feminism, Psychoanalysis* (New York: Routledge, 1993), where she argues that Miriam is associated with the devouring "archaic" mother.

46.   See Rice's "Vampire Chronicles," including *Interview with the Vampire* (New York: Knopf, 1976), *The Vampire Lestat* (New York: Ballantine Books, 1985), *Queen of the Damned* (New York: Knopf, 1988), and *The Tale of the Body Thief* (New York: Knopf, 1992). Not surprisingly, a number of difficulties have plagued the translation of Rice's polymorphous, polysexual literary vampires into film.

Index